THRESHOLDS AND PATHWAYS BETWEEN JUNG AND LACAN

This groundbreaking book was seeded by the first-ever joint Jung–Lacan conference on the notion of the sublime held at Cambridge, England, against the backdrop of the 100th anniversary of the outbreak of the Great War. It provides a fascinating range of in-depth psychological perspectives on aspects of creativity and destruction inherent in the monstrous, awe-inspiring sublime.

The chapters include some of the outcrop of academic and clinical papers given at this conference, with the addition of new contributions that explore similarities and differences between Jungian and Lacanian thinking on key topics such as language and linguistics, literature, religion, self and subject, science, mathematics and philosophy.

The overall objective of this vitalizing volume is the development and dissemination of new ideas that will be of interest to practising psychoanalysts, psychotherapists and academics in the field, as well as to all those who are captivated by the still-revolutionary thinking of Jung and Lacan.

Ann Casement LP is a Professor at the Oriental Academy for Analytical Psychology, China; a member of the International Association for Analytical Psychology, where she served on its Executive and Ethics Committees; and a senior member of the BJAA. She lectures worldwide and has published extensively, including *Who Owns Psychoanalysis*, which was nominated for the Gradiva Award in 2005, and contributes to *The Economist* and international psychoanalytical journals.

Phil Goss is Associate Professor and Director of Counselling and Psychotherapy at Warwick University, UK. He is the author of *Jung: A Complete Introduction* (2015) and *Men, Women and Relationships: A Post-Jungian Approach* (2010) and has published on a range of topics from a Jungian perspective, including education and learning difficulties, gender and spirituality.

Dany Nobus is Professor of Psychoanalytic Psychology at Brunel University London, UK, Founding Scholar of the British Psychoanalytic Council, and Former Chair and Fellow of the Freud Museum London. He is the author of numerous books and papers on the history, theory and practice of psychoanalysis, most recently *The Law of Desire: On Lacan's 'Kant with Sade'* (2017).

"It seems so obvious, but it has taken many decades before a serious scholarly engagement between Lacan and Jung could take place. This book conducts such an important and fraught encounter, by focusing on the idea of the sublime, and illuminating the convergences and differences this concept reveals in each. With the continuing publication and translation of Lacan's *Seminars*, along with the publication of Jung's *The Red Book*, both thinkers continue to offer untapped resources for understanding what psychoanalysis is and can be. Excellent and wide-ranging, rich in theoretical and cultural-artistic implications, this volume is not to be missed!"

Clayton Crockett, University of Central Arkansas, USA

"'Jung and Lacan'? This ground-breaking and brilliant book answers the question with a resounding YES. The notion of the sublime has been gently eased into place as a bridge between these two traditions and is the clear result of years of thinking by the skilled editors and erudite contributors. In addition, not to put too fine a point on it, there has been less apparent but much-needed professional and academic agitation and persuasion on their part. Fields that will benefit from an engagement with the book include clinical work, politics, art and creativity, history of ideas, and contemporary spiritualities."

Andrew Samuels, Former Professor of Analytical Psychology, University of Essex, UK; Author of *Jung and the Post-Jungians*

THRESHOLDS AND PATHWAYS BETWEEN JUNG AND LACAN

On the Blazing Sublime

Edited by

Ann Casement, Phil Goss and Dany Nobus

LONDON AND NEW YORK

First published 2021
by Routledge
2 Park Square, Milton Park, Abingdon, Oxon OX14 4RN

and by Routledge
52 Vanderbilt Avenue, New York, NY 10017

Routledge is an imprint of the Taylor & Francis Group, an informa business

© 2021 selection and editorial matter, Ann Casement, Phil Goss and Dany Nobus; individual chapters, the contributors

The right of Ann Casement, Phil Goss and Dany Nobus to be identified as the authors of the editorial material, and of the authors for their individual chapters, has been asserted in accordance with sections 77 and 78 of the Copyright, Designs and Patents Act 1988.

All rights reserved. No part of this book may be reprinted or reproduced or utilised in any form or by any electronic, mechanical, or other means, now known or hereafter invented, including photocopying and recording, or in any information storage or retrieval system, without permission in writing from the publishers.

Trademark notice: Product or corporate names may be trademarks or registered trademarks, and are used only for identification and explanation without intent to infringe.

British Library Cataloguing-in-Publication Data
A catalogue record for this book is available from the British Library

Library of Congress Cataloging-in-Publication Data
A catalog record for this book has been requested

ISBN: 978-0-367-54544-4 (hbk)
ISBN: 978-0-367-54543-7 (pbk)
ISBN: 978-1-003-08966-7 (ebk)

Typeset in Sabon
by Apex CoVantage, LLC

Contents

NOTES ON CONTRIBUTORS   vii

	Introduction	1
PART I	Theory	5
Chapter 1	Simply sublime? Lacan, Jung and *The Red Book* PAUL BISHOP	6
Chapter 2	Sublime anxiety BERNARD BURGOYNE	31
Chapter 3	The complex pleasure of the sublime ANN CASEMENT	50
Chapter 4	Jung, the sublime and apophatic mysticism in psyche and art JOHN DOURLEY	64
Chapter 5	The subjective sublime: "like a diamond"? PHIL GOSS	76
Chapter 6	The sublime: opportunity for the integration of otherness NAMI LEE	94
Chapter 7	The hermetic subtle body and the sublime in Jung and Lacan ALBERT MORELL	108
Chapter 8	Lacan's clinical artistry: on sublimation, sublation and the sublime DANY NOBUS	123

Chapter 9	A crumpled note or purloined letter? Sublime and feminine creativity in destruction in Jung and Lacan SUSAN ROWLAND	153
PART II	Culture	165
Chapter 10	The object of Victor Frankenstein's desire LIONEL BAILLY	166
Chapter 11	The Soviet Antigones: the poets versus the state HELENA BASSIL-MOROZOW	175
Chapter 12	*Thunder, Perfect Mind*: entering the land of the sublime ISABELLE M. DeARMOND	186
Chapter 13	Unconscious processes, instrumental music and the experience of the sublime: an exploration through Messiaen's *Quartet for the End of Time* GIORGIO GIACCARDI	199
Chapter 14	The *Sinthome* and the work of Imre Kertész SHARON R. GREEN	218
Chapter 15	Expressing the inexpressible: art as a challenge to its own object NIHAN KAYA	229
Chapter 16	The *Nibelungenlied*: a Germanic myth and the sublime ARTHUR NIESSER	245
Chapter 17	James Joyce's "The Dead" and paleo-postmodernism: a Lacanian/Jungian reading CATRIONA RYAN	257
Chapter 18	Apostolic actuality: David Jones and sublimation LUKE THURSTON	268
INDEX		282

Contributors

Lionel Bailly is a psychoanalyst and a child and adolescent psychiatrist. He is a member of the *Association Lacanienne Internationale* and a Clinical Associate of the British Psychoanalytic Society. He teaches and supervises students at the UCL Psychoanalysis Unit and is the author of *Lacan: A Beginner's Guide* (Oneworld, 2009) and co-editor (with David Lichtenstein and Sharmini Bailly) of *The Lacan Tradition: Lines of Development – Evolution of Theory and Practice over the Decades* (Routledge, 2018).

Helena Bassil-Morozow is a cultural philosopher, media and film scholar, and academic author. Her many publications include *Tim Burton: The Monster and the Crowd* (Routledge, 2010), *The Trickster in Contemporary Film* (Routledge, 2011), *The Trickster and the System: Identity and Agency in Contemporary Society* (Routledge, 2014), *Jungian Film Studies: The Essential Guide* (co-authored with Luke Hockley) (Routledge, 2016) and *Jungian Theory for Storytellers* (Routledge, 2018).

Paul Bishop is William Jacks Chair of Modern Languages at the University of Glasgow. He has written on various topics in German intellectual history (including Cassirer, Goethe, Thomas Mann, Nietzsche and Schopenhauer). He has recently published *German Political Thought and the Discourse of Platonism: Finding the Way Out of the Cave* (Palgrave, 2019), *Ludwig Klages and the Philosophy of Life: A Vitalist Toolkit* (Routledge, 2017), and *On the Blissful Islands: With Nietzsche & Jung in the Shadow of the Superman* (Routledge, 2017).

Bernard Burgoyne is a psychoanalyst practising in London. He was educated at the University of Cambridge, the London School of Economics and the University of Paris. He is Emeritus Professor of Psychoanalysis at Middlesex University, and is currently interested in how frontiers of desire are determined by general topological properties of the structure of the mind.

viii   Contributors

Ann Casement is a member of the International Association for Analytical Psychology, where she served on its Executive and Ethics Committees, and a senior member of the BJAA and JPA (New York). She lectures worldwide and has published widely, including *Who Owns Psychoanalysis?* (Karnac, 2004), which was nominated for the 2005 Gradiva Award. She contributes to *The Economist* and international psychoanalytical journals

Isabelle M. DeArmond is a physician, a psychologist in private practice in Berkeley, CA, and a candidate at the C.G. Jung Institute of San Francisco. She has published on the archetypal aspects of the transference at the end of life and the role of places for individuation, among other subjects.

John Dourley was a Roman Catholic priest and a member of the Oblates of Mary Immaculate. He was also a member of the Ontario Association of Jungian Analysts, wrote prolifically and lectured widely in Jungian and academic circles. John died on 22 June 2018, aged 82.

Giorgio Giaccardi is a Jungian analyst in private practice in London (BJAA) and Milan (ARPA). He previously published a paper on Dionysian and Apolline pathways to the numinous. He writes, teaches and presents on aspects of post-Jungian theory, with a particular focus on symbolisation, gender and sexuality, on which he contributed chapters to two edited volumes published by Routledge in 2019.

Phil Goss is Director of Counselling and Psychotherapy at the University of Warwick and a Jungian analyst (AJA, London). He is the author of *Jung: A Complete Introduction* (Hodder and Stoughton, 2015) and *Men, Women and Relationships: A Post Jungian Approach* (Routledge, 2010) and has published on a range of topics from a Jungian perspective, including education and learning difficulties, gender and psychotherapy, holism and spirituality.

Sharon R. Green is a psychoanalyst in private practice in Seattle, WA, and a founding director of the New School for Analytical Psychology (www.nsanpsy.com), a multidisciplinary consortium of clinicians and scholars. Her published work includes a chapter in the award-winning book *Temporality & Shame* (L. Hinton and H. Willemsen, Eds., Routledge, 2017).

Nihan Kaya is the author of fourteen books in Turkish: five novels, two collections of short stories and three non-fiction works about creativity, aesthetic theory and the child archetype. She contributed a chapter on creativity to *Dreaming the Myth Onwards* (Lucy Huskinson, Ed., Routledge, 2010). She is currently teaching at the MEF University Psychology Department in Istanbul.

Contributors   ix

Nami Lee is a psychiatrist and Jungian analyst who teaches at Seoul National University Hospital, and who is also working as the director of a human rights centre. She has published 25 books on mythology, fairy tales, religion and society from Jungian perspectives. Her books have been translated into Chinese, Thai and Vietnamese. She is currently a board member and supervising analyst at the Jung Institute of South Korea.

Albert Morell is a Lacanian clinical and research psychoanalyst in private and institutional practice. He is a former university lecturer in literature, philosophy, comparative religion and film studies, as well as a former screenwriter. He is co-editor of *The Los Angeles Psychologist*, and founder of the California Forum of the *Internationale des Forums – École de Psychanalyse des Forums du Champ Lacanien* (IF-EPFCL), based in Paris.

Arthur Niesser is a professional member and a former Chair of the Association of Jungian Analysts in London. After training in Stuttgart in his native Germany and in London, he now works in private analytic practice in Porthmadog in North Wales. As a retired general practitioner, he is particularly interested in the interface between biology and psyche. He is concerned with the application of Jungian concepts to developments in society and in a political context.

Dany Nobus is Professor of Psychoanalytic Psychology at Brunel University London, Founding Scholar of the British Psychoanalytic Council, and Former Chair and Fellow of the Freud Museum London. He is the author of numerous books and papers on the history, theory and practice of psychoanalysis, most recently *The Law of Desire: On Lacan's "Kant with Sade"* (Palgrave, 2017).

Susan Rowland is co-Chair of the MA in Engaged Humanities and the Creative Life at the Pacifica Graduate Institute. Author of nine books on C.G. Jung in relation to creativity, modernity and transdisciplinary studies, her latest book is *Jungian Literary Criticism: the Essential Guide* (Routledge, 2019). She was founding Chair of the International Association for Jungian Studies (IAJS jungstudies.net) from 2003 until 2006. Educated in the UK at the Universities of Oxford, London and Newcastle, she now lives in California, USA.

Catriona Ryan SFHEA is the Director of Scriptor Cube Ltd., which embeds well-being into its research and learning courses for university students and academic staff. She is also an Irish poet, a published academic, a critical theorist and a world leading authority on the work of Tom MacIntyre, with an international standing in Irish Studies. She is a Senior Fellow of the HEA, an Honorary Research Fellow at UWTSD and a Student Experience specialist. She has worked in three universities in Ireland and the UK over the last 12 years.

Luke Thurston is Senior Lecturer in Modern Literature at Aberystwyth University. His most recent publications include the *Routledge Handbook to the Ghost Story* (co-edited with Scott Brewster, Routledge, 2018) and a translation of Jean Laplanche's *The Unfinished Copernican Revolution* (2019).

Introduction

The current book evolved out of the joint Jung/Lacan Conference that was organized in the Autumn of 2014 at St John's College, University of Cambridge, by two Lacanian psychoanalysts, Bernard Burgoyne and Lionel Bailly, and Phil Goss and Ann Casement from the Jungian orientation. The venue for the conference was chosen for its association with the English Romantic poet William Wordsworth, who attended St John's and whose poetry was influenced by ideas about the sublime. A previous conference on *The Sublime and the Numinous* had been held in 2011 in the English Lake District, Wordsworth's home and creative inspiration for his poetry, and had provided the spur to explore the issue further. The 2014 Cambridge conference was entitled *The Notion of the Sublime in Creativity and Destruction*, and it included contributions by psychoanalysts and scholars from the two traditions of psychoanalysis, quite a few of whom have chapters in this book. In addition, Dany Nobus, Psychoanalytic Psychotherapist and former Chair of the Freud Museum London, with expertise in the Lacanian field, has joined Ann Casement and Phil Goss as one of the editors of the book.

According to Élisabeth Roudinesco, Jacques Lacan met Carl Gustav Jung in 1954 at his home in Küssnacht, yet very little is known about what the two men talked about, other than their meeting having been facilitated by Roland Cahen, a French psychiatrist with a joint interest in analytical psychology and Freudian psychoanalysis, and Lacan subsequently claiming in a lecture in Vienna that Jung had disclosed to him how Freud had greeted their arrival in New York harbour, back in 1909, with the words: "They don't realize we're bringing them the plague" (Lacan, 2006[1956], p. 336). Following the 2014 Conference, Jung and Lacan meet again in this book, in order to explore the enigmatic notion of the sublime. However, "creativity" and "destruction" were added to the theme of the 2014 Conference, owing to its coinciding with the centenary of the outbreak of the Great War and by way of tribute to Edmund Burke's notion of the sublime as an innovative way of thinking about excess as the key to a new kind of subjectivity. In relation to this, the Freud Museum London had also opened a small exhibit on psychoanalysis and war in July 2014, based on some correspondence

2 Introduction

between Sigmund Freud and Albert Einstein from 1932. At the time, Einstein was attached to the League of Nations and asked Freud the burning question: "Is there any way of delivering mankind from the menace of war?" He further asked: "Is it possible to control man's mental evolution so as to make him proof against the psychoses of hate and destructiveness? . . . Experience proves that it is rather the so-called "Intelligentzia" [*sic*] that is most apt to yield to these disastrous collective suggestions" (Einstein, 1960[1932], p. 201). Freud replied one month later, first of all citing human instincts as being of two kinds: "those which seek to preserve and unite – which we call "erotic" . . . and those which seek to destroy and kill" (Freud, 1960[1933b], p. 209). Summarizing an argument he had made previously in *Civilization and Its Discontents* (1964[1930a]), Freud then went on to state that the cultural development of mankind leads to all that is best in the human condition but also to much that makes for human suffering. Finally, he proposed that amongst "the psychological characteristics of civilization two appear to be the most important: a strengthening of the intellect, which is beginning to govern instinctual life, and an internalization of the aggressive impulses, with all its consequent advantages and perils" (Freud, 1960[1933b], pp. 214–215). Freud concluded by saying that man's cultural disposition as well as a well-founded human dread of the forms that future wars will take may serve to put an end to war in the near future. Needless to say, that was not to be, since by the time the exchange between these two self-acknowledged pacifists was published in 1933 under the title *Why War?*, Adolf Hitler, who was to drive both men into exile, had already been appointed as Chancellor, and the letters never achieved the wide circulation intended for them.

The 2014 Conference was an inspiring event, at which Jungians and Lacanians came together both in acknowledging their joint origin in the genius of Freud and in expressing their divergent views of psychoanalysis in their different languages. Participants from the Jungian tradition explored notions such as the collective unconscious, archetypes, alchemy, the numinous and the shadow, whereas from the Lacanian tradition there were contributions on the Symbolic, the Imaginary and the Real, the signifier, the sinthome, the objet *a*, desire and jouissance. Since the initiative was also taken to compare and, where applicable, bridge the two differing theoretical frames of reference around the subject of the sublime, lively discussion was generated, and further questions and debate were provoked – far beyond the confines of the conference hall – which not only confirmed the enduring value of this topic, but also promoted ongoing dialogue between these two traditions within psychoanalysis.

The chapters in this book reflect the range of ways in which the sublime can be understood and applied, reaching back to pivotal influences, including Edmund Burke and Immanuel Kant, whilst also drawing on more recent thinkers, from Jacques Derrida to Slavoj Žižek. We hope that the diverse ways in which the notion of the sublime can be defined, deployed and deconstructed will offer the reader a panoply of creative ideas and stimulating lines of thought. The book is organized to reflect this dazzling scope, bringing together expert perspectives from the academy and the clinical field under two main parts: Theory and Culture. With the inherent philosophical and theoretical tensions between Jungian and Lacanian perspectives offering a dynamic backdrop, this book unpacks multifarious readings of the sublime and demonstrates their relevance for a wide range of contemporary themes. These include limit, possibility and excess; the relationship between the human and the natural world; reason and the interpretation of aesthetic and phenomenological experience; creativity and destructiveness; the nature and varieties of unconscious processes; depth psychological readings of the sublime as manifested in art, literature and culture; and the enduring fascination with the mysterious, the terrifying and the numinous. The book speaks to the importance of upholding the value of scrutinizing what is beyond the limits of the ordinary: the blazing sublime.

References

Einstein, A. (1960[1932]). Why War? In J. Strachey (Trans.), *The Standard Edition of the Complete Psychological Works of Sigmund Freud*, vol. 18 (pp. 199–202). London: The Hogarth Press and the Institute of Psycho-Analysis.

Freud, S. (1960[1933]). Why War? In J. Strachey (Trans.), *The Standard Edition of the Complete Psychological Works of Sigmund Freud*, vol. 22 (pp. 203–215). London: The Hogarth Press and the Institute of Psycho-Analysis.

Freud, S. (1964[1930]). Civilization and Its Discontents. In J. Strachey (Trans.), *The Standard Edition of the Complete Psychological Works of Sigmund Freud*, vol. 21 (pp. 57–145). London: The Hogarth Press and the Institute of Psycho-Analysis.

Lacan, J. (2006[1956]). The Freudian Thing, or the Meaning of the Return to Freud in Psychoanalysis. In B. Fink (Trans.), *Écrits* (pp. 334–363). New York: W. W. Norton & Company.

PART I
THEORY

ONE

Simply sublime? Lacan, Jung and *The Red Book*

Paul Bishop

The starting point of this chapter is the famous question, *Wie hast du es mit der Religion*, posed by Gretchen in Part One of Goethe's *Faust*.[1] Here, in the scene in Martha's garden, we find the following exchange:

MARGARETA: Promise me, Heinrich.

FAUST: Whatever I can!

MARGARETA: Then tell me, how is't with thy religion, pray?
> Thou art a good and kindly man,
> And yet, I think, small heed thereto doth pay.

(Goethe, 1908, p. 164)

Gretchen's question is entirely pertinent, since Faust is a man who is in league with the devil! In this respect, Gretchen's question pushes against the theological framework of Goethe's entire text (reflected in the "Prologue in Heaven" of Part One and in the famous concluding scene, "Amid Mountain Gorges", at the end of Part Two). But Gretchen's question is also, it seems to me, a good question to put to Lacan and to Jung.

After all, an important dimension of psychoanalysis is its reactivation and revival of ancient traditions and doctrines, especially the notion of divinity. There already exists a body of scholarship in this field of enquiry: for instance, on Freud and Empedocles (Tourney, 1956) or on Jung and Heraclitus (Bodlander, 1990), and in his recent work Peter Kingsley has placed fresh emphasis on the significance for Jung of both Heraclitus and Empedocles (Kingsley, 2018, pp. 197–198, 608–610, 602–603). The writings of Jung positively teem with references to antiquity; *Psychological Types*, for instance, is rich in references to the problem of types in history of classical and medieval thought, including the figures of Tertullian and Origen, theological disputes of the ancient Church, the problem of transubstantiation, the Scholastic debate between nominalism and realism, and the Communion controversy between Luther and Zwingli.

For his part, Lacan also moves at ease across various epochs of intellectual history, among which his references to Plato (especially the *Symposium*) for a definition of *desire* as *lack*, are especially important. When Socrates says

Simply sublime? Lacan, Jung & *The Red Book*   7

in the *Symposium* (200a), "Everything longs for what it lacks, and . . . nothing longs for what it doesn't lack" (Plato, 1989, p. 552), we find stated with eminent clarity the central thesis of Lacanian psychoanalysis. Then again, in his seminar of 1960–1961 on the transference, Lacan explained the *objet petit a* in terms of the *agalma* from the *Symposium*. In Greek, an *agalma* is an ornament, offering or gift left in a temple for the gods; for Lacan, it is above all "a precious object, a jewel, something which is inside" (cf. Lacan, 1991a, p. 167). So when, in the *Symposium* (216e-217a), Alcibiades describes how he had once seen "the little images . . . so golden, so beautiful, and so utterly amazing" inside Socrates, famed for his ugliness (Plato, 1989, p. 568), Lacan sees in this something fundamental about the dynamics of desire. As Lionel Bailly explains, desire's "ultimate but unattainable object is the *agalma* within Socrates, its subject is the castrated (symbolically – wanting, drunken, and demanding) Alcibiades, who uses as a lure for a secondary object of desire (Agathon) his own desire or neediness, which he knows makes him desirable" (Bailly, 2009, p. 131).

So this chapter takes as its working assumption the belief that seeing Lacan and Jung in an intellectual-historical light can elucidate their common features as well as their differences and help establish a framework for approaching both thinkers in a way that can open up a dialogue that is at once constructive and critical. This is possible because the common ground between Lacan and Jung is, I shall argue, larger than is often assumed to be the case, as a consideration of three topics – language, desire and the quaternity – indicates. Yet as I shall also suggest, there are significant differences between Jung and Lacan that emerge in their respective relation to religion – and to the sublime.

Affinities: language

For Lacan, the unconscious is structured like a language. As he puts it in *The Four Fundamental Concepts of Psycho-Analysis* (1964), "[I]f psychoanalysis is to be constituted as the science of the unconscious, one must set out from the notion that the unconscious is structured like a language" (Lacan, 1978, p. 203; cf. pp. 20–23). In fact, his entire account of psychosexual development is predicated on the subject's entrance into the realm of the visual (the imaginary) and language (the symbolic). And Lacan is interested not just in the structure of language, but in the structures within which we use language: for the use of language always implies a relationship of one kind or another to an interlocutor.

Consequently, for Lacan, language involves both a symbolic *and* an imaginary dimension. In his famous diagram he introduced in 1955 in his *Seminar*, known as "schema L", the axis A-S (from Other to S/Es, or language in its symbolic dimension) has a corresponding axis, from *a'* to *a* (from ego to other, or an imaginary axis). On this account, "the subject is separated from the Others, the true ones, by the wall of language", and hence it is, for

Lacan, a mistake to see language as something fundamentally communicative or referential: on his account, "language is as much there to found us in the Other as to drastically prevent us from understanding him" (Lacan, 1991b, p. 244).

The problem of language is one for Jung as well. At first glance, Jung approaches the problem from a different angle – from the problem of meaning. As he puts it in *Archetypes and the Collective Unconscious* (1934; 1954), "[F]rom whatever side we approach this question" – i.e. the question of meaning (*Sinn*) – "everywhere we find ourselves confronted with the history of language, with images and motifs that lead straight back to the primitive wonder-world" (Jung, 1968a, para. 67). This is so, Jung argues, because "the forms we use for assigning meaning are historical categories that reach back into the mists of time", and hence "interpretations make use of certain linguistic matrices that are themselves derived from primordial images" (Jung, 1968a, para. 67). Jung insists on the *historical* context of language, which is a dimension absent from Lacan's structuralist (and hence synchronic) approach to language. Yet for all his talk of "the mists of time", Jung is also appealing to a timeless (or synchronic) dimension by describing the "images" from which "linguistic matrices" derive as "primordial".

Both Lacan and Jung were aware of the importance of analogy. For Lacan, the unconscious *is* not a language; it is not structured *as* a language; it is structured *like* a language, and in this respect, we might note Jung's interest, in *Symbols and Transformations of the Libido* (1911/1912), in the importance of analogy in general and, in particular, the term *gleich-wie* (i.e. "like"). As he puts it, citing the German philologist and philologist Hermann (or Heymann) Steinthal (1823–1899) as his authority, "[A]n absolutely overweening importance must be granted to the little phrase "Gleich wie" (even as) in the history of the development of thought" (Jung, 1991, para. 236).[2] The reason for this, as Jung adds, is that his own central thesis will be that "the carryover of the libido to a phantastic correlate has led primitive man to a number of the most important discoveries" (Jung, 1991, para. 236).

This is why Jung – in this respect, similar to Martin Heidegger (1889–1976) – is interested in the way linguistic connections can alert us to the hidden dimensions of concepts or fantasies. In *The Psychology of the Unconscious*, he suggests that "Prometheus, the fire-bringer, may be a brother of the Hindu Pramantha, that is to say, of the masculine fire-rubbing piece of wood" (Jung, 1991, para. 241). After tracing a complicated etymological path, Jung concludes that "the path from Pramantha to Prometheus passes not through the word, but through the idea" (Jung, 1991, para. 241). So here lies an important difference between Lacan and Jung: over and above language, Jung asserts the dimension of the *idea*. And Jung is very much aware of the etymological implications of his own terminology: for instance, he notes in relation to the question as to whether God is archetype that the word "type" is derived from *typos* = "blow", "imprint'; concluding that "an archetype presupposes an imprinter" (Jung, 1968b, para. 15).

Affinities: desire

Desire is clearly a master category for Lacan, and as a concept he distinguishes it from need or biological instinct and from demand, made in relation to the Other. (Seen in this way, Lacan follows the etymology of the word "desire" as meaning "to wish for, long for, or to regret something that is absent'). As well as being indebted to Plato, Lacan derives his specific concept of desire from Spinoza, for whom "desire [*cupiditas*] is the essence itself of man" (*Ethics*, Part III, "Definitions of the Affects", def. 1; Spinoza, 1928, p. 266). (On Lacan's fascination with Spinoza, see Homer, 2005, pp. 3–4, 72.) And Lacan refines it via Hegel, who explores how desire involves a relation to the Other, via Alexandre Kojève, who "existentializes" Hegel's thinking. (For a fuller discussion, see the entry on "desire" in Evans, 1996, pp. 35–39; as well as Lacan, 2002.)

In Jung's approach, we find a different understanding of desire, one that perhaps the alternative etymology of the word as meaning "to await what the stars will being" (from *de* + *sidere*, "from the stars'). For Jung, desire is linked to notion of *libido*; which, in turn, in *Transformations and Symbols of the Libido* (i.e. *The Psychology of the Unconscious*) is intriguingly linked to idea of *will*: "Originally taken from the sexual sphere, this word [i.e. *libido*] has become the most frequent technical expression of psychoanalysis, for the simple reason that its significance is wide enough to cover all the unknown and countless manifestations of the Will in the sense of Schopenhauer" (Jung, 1991, para. 212). Elsewhere, Jung remarks that the conception of a continuous life impulse or the will-to-live "coincides with the idea of the Will in Schopenhauer, for we can conceive the Will objectively, only as a manifestation of an internal desire" (Jung, 1991, para. 223). (Seen in this light, Schopenhauer might also be seen as a highly Lacanian figure, emphasizing the constitutive function of desire yet recognizing the impossibility of satisfying it.)

And in this same chapter Jung goes on to adopt "the exact classical significance" of the word *libido* as it is used, "in a very wide sense", in such authors as Cicero, Sallust and St Augustine. (To be precise: Jung refers to Cicero's *Tusculan Disputations*, Book 4, Chapter 6 (with reference to Pythagoras, Plato and the Stoics, especially Zeno), where a distinction is made between delight with a present and with a future good; to Sallust's observation that "rage is part of a desire", a definition developed in *The War with Catiline*, Chapter 7, and his *Letter to Caesar*, Chapter 13 [for further discussion of this aspect of desire, see Harris, 2001, esp. 207] and St Augustine's *The City of God*, Book 14, Chapter 15 [Jung, 1991, paras. 212–217].)

Yet Jung does not simply rely on classical texts: once again, following the hints provided by language, he notes that "this general classical application of the conception" is confirmed by "the corresponding etymological context of the word", namely, *libido* or *lubido* (with *libet*, or the older *lubet*) = "it pleases me", and *libens* or *lubens* = "gladly, willingly" (Jung, 1991, para. 218). Here Jung might also be thinking of Jakob Böhme's use

10   Paul Bishop

of the term "*lubet*" in the initial chapters of his *Mysterium Magnum* to mean pleasing or pleasurable delight. (For further discussion, see Cardew, 2012, p. 131.)

In a chapter of *The Psychology of the Unconscious* entitled "The Conception and the Genetic Theory of Libido", Jung notes, with reference to Freud's *Three Contributions to the Sexual Theory* (1905), how libido is conceived here "in the original sense of sexual impulse, sexual need" (Jung, 1991, para. 219). Does this conception interpret libido as "everything sexual'? Jung thinks not, remarking that "the hypothetical idea at the basis is the symbol of the "Triebbündel" [bundle of impulses], wherein the sexual impulse figures as a partial impulse of the whole system, and its encroachment into the other realms of impulse is a fact of experience" (Jung, 1991, para. 219). As Jung goes on to write, however, "since the appearance of the *Three Contributions*, in 1905, a change has taken place in the libido conception; its field of application has been widened" (Jung, 1991, para. 219). Polemically, even provocatively, Jung associates himself with this conceptual "widening" of the notion of the libido by citing Freud again, this time from his study of Schreber, *Psycho-Analytic Notes on an Autobiographical Account of a Case of Paranoia (Dementia Paranoides)* (1911). So, for Freud – and for Jung, too, in his *The Psychology of Dementia Præcox* (1907) – paranoid schizophrenia reveals another aspect to libido, one that sounds remarkably proto-Lacanian:

> The fact is that in many cases [of paranoid schizophrenia] reality disappears entirely, so that not a trace of psychological adaptation or orientation can be recognized. Reality is repressed under these circumstances and replaced by the contents of the complex. One must of necessity say that not only the erotic interest but the interest in general has disappeared, that is to say, the whole adaptation to reality has ceased.
>
> *(Jung, 1991, para. 220)*

What else is the libido for Jung? Elsewhere he says that "the conception of libido as developed in the new work of Freud and of his school has functionally the same significance in the biological territory as has the conception of energy since the time of Robert Mayer in the physical realm" (Jung, 1991, para. 218), and it is in this sense that Jung himself develops the term "psychic energy" (cf. Jung, 1991, para. 221).

But he also has recourse to mythology, and to those Neoplatonic systems that draw on the ancient cosmogonies of Hesiod and of Plato. For libido (as he conceives it) reminds Jung, or so he says, of "the cosmogenic meaning of Eros in Plato and Hesiod" (a footnote refers us to the *Theogony*), "and also of the Orphic figure of Phanes, the *shining one*, the first created, the 'father of Eros' " (Jung, 1991, para. 223). And he goes on, via the figure of Phanes, and the associated figures of Priapus and Dionysos Lysios (i.e. the Liberator or Deliverer, the god of "letting go"), to relate these representations of libido to two further traditions: first, the Indian figure of *kâma*, the god of love, and second, the Neoplatonic doctrine of Plotinus. (See Drews, 1907, p. 127; cf. Plotinus, *Enneads*, II.4.3–5 and 16.)

On Jung's account of Plotinus, the "world-soul" is "the energy of the intellect" (Jung, 1991, para. 223), and seen in these Plotinian terms, libido can be conceived as the One, as "the creative primal principle" (as Jung puts it) and as "light in general": within this system, the intellect can be compared with the (masculine) sun, the world-soul with the (feminine) moon (Jung, 1991, para. 223). Elsewhere, Plotinus explains that "the world-soul has a tendency towards a divided existence and towards divisibility, the *conditio sine qua non* of all change, creation and procreation"; it is "an 'unending all of life' and wholly energy", it is "a living organism of ideas, which attain in it effectiveness" (Jung, 1991, para. 223; cf. *Enneads*, II.5.3). For Plotinus, "the intellect is its procreator, its father, which, having conceived it, brings it to development in thought" (Jung, 1991, para. 223; cf. *Enneads*, IV.8.3). Or as Plotinus writes (in a passage directly cited by Jung): "What lies enclosed in the intellect, comes to development in the world-soul as logos, fills it with meaning and makes it as intoxicated with nectar" (*Enneads*, III.5.9; cited in Jung, 1991, para. 223).

In the course of this discussion it becomes evident that Jung has a very clear sense of the difference between *repression* and *sublimation*. In *The Psychology of the Unconscious*, for instance, he notes:

> The process of transformation of the primal libido into secondary impulses always took place in the form of affluxes of sexual libido, that is to say, sexuality became deflected from its original destination and a portion of it turned, little by little, increasing in amount, into the phylogenetic impulse of the mechanisms of allurement and of protection of the young. This diversion of the sexual libido from the sexual territory into associated functions is still taking place. Where this operation succeeds without injury to the adaptation of the individual it is called *sublimation*. Where the attempt does not succeed it is called *repression*.
>
> *(Jung, 1991, para. 228)*

Here again, the difference between Lacan and Jung emerges along the fault line of the concept of adaptation: for Jung, adaptation to the world is a sign of success, whereas for Lacan, adaptation locks the individual into a permanent state of self-alienation.

Affinities: quaternity

It turns out that, curiously enough, both Lacan and Jung have an interest in fourfold structures. In "Kant avec Sade" (1963), Lacan explains why his diagrams so frequently involve a quaternity: "A quadripartite structure has, since the introduction of the unconscious, always been required in the construction of a subjective ordering" (Lacan, 1996, p. 774); in this case, the four elements involved are the will to enjoy (*V*), the subject (*S*), the "barred subject" (barred *S*), and the object (*a*). In addition to the quadripartite structure of the Oedipus Complex (mother, child, father, phallus), his "schema L" has four nodes (*S* [or *Es*], *objet petit a*, ego, and the Other); there are four discourses (of the master, the university, the hysteric, and the analyst); there are four fundamental concepts of psychoanalysis (the unconscious, repetition, the transference, and the drive); and the *sinthome* constitutes the fourth, virtual ring in the Borromean knot (of the three orders of Real, Symbolic, and Imaginary) that ties the three other rings together (see Evans, 1996, pp. 158–159).

In this respect, Lacan shares a core interest with Jung, for throughout the development of his psychological system, Jung demonstrated a remarkable passion for the detection of opposites and their resolution through the constellation of quaternities (see McLynn, 1996, pp. 474–475). Not only are there the four psychic functions of thinking, feeling, sensation and intuition, but he pointed to Empedocles's four elements, Hippocrates's four "humours", the ascending quaternity of *anima* figures (Eve, Helen, Mary, Sophia), the four figures of the Trinity together with the Virgin Mary, and he frequently quoted the lines from the "Kabeiroi Scene" of Goethe's *Faust II*: "Three we took off beside us,/The fourth of them denied us" (*Faust II*, ll. 8186–8187; Goethe, 2001, p. 232). Could this schematic interest in the quaternity mark the point where a *rapprochement* between Jungian and Lacanian psychology might take place?

Yet the heart of the major conceptual (and also clinical?) difference between Lacan and Jung might, however, be expressed by examining their attitude to a theme on which we have already touched – namely, religion; and, in particular, in their relation to the intellectual currents of the first three or four centuries of the Common Era, Gnosticism and Neoplatonism.

Lacan, Jung and Gnosticism?

Does, one wonders, Lacan really understand the religious? (One feels obliged to ask this question despite – or perhaps because of – his flirtation in various ways with Roman Catholicism; see Pound, 2008, pp. 13–16, 88–90, 137–141.) Consider, for instance, his (in)famous discussion of Bernini's remarkable statue, *The Ecstasy of Saint Teresa*, at the end of his sixth session in Seminar XX, *Encore*:

> You need but to go to Rome and see the statue by Bernini
> to immediately understand that she's coming. There's no
> doubt about it. What is she getting off on? It is clear that
> the essential testimony of the mystics consists in saying
> that they experience it, but know nothing about it.
>
> *(Lacan, 1998, p. 76)*

To this analysis of Bernini's statue, one might reply with Jung that "the unconscious recasting of the erotic into something religious lays itself open to the reproach of a sentimental and ethically worthless pose" (Jung, 1991, para. 126). Leaving aside the question of ethics, Lacan's comments on Bernini's *The Ecstasy of Saint Teresa* seem to point to an aesthetic deficit, or to a religious deficit, or possibly even to both.

Nevertheless, according to some commentators there are significant affinities between Lacan and Gnosticism. For Daniel Burston, for instance, there are elements of Gnosticism in Lacan's characterization of the ego as an "imaginary function", as a creature of "specular identification", or as an illusory, artificial construct embedded in "the discourse of the other". The goal of Lacanian analysis – the deconstruction of the ego, not its support and strengthening – echoes "the ancient Gnostic view that all but a handful of *cogniscenti* fundamentally misrecognize themselves and their condition" (Burston, 2000, p. 122). Now one of the most striking characteristics of Gnosticism is its antagonism to the body. (In this respect, it is useful to compare Plotinus' attack on the Gnostics in his *Enneads*, II.9, "Against the Gnostics; or Against Those that Affirm the Creator of the Cosmos and the Cosmos Itself to be Evil"). One might see here a key affinity on the part of Gnosticism with Lacan, who is not really interested in the body (except in its "symptoms"), and especially not in biological instincts. (For further discussion, and a defence of the view that for Lacan the body is "a reality", see Soler, 1995.)

Lacan distinguishes strictly between instincts and drives, associating *Instinkte* in his early writings with biology (and, in his later writings, differentiating between demand, desire and pre-linguistic need) and using *Triebe* as cultural and symbolic constructs. Surely we cannot get any further away from Jung than when, in *The Four Fundamental Concepts of Psycho-Analysis*, Lacan informs his listeners that his teaching invites them, if they are to "understand the unconscious", to "renounce" any "recourse" to "a reference to some ultimate given, something archaic, primal" (Lacan, 1978, p. 162). Lacan's thought is a de-biologized thought – and is not just this. He is interested in *structures*, and these structures are (somehow) disembodied, so Lacan's thought is a non-anatomical, non-physiological thought as well. (As a consequence, this would arguably give rise to the question: can then there be such a thing as a Lacanian aesthetics?)[3]

This absence of an interest in the body in Lacan's thought marks out its strongest affinity with Gnosticism, and it also seems to me that a further hallmark of Gnosticism is that, like Lacan, it does not really have a concept of the sublime (cf. Costelloe [Ed.], 2013), for strangely enough, the sublime as a category is missing from Lacan's thought. This point is made by Philip Shaw in his extremely useful primer on the subject of the sublime, where he points out that although in his *Seminar*, volume 7, *The Ethics of Psychoanalysis* (1959–1960), Lacan notes that the "conjunction" of *the sublime* (as it is defined by Kant) and *sublimation* is "probably not simply an accident nor simply homonymic" (Lacan, 1992, p. 301), he does not actually explain what the significance of that conjunction is (Shaw, 2006,

p. 132). (Indeed, in an earlier session, Lacan had passed, in a masterful act of delegation, the task of talking about the beautiful and the sublime in Kant to another seminar participant, Pierre Kaufmann (Lacan, 1992, pp. 286–287).) This is a point to which I shall return.

For his part, and by contrast, Jung has a reputation for being *all too* gnostic, a reputation whose origins can be traced with some precision. In the late 1950s, at around the time that he was working on his *Answer to Job* (1952), Jung became caught up in a controversy with the Jewish philosopher Martin Buber (1878–1965). Buber's accusation that Jung was a Gnostic was one that he, Jung, strongly rejected and, one might add, hotly disputed.[4] Yet one can see why Buber was suspicious. After all, Jung does use Gnostic vocabulary, not least in the text privately published as the *Septem Sermones ad mortuous*, which opens with the notions of Pleroma and Creatura, and features the figure of a Gnostic deity, Abraxas. For Peter Kingsley, Jung belongs firmly in the tradition of Gnosticism, to which alchemy was the crucial bridge back (Kingsley, 2018, pp. 586–590, 606–608). And in the light of the publication of *The Red Book*, we can clearly see how this deployment of Gnostic vocabulary is part and parcel of a larger engagement with world mythology, as evidenced, for instance, by the figure of Izdubar. Moreover, *The Red Book* is the text that makes my case: that Jung is interested in BEAUTY, to be sure, but he is also interested in the RELIGIOUS SUBLIME. I shall argue that it is *here* that the real dividing line between Lacan and Jung should be seen.

It is surely telling that when Lacan does try to develop an approach to art, he does so with reference to the theme of "the Thing" (*la chose* = *das Ding*) – and by invoking the notion, not of the *sublime*, but of *sublimation*. In his Seminar on *The Ethics of Psychoanalysis*, Lacan tells us:

> "This Thing, all forms of which created by man belong to the sphere of sublimation, this Thing will always be represented by emptiness, precisely because it cannot be represented by anything else – or, more exactly, because it can only be represented by something else. But in every form of sublimation, emptiness is determinative"
>
> *(Cette Chose, dont toutes les formes créées par l'homme sont du registre de la sublimation, sera toujours représentée par un vide, précisément en ceci qu'elle ne peut pas être représentée par autre chose – ou plus exactement, qu'elle ne peut qu'être représentée par autre chose. Mais dans toute forme de sublimation, le vide sera déterminatif)*
>
> *(Lacan, 1992, pp. 129–130).*[5]

While it is true that, as Michel Cazenave has suggested, the "Thing" can be read as the equivalent of some kind of originary maternal (Cazenave, 2012, comments at 27:00), it is striking that Lacan, in an entirely characteristic way, emphasizes its emptiness – *le vide*. Indeed, he thematizes it, declaring that "all art is characterized by a certain mode of organization around this emptiness", while adding (in a way that is highly significant for our discussion here) that "religion in all its forms consists of avoiding this emptiness" (Lacan, 1992, p. 130).

Now it is true that an alternative view of sublimation and the sublime from a Lacanian perspective is offered by Paul Allen Miller, when he discusses Lacan's presentation in his Seminar on *The Ethics of Psychoanalysis* of Sophocles' *Antigone* as a pure model of desire. This is because, for Miller, Sophocles' *Antigone* "presents", "in its beauty", "what Lacan defines as a 'Sublime Object'" (Miller, 2007, p. 2), yet this term is not actually one used by Lacan, but rather by Slavoj Žižek, who defines it in *The Sublime Object of Ideology* as "an object raised to the level of the (impossible-real) Thing" (Žižek, 1989, pp. 202–203). Although the title of Žižek's book is indebted, as has been argued, to Lacan's *objet petit a*, understood as "an unconscious and unattainable fantasy that takes a distinct form for each individual" (Parker, 2011; Parker, 2004, p. 107), the actual context of Žižek's discussion is Kant's third *Critique*, rather than Lacan on Sophocles.

In his Seminar on *The Ethics of Psychoanalysis*, Lacan does describe the figure of Antigone in a way that associates her with the sublime – she has an "unbearable splendor", he says, "she has a quality that both attracts us and startles us, in the sense of intimidates us; this terrible, self-willed victim disturbs us" (Lacan, 1992, p. 247). Nevertheless, it is Žižek who really supplies the definition of the sublime in Lacanian terms, not Lacan himself. For Žižek, who is drawing on Kant and Hegel rather than directly on Lacan, the sublime is conceived, "not . . . as a transcendent "Thing-in-itself" beyond the field of representation" but rather as "an indicator of the traumatic emptiness, the primordial lack, residing at the heart of all forms of symbolization" (Shaw, 2006, p. 138). Thus, on Žižek's reading of Lacanian psychoanalysis, the sublime is "identified, via Hegel, as the 'reified' effect of the inconsistency of the symbolic order", and its fascination derives from "its status as an indicator of the Thing, the emptiness at the heart of the Real without which signification could not occur" (Shaw, 2006, p. 147). Nevertheless, the sublime as a concept is not so much an absence *for* Lacan as it is absent *from* him (yet supplemented by Žižek). One might say that when one looks for the sublime in Lacan, all one finds is an absence.

By contrast, the sublime is very much present in Jung – not as a concept (for we run here into Jung's reluctance to deal with aesthetic concepts or to conceptualize his own work in aesthetic terms),[6] but through something even more important: its ENACTMENT. One can already detect the sublime in the soaring rhetoric that Jung, from time to time, deploys: one thinks, for example, of the opening paragraphs of *Transformations and Symbols of the Libido*:

> The impression made by [Freud's] simple reference [to the Oedipus legend] may be likened to that wholly peculiar feeling which arises in us if, for example, in the noise and tumult of a modern street we should come across an ancient relic – the Corinthian capital of a walled-in column, or a fragment of inscription. Just a moment ago we were given over to the noisy ephemeral life of the present,

16   Paul Bishop

> when something very far away and strange appears to us, which turns our attention to things of another order; a glimpse away from the incoherent multiplicity of the present to a higher coherence in history.
>
> *(Jung, 1991, para. 1)*

Or, then again, in the conclusion to *Answer to Job*, in a passage which in its own way exemplifies the sublime:

> Even the enlightened person remains who he is, and is never more than his own limited ego before the One who dwells within him, whose form has no knowable boundaries, who encompasses him on all sides, fathomless as the abysms of the earth and vast as the sky.
>
> *(Jung, 1969, para. 758)*

Yet the sublime is most unmistakeably, patently and self-evidently present in its most tangible form in the case of Jung's *The Red Book* (Jung, 2009).

For while *The Red Book* is, as I have argued elsewhere, above all a quest for beauty (Bishop, 2014), this beauty is, as I have also tried to suggest, a special kind of beauty: it is a beauty beyond beauty, and from *a certain point of view* this quest for beauty also involves the sublime. And if we rightly understand the relation between the beauty and sublimity, we can understand the role that both beauty and sublimity play in the psychoanalytic outlook expounded by Jung. To understand this, however, we must not confuse the sublime as a *discourse* with the sublime as an *affect*.

Schiller on the sublime

Within the long and complicated history of the discourse on the sublime, from Longinus via Burke, Kant, Hegel, to Lacan and Žižek, we should not overlook the contribution of a leading poet, playwright and aesthetician in the classical period of German culture, Friedrich Schiller (1759–1805). On the topic of the sublime, Schiller contributed two important essays, "On the Sublime" (*Vom Erhabenen*) (1793) and "Concerning the Sublime" (*Über das Erhabene*) (pub. 1801, but composed between 1794 and 1796) (Schiller, 2005a, pp. 22–44, 70–85). (For further critical discussion of these works, see Barnouw, 1980 and Hinnant, 2002). In both these essays, Schiller makes insightful remarks on beauty as well as the sublime, and it is clear that, for Schiller, beauty and the sublime are *separate*, albeit *clearly related*, concepts.

In his second essay, Schiller explains the relation of the sublime to the beautiful as follows:

> Nature gives us two genii to accompany us through life. The one, sociable and comely, shortens our trouble-filled journey with its cheerful games; it eases the bonds of necessity

for us, and in the midst of joy and levity it guides us to those dangerous places where we must act as pure spirits and lay aside everything corporeal, in other words, it leads us to the knowledge of truth and to the exercise of duty. Here it abandons us, since its realm is only the world of the senses and its earthly wings cannot carry it beyond this world. But then another genius steps forward, a strong-armed genius, serious and silent, that carries us across the dizzying depth.

(Schiller, 2005a, p. 73)

Of course, the first of these genii is "the feeling of the beautiful", the second is "the feeling of the sublime". What exactly *is* the sublime for Schiller? He defines it as "a mixed feeling" – "a combination of *being in anguish* (at its peak this expresses itself as a shudder) and *being happy* (something that can escalate to a kind of ecstasy)" which, "although it is not actually pleasure, is still preferred by noble souls over all pleasure", and he distinguishes two kinds of "sublime object", those that relate to "our *powers of comprehension*" and those that relate to "our *powers of living*" (Schiller, 2005a, p. 74). Elsewhere in this essay Schiller distinguishes the beautiful from the sublime as follows: "Reason and sensuality harmonize in the case of what is beautiful, and only on account of this harmony does it hold any charms for us". By contrast, "in what is sublime . . . there is *no* harmony of reason and sensuousness and the spell that captivates our minds lies precisely in this contradiction" (Schiller, 2005a, p. 75).

So these statements might prompt one to ask: why do we need the sublime at all? As Schiller explains,

In this way nature has wielded a sensuous means to teach us that *we are more than simply sensuous*. It has known how to employ even sensations to lead us to the realization that we have been subjected to their brute force in nothing less than the manner of a slave. This is a completely different effect than can be accomplished by beauty, namely, by the beauty of the actual world, since *even the sublime must lose itself in something ideally beautiful.*

(Schiller, 2005a, p. 75)

In other words, the sublime is related (as is beauty, albeit in a different way) to the great Schillerian theme of *freedom*:

The sublime thus fashions for us a beautiful point of departure from the sensuous world in which the beautiful would gladly detain us forever. Not gradually (since there is no transition from dependency to freedom), but only suddenly and through a kind of shock, does something sublime tear the independent spirit loose from the net a sophisticated sensuousness uses to ensnare it.

(Schiller, 2005a, p. 77)

In order to explain how this works, Schiller has recourse – as he so often does – to the classical realm, and specifically to Homer:

> Beauty in the shape of the goddess Calypso had enchanted the courageous son of Ulysses, and by the power of her charms she long held him captive on her island. Although he was simply lying in the arms of lust, he long believed he was paying homage to an immortal divinity. But suddenly, in the shape of Mentor, a sublime impression took hold of him; he recalled his higher calling, dove into the waves, and was free.
>
> *(Schiller, 2005a, p. 77)*

And Schiller makes use of a further classical image to convey his message, in a way that would surely have been congenial to Jung – "as long as the human being was merely a slave of physical necessity" and "as long as he found no way out of the narrow circle of needs", the human being does not have a clue about "the lofty *daimonic* freedom lurking in his heart": that is, "something enduring in his own being" or "the absolute grandeur within him" (Schiller, 2005a, p. 78; translation modified), what Schiller earlier calls "the absolute grandeur within us" or "this discovery of an absolute, moral capability" (Schiller, 2005a, pp. 75–76).[7] (Indeed, on Schiller's account the discovery of this capacity *is* the sublime: "the melancholy feeling. . . , that completely distinctive, unspeakable charm, that *sublimity* that no pleasure of the sense, however noble it be, can ever compete with" [Schiller, 2005a, p. 77].)

Hence, for Schiller, the sublime appeals to the *daimon* within each of us: indeed, on his account there is something about the sublime that lies beyond the purely human:

> The capacity to feel the sublime is thus one of the most glorious dispositions in human nature, deserving our *respect* due to its origin in a self-sufficient capacity to think and will; because of its influence on moral human beings, it deserves as well to be developed in the most complete possible manner. The beautiful renders itself deserving on the account of the *humaneness* in a human being, the sublime on account of the *purely daimonic* in him.
>
> *(Schiller, 2005a, p. 83; translation modified)*

Thus, the sublime completes the "aesthetic education" which, in his major treatise of 1795, *On the Aesthetic Education of Man in a Series of Letters*, Schiller had so closely related to the beautiful:

> Because it is our calling to orient ourselves, in the face of all sensuous limitations, according to the lawbook of pure spirits, the sublime must come to the assistance of the beautiful in order to make the *aesthetic education* a

complete whole and expand the human heart's sensitivity
to the entire scope of our calling, extending even beyond
the world of the senses.

(Schiller, 2005a, pp. 83–84)

Seen in these Schillerian terms, how do Lacan and Jung contribute to our "aesthetic education"? Lacan, it would seem, has little to contribute, whereas Jung, by contrast, has an enormous amount to contribute. For it would be impossible to overstate the importance to Jung of beauty. In *The Psychology of the Unconscious*, for instance, he argues:

It is rather the *incapacity to love which robs mankind of his possibilities*. This world is empty to him alone who does not understand how to direct his libido towards objects, and to render them alive and beautiful for himself, for Beauty does not indeed lie in things, but in the feeling that we give to them.

(Jung, 1991, para. 284)

Because of this investment in "objects" and the "feeling" we give them, Jung does not share Lacan's antagonism toward the body. After all, the archetypes are not simply structures, but they are structures that must be embodied.

Over recent years a number of commentators have begun reading Jung in the light of Neoplatonism.[8] From the point of view of our discussion here, the important thing about the Neoplatonic tradition is that it takes a very sophisticated approach to the body and to the soul (or psyche). Its belief in order, teleology, and hierarchy, coupled with its interest in the problem of the One and the Many, are all hallmarks of Jungian analytical psychology. Furthermore, the emphasis on the divine within in Platonic thought is entirely compatible with Jung's notion of individuation as the path to salvation. And this leads me to a concluding point: Jung can have a notion of religion, because Jung is open to the experience of the sublime. Hence the sublime is *the* key to the decisive difference between Lacan and Jung.

Conclusion

"And the Word became flesh, and dwelt among us". Ultimately Jung is the inheritor of this tradition, not Lacan. This difference is reflected in their approach to the sublime: in Lacan, the sublime is neither theorized nor practised; for Jung, it is not theorized, but it is nevertheless practised.

For Lacan, human subjectivity is based on a split or organized around an absence. Just as entry into the Imaginary involves a moment of joy in a moment of self-(mis)recognition, followed by the devastating realization that the "ideal I" is unattainable, so the entry into the Symbolic is marked by another structuralization of loss. The *objet petit a* is (always already) missed or missing, and at the heart of the Symbolic lies a void or the "Thing", something that can never be represented yet must nevertheless be presupposed in order for reality to cohere (cf. Shaw, 2006, p. 134). As Lacan puts it in his seminar on *The Ethics of Psychoanalysis*, "the fashioning of the signifier and the introduction of a gap or a hole in the real is identical", and correspondingly "the Thing is characterized by the fact that it is impossible for us to imagine it" (Lacan, 1992, pp. 121, 125). Or as Philip Shaw has argued, "the Thing for Lacan is a kind of non-thing; we become aware of it as a kind of void or absence residing at the heart of signification" (Shaw, 2006, p. 135).

By contrast, what Jung discovers in *The Red Book* – and what he actually *shows* us in *The Red Book*, both in its various details and in the sheer fact of its existence – is the exact opposite. Within the overall economy of *The Red Book*, a crucial turning point comes in the moment when Jung comes to identify the tower which the Kabeiroi have constructed for him: "I set foot on new land. . . . I serve myself and I myself serve. Therefore I have what I need" (Jung, 2009, p. 321). This tower is remarkable not least because of how it has been constructed: "It has not arisen from a patchwork of human thoughts, but has been forged from the glowing heat of the innards; the Kabeiroi themselves carried the matter to the mountain and consecrated the building with their own blood", after which Jung himself "built it out of the lower and upper beyond" – recall the etymological origin of "the sublime" from the Latin *sublimis* = *sub* ("up to') and *limen* ("lintel", or top piece of a door) – "and not from the surface of the world" (Jung, 2009, pp. 321–322). Yet the tower in *The Red Book* is equally remarkable for what it represents, namely, "the happiness of h[im] who surveys things . . . and who lives from himself" (*die Herrlichkeit des Schauenden und des aus sich selber Lebenden*) (Jung, 2009, p. 321). Jung tells us how, with the construction of the tower, he has acquired a kind of Goethean "permanence in change", or *Dauer im Wechsel* (Goethe, 1998, pp. 84–87), which he defines in terms of solidity:

> Thus I built a firm structure. Through this I myself gained stability and duration and could withstand the fluctuations of the personal. Therefore the immortal in me is saved [*Dadurch ist das Unsterbliche an mir gerettet*].
> *(Jung, 2009, p. 323)*

Now by speaking of how he has saved what is immortal about him, Jung touches on an extremely important theme in the work of earlier thinkers, including Spinoza and Schelling, that can be traced back to Plato and finds its classic statement in a dialogue attributed to him, *Alcibiades I*.[9] For reasons of space, let me concentrate here on Spinoza, Schelling, and Schiller.

In a famous passage in the fifth and final part of his *Ethics* (pub. 1677), Baruch Spinoza (1632–1677) tells us that we know – indeed, that we *experience* – that we are "eternal":

> We feel and know by experience that we are eternal. . . .
> Although, therefore, we do not recollect that we existed

before the body, we feel that our mind, insofar as it involves the essence of the body under the form of eternity, is eternal, and that this existence of the mind cannot be limited by time nor manifested through duration.

(Ethics, part 5, proposition 22, scholium;
Spinoza, 1928, p. 385)

When we read the question posed in Jung's *Memories, Dreams, Reflections*, "Are you related to something infinite or not?" (Jaffé, 1963, p. 356), we might well hear in it not just an echo, but a reformulation of Spinoza's invitation in this fifth part of his *Ethics* to regard the world (as he repeatedly puts it) *sub specie aeternitatis*, "under the form of eternity" (*Ethics*, part 2, proposition 44, corollary 2, and part 5, propositions 22, 23, 29 and 30; Spinoza, 1928, pp. 191, 384–385, 387–389). (For further reflections on Jung's view on the eternal, see Jaffé, 1963, p. 327.)

Spinoza's argument about the experience of our eternity recurs in a work by F.W.J. Schelling. In his *System of Transcendental Idealism* (1800), we find Schelling, in the context of a discussion of the categorical imperative (or the moral law), writing about what he calls "the eternal in me" as follows:

> [In transcendental philosophy] even the moral law is merely deduced as a condition of self-consciousness. This law originally applies to me, not insofar as I am this particular intelligence, for indeed it strikes down everything that belongs to individuality and completely destroys; it applies to me, rather, as an intelligence in general, to that which has as its immediate object the purely objective, the eternal in me [*das Ewige . . . in mir*].
>
> (Schelling, 1978, p. 188)

In other words, the moral law applies to the individual not *qua* individual, but rather to the individual as a vehicle for, or as a bearer of, immortality; and thereby it makes us aware of what is "eternal" within us.

As we have seen, this is an important notion for Schiller as well, when he speaks of "the lofty *daimonic* freedom lurking in [our] heart", "something enduring in [our] own being", or "the absolute grandeur within us". Elsewhere Schiller strikingly depicts this idea, writing in his poem entitled "The Ideal and Life" (*Das Ideal und das Leben*):

> When thou art weigh'd down by human care,
> When the son of Priam there
>   Strives against the snakes with speechless pain,
> Then let man revolt! Then let his cry
> To the canopy of heav'n mount high, –
>   Let thy feeling heart be rent in twain!
> Let the radiant cheek of joy turn pale,
>   Nature's fearful voice triumphant be,

And let holy sympathy prevail
O'er thine immortality! [*das Unsterbliche in euch!*]
(Schiller, 1874, pp. 198–199)

If we trace this tradition even further back to its Platonic and Neoplatonic sources, its affinity with Jung's thinking becomes even clearer. In the section of the second speech of Socrates in the *Phaedrus* devoted to the soul, Socrates offers an account of "that place beyond the heavens [of which] none of our earthly poets has yet sung, and [of which] none shall sing worthily" (*Phaedrus*, 247c; Plato, 1997, p. 494). On this mythical account, the moral forms are to be found in this "place beyond the heavens", and it is here that the soul may behold them:

> It is there that true being dwells, without color or shape, that cannot be touched; reason alone, the soul's pilot, can behold it, and all true knowledge is knowledge thereof. . . . And while [the soul] is borne round she discerns justice, its very self, and likewise temperance, and knowledge. . . , the veritable knowledge of being that veritably is. And when she has contemplated likewise and feasted upon all else that has true being, she descends again within the heavens and come back home.
> *(Phaedrus, 247c-e; Plato, 1997, p. 494)*

In the philosophy of Plotinus, however, this account undergoes a remarkable transformation. For here, the moral forms are to be found, not in "that place above the heavens", but within the soul itself, and what, in Plato, the soul sees as transcendent realities are, in Plotinus, introjected within and made part of the soul's self-vision (see editorial footnote in Plotinus, 1984, pp. 384–385):

> For it is not by running hither and thither outside of itself that the Soul understands morality and right conduct: it learns them of its own nature, in its contact with itself, in its intellectual grasp of itself, seeing deeply impressed upon it the images of its primal state.
> *(Ennead IV.7, §10; Plotinus, 1956, p. 354)*

It is precisely this move that Jung makes in *The Red Book*: turning from the world without to the world within, letting himself "drop" (as he puts it in *Memories, Dreams, Reflections*), and discovering an entire world of visions, images, forms and principles *within himself* – a vision that may, stylistically speaking, be properly described as *sublime*.

Moreover, what we find time and again in this remarkable work are expressions of a RELIGIOUS SUBLIME. In the very first chapter of *Liber primus*, "The Way of What is to Come", we are told: "The way is within us, but not in Gods, or in teachings, nor in laws. Within us is the way, the truth, and the life" (Jung, 2009, p. 231). In the third chapter, "Soul and God", Jung cries out to his own soul:

> I am weary, my soul, my wandering has lasted too long, my search for myself outside of myself. Now I have gone through events and find you behind all of them. For I made discoveries on my erring through events, humanity, and the world. I found men. And you, my soul, I found again, first in images within men and then you yourself. I found you where I least expected you. You climbed out of a dark shaft. You announced yourself to me in advance in dreams [which were dark to me, and which I sought to grasp in my own inadequate way]. They burned in my heart and drove me to all the boldest acts of daring, and forced me to rise above myself. You let me see truths of which I had no previous inkling. You let me undertake journeys, whose endless length would have scared me, if the knowledge of them had not been secure in you.
>
> *(Jung, 2009, p. 233)*

Further on in *Liber primus*, in the chapter entitled "Descent into Hell in the Future", Jung comments on his vision of a blond hero, a black scarab, and a stream of thick red blood that he had had on the night of 12 December 1913:

> Depths and surface should mix so that new life can develop. Yet the new life does not develop outside of us, but within us. What happens outside us in these days is the image that the peoples live in events, to bequeath this image immemorially to far-off times so that they might learn from it for their own way, just as we learned from the images that the ancients had lived before us in events.
> Life does not come from events, but from us. Everything that happens outside has already been.
>
> *(Jung, 2009, p. 239)*

In the final chapter of *Liber primus*, "Resolution", we read: "Man doesn't only grow from within himself, for he is also creative from within himself. The God becomes revealed in him" (Jung, 2009, p. 253), and shortly later in this chapter Jung declares:

> In the end I found that I wanted myself in everything, but without looking for myself. Therefore I no longer wanted to seek myself outside of myself but within. Then I wanted to grasp myself [*mich selber fassen*] and then I wanted to go on again, without knowing what I wanted, and thus I fell into the mystery [*so fiel ich ins Mysterium*].
>
> *(Jung, 2009, p. 254)*

24 Paul Bishop

In the conclusion to the fourth chapter of *Liber secundus*, "One of the Lowly", we find one of the most sublime moments of this most sublime of works:

> The moon is dead. Your soul went to the moon, to the preserver of souls. Thus the soul moved toward death. I went into the inner death and saw that outer dying is better than inner death. And I decided to die outside and to live within. For that reason I turned away [from death] and sought the place of the inner life.
>
> *(Jung, 2009, p. 267)*

And the sublimity of Jung's writing becomes more sublime still when in the central chapter of *Liber secundus*, "The Remains of Earlier Temples", he himself undergoes a transformation into a Green Man:

> But I was no longer the man I had been, for a strange being grew through me. This was a laughing being of the forest, a leaf green daimon, a forest goblin and prankster, who lived alone in the forest and was itself a greening tree being, who loved nothing but greening and growing, who was neither disposed nor indisposed toward men, full of mood and chance, obeying an invisible law and greening and wilting with the trees, neither beautiful nor ugly, neither good nor bad, merely living, primordially old and yet completely young, naked and yet naturally clothed, not man but nature, frightened, laughable, powerful, childish, weak, deceiving and deceived, utterly inconstant and superficial, and yet reaching deep down, down to the kernel of the world.
> [. . .]
> Within myself I had become one as a natural being, but I was a hobgoblin who frightened the solitary wanderer, and who avoided the places of men. But I greened and bloomed from within myself. I had still not become a man again who carried within himself the conflict between a longing for the world and a longing for the spirit. I did not live either of these longings, but I lived myself, and was a merrily greening tree in a remote spring forest. And thus I learned to live without the world and spirit; and I was amazed how well I could live like this.
>
> *(Jung, 2009, pp. 276–277)*

This is to say nothing of the further transformations that Jung undergoes in the remainder of this work. What Jung "sees", paints, describes and transcribes in *The Red Book* – in all senses, its "vision" – is captured well in the quotation from Coleridge that Hull felt prompted, after reading *The Red Book*, to propose as the motto that now prefaces Jaffé's introduction to *Memories, Dreams, Reflections* – "He looked into his own soul with a telescope. What seemed all irregular, he saw and shewed to be constellations: and he added to the consciousness hidden worlds within worlds" (Bair, 2003, p. 617; cf. Coleridge, 1957, no. [1798]). (For further discussion of the affinities between Coleridge and Jung, see Toor, 2012.)

To summarize the conclusions of this chapter: *if* there is a Lacanian sublime (and it is by no means clear that there necessarily is one), then it is a sublimity of absence: a dizzying void, a gnawing absence, or a "primordial lack". By contrast, there certainly *is* a Jungian sublime, and it is a sublimity of a profoundly religious kind. For *The Red Book* is many things – such as a "quest for beauty", an expression of Jung's status as a "mystical fool" (cf. Jung's unpublished letter of 1975; Adler, 1875, p. 12), a "cathedral" for "the silent spaces of your spirit where you will find renewal" (cf. Jung's remark to Christiana Morgan; Jung, 2009, p. 216), or even something utterly, gloriously mad (cf. Richard Hull's comment to William McGuire; Jung, 2009, p. 221).[10] But it is also an exercise in sublimity, albeit one that, from time to time, risks slipping from the sublime to the ridiculous. Could this be how we should also see *The Red Book*, as an exercise in taking risks – the ultimate form of the sublime?

Notes

1 I should like to thank the organisers and participants at the Joint Jung/Lacan Conference, "The Notion of the Sublime in Creativity and Destruction", for their comments and feedback. An earlier version of this chapter was first published as "*Wie hast du es mit der Religion?* Lacan, Jung, and the Religious Sublime" in Robin S. Brown (ed.), *Re-Encountering Jung: Analytical Psychology and Contemporary Psychoanalysis*, London and New York: Routledge, 2018, pp. 195–217, and I am grateful for permission to republish this paper here in a slightly revised form.

2 The German philologist and philosopher Steinthal was a pupil of Wilhelm von Humboldt, whose writings on linguistics he edited. Himself a Jew, and one of the directors of the Deutsch-Israelitische Gemeindebund, in 1860 he founded, together with German philosopher and psychologist (and his brother-in-law) Moritz Lazarus (1824–1903) the *Zeitschrift für Völkerpsychologie und Sprachwissenschaft*, a journal dedicated to the "science" of racial psychology. In *Transformations and Symbols of the Libido*, Jung cites two papers by Steinthal (see Steinthal, 1862a; Steinthal, 1862b).

3 Compare with Ruth Ronen's observation regarding Lacan's seminar on anxiety: "Lacan's aesthetics is in this sense derivative and cannot be straightforwardly applied to the aesthetic dilemma. The fact that Lacan's thought on art does not constitute an aesthetic theory yet somewhat paradoxically points at its affinity rather than distance from Kant" (Ronen, 2009, p. 26).

4 For further discussion of the Jung/Buber debate and the issues involved, see Sborowitz, 1956; Progoff, 1966; Erlenwein, 1987; Dourley, 1994.

5 For the context of these remarks, see Lacan's earlier comments:

> "As far as the signifier is concerned, the difficulty is to avoid leaping on the fact that man is the artisan of his support system.

> For many years now, I have habituated you to the notion, the primary and dominant notion, that the signifier as such is constituted of oppositional structures whose emergence profoundly modifies the human world. It is furthermore the case that those signifiers in their individuality are fashioned by man, and probably more by his hands than by his spirit. And here we encounter the linguistic usage that, at least in connection with sublimation in the sphere of art, never hesitates to speak of creation. We must now, therefore, consider the notion of creation with all it implies, a knowledge of the creature and of the creator, because it is central, not only for our theme of the motive of sublimation, but also that of ethics in its broadest sense. I posit the following: an object, insofar as it is a created object, may fill the function that enables it not to avoid the Thing as signifier, but to represent it"
>
> (*La difficulté concernant le signifiant est de ne pas se précipiter sur le fait que l'homme est l'artisan de ses supports. Pendant de longues années, je vous ai pliés à la notion, qui doit rester première et prévalente, de ce qui constitue le signifiant comme tel, à savoir les structures d'opposition dont l'émergence modifie profondément le monde humain. Il reste que ces signifiants sont, dans leur individualité, façonnés par l'homme, et probablement avec ses mains plus encore qu'avec son âme. C'est ici notre rendez-vous avec l'usage du langage, qui, tout au moins pour la sublimation de l'art, n'hésite jamais à parler de création. La notion de création doit être maintenant promue par nous, avec ce qu'elle comporte, un savoir de la créature et du créateur, parce qu'elle est centrale, non seulement dans notre thème, le motif de la sublimation, mais dans celui de l'éthique au sens le plus large. Je pose ceci, qu'un objet peut remplir cette fonction qui lui permet de ne pas éviter la Chose comme signifiant, mais de la représenter, en tant que cet objet est créé*).
>
> (Lacan, 1992, p. 119)

For further discussion, see Saint-Cyr, 2010.

6   Peter Kingsley dismisses Aniela Jaffé's portrayal in *Memories, Dreams, Reflections* of Jung's *Red Book* as "aesthetic elaboration" (2018, p. 424, cf. pp. 788–790, n. 57), castigating those who promote a "textual Jung" (p. 74). So the question remains: is what we are confronted with in *The Red Book* (to use the terms of the Swiss classicist, Maria Laura Gemelli Marciano et al., 2013, pp. 231–233, 280) a question of "literary concepts" or "attitudes", or is it a question of "hard inner experience" (Kinsgley, 2018, pp. 493–494, n. 52)? Or is this itself a false binary?

7   Similarly, in his essay "On Grace and Dignity" (1793), Schiller describes love as "*absolute greatness* itself, . . . the legislator himself, the God in us, who plays with his own image in the world of senses" (Schiller, 2005b, p. 166), a turn of phrase echoed by Jung when, in *The Relations between the* Ego *and the Unconscious* (1928), he writes of the self as something "strange to us and yet so near, wholly ourselves and yet unknowable" and indeed as "the god within us" (Jung, 1953, paras. 398–399).

8 For further discussion of Jung's interest in Neoplatonism in general and in Plotinus in particular, see Barnes, 1945; Schwyzer, 1975a; Schwyzer, 1975b; Williamson, 1985; Robertson, 2002; and MacLennan, 2006. In *Revisioning Psychology*, James Hillman drew links between Renaissance Neoplatonism and archetypal psychology (Hillman, 1975, pp. 193–211), and for the most recent discussion, see Henderson, 2014; Shaw, 2016; Weldon, 2017; Cardew, 2018; and Kinsgley, 2018, pp. 559, 609, 617, 792–797.

9 In the crucial passage in this dialogue attributed to Plato, Socrates discusses with his eponymous interlocutor the question of how the soul can know itself. In the immediately following passage, subsequently added by a later Neoplatonist, this argument is linked to a preceding discussion about the injunction of the Delphic Oracle, "know thyself", and the role of vision as a model of knowledge (*Alcibiades I*, 133c; in Plato, 1997, p. 592).

10 For further discussion of *The Red Book* in relation to the theme of madness, see Bishop, 2017a; and Kinsgley, 2018, pp. 492–494. In "Nox tertia", Jung's soul tells him that "madness is a special form of the spirit and clings to all teachings and philosophies, but even more to daily life, since life itself is full of craziness and at bottom utterly illogical" (Jung, 2009, p. 298). Later, Jung restates this idea in "Archetypes of the Collective Unconscious" (1934a, 1954) with reference to the archetype of *anima* as the archetype of life itself: "In elfin nature wisdom and folly appear as one and the same; and they *are* one and the same as long as they are acted out by the anima. Life is crazy and meaningful at once" (Jung, 1968a, para. 65). For the indebtedness of Jung's understanding of *anima* to Nietzsche's allegorical figure of Life, see Bishop, 1994, p. 204.

Bibliography

Adler, G. (1975). Aspects of Jung's Personality and Work. *Psychological Perspectives*, 6(1): 11–21.

Bailly, L. (2009). *Lacan: A Beginner's Guide*. London: Oneworld.

Bair, D. (2003). *Jung: A Biography*. Boston, London and New York: Little, Brown.

Barnes, H.E. (1945). Neo-Platonism and Analytical Psychology. *The Philosophical Review*, 54(6): 558–577.

Barnouw, J. (1980). The Morality of the Sublime: Kant and Schiller. *Studies in Romanticism*, 19(4): 497–514.

Bishop, P. (1994). *The Dionysian Self: C.G. Jung's Reception of Friedrich Nietzsche*. Berlin and New York: de Gruyter.

Bishop, P. (2014). Jung and the Quest for Beauty: *The Red Book* in Relation to German Classicism. In T. Kirsch and G. Hogenson (Eds.), *The Red Book: Reflections on C.G. Jung's "Liber Novus"* (pp. 11–35). London and New York: Routledge.

Bishop, P. (2017a). In a World That Has Gone Mad, Is What We Really Need . . . A Red Book? In M. Stein and T. Arzt (Eds.), *Jung's Red Book for Our Time: Searching for Soul Under Postmodern Conditions* (pp. 125–142). Asheville, NC: Chiron.

Bishop, P. (2017b). *On the Blissful Islands: With Nietzsche & Jung in the Shadow of the Superman*. London and New York: Routledge.

Bodlander, R.C. (1990). Heraklit und Jung. *Analytische Psychologie*, 21(2): 142–149.

Burston, D. (2000). *The Crucible of Experience: R.D. Laing and the Crisis of Psychotherapy*. Cambridge: Harvard University Press.

Cardew, A. (2012). The Archaic and the Sublimity of Origins. In P. Bishop (Ed.), *The Archaic: The Past in the Present* (pp. 93–146). London and New York: Routledge.

Cardew, A. (2018). Antiquity and Anxiety: Freud, Jung, and the Impossibility of the Archaic. In P. Bishop and L. Gardner (Eds.), *The Ecstatic and the Archaic: An Analytical Psychological Inquiry* (pp. 56–76). London and New York: Routledge.

Carus, P. (1911). The Ideal and the Life: By Friedrich Schiller. *The Monist*, 21(2): 278–284.

Cazenave, M. (2012). *Continents intérieurs*. La beauté, reflet du divin. Retrieved from www.continents-interieurs.info/Michel-Cazenave/La-beaute-reflet-du-divin.

Coleridge, S.T. (1957). *The Notebooks, 1794–1804*, vol. 1, Ed. K. Coburn. London: Routledge and Kegan Paul.

Costelloe, T.M. (Ed.) (2013). *The Sublime: From Antiquity to the Present*. Cambridge: Cambridge University Press.

Dourley, J.P. (1994). In the Shadow of the Monotheisms: Jung's Conversations with Buber and White. In J. Ryce-Menuhin (Ed.), *Jung and the Monotheisms: Judaism, Christianity and Islam* (pp. 125–145). London and New York: Routledge.

Drews, A. (1907). *Plotin und der Untergang der antiken Weltanschauung*. Jena: Diederichs.

Erlenwein, P. (1987). Individuation und Begegnung: Überlegungen zum Verhältnis von Tiefenpsychologie und Religion an Hand der Werke C.G. Jungs und M. Bubers. *Zeitschrift für Religions- und Geistesgeschichte*, 39: 69–83.

Evans, D. (1996). *An Introductory Dictionary of Lacanian Psychoanalysis*. London and New York: Routledge.

Fowler, F.M. (Ed.) (1969). Notes. In *Schiller: Selected Poems* (pp. 111–169). London: Macmillan; New York: St Martin's Press.

Gemmelli Marciano, M.L. et al. (2013). *Parmenide: suoni, immagini, esperienza*. Sankt Augustin: Academia Verlag.

Goethe, J.W. (1908). *Faust, Parts I and II*, Trans. Albert G. Latham. London and New York: Dent and Dutton.

Goethe, J.W. (1998). *Selected Poems*, Trans. J. Whaley. London: Dent.

Goethe, J.W. (2001). *Faust*, Ed. C. Hamlin, Trans. W. Arndt. London and New York: Norton.

Harris, W.V. (2001). *Restraining Rage: The Ideology of Anger Control in Classical Antiquity*. Cambridge: Harvard University Press.

Henderson, D. (2014). *Apophatic Elements in the Theory and Practice of Psychoanalysis: Pseudo-Dionysius and C.G. Jung*. Hove and New York: Routledge.

Hillman, J. (1975). *Revisioning Psychology*. New York: Harper & Row.

Hinnant, C.H. (2002). Schiller and the Political Sublime: Two Perspectives. *Criticism*, 44(2): 121–138.

Homer, S. (2005). *Jacques Lacan*. Abingdon and New York: Routledge.

Jaffé, A. (Ed.) (1963). *Memories, Dreams, Reflections of C.G. Jung*, Trans. R. Winston and C. Winston. London: Collins, Routledge and Kegan Paul.

Jung, C.G. (1953). *Two Essays on Analytical Psychology* [*Collected Works of C.G. Jung*], vol. 7, Trans. R.F.C. Hull. London: Routledge & Kegan Paul.

Jung, C.G. (1968a). *The Archetypes and the Collective Unconscious* [*Collected Works of C.G. Jung*], vol. 9/i, Trans. R.F.C. Hull. Princeton, NJ: Princeton University Press.

Jung, C.G. (1968b). *Psychology and Alchemy* [*Collected Works of C.G. Jung*], vol. 12, Trans. R.F.C. Hull. London: Routledge & Kegan Paul.

Jung, C.G. (1969). *Psychology and Religion: West and East* [*Collected Works of C.G. Jung*], vol. 11, Trans. R.F.C. Hull. London: Routledge and Kegan Paul.

Jung, C.G. (1991). *Psychology of the Unconscious: A Study of the Transformations and Symbolisms of the Libido: A Contribution to the History of the Evolution of Thought*, Trans. B.M. Hinkle, Intro. W. McGuire. London: Routledge.

Jung, C.G. (2009). *The Red Book: Liber Novus*, Ed. S. Shamdasani, Trans. M. Kyburz, J. Peck, and S. Shamdasani. London and New York: Norton.

Kingsley, P. (2018). *Catafalque: Carl Jung and the End of Humanity*, 2 vols. London: Catafalque Press.

Lacan, J. (1978). *Four Fundamental Concepts of Psycho-Analysis*, Ed. J.-A. Miller, Trans. A. Sheridan. New York: Norton.

Lacan, J. (1991a). *Le Séminaire de Jacques Lacan. Livre VIII: Le Transfert, 1960–1961*, Ed. J.-A. Miller. Paris: Seuil.

Lacan, J. (1991b). *The Seminar: The Ego in Freud's Theory and the Technique of Psychoanalysis, 1954–1955*, vol. 2, Ed. J.-A. Miller, Trans. S. Tomaselli. London and New York: Norton.

Lacan, J. (1992). *The Seminar. Book 7: The Ethics of Psychoanalysis, 1959–1960*, Ed. J.-A. Miller, Trans. D. Porter. London and New York: Norton.

Lacan, J. (1996). Kant avec Sade. In *Écrits* (pp. 765–790). Paris: Seuil.

Lacan, J. (1998). *Seminar. Vol. 20: Encore 1972–1973: On Feminine Sexuality; The Limits of Love and Knowledge*, Trans. B. Fink. London and New York: Norton.

Lacan, J. (2002). *The Seminar. Book VI: Desire and its Interpretation, 1958–1959*, Trans. C. Gallagher. London: Karnac Books.

MacLennan, B.J. (2006). Individual Soul and World Soul: The Process of Individuation in Neoplatonism and C.G. Jung. In T. Arzt and A. Holm (Eds.), *Wegmarken der Individuation* [Studienreihe zur Analytischen Psychologie, 1] (pp. 83–116). Würzburg: Königshausen and Neumann.

McLynn, F. (1996). *Carl Gustav Jung: A Biography*. London: Bantam Press.

Miller, P.A. (2007). Lacan's *Antigone*: The Sublime Object and the Ethics of Interpretation. *Phoenix*, 61(1–2): 1–14.

Packer, J.M. (2006). "Zwischen Sinnenglück und Seelenfrieden": Chiasmus and Symmetry in Schiller's "Das Ideal und das Leben". *Colloquia Germanica*, 39: 257–273.

Parker, I. (2004). *Slavoj Žižek: A Critical Introduction*. London and Sterling, VA: Pluto Press.

Parker, I. (2011). Slavoj Žižek. In *Encyclopædia Britannica*. Retrieved from www.britannica.com/Ebchecked/topic/1446643/Slavoj-Zizek/301049/The-Sublime-Object-of-Ideology.

Plato (1989). *Collected Dialogues*, Eds. E. Hamilton and H. Cairns. Princeton, NJ: Princeton University Press.

Plato (1997). *Complete Works*, Ed. J. M. Cooper. Indianapolis and Cambridge: Hackett.

Plotinus (1956). *The Enneads*, Trans. S. MacKenna, Revised B.S. Page. London: Faber and Faber.

Plotinus (1984). *Ennead IV*, Trans. A.H. Armstrong. Cambridge and London: Harvard University Press.

Pound, M. (2008). *Žižek: A (Very) Critical Introduction*. Grand Rapids, MI: Eerdmans.

Progoff, I. (1966). The Man who Transforms Consciousness: The Inner Myth of Martin Buber, Paul Tillich, and C.G. Jung. *Eranos-Jahrbuch*, 35: 99–144.

Robertson, R. (2002). Stairway to Heaven: Jung and Neoplatonism. *Psychological Perspectives: A Quarterly Journal of Jungian Thought*, 44(1): 80–95.

30 Paul Bishop

Ronen, R. (2009). *Aesthetics of Anxiety*. Albany, NY: State University of New York Press.

Saint-Cyr, V.M. (2010). La sublimation chez Lacan: Destruction créatrice du sujet. *Psychoanalytische Perspektiven*, 28(1–2): 163–188.

Sborowitz, A. (1956). *Beziehung und Bestimmung: Die Lehren von Martin Buber und C.G. Jung in ihrem Verhältnis zueinander*. Darmstadt: Gentner.

Schelling, F.W.J. (1978). *System of Transcendental Idealism*, Trans. P. Heath. Charlottesville: University Press of Virginia.

Schiller, F. (1874). *Poems*, Trans. Edgar A. Bowring. London: Bell.

Schiller, F. (2005a). On the Sublime, Concerning the Sublime. In W. Hinderer and D.O. Dahlstrom (Eds.), *Essays* (pp. 22–44 and 70–85). New York: Continuum.

Schiller, F. (2005b). *Schiller's "On Grace and Dignity" in its Cultural Context: Essays and a New Translation*, Eds. J.V. Curran and C. Fricker. Rochester: Camden House.

Schwyzer, H.-R. (1975a, July 25–26). Archetyp und absoluter Geist: C.G. Jung und Plotin. *Neue Zürcher Zeitung*, "Literatur und Kunst", 38.

Schwyzer, H.-R. (1975b). The Intellect in Plotinus and the Archetypes of C.G. Jung. In J. Mansfeld and L.M. de Rijk (Eds.), *Kephalaion: Studies in Greek Philosophy and its Continuation Offered to Professor C.J. de Vogel* (pp. 214–222). Assen: Van Gorcum.

Shaw, G. (2016). Archetypal Psychology, Dreamwork, and Neoplatonism. In H.T. Hakl (Ed.), *Octagon: The Quest for Wholeness: Mirrored in a Library Dedicated to Religious Studies, Philosophy and Esotericism in Particular*, vol. 2 (pp. 327–358). Gaggenau: scientia nova.

Shaw, P. (2006). *The Sublime*. London and New York: Routledge.

Soler, C. (1995). The Body in the Teaching of Jacques Lacan. *Journal of the Centre for Freudian Analysis and Research*, 6: 6–38.

Spinoza (1928). *Selections*, Ed. J. Wild. London: Scribner.

Steinthal, H. (1862a). Die ursprüngliche Form der Sage von Prometheus. *Zeitschrift für Völkerpsychologie und Sprachwissenschaft*, 2: 1–29.

Steinthal, H. (1862b). Die Sage von Simson. *Zeitschrift für Völkerpsychologie und Sprachwissenschaft*, 2: 129–178.

Toor, K. (2012). Dream Weaver: Samuel Taylor Coleridge and the prefiguring of Jungian Dream Theory. Retrieved from www.friendsofcoleridge.com.

Tourney, G. (1956). Empedocles and Freud, Heraclitus and Jung. *Bulletin of the History of Medicine*, 30: 109–123.

Weldon, J. (2017). *Platonic Jung and the Nature of Self*. Asheville, NC: Chiron.

Williamson, E. (1985). Plato's "Eidos" and the Archetypes of Jung and Frye. *Interpretations*, 16(1): 84–104.

Žižek, S. (1989). *The Sublime Object of Ideology*. London and New York: Verso.

TWO

Sublime anxiety

Bernard Burgoyne

1

A space in general will contain a part, but not all of its boundary. The same can be expected from the spaces of the mind: the psychic apparatus – the human soul – is a space that contains a part, but not all of its boundary (see Figure 2.1).

Pathways through this space can be constructed, and some of them will end on a part of the boundary that is contained within the space. A different experience can be expected from a pathway that approaches a boundary point that is missing. Any region that for the space is a region of lack I will take to be a region of desire. Psychoanalysis aims to construct pathways that approach such previously unattainable regions; the same attempt can also be part of the experiences and struggles of everyday life (see Figure 2.2).

2

There is some connection between anxiety and boundaries or borders. The experience of anxiety could be formulated as that of encountering a boundary in a locality where it was not expected to be.

Anxiety can be mild, or it can be severe: severe anxiety can tear the edges off the framework of your world. Severe anxiety in someone who is psychotic can propel them over the edges of an abyss. A milder anxiety can be beneficial – it can serve desire, and it can manage someone's pathways through the world.

The sublime also has to do with borders, or what comes at an edge. This is present in the very origins of the term. The word itself, in its original Greek as well as in Latin, indicates height, grandeur, elevation. If you look up at a frieze over a pillar, the highest parts of the pillar meet a line that is on a par with the horizon. This line appears unlimited, sweeping out into the spaces of the sky, and at times into the space of the sea. While the sublime may extend indefinitely, it can be infinitely approached, but not reached. The approach to the sublime seems to be a closing towards an edge of perception that is encountered with intimations and awe.

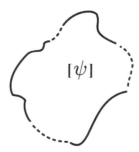

Figure 2.1   The psychic apparatus

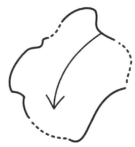

Figure 2.2   Psychoanalytic pathways

The sublime, whether in its ancient or modern conceptions, has certain characteristics: they are found in every episode involving the sublime. Going into the Greek camp at night to ask for the body of his murdered son Hector, Priam has a sublimity. His action has a greatness to it. He is at an extreme. Or, in a contemporary mode, one that is more elegiac, here are some lines from Wallace Stevens's poem "The Idea of Order at Key West": "She sang beyond the genius of the sea./The water never formed to mind or voice,/Like a body wholly body, fluttering/Its empty sleeves; and yet its mimic motion/Made constant cry, caused constantly a cry,/That was not ours although we understood,/Inhuman, of the veritable ocean" (Stevens, 2015[1936], p. 136).

The sublime is built from great words: "high words . . . high speech . . . high action" (Longin, 1993; Russell, 1964, pp. xxx–xlii). And the question arises: how can you approach something that is so high? There is a frontier between the various forms of such a skill, says Longinus, and this frontier can move. In trying to discover it, you disclose the various states of the soul: in investigating the sources of the experience of the sublime, you investigate the nature of the soul.

There are relations, then, between these terms: the sublime, anxiety, the soul. And these relations involve boundaries as well as limits. But we are moving a little fast. To explain some of this, let me take you back a little while ago, to some ancient views on the nature of the soul.

3

Throughout the post-Socratic era in Greek philosophy there was a focus on what can be called "striking perceptions". The clearest account of this is found in the epistemology and the psychology of the Stoic philosophers. The term there, which contains the apparatus of perception, and which represents a part of the agency of the German term *Vorstellung* (representation), is *phantasia*.[1] We will need to look at the structure of these *phantasia*, at how some of them become particularly strong, and at how this relates to the experience of the sublime (see Figure 2.3).

The German texts of Freud and Jung are full of references to these *Vorstellung* entities: while English translators have often – abysmally – translated this term as *idea*, I will keep it as *Vorstellung*, or simply *V*. The work of the various Stoic philosophers, with their distinction between "signifier" and "signified", is probably what led Lacan to replace this term *Vorstellung* with "signifier".

We are here in a world far removed from that of the common-sense theories of the Lockean traditions of English philosophy. In the research tradition that we are looking at, there is no commonsensical individual with a natural and largely truthful experience of the objects surrounding them. Instead, in our Greek tradition, any individual has an experience of the world which leads them to have these images or *phantasia*. The question arises: How do these images get close to the truth? How does a representation of the world catch something of the real? And to change the register for a moment: How does fantasy – while hiding truth – come close to it?

Of course, these questions also arise for theories, like Freud's, that take the *Vorstellung* to be the constitutive element of a human experience of the world. The structure of the human mind has been investigated in this form in a modern research tradition that starts with Leibniz, and then – via Kant – moves to the work of Fichte, Schelling and Hegel, before acquiring a more current vocabulary in the work of the post-Kantian philosopher Herbart. Many of the central themes of Herbart's work were taken up by Freud.

To go back to these ancient accounts of the nature of the soul, the historian of ancient psychotherapy and psychiatry Jackie Pigeaud has documented many of their elements (Pigeaud, 1987; Longin, 1993). The Stoics distinguished four elements in the perception of reality: *phantaston* and *phantasia*, *phantasma* and *phantastikon*. The *phantasia* is the field of representation – and of its corresponding affect – that is produced in the human soul. The *phantaston* is what produced it. The *phantastikon* is a state of the subject who is stretched or rendered haggard, not by a perception of what is

Figure 2.3   Phantasia

actual, but by an emptiness. It is this emptiness that constructs a *phantasma* (see Figure 2.4).

So Orestes says to his mother: "Mother, I beg you, don't allow them to come to me these virgins with bloody eyes and their serpents: they are here – see them leaping towards me" (cited by Pigeaud in Longin, 1993, p. 137). He sees a *phantasma* in this moment of sublime terror. The Stoic Chrysippus comments: "He sees this because he is prone to mania. . . [I]n reality he sees nothing, but he believes that he sees it" (Ibid., p. 137). In a more modern terminology – not necessarily a more accurate one – the Stoics were able to distinguish the field of neurosis from that of the psychoses, the field of illusion from the field of hallucination. So these Greek commentators were well aware that some phenomena were more veridical than others; they were well aware of hallucinatory phenomena and of being gripped by a *phantasma*.

The next term I would like to look at is *phantasia kataleptike*. It is the title of a paper by the renowned classicist (Francis) Henry Sandbach (1996[1971]). How to translate *kataleptike*? It is a term which means that in the moment of apprehension the perceiver is grasped: as in a cataleptic psychosis the body is grasped. It is clear from this term that such an experience contains awe, insofar as it immediately borders on it. There have been classical (and modern) disputes as to the active or passive nature of this experience, yet what is clear in all of these versions is that the experience is made up of a presentation that grips the participant and drags him to give his assent to its perception. Pigeaud points out that this is the "ideal form" of perception for the Stoics (Pigeaud, 1987, p. 122). For them, the ideal *phantasia* is what they called this *phantasia kataleptike*: a seizing of the body by a perception (see Figure 2.5).

This was a widely understood schema within a century of the founding of Alexandria by Alexander the Great. Although the schema draws on pre-Socratic influences, it had to compete with a contrary scheme of things drawn up by Alexander's tutor – Aristotle. The two programmes differ as regards the nature and bounds of reason and the limits encountered within

Figure 2.4 *Phantasma*

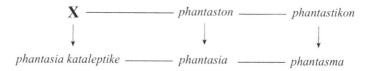

Figure 2.5 *Phantasia kataleptike*

the human soul. But let us stay a little with the text by Longinus on the sublime. It is a first-century CE text, and the author was well aware – 400 years after Alexander – of the questions that we have been discussing. Sublimity in speech leads, says Longinus, to the highest point – the eminence – of a discourse, and it leads not to persuasion, but to ecstasy. It acts as a vehicle for the presence of greatness, and it brings into play irresistible forces which go well beyond those possessed by the listener. But such a discourse catches only a trace of what is real. What is really sublime in the world creates a strong effect in the subject: what is great "is difficult – and even impossible – to resist, and it leaves a strong memory, which is difficult to erase" (Longin, 1993, p. 61).

This greatness can be found in Oedipus, where the effect is one of stupor, shock, desire, love and terror – a terrible access to the nature of the soul, the representation of which is, according to Aristotle, accompanied by pleasure (Aristotle, 1995, p. 75; Dupont-Roc and Lallot, 1980). The boundaries that previously contained the world have been shaken, but sometimes what is great can be found in a context which is more elegiac: "as when Ocean retires into himself, and is left lonely around his own limits" (Longin, 1993, p. 69). The borders of the tide have changed, the ebbing of Ocean becomes dry land. Longinus is here describing the *Odyssey*. He refers to Homer's text as a "current of passion poured upon passion", as a "throng of images all drawn from the truth" (Ibid., p. 64). And it is in this passage that we find the famous phrase used by Longinus: "the sublime is the echo of the grandeur of the soul" (Ibid., p. 64).

Now, this "greatness". Pigeaud says that it can be subject to mathematics, and for that one needs a *kairos* – a measure. *Kairos* (measure) is clearly not determined by numbers. So what kind of measurement is involved in this assessment of what is great? You do not take a stick to measure the Gods. And you do not take a metre rule to measure the soul. What is involved, here, is an operation on spaces of the soul, on topologies. The "X" with its arrows that appears in my final version of the Stoic schema (see Figure 2.5) is operative only within these spaces of the soul, as are the other arrows in all the previous forms of this schema, which aims to measure the differences between perception and reality.

Pigeaud, as he raises this issue, seems to think that the *kairos*, the measurement, is done with *adynata*, impossibilities. For sure, impossibilities are one way of approaching what is real. Pigeaud sets this term in relation to others: *krisis* (judgment of difference) and *ametron* (that which goes beyond what reason can subject to measure). Some of these terms go back to the earliest times of pre-Socratic cosmologies. The poet Sappho, he says, also uses such a measure: she takes the most eminent elements to put into her lines, those that create the most tension.[2] She takes them in fact out of her body, and puts them into the body of the poem.

The technique of the poet approaches the limits of these bodies: the sublime reaches out to these limits and is ready to go beyond them. Longinus refers to more than one type of measure here: human measures are only echoes of the measures of the God (Ibid., p. 65). As a human being

36   Bernard Burgoyne

contemplates the sea, the measure at play is "the leaping of the neighing horses of the Gods" (Ibid., p. 65). The sublime involves an apprehension of limits that go beyond old boundaries. Established boundaries inhibit the approach to desire; as boundaries shift, the soul is subjected to a new framing of the world. In this context, Longinus speaks of a delirium of enthusiasm.

The sublime is a point at which an external border is about to be brought into the interior. In this sense, the sublime is the creator of new borders and the destroyer of old bounds. Proximity to the incestuous object can create such an effect. But the ancients insist that this horror that is present in both anxiety and the sublime can be measured. And the soul can be measured because it is infused with language. Its words make a network that constitutes psychic space. At this point, I therefore ought to say something about the relation between the structure of *phantasia* and speech.

"The term *phantasia* is used generally for anything which in any way suggests a thought which is productive of speech" (Ibid., p. 65). So a first point to make would be that a *phantasia* engenders speech. Secondly, the *phantasia* constitutes a framework, and there is a close relationship between this framework and the ordered structure of representations that constitutes a world.[3] Claude Imbert, a contemporary historian of classical philosophy, puts it as follows: "A *phantasia* is . . . a vision which can be communicated in its entirety by language: language makes *phantasiai* explicit, and *phantasiai* bring language into existence" (Imbert, 1980[1978], p. 182).[4] The semantic force of a phrase, she says, derives wholly from the *phantaston* of the representation that gives rise to it. When this representation is cataleptic in its force, the phrase gives access to what is real.

The combination of representations by various forms of synthesizing, which introduce the forming of complexes and the blending of representations, involves the functions of "analogy, transference, composition, contrariety, and transition (*metabasis*)" (Ibid., p. 182). The relation between language and the space of representations involves a "mapping function, which relies on the structure of Stoic logic" (Ibid., p. 190). So a mathematical function is operative within the space of representations: a mathematical function that parallels the structuring of transference and, more generally, the art of rhetoric and the structure of logic.

Pigeaud's commentary had been as follows: "[T]he sublime is the perception of limit situations" (Longin, 1993, p. 20). The experience of the sublime tends therefore to represent the impossible (*adynata*) as coming within reach. If this limit could be reached, the beyond also could be reached. Hence the horror and the shock and the uncanny nature of an encounter with the sublime. In this context, Longinus speaks of the "separation of the world" and of the limits of space (Longin, 1993, p. 66). Later generations would recognize these notions – of limit and separation – as topological. In his text, Longinus represents them as dramatic – not that these two ways exclude one another. So the sublime is a structure that takes someone to the boundaries of their world; it is this structure that "possesses a poet's body and determines his words" (Ibid., p. 23).

The Stoic reading of *phantasia kataleptike* had taken it to be a strong representation, thought about which engenders speech, and Longinus was clearly aware of this usage in constructing his treatise (Russell, 1964, p. 120). The tradition on which he drew involves the whole field of Stoic theories of representation and in particular the relation of representations to the body. Imbert puts this strongly: "The action of sensorial catalepsis involves the effect of voice on the body. There is a force in the body which involves a voice: 'Voice is the physical condition of dialectical exchange. [A voice] is a body, according to the Stoics . . . for every active agent is a body, and a voice acts in going from the one who speaks to the listener'" (Imbert, 2006[1976], p. 93).[5]

What we have so far discovered about the sublime, then, involves this: (1) The experience contains within it a limit phenomenon, an extreme of "being grasped" by elements which underlie knowledge, (2) It involves a subsequent apparatus of judgment (*krisis*) which introduces both the space of memory and a corresponding access to truth (*aletheia*), (3) There are echoes in all of this that stem from the modern terminology that I mentioned earlier. Catalepsy is a grasping of the body by a force in the external world: catalepsy is where the body – to use Lacanian terms – is limited and crushed under the weight of the Other. We could call this cataleptic force on the body KAT.

So far we have mentioned, from ancient times, mania (we could also have added melancholia (Pigeaud, 1987)), delirium and cataleptic states. Let me now move on to Kant in 1764. This next topic, then, could well be called "From KAT to Kant".

4

I will discuss Kant's "Essay on the Maladies of the Head", from 1764 (Kant, 2011[1764]). But first an introductory note. Throughout his work, Kant attempted to chart the progress of reason. In this, he was repeatedly led to raise the question we have already raised with respect to the Greeks. How can the structure of the elements of representation – the *Vorstellungen* – give access to what is real? In a sense, his three *Critiques* represent an answer to this question, but they come later (Kant, 1998[1781], 1997[1788], 2002[1790]).[6] In 1764, as he took up the question of Rousseau's "General Will", Kant associated it with the sublime. This "true virtue alone", he said, "is sublime", and "true virtue can only be grafted upon principles, and it will become the more sublime and noble the more general they are" (Kant, 2011a[1764], pp. 22, 24).

By 1790, Kant was led to associate the sublime with mathematics. He started his "Analytic of the Sublime" in the *Critique of the Power of Judgment* (Kant, 2002[1790]) with three sections on the relations between mathematics and the sublime. In the sublime, he claimed, the unlimited and the boundless are represented: these mathematical notions – limit and bound – form part, then, of what he termed the "mathematical sublime"

38   Bernard Burgoyne

(Ibid., pp. 131–140). In contrast, he located, beyond the mathematical, the "dynamically sublime" in nature (Ibid., pp. 143–144). In the experience of nature, the sublime will always excite fear. In this process, he claimed, we find our own limitation, and in the sublime there is therefore always a feeling of pain. Kant had already brought together these two notions – of mathematics and of nature – in the content of a dream report that he gave at the start of his *Observations on the Feeling of the Beautiful and Sublime*. The dream is so remarkable that I am inclined to call it a "topological dream".[7] The second part of the dream, as Kant presents it, has a mathematical mise-en-scène:

> I quickly left innumerable worlds behind me. As I approached the most extreme limit of nature, I noticed that the shadows of the boundless void sank into the abyss before me. . . . The mortal terrors of despair increased with every moment, just as every moment my distance from the last inhabited world increased. I reflected with unbearable anguish in my heart that if ten thousand thousand years were to carry me further beyond the boundaries of everything created, I would still see forward into the immeasurable abyss of darkness.
>
> *(Kant, 2011a[1764], p. 17, note 9 cont.)*

The terror of separation (from nature) is couched by the dream in mathematical and topological terms: "innumerable", "extreme", "limit", "boundless", depths, "distance", "void", "boundary" and even the "immeasurable abyss" of despair.

By 1764, the year of his *Observations on the Feeling of the Beautiful and Sublime*, Kant's investigations had also led him to some conclusions regarding mental illness. Each mental illness, he says, occurs as a result of troubles affecting one of two faculties: those of perception and of judgment (Kant, 2011b[1764], p. 210). The three types of mental pathology that he distinguished on this basis were hallucination, delirium and mania.

As far as hallucinations are concerned, it is natural, says Kant, to have chimerical representations of the world. In order to see why this does not disorient the workings of reason, he looks at the differences between the waking state and the dream. In a waking state, he says, the vividness of any current impressions "obscure and render unrecognizable the more fragile, chimerical images" (representations) of things (Ibid., p. 210).[8] In a state of sleep this obscuring does not happen. But in both dreaming and waking states it can be that a strong sensory representation is obtained of something which is not there. Kant refers to it as a "phantom" representation (Ibid., pp. 210–211). Someone with strong reason can tolerate this, but otherwise (in Kant's phrase) someone who hallucinates is "a dreamer in waking" (Ibid., p. 211). Depending on whether this intrusion into reasoned perception is mild or severe, you get a spectrum, says Kant, of dispositions: *phantasia*, exaltation, enthusiasm, inspiration, some forms of melancholy and hypochondria (Ibid., p. 211).

The melancholic, Kant says, is a *phantasist* "with respect to life's ills" (Ibid., p. 212). Enthusiasm in politics – and this is before the French Revolution, so his reflections are about Rousseau rather than Robespierre – can be put down to *phantasism*. But in all of this, the faculty of judgment is not affected, merely the strength of perception. Judgment, however, can be affected, as in a delirium. At this point, Kant is principally thinking of paranoia, but also of what nowadays would be seen as the psychotic structure of melancholia. Judgment is also affected by the ravaging effects of mania. The spectra that Kant produces here are effectively derived from the notions of *phantasia* and *phantastikon*. Some of the spectra are applied to "debilities" of the mind, some to everyday perceptions of the world. In matters of everyday life, he says, love can make a *phantasist* of everyone (Ibid., p. 212).

5

In his 1912 text on transformations of the libido, Jung distinguished two types of thinking (Jung, 1967[1912], p. 7). What he called "thinking with directed attention" (Ibid., p. 11), and a further kind of thinking he called "subjective thinking", which "sets free", he says "subjective tendencies" (Ibid., p. 18). Frequently he calls this second type of thinking "dream thinking" or "*phantasia* thinking" (Ibid., p. 26). He will also call it "symbolic representation" (Ibid., p. 8). Jung set out to distinguish these two forms of thinking, whilst maintaining that the second is presupposed by the first. Now certainly they are distinct, and it seems that both of them are aspects of the activity of thinking. Let us start, then, by comparing some of Lacan's formulations of these themes with those that I take to be constructed in Jung's work. It is well known that Lacan, apart from in his late work, subordinated the Imaginary to the Symbolic. The work of analysis starts with the Symbolic implicit, and dominated by the Imaginary. The analysis leads to the predominance of the Symbolic over the Imaginary, and this will, at length, give an access to the Real:

Analysis: I/S $\rightarrow$ S/I $\rightarrow$ R

Jung, I think, may have chosen this *phantasia* term so as to give his theory access to an approach to the real. In doing so, it seems to me that he takes all *Vorstellung* elements, all concepts and all images to be translated into the language of the unconscious:

Translation: {V, C. I} $\rightarrow$ (M)Un $\rightarrow$ R

Here, (M)Un stands for the mythological structure of the unconscious. We could reformulate one aspect of this as follows:

Logic: Lg (V, C, I) $\rightarrow$ [R]

In this formula, Lg equals Directed Thinking (Logic), and [R] is the access to the real provided by the restricted circuits of the constitutions of reality.

40   Bernard Burgoyne

So when Jung uses a phrase such as "close to the mother or in her", the notion he is working with would seem to call for a topology.[9] But the mixing of Symbolic and Imaginary elements – representation, concept, image – would debar it: the structure of these combined elements does not allow for a topology, whereas the structure of signifiers does.[10]

There is directed thinking and, underneath it, symbolic thinking, which Jung says "obeys very special laws which have their own aim quite other than those of consciousness" (Jung, 1967[1912], p. 8). And when these latent laws manifest themselves, what is their aim? Jung is very precise. Their aim is to hide something precious. It is to hide the desire that is hidden within them, and which is their source. In this, both Jung, and later, Lacan would be in strong agreement. Where they will disagree, is on the nature of the laws that this symbolic is subject to. In the first instance, then, there is directed thinking, which Jung takes to operate only in consciousness, and which is itself subject to a number of laws, one of which is that it is subjected to "subordination to a ruling idea" (Ibid., p. 9). Jung takes it that this directed thinking elaborates itself in a language, the aim of which is to communicate. But it is otherwise with the underlying symbolic thinking: "originally, language is basically only a system of signs or symbols which designate real events and phenomena, or their echo in the human soul" (Ibid., p. 10). Jung supposes it to be of great importance to have access to these original strata, in order to be in possession of the fullness of the structure of language as it operates within the human soul. It is a contact with these earlier strata of symbolical thinking that gives an access to the "oldest layers of the human mind" (Ibid., p. 27). He cites the American philosopher and psychologist James Mark Baldwin in describing language as a "treasury of previous acquisitions" (Ibid., pp. 14–15). But Jung, as he does this, includes science within the spheres of directed thinking.[11] His claim is that symbolic thinking "uncovers creative forces", whereas – particularly post-Renaissance – science he assumes to have been organized around the "coldness and disillusionment" of directed thinking (Ibid., p. 19).[12] Directed thinking attempts to act within the confines of reality, whereas symbolic thinking liberates subjective desires. Jung's claim about directed thinking, then, is that it gives an access – but not the only access and, even then, a constrained access – to the real.[13]

Jung uses Kleinpaul's text from the late nineteenth century *The Life of Language* (Kleinpaul, 1893), and what he will draw from this gives him a further access to the real, one beyond the resources of directed thinking. Language is made up of signs which, whatever their origin, have connectivities and allusiveness, as they are taken up by the human subject. These two functions together construct a network which allows an access to the real, and to what Jung had called "its echo in the human soul" (Jung, 1967[1912], p. 10). There is another echo here, notably of the phrase used by Longinus to designate the sublime. I think this is no accident.

Within these connectivities, there are strata, and Jung seems to equate the most ancient of these strata with the unconscious. The relics of the infantile life of the individual are then given form – in fact they are "re-animated" – by these ancient types of symbolization. And it is these "most ancient foundations of the human spirit" that give a foundation for this "*phantasia-thinking*" which, unlike directed thinking, infiltrates into both unconscious and conscious forms of thinking. What differentiates Lacan (and the Stoics) from Jung, is that they take current language structures to be operative within the constitution of these *phantasia*.

But there is a more major difference between Lacan and Jung, namely in the assumptions they make about science. Jung finds in ancient science something that he takes to stand in opposition to the nature of modern science – the forms of mythology. Lacan, on the other hand, finds in ancient science the operation of Eleatic (and Socratic) dialectic, something which, as it turns out, is quite consonant with the structure of modern science and with mathematics.

Schrödinger cites the following passage from Jung, in lectures that were presented as the Tarner Lectures in October 1936 at Trinity College Cambridge:

> All science . . . is a function of the soul, in which all knowledge is rooted. The soul . . . is the *conditio sine qua non* of the world as an object . . . the Western world (apart from very rare exceptions) seems to have so little appreciation of this being so. The flood of external objects . . . has made the subject of all cognizance withdraw to the background, often to apparent non-existence.
>
> *(Schrödinger, 1958, p. 40)*[14]

Schrödinger comments: "Of course Jung is quite right". But he adds a proviso that "a rapid withdrawal from the position held for over 2,000 years is dangerous" (Ibid., p. 40). "The position held for over 2000 years" is the rise of the science of nature, accompanied by what seems, at first glance, to be an exclusion of the study of the nature of the soul. But the study of the "functions of the soul" is clearly organized around the notion of function; and function is a mathematical term, as are limit and boundary.[15] These terms appear early with the Greeks, and this is so despite the protestations of Heidegger, who deliberately turned his back on this rich cultural heritage of mathematics. Greek cosmology transfers its mathematical instruments to the study of the soul. It follows from this that mathematics can grasp the structure of the unconscious. Moreover, to paraphrase Herbart (2001[1822]), it is necessary that it do so.

Let us now see how this affected Sabina Spielrein, in her remarkable work *Die Destruktion als Ursache des Werdens* from 1912 (Spielrein, 2019[1912]). In this text, she claims the following: the content of every conscious thought (*Gedanken oder Vorstellungsinhalt*) is accompanied by unconscious content, by means of which the conscious content is translated into the unconscious. She is explicit that there is no means by which what could be a topological analysis of this could be done: "there is no boundary between these two domains" (Ibid., p. 218).

But as this translation is brought about, the differentiated *Vorstellungen* of consciousness find themselves transformed backwards into an undifferentiated domain, a domain that she says was familiar to the earliest pre-Socratic philosophers. Moreover, it is a very particular domain: "every particle of our being longs for such a back-transformation" (Ibid., p. 218).[16] There is a loss of differentiation in this archaic domain, whose content is made up of ancient kinds of *Vorstellungen* or Types.[17] Now this distinction between those *Vorstellungen* where separation is possible, and those where it is not, can be analyzed topologically, but of course this is not the way that her thinking progressed in 1912.[18] Her conclusion only alludes to space, but it runs as follows: when there is an established way of representing the world, every *Vorstellung* composing it is seeking unconscious material into which it can dissolve itself. There is thus a destruction attached to every achieved way of relating to the world. Destruction is part of a cycle that every representation of the world immediately falls prey to. I do not know of any reference to the death-drive earlier than this. She introduces a cycle of repetition (Figure 2.6).

This cycle of destruction will of course be found in the work of the artist, but also in every experience of the sublime. In *Part III* of her paper, she restates her main point. The nature of the V-structures (*Vorstellungen*) found in the unconscious is different from that of our current and conscious V-structures. So the unconscious cannot be understood by means of this current V-thinking. In order to understand it, we need access to the forms of thinking of our ancestors. And where I would like to draw on the "oldest topologies", she draws on the oldest myths.

In her thesis of 1911 she had drawn on the psychoanalytical work available to her: Jung, certainly, but also "Freud, Riklin, Rank and Abraham have drawn our attention to the similarity between the mechanisms of dreams of our time and mythical thought" (Spielrein, 1995[1911], p. 92).[19] She referred, in her conclusion to this thesis, to a theme which is straight out of the pre-Socratic cosmology of Empedocles. In the concluding lines of her thesis, she formulates her key concept as that of "the two antagonistic components of sexuality" (Ibid., p. 95).[20] She further refers in this conclusion to the tendency of a complex to dissolution, to "being emptied of all

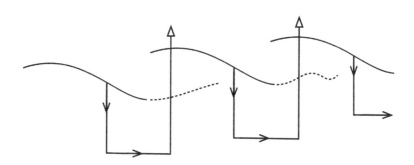

Figure 2.6   Cycle of repetition

that is personal" (Ibid., p. 94). And she adds at this point (in a footnote): "[This] transformation of each individual complex is the moving force of poetry, of painting, of every form of art" (Ibid., p. 94).

But only later, in her paper on time – "Time in Subliminal Psychic Life" (Spielrein, 2019[1923]) – does she take up the work of twentieth-century theorists of language.[21] In this paper, she refers to the work of Charles Bally, who had discussed a number of linguistic themes with her in Geneva.[22] She seems to be aware that mathematical language is also involved in this, because she discusses arithmetic functions and geometric shapes. Ten years earlier, in 1912, she had already referred to algebraic symbolism (Spielrein, 2019[1912], p. 242). Her primary focus in this text is the language of the child, but she also takes up the question of the relation between language and thinking, and the dependent relations that exist between each of these, and the structure of the mind.

Sublimation and the sublime both reach out towards the boundaries that Spielrein had earlier failed to notice. Of course, these two are not identical. However, they do have a large domain in common. They are centred on the experience of borders, of frontier, of barrier, of interior, of outside. With the sublime in particular, there is the experience of something that is great: of greater and less, of a partial (incomplete) ordering that is equipped with limits. Mathematicians work with this, as they do with general theories of space.

Mathematicians and poets follow the same pathways; artists and scientists pass through the same domains. In each case their search aims at a discovery and in each case their pathways towards it encounter impasse and overcoming, drama and renewal. A science of psychoanalysis, it seems, must therefore concern itself with the experience of poets. Poetry tests the impossibility of saying, and both mathematician and poet try to approach the real (Figure 2.7).

Anxiety is central to Lacan's work: its pathways give indications of what is real. Anxiety is the limit affect *par excellence*, as Marcus Vieira puts it (Vieira, 1998). As you move towards a limit, something grand appears which makes you very susceptible to a change of boundary. Anxiety becomes even stronger if a point on the border is reached – actually changing the structure

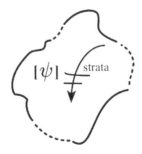

Figure 2.7 Approaching the real

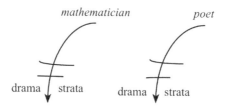

Figure 2.8   Artists become scapegoats

of desire. For Lacan, the limit-point of sublimation separates and conjoins beauty and horror. In sublime anxiety the horror is clear: the "great" aspect of the experience leads *beyond* the more earthly topology. The artist finds new representations, a new impetus to what is real. So in this fundamental respect, Spielrein was right. There is artistic creativity in the destructivity of the sublime. But because of the work that they create, artists may also become scapegoats, outside of the city's bounds (Figure 2.8).

6

In 1930, Freud published his text on what lies within and beyond the city's bounds: "The Discontent within Culture" is the title that he gave it (Freud, 1961[1930*a*]). In Chapter One, he writes as follows:

> It is impossible to escape the impression that people commonly use false standards of measurement. . . . There are a few men from whom their contemporaries do not withhold admiration, although their greatness rests on attributes and achievements which are completely foreign to the aims and ideals of the multitude.
> *(Freud, 1961[1930a], p. 64)*

One of my friends, says Freud, has suffered this fate; he described to me a sentiment of something "limitless", without bounds, an "oceanic sentiment", a sentiment of belonging to the totality of the external world. Freud then raises this question of boundaries in relation to the ego. Externally to the ego, he says, it "seems to maintain clear and sharp lines of demarcation" (Ibid., p. 66). With respect to the internal boundaries, however, this is much less clear. On these grounds, Freud claims that this appearance of the ego – of being clearly separated from what is outside of it – appears itself to be a lure. So these boundaries of the ego are problematic, rather than clear.

These frontiers have a history behind them, claims Freud. The child at the breast has a different version of the external world and the child's first objects appear at the same time as the first of these frontiers. Of these representations and objects, the painful ones are "expelled" (like a scapegoat beyond the city walls). The "pure pleasure-ego" so formed has its own frontiers that are themselves re-formed by the experience of pain. So in the beginning, the ego contains all, and by these processes it separates itself from an external world.[23]

So the sum of our actual sentiments of the world is but a feeble remainder of a more largely extended sentiment of the world. With some people, this original sentiment is still in place, remaining behind the more closed-up boundaries that have been brought into being by the ego's attempts at mastery of the world. And when this primary sentiment continues, there needs to be a wider class of spaces available than the ones allowed access to by the structuring of the ego. "[T]he same space", Freud says "cannot have two different contents" (Ibid., pp. 70–71). These primary spaces exist then, says Freud. There are these spaces, these sentiments, whose history has been one of repeated destruction, even when the relics of them survive. But he makes a call to arms: avoid aiming for a retreat into these primary spaces. He cites a Homeric reference by Schiller, in order to encourage the exploration of the present: "Let him rejoice who breathes up here in the roseate light!" (Ibid., p. 73).

Now for this theme of "oceanic sentiment". Henri and Madeleine Vermorel have documented Freud's relation with the author of this term, Romain Rolland. Freud wrote to Rolland on 19 January 1930: "We seem very far from each other in the way we evaluate intuition. Your mystics turn to it in order to find the solution of the enigmas of the universe; how I take it is that intuition can show us nothing but primitive dynamics and attitudes, close to the drive – this is very precious, when one understands it well, for an embryology of the soul, but not something that we can use to orientate ourselves in an external world which is strange to us" (Vermorel and Vermorel, 1993, pp. 313–314).

For Rolland, on the other hand, "mystical introversion [had a] scientific value in gaining knowledge of the real" (Ibid., p. 315). In his text on Empedocles he had claimed that the cycle of repetition inherent in the conflict between *philia* and *neikos* could be broken by a knowledge gained from contemplation (Rolland, 1931). Rolland and Freud may on several of these issues be a distance apart, but even a disquieting distance can be bridged. On 5 December 1927, Rolland had written to Freud (in response to Freud having sent him one of his books): "By "oceanic sentiment" . . . I understand . . . the simple and direct fact of the *sensation of the "eternal"*, which can very well not be eternal, but simply be *without perceptible bounds, and* [on account of this] *oceanic*" (Vermorel and Vermorel, 1993, p. 304). Freud replied to this, but almost two years later, on 14 July 1929. Your introduction of this term, he said at the start of his letter "has left me with no peace" (Ibid., p. 308).

The correspondence was to continue until 1936. Other events "within the city" were to leave neither of the correspondents with peace. But the pretence of a fundamental conflict between artistic sense and science continues to this day. Both science and art deal with problems of frontier, of border, of exterior and of interiority. Both the artist and the scientist address problems of resistance and inertia, encountering as they do so questions of boundary and limit. Both deal with the conflict of forces, and both attempt to represent this conflict within the structure of the mind: as they do, they find these conflicts present in the mind itself. The attempt to separate these two domains with the claim that they have little or nothing in common is untenable. I hope to have demonstrated, at least to some extent, that the attempt to discriminate and separate these two spheres of human activity misrepresents their true nature and elides the spatial reality of the human mind.

Notes

1 The term *Vorstellung* is common in German (and Austrian) psychology and philosophy from the seventeenth century.
2 See the section entitled "The Reconstituted Body" in Longin (1993, pp. 23–25). These remarks on the relation of body and mind had been instigated by a section of Longinus's text in which he commented on the relations at play in "the assemblage of passions" created in the poem (Prickard, 1930, pp. 23–24; Russell, 1964, pp. 100–101). The poem quoted by Longinus appears as Poem 20 in Sappho (1984), and as Poem 31 in Sappho (2003).
3 In mathematical terms, a measure (*kairos*) within the soul would presumably make use of this (partial) order relation within V, the space of representations.
4 This paper was first delivered at a conference in Oriel College Oxford in March 1978. It is the second of a pair of papers, the first being Imbert (2006[1976]), which was presented at a conference in Chantilly, France, in September 1976.
5 The citation in this passage is from Diogenes Laertius. "The voice which acts in going from the one who speaks to the listener" describes the situation of the child in the womb who introjects surrounding voices, and in particular that of the mother. It is also descriptive both of the psychoanalytical setting and the setting of Socratic dialectic. Lacan claims that, at least in part, these last two are identical. See Burgoyne (2018, 2020).
6 For a discussion of these themes in relation to contemporary problems of psychoanalysis, see Miller (2011), particularly Section IV, "Le statut du réel".
7 The dream is usually referred to as "Carazan's Dream". For an extensive account of this dream, and for the relation that Kant proposes between sublimity, ethical sentiment and melancholia, see Luftig (2011).
8 This notion of the obscuring and rendering inaccessible of representations will later be taken up by Herbart, during the early years of the nineteenth century, in his theory of the constitution of the unconscious by means of psychic conflict. See Herbart (2001[1822]). Herbart's theory itself will later form the basis of Freud's theory of repression.
9 Part II, Chapter VI, "The Battle for Deliverance from the Mother". This phrase occurs in the French version of the text (Jung, 1931[1912], p. 265), but it is absent in the later English translations.
10 This helps to explain the subsequent divergence between the formulations of Jung and those of Lacan.
11 He even cites the programmes of Kepler and Bruno in this respect.
12 Jung claimed that antiquity was hostile to science. But what he calls "the antique spirit", far from being organized around mythological themes, found

the structures taken up in early Greek cosmology, when it became organized around mathematical notions: limit, boundary, transgression of boundary, retributive force.

13 The type of access to the real that he is invoking here, he formulates as *"das Wie der wirklichen Welt"*.

14 Schrödinger (1958). The passage is from the *Eranos Jahrbuch* for 1946. The six lectures were presented by John Wisdom of the University of Cambridge, Schrödinger himself remaining in Vienna, as he was too ill at the time to travel to England.

15 The mapping referred to by Claude Imbert in her survey of the relations between representation and language is a function in this sense (Imbert, 2006[1976]).

16 In this context, Spielrein refers to pre-Socratic Greek cosmologists such as Anaxagoras, who proposed that the early structuring of the cosmos can be found "in the process of Being differentiating itself from the primal parts [*in der Differenzierung des Seinden aus dem Urelemente*]" (Spielrein, 2019[1912], p. 213). Freud had also cited Anaximander in this respect (1958[1912–13], p. 153). The separation described here is, as I have mentioned before, a mathematical notion.

17 The translators of the English version of this text (Bettina Mathes and Pamela Cooper-White) point out that by this term *Type*, Spielrein is probably referring to Jung's term "archetype".

18 Apart from anything else, the elements of the mathematical theory of general spaces – the field that is now called general topology – were still being put into place in 1912. Moreover, no more than a handful of people were thinking of treating psychoanalysis topologically at this point.

19 This concluding section is not translated in the available English excerpts of her thesis (Spielrein, 2019[1911])].

20 Freud was later to make this reference to Empedocles very explicit. In his "Analysis Terminable and Interminable" of 1937 he organizes his themes around Empedocles's notion of the two separated and antagonistic powers: love and strife, *philia* and *neikos* (Freud, 1964[1937c], pp. 245–247).

21 This paper on sublimation was given at the Berlin Congress of the International Psycho-Analytic Association in September 1922.

22 Bally was a student of Ferdinand de Saussure, and the co-editor of Saussure's *Course in General Linguistics* (de Saussure, 1960[1916]). Spielrein had drawn on (late nineteenth-century) linguistic theories before this, such as the *Völkerpsychologie* of Kleinpaul (1898). Freud had referred to this text in his letter to Fließ of 12 December 1897: "Let me recommend to you a book by Kleinpaul, *Die Lebendigen und die Toten* [The Living and the Dead]" (Masson, 1985, p. 286).

23 The allusions made here to early Greek cosmology are, I think, intentional.

References

Aristotle (1995). *Poetics*, Trans. S. Halliwell. Cambridge and London: Harvard University Press.

Burgoyne, B. (2018). The Changing Forms of a Research Programme. In L. Bailly, D. Lichtenstein and S. Bailly (Eds.), *The Lacan Tradition* (pp. 5–47). London and New York: Routledge.

Burgoyne, B. (2020). Presentation on Transference. In C. Neill, S. Vanheule and D. Hook (Eds.), *Reading Lacan's* Écrits: *From 'Seminar on "The Purloined Letter"'*

48   Bernard Burgoyne

to *'Response to Jean Hyppolite's Commentary on Freud's "Verneinung"'*. London and New York: Routledge.

de Saussure, F. (1960[1916]). *Course in General Linguistics*, Eds. Ch. Bally and A. Séchehaye, Trans. W. Baskin. London: Peter Owen.

Dupont-Roc, R. and Lallot, J. (Eds.) (1980). *Aristote. La poétique*. Paris: du Seuil.

Freud, S. (1958[1912–'13]). *Totem and Taboo*. In J. Strachey (Ed.), *The Standard Edition of the Complete Psychological Works of Sigmund Freud*, vol. 13 (pp. 1–162). London: The Hogarth Press and the Institute of Psycho-Analysis.

Freud, S. (1961[1930a]). Civilization and its Discontents. In J. Strachey (Ed.), *The Standard Edition of the Complete Psychological Works of Sigmund Freud*, vol. 21 (pp. 57–145). London: The Hogarth Press and the Institute of Psycho-Analysis.

Freud, S. (1964[1937c]). Analysis Terminable and Interminable. In J. Strachey (Ed.), *The Standard Edition of the Complete Psychological Works of Sigmund Freud*, vol. 23 (pp. 216–253). London: The Hogarth Press and the Institute of Psycho-Analysis.

Herbart, J.F. (2001[1822]). De la possibilité et de la nécessité d'appliquer les mathématiques à la psychologie. J. F. Herbart (1776–1841). Métaphysique, psychologie, esthétique. In C. Maigné (Ed.), *Cahiers de Philosophie de l'Université de Caen*, vol. 36 (pp. 127–163). Caen, France: Presses Universitaires de Caen.

Imbert, C. (1980[1978]). Stoic Logic and Alexandrian Poetics. In M. Schofield, M. Burnyeat and J. Barnes (Eds.), *Doubt and Dogmatism: Studies in Hellenistic Epistemology* (pp. 182–216). Oxford: The Clarendon Press.

Imbert, C. (2006[1976]). Théorie de la représentation et doctrine logique dans le Stoïcisme ancien. In J. Brunschwig (Ed.), *Les Stoïciens et leur logique* (pp. 79–108). 2e édition revue et augmentée. Paris: Vrin.

Jung, C.G. (1931[1912]). *Métamorphoses et symboles de la libido*, Trans. L. Vos-Aubier. Paris: Montaigne.

Jung, C.G. (1967[1912]). *Symbols of Transformation*, Trans. G. Adler and R.F. C. Hull. Princeton, NJ: Princeton University Press.

Kant, I. (1997[1788]). *Critique of Practical Reason*, Trans. M. Gregor. Cambridge: Cambridge University Press.

Kant, I. (1998[1781]). *Critique of Pure Reason*, Ed. and Trans. P. Guyer and A.W. Wood. Cambridge: Cambridge University Press.

Kant, I. (2002[1790]). *Critique of the Power of Judgment*, Ed. P. Guyer, Trans. P. Guyer and E. Matthews. Cambridge: Cambridge University Press.

Kant, I. (2011a[1764]). Observations on the Feeling of the Beautiful and Sublime. In P. Frierson and P. Guyer (Eds.), P. Guyer (Trans.), *Observations on the Feeling of the Beautiful and Sublime and Other Writings* (pp. 9–62). Cambridge: Cambridge University Press.

Kant, I. (2011b[1764]). Essay on the Maladies of the Head. In P. Frierson and P. Guyer (Eds.), H. Wilson (Trans.), *Observations on the Feeling of the Beautiful and Sublime and Other Writings* (pp. 203–217). Cambridge: Cambridge University Press.

Kleinpaul, R. (1893). *Das Leben der Sprache und ihre Weltstellung*. Leipzig: Verlag von Wilhelm Friedrich.

Kleinpaul, R. (1898). *Die Lebendigen und die Toten in Volksglauben, Religion und Sage*. Leipzig: G. J. Gröschen'sche Verlagshandlung.

Longin (1993). *Du sublime*, Trans. J. Pigeaud. Paris: Rivages.

Luftig, J. (2011). Fiction, Criticism and Transcendence: On Carazan's Dream in Kant's *Observations on the Feeling of the Beautiful and Sublime. MLN*, 126(3): 614–629.

Masson, J.M. (Ed.) (1985). *The Complete Letters of Sigmund Freud to Wilhelm Fließ: 1887–1904*. Cambridge and London: The Belknap Press of Harvard University Press.

Miller, J.-A. (2011). Progrès en psychanalyse assez lents. *La Cause Freudienne*, 78: 151–206.

Pigeaud, J (1987). *Folie et cures de la folie chez les médecins de l'Antiquité Gréco-Romain. La Manie*. Paris: Les Belles Lettres.

Prickard, A.O. (Ed.) (1930). *Longinus on the Sublime*. Oxford: Clarendon Press.

Rolland, R. (1931). *Empédocle, suivi de L'éclair de Spinoza*. Paris: du Sablier.

Russell, D.A. (Ed.) (1964). *"Longinus": On the Sublime*. Oxford: The Clarendon Press.

Sandbach, F.H. (1996[1971]). Phantasia Kataleptike. In A.A. Long (Ed.), *Problems in Stoicism* (pp. 9–21). London and Atlantic Highlands, NJ: The Athlone Press.

Sappho (1984). *Sappho: Poems and Fragments*, Trans. J. Balmer. London: Brilliance Books.

Sappho (2003). *If Not, Winter: Fragments of Sappho*, Trans. A. Carson. London: Virago.

Schrödinger, E. (1958). *Mind and Matter*. Cambridge: Cambridge University Press.

Spielrein, S. (1995[1911]). Extraits de sa thèse de doctorat en médecine: "Sur le contenu psychologique d'un cas de schizophrénie (Dementia Praecox)". *L'Évolution psychiatrique*, 60(1): 69–98.

Spielrein, S. (2019[1911]). On the Psychological Content of a Case of Schizophrenia (Dementia Praecox) (An Excerpt). In P. Cooper-White and F. Brock Kelcourse (Eds.), *Sabina Spielrein and the Beginnings of Psychoanalysis: Image, Thought, and Language* (pp. 197–208). New York: Routledge.

Spielrein, S. (2019[1912]). Destruction as the Cause of Becoming. In P. Cooper-White and F. Brock Kelcourse (Eds.), *Sabina Spielrein and the Beginnings of Psychoanalysis: Image, Thought, and Language* (pp. 209–253). New York: Routledge.

Spielrein, S. (2019[1923]). Time in Subliminal Psychic Life. In P. Cooper-White and F. Brock Kelcourse (Eds.), *Sabina Spielrein and the Beginnings of Psychoanalysis: Image, Thought, and Language* (pp. 279–294). New York: Routledge.

Stevens, W. (2015[1936]). The Idea of Order at Key West. In *The Collected Poems of Wallace Stevens* (pp. 136–138). New York: Vintage Books.

Vermorel, H. and Vermorel, M. (Eds.) (1993). *Sigmund Freud et Romain Rolland. Correspondance 1923–1936. De la sensation océanique au Trouble du souvenir sur l'Acropole*, Trans. P. Cotet and R. Lainé. Paris: Presses Universitaires de France.

Vieira, M.A. (1998). *L'éthique de la passion. L'affect dans la théorie psychanalytique avec Freud et Lacan*. Rennes: Presses Universitaires de Rennes.

THREE

The complex pleasure of the sublime

Ann Casement

Preface

The ambiguous nature of the *sublime* resonates with the ambiguous nature of C.G. Jung's alchemical approach to *psyche*. This attribute is exemplified in his concept of the *syzygy*, the yoked *anima/animus* representing twinned archetypes denoting the feminine/masculine principles. According to Jung, the union symbolized by the *syzygy* leads to a bisexual being in which consciousness and unconsciousness are integrated – the ultimate product of that union culminating in the metaphorical figure of the *hermaphrodite*, the outcome of a lengthy psychological alchemical process. Jung goes on to describe the *hermaphrodite* as a "monstrous and horrific image" as alchemy was compensating for the cleaned-up images of Christianity, the latter being "the product of spirit, light and good', whereas alchemical figures are "creatures of night, darkness, poison and evil" (Jung, 1954, p. 316). The latter links to the eighteenth-century philosopher and political theorist Edmund Burke's thinking that depicted the *sublime* in terms of terror and horror, the precursor of Gothic horror. This Burkean aspect will be explored at greater length further in the chapter along with the absence of Kantian thinking on the *sublime* in Jung's *Collected Works*.

Reflections on the sublime

The present chapter represents another attempt at a reworking of the notion of the *sublime* "for what subject does not branch out to infinity?" (Burke, 1990, p. xii). In 2011, I was invited to speak at a conference organized by Phil Goss at the Wordsworth Centre set in the sublime landscape of the Lake District of England. The topics were the notions of the *sublime* and the *numinous* at that conference, during the course of which my paper explored Jung's extensive usage in his writings of the second term in contrast to the absence of the first. Yet another version of this chapter was presented at the first Wolfgang Giegerich conference in Berlin in 2012; that version was an account of the *sublime* in the creation of a new kind of subjectivity. In exploring the *sublime* for these purposes, it became clear that it appeared to hold little interest for Jung which, in itself, was intriguing, particularly so as he declared himself

50

The complex pleasure of the sublime   51

to be a Kantian. The latter's *Critique of Judgment* has much to say on the *Mathematically* and the *Dynamically Sublime*, though Jung paid little attention to that in much of his written work. This is all the more intriguing as the Jung scholar Dangwei Zhou, currently doing a PhD with Sonu Shamdasani at University College London, informed me that Shamdasani confirmed that Jung had a copy of the *Critique of Judgment (Kritik der Urteilskraft)* in his library at Küsnacht, which volume includes his annotations.

I turned to Paul Bishop to cast a critical eye over the first draft of what I had written on Kant. Bishop generously sent me two chapters from his book entitled *Synchronicity and Intellectual Intuition in Kant, Swedenborg, and Jung*. These chapters are critical of Jung's "cavalier" misuse of Kant on several counts, although the focus in my chapter is specifically on why there is no reference to Kant's third *Critique* in Jung's writings published in the *Collected Works*; nonetheless, Jung's description of a late stage in the alchemical process does include a rare reference to the "sublimed and exalted" (Jung, 1954, p. 300).

The *sublime* is a vast, wide-ranging topic that lends itself to no one single definition; hence its ambiguous nature that will become apparent in each of the sections in this chapter. One recent event that has fed into this latest version of my thinking on the topic is the publication of a scholarly work by Robert Doran entitled *The Theory of the Sublime*, which references some of the thinkers that feature in this chapter, viz., Longinus, Burke and Kant, as well as relevant material from French thinkers such as the seventeenth-century Nicolas Boileau to postmodern thinkers like Derrida and Lyotard. These latter will not feature in this chapter, as it grapples with sufficient theorists on the *sublime*, though it is worth mentioning that Boileau was "the midwife, champion, and populariser of this concept" (Doran, 2015, p. 97).

In addition to Longinus, Burke and Kant, the chapter will pay a passing nod in the direction of Rudolf Otto because of his impact on Jung. The latter's privileging of the notion of the *numinous* over that of the *sublime*, is illustrated by the fact there is no mention of the *sublime* in the *General Index*, Volume 20 of Jung's *Collected Works* despite its "mystic-religious resonances" (Doran, 2015, p. 1). This chapter sets out to explore why Jung largely eschewed the use of the *sublime* in his writing even though he drew extensively on the work of Kant. In so doing, he focused on the latter's theory of knowledge whilst choosing to ignore his thinking on aesthetics, and, in particular, the *sublime*, to which a significant portion of Kant's third *Critique of Judgment* is dedicated.

On the other hand, the English Romantic poet William Wordsworth integrated Kantian thinking on both knowledge and aesthetics into some of his poetry, this combination holding the key to the dynamical subjectivity of the English Romantic movement. Wordsworth, Coleridge and the other Romantics were well acquainted with the *Critique of Judgment* and grasped its relevance for their own creativity. At the outset, it is important to note that all the references to Kant and Jung are from translations of their works, as my knowledge of the German language is even more rudimentary than Wordsworth's.

Rudolf Otto and Jung

Published in 1917, *The Idea of the Holy* by Rudolf Otto, the eminent German Lutheran theologian, philosopher, and comparative religionist, played a significant role in Jung's thinking as he borrowed from it the neologism *numinous*, a term derived from the Latin *numen* meaning divine will. As elaborated by Otto, this concept was to become a central component in Jung's religious thinking whilst the notion of the *sublime*, as already mentioned, is completely absent. It is this absence that leads one to wonder why Jung chose to ignore the point Otto makes that

> the connexion of the sublime and the holy becomes firmly established . . . and is carried on into the highest forms of religious consciousness – a proof that there exists a hidden kinship between the numinous and the sublime . . . to which Kant's *Critique of Judgement* bears distant witness.
> *(Otto, 1958, p. 63)*

Otto goes on to make further comparisons between the *numinous* and the *sublime*, stating that both are humbling, though at the same time exalting, and causing rejoicing whilst also provoking feelings of fear. He acknowledges the two concepts are similar inasmuch as each excites the other and tends to pass over into the other.

The notion of the sublime *and the concept of dread*

The feeling of *dread* provides us with another link between the *numinous* and the *sublime*, which I addressed in a book entitled *Post-Jungians Today* (1998), while inquiring into another largely absent piece of thinking from Jung's oeuvre, viz., the concept of dread as conceptualized by the Danish philosopher, Kierkegaard. In his writings on this topic, Kierkegaard takes up the question of sin, guilt and freedom, the latter notion being a favourite of Kant's which we shall come to later in this chapter. Kierkegaard postulates that *dread* is a *prelude* to sin not its *sequel*, that it has a portentous quality and hence may precede a shift from a state of ignorance to attainment of new knowledge.

> It follows from this that innocence is ignorance so that when it is stated in the *Book of Genesis* that God said to Adam: "Only from the tree of the knowledge of good and evil you must not eat", Adam does not understand, for the distinction between the two would follow as a result of his eating the fruit. Thus, Adam is in a state of ignorance when the voice of prohibition awakens in him a new set of possibilities, including the possibility of disobedience.
> *(Casement, 1998, p. 70)*

The complex pleasure of the sublime   53

Edmund Burke says something not dissimilar in his *Enquiry* as follows: "Hence arises the great power of the sublime, that far from being produced by them, it anticipates our reasonings, and hurries us on by an irresistible force" (Burke, 1990, p. 53).

The *dread* experienced by Adam is the end of his ignorance, the beginning of his ethical responsibility and a portent of the prelude to sin. It may be useful to draw a distinction between three different kinds of affect, namely, *fear*, which is focused on an object; *anguish*, which is retrospective; and *dread*, which is prospective, objectless and free-floating. The point being made here is that it is primarily a feeling of *dread* linked to the portentous, which is to be found in the *sublime*.

Longinus and Burke

It is generally acknowledged that the earliest known study of the sublime, *On the Sublime*, dates from the first century CE. Its authorship is attributed to Longinus, a Greek teacher of rhetoric and in some accounts a literary critic. *On the Sublime* references Greek sources, viz., Homer, Demosthenes and Plato, as well as biblical ones. It was unknown for many centuries but was rediscovered in the sixteenth century, since which time it has had an enduring impact on thinkers up to the present, including French philosopher and literary critic Jean-François Lyotard and American literary critic Harold Bloom. *On the Sublime* used *sublime* to describe great, elevated or lofty thought or language that inspires awe, dread and veneration: "For, as if instinctively, our soul is uplifted by the true sublime" (Longinus, 1899, p. 55).

The author's conclusion was that the dearth of sublime writers was the result of the contemporary pursuit of wealth and cheap popularity, a view that highlighted the fact that he had a negative view of the times in which he dwelt. Jung's opinion of the times he lived in was no more favourable, as may be seen in the following quotation from *The Red Book*: "Filled with human pride and blinded by the presumptuous spirt of the time, I long sought to hold that other spirit away from me" (Jung, 2009, p. 231).

In the eighteenth century, Longinus's text was referenced in Edmund Burke's book *A Philosophical Enquiry into the Origin of Our Ideas of the Sublime and the Beautiful (1757)*. The Anglo-Irish liberal thinker lived at the time of the French Revolution (1789–1799), as did Kant and Wordsworth. That event led to the "destruction of the feudal order . . . which consolidated the power of the bourgeoisie as the dominant social class which overlaps with the period of the most intense interest in sublimity" (Doran, 2015, p. 20). Although this momentous historical time followed Burke's book on the sublime by 30 years, Adam Phillips posits in his *Introduction* to it that both Burke and Kant share what was to become a fundamental modern preoccupation that "the Sublime was a way of thinking about *excess* as the key to a new kind of subjectivity" (Burke, 1990, p. ix).

According to Burke, the sublime is different from the beautiful in that the former always includes in itself something of terror. He goes on to say: "I know of nothing sublime which is not some modification of power . . . which may equally belong to pain or to pleasure" (Burke, p. 59). He suggests that pain and pleasure are of a "positive nature", in that one is not simply the absence of the other. This latter anticipates twentieth-century psychoanalytic thinking an example being Jung's critique of the theological doctrine of the *privatio bono*, viz., that evil is merely the absence of good – the former being viewed as insubstantial; while the pain-in-pleasure can be seen at work in the notion of *jouissance* to be found in Lacanian psycho-analysis. *Jouissance* is most readily, if only partially, grasped in English as denoting enjoyment and derives from the French verb *jouir*, that is, "to come" in the sexual sense of the term, wherein it manifests as the pleasure-in-pain or the pain-in-pleasure. *Jouissance* means transgressing the *pleasure principle* whereby pleasure may become painful, and pain may be pleasur-able. It is unsurprising that Kant viewed Burke's contribution to the sublime as more psychological than philosophical.

Kant's own thinking on pain-pleasure goes as follows: "The feeling of the Sublime is therefore a feeling of pain, arising from the want of accordance between the aesthetical estimation of magnitude formed by the Imagination and the estimation of the same formed by Reason" (Kant, 2005, p. 72). "There accompanies the reception of an object as sublime a pleasure, which is only possible through the medium of pain" (Ibid: p. 74).

This echoes Burke's pleasure-in-pain, though for Kant that arises from the fact that the *sublime* is the highest faculty relating to morality, as the experience of the *sublime* is only possible in one who is formed by a culture of morality. This, in turn, is dependent on freedom, as without that, moral evaluation is vacuous and meaningless. Physically, humanity can be over-whelmed by forces in nature, but through freedom, which is embedded in ideas of reason, i.e. what is properly sublime, humanity need not be; hence the duality of pain as well as pleasure in the *sublime*. Thus, sublimity resides not in the object, viz., the transcendent might of Yahweh or the force of the storm but in ideas of reason, which allow humanity the freedom to rise above these forces.

Jung incorporates the notion of pain-pleasure into his development of the different faculties at work in human behaviour and relates it to the faculty of *feeling* as follows: "The pain-pleasure reaction of feeling marks the highest degree of subjectivation of the object. Feeling brings subject and object into such a close relationship that the subject must choose between acceptance and rejection" (Jung, 1960, p. 123).

The sublime Proust includes a pain-in-pleasure account of a sexual encounter between Jupien and M. de Charlus in his magisterial work on time as follows:

> From what I heard at first in Jupien's quarters, was only a series of inarticulate sounds, I imagine that few words had been exchanged. It is true that these sounds were so violent that, if they had not always been taken up an octave higher by a parallel plaint, I might have thought that one

> person was slitting another's throat. .... I concluded from this later on that there is another thing as noisy as pain, namely pleasure.
>
> *(Proust, 1992, p. 10)*

To return to Burke, his book cites a passage from the *Book of Job* which he calls "amazingly sublime":

> In thoughts from the visions of the night, when deep sleep falleth upon men, fear came upon me and trembling, which made all my bones to shake. Then a spirit passed before my face. The hair of my flesh stood up. It stood still, but I could not discern the form thereof; an image was before my eyes; there was silence; and I heard a voice, – Shall mortal man be more just than God?
>
> *(Burke, 1990, p. 58)*

This theme has been taken up by religious thinkers through the ages, including Jung in *Answer to Job*, as evidenced by the following quotations from that late work: "From the human point of view Yahweh's behaviour is so revolting"(Jung, 1973, p. 13); "Without knowing or wanting it, Job shows himself superior to his divine partner both intellectually and morally"(Ibid: p. 10); and: "Yahweh displays no compunction, remorse, or compassion, but only ruthlessness and brutality" (Ibid: p. 14). Without altering a word of these passionate outpourings, it is not difficult to recognize that the object of them on Jung's part could be Freud thinly disguised as Yahweh.

"Kant is my philosopher"

The quotation in this heading is a reference to a personal comment made by Jung to John Phillips, a student at the Jung Institute at Zürich in the 1950s, which Phillips reported to the Jung scholar Sonu Shamdasani, who recorded it in his work *C.G. Jung: A Biography in Books*. This section will seek to find out what Jung meant by this statement.

The following Kantian notions, viz., the thing-in-itself (Kant, 2007, p. 490), treasure in the realm of shadowy thoughts (Ibid: p. 309) and pure borderline concept (Ibid: p. 601), are used by Jung to denote what he variously called "the unconscious", "the Self", or "the God image" – in other words, all that is unknowable and boundless. As Jung states: "We cannot know the boundaries of something unknown to us" (Jung, 1953, p. 182). In creating these concepts, he acknowledges that he was influenced by Kant's thinking on the thing in itself. As Jung puts it, the self as "totality transcends our vision. .... Consequently the "self" is a pure borderline concept similar to Kant's thing in itself" (Jung, 1953, p. 182). The third reference to the treasure in the realm of shadowy thoughts is applied by Jung to his concept of archetypes "the *a priori* conditioning factors of unconscious whose innermost nature is inaccessible to experience" (Jung, 1971, p. 659). In this way, Jung was using Kantian ideas to underwrite, and, subsequently, unify his concepts of "self", "unconscious" and "archetypes" into an overarching theory about the "Other". As already noted, Jung's usage of Kant's epistemological theory has been the subject of criticism from Paul Bishop.

The quotations just mentioned were based by Jung on the first two of Kant's *Critiques*: the *Critique of Pure Reason* (1781) and the *Critique of Practical Reason* (1788). A summary of what Kant is aiming at in these two works goes as follows. The two works encapsulate his attempt to transcend the divide between the rationalist philosophy of the seventeenth century as exemplified by Descartes, Spinoza and Leibniz, and the seventeenth and eighteenth-century empiricism of Locke and Hume. Instead, Kant invites us to reconsider the proposition that the nature of objectivity is dependent on our subjectivity. In other words, we can know nothing beyond what the mind has made of it, so that *all* objectivity of our knowledge is a subjective construct, and we can *know* nothing beyond what the mind has projected into reality. Kant's approach depicts a mental realm that precedes the empirical, which makes experience possible. This is what he meant by *transcendental idealism*, and it is this, along with his other related discoveries, that he claimed was his Copernican Revolution. Excluded from subjectivity is *the thing in itself*, which remains outside our knowledge and apprehension – hence the dualism that has been ascribed to his philosophy. This is an all too rough summary of the thinking of arguably the greatest philosopher since Plato, Descartes aside, from whom philosophical thinking has since descended.

Kant's *Critique of Judgment* (1790) is his attempt to unify all philosophy through the *a priori* concept of judgment, which can mediate between *theory*, as set out in the first *Critique*, and *practice*, which is to be found in the second *Critique*. Contrary to the criticism of him by Johan Georg Hamann, a key figure in German Romanticism, whose ideas supported the *Sturm und Drang* movement and who saw faith and belief as the determinants of human action, Kant is on the side of the Romantics where, for instance, he found it necessary to deny knowledge in order to make room for faith. He is, however, *critically* sympathetic to the Romantics in insisting that the production of an ideal object is for our satisfaction as cognitive beings evidenced in the following: "*The sublime is that, the mere ability to think which, shows a faculty of the mind surpassing every standard of sense*" (Original italics: Kant, 2005, p. 66). "The sublime is not to be sought in the things of nature, but only in our ideas" (Ibid: p. 65). Later in the chapter, these statements are made manifest in an extract from a poem by Wordsworth.

According to Doran "[B]y *virtually* conquering our natural inclinations we show ourselves to be (morally/spiritually) stronger than the nature that threatens us, the Dynamically Sublime demonstrates, makes "palpable", to use Kant's term, the *transcendence* of our sensuous self by our moral self (our freedom to resist), and therefore the "humanity in our person" is not only "undemeaned" but is also *exalted* in this virtual conquest of nature. Although both the Mathematically and the Dynamically Sublime reveal our *superiority* to nature, the Dynamically Sublime additionally reveals our *independence from* nature (within and without), that is our *autonomy*, and for this reason is more directly connected with morality" (Doran, 2015, p. 146).

Although Kant's third *Critique* is not referenced in the *General Index* of the English edition of Jung's *Collected Works*, as already stated, Jung owned and knew the work, which is evidenced in the many ideas from it that appear in his writings such as God, soul, archetype, symbol, teleology, *summum bonum*, morality, unity and judgment, though these also feature in Kant's earlier work. On the other hand, the concept of the sublime, which is a key theme in the third *Critique*, does not feature in Jung's writing. As Kant posits that the sublime is central to the faculty of judgment, which he sees as a constitutive principle of the mental apparatus, this deficit on Jung's part appears surprising. Before moving on to explore possible reasons why he did not so do, I would like first to further elaborate the concept of the sublime as embraced by Kant.

Kant's concept of the sublime

The following quotations taken from Kant's *Critique of Judgment* illustrate some of his thinking on the *sublime*.

> The mind feels itself moved in the representation of the sublime in nature.
>
> *(Kant, 2005, p. 72)*

> If nature is to be judged by us as dynamically sublime, it must be represented as exciting fear.
>
> *(Ibid: p. 74)*

> We readily call these objects sublime, because they raise the energies of the soul above their accustomed height.
>
> *(Ibid: p. 75)*

> The sublime is the presupposition of the moral feeling in man.
>
> *(Ibid: p. xiv)*

In this work he posits that the faculty of judgment derives from the notion of the sublime. In referencing Kant's third *Critique*, the focus of the chapter will be on his concepts of the *Mathematically* and *Dynamically Sublime*, which postulate that the mind recoils at objects in nature that are immeasurably greater or more powerful than humanity, for instance, a violent storm. In Job's – and by extension Jung's – case, this all mighty force would be represented by Yahweh/Freud. The sense of physical danger aroused by powerful natural objects prompts an awareness in the human mind that it is not just a physical material being but a moral one as well.

58   Ann Casement

To put it another way, sublimity enables humanity to get its head around overwhelming experiences, bringing us back to what was said earlier about the relationship of the *sublime* to *excess*. In this way, the *sublime* personifies nobility of mind and is the supreme aesthetic virtue that allows for an affective as well as a cognitive response. To conclude this part of the chapter, it is possible to assert that the higher purpose of subjectivity resides in what Kant calls the "super-sensible destination" (Kant, 2005, p. 72) of humanity's faculties deriving from the *Mathematically* and the *Dynamically Sublime*.

This echoes Burke's pleasure-in-pain, though for Kant, arises from the fact that the *sublime* is the highest faculty relating to morality as the experience of the *sublime* is only possible in one who is formed by a culture of morality. This, in turn, is dependent on freedom, as without that, moral evaluation is vacuous and meaningless. Physically, humanity can be overwhelmed by forces in nature, but through freedom, which is embedded in ideas of reason, i.e. what is properly sublime, humanity need not be; hence the duality of pain as well as pleasure in the sublime. Thus, sublimity resides not in the object, viz., the transcendent might of Yahweh or the force of the storm but in ideas of reason, which allow humanity the freedom to rise above these forces. For Kant, this results in the higher morality of subjectivity that is based on "moral" religion as opposed to mere superstition, so that humans vibrate between painful feelings of fear and pleasurable ones of freedom from fear. Thus, sublimity may be seen as the key to a new subjectivity that transcends each of these. Furthermore, by mediating between theoretical and practical reason, Kant posited that sublimity could also unite philosophy.

A crucial point being explored in this chapter is the difficulty arising from Jung's reliance on Kant's epistemological theory as set out in the first *Critique*. In relation to this, Wolfgang Giegerich, the erudite Jungian psychoanalyst from Berlin, states that Jung hypostasizes "*the* unconscious" and "*the* archetypes", in this way treating unconsciousness as a positive fact, as if it were some kind of author of dreams, visions, myths, ideas. He does the same with his concept of "*the Self*" as Other, which presupposes a "positivistic" interiorization into the human being as an "It"(Casement, 2011, p. 541). Jung's reification of these concepts sits uncomfortably alongside Kant's epistemology, in which the latter does *not* claim that objective reality is contained in the ideas of reason but speaks rather of the conditions of the possibility of knowledge.

Along the same lines, Paul Bishop sent me the following quotation for this chapter:

> Whilst claiming to remain within Kantian boundaries, Jung shows his true Romanticism in constantly yearning to go beyond them. For as many times as Jung insists on the impossibility of knowing anything directly about the unconscious psyche, he makes qualifications and claims

The complex pleasure of the sublime 59

insights into the nature of the collective unconscious, such
as, for instance, that it is structured by archetypes.

(Bishop: Synchronicity and
Intellectual Intuition, *p. 185)*

In this chapter, what is being proposed, instead, is that Kant's concept of
the *sublime* would have been more suited to Jung's thinking on his central
ideas to do with God, *Self* and morality. "The Sublime . . . is to be found in
a formless object, so far as in it or by occasion of its *boundlessness* is represented, and yet its totality is also present to thought" (Kant, 2005, p. 61).
As already stated, however, there are no references to the sublime in the
General Index. This appears curiously lacking on Jung's part, particularly
after the publication of *Liber Novus*, which shows him to be a gifted artist.
When the English edition was launched in October 2009, my editor at *The
Economist*, for which I was reviewing the book, asked if Jung had actually
painted the images contained in it himself, as they were of such high artis-
tic merit. Instead, Jung's disparaging allusion to aesthetics in *Memories,
Dreams, Reflections* states as follows:

> In the *Red Book* I tried an aesthetic elaboration of my fan-
> tasies, but never finished it . . . I gave up the aestheticizing
> tendency in good time, in favour of a rigorous process of
> *understanding.*
>
> *(p. 213, original italics)*

I suggest there are problems in this quotation from Jung. For one thing,
he appears to be dismissing aesthetics with the demeaning term "the aes-
theticizing tendency". For another, he appears to be underrating his own
achievements that followed *The Red Book*, which consist of volumes of
rich, dense, allusive writing, by reducing them to "a rigorous process of
understanding".

Furthermore, Jung not only eschewed aesthetics but was even negative in
his view of it. For instance, he tellingly says the following:

> Aestheticism can, of course, take the place of the religious
> function. . . . Even though aestheticism may be a very noble
> substitute, it is nevertheless only a compensation for the
> real thing that is lacking.
>
> *(*Psychological Types, *p. 141)*

It may be that one answer to the question of why Jung chose to ignore Kant's
theory on aesthetics in the *Critique of Judgment*, paradoxically lies in the
very fact that Jung was a gifted artist. In a private seminar led over four
days by Sonu Shamdasani in the bucolic English countryside in the summer
of 2009 shortly before the publication of *Liber Novus*, Shamdasani pointed
to the fact that a number of individuals in the close circle around Jung in

60 Ann Casement

Zürich were "going off" into aestheticism. These included Maria Molzer and Franz Riklin, about the latter of whom Jung stated:

> Indeed, he vanished wholly in his art, rendering him utterly intangible. His work was like a wall over which water rippled. He could therefore not analyse, as this required one to be pointed and sharp-edged like a knife. He had fallen into art.
>
> *(Introduction to* Liber Novus *p. 204)*

Above all, Jung wanted to be a psychologist of religion not an artist. It would appear that being artistically gifted made Jung wary of being seduced by art, which he feared would render him ineffectual as a psychologist. The claim in his 1917 paper *The Transcendent Function* (CW:Vol.8) that "the danger of the aesthetic tendency is overvaluation of the formal or "artistic" worth of fantasy-productions" (p. 84) is, I suggest, a warning to himself to beware the lure of aestheticism.

* * *

Let us turn now to the work of the eighteenth- and nineteenth-century English Romantic poet William Wordsworth. The latter, along with Samuel Taylor Coleridge, who had a good grasp of the German language and who introduced German Idealist philosophy to England, were founders of the English Romantic poetry movement.

As the extract I will be using in this section is from a poem of Wordsworth's, I shall now focus entirely on him. Wordsworth went to Germany in 1798 with Coleridge in order to learn more about Kantian ideas. For much of the time he was there, he was isolated and lonely, being incarcerated at Goslar with his sister, Dorothy, neither of them being able to speak German well. In the meantime, Coleridge went about meeting philosophers and academics. This not altogether happy experience did not dampen Wordsworth's enthusiasm for Kantian ideas, as we shall see from the following extract from his poem *A few lines composed above Tintern Abbey*, which was written after his return from Germany in 1798 (*Poems of Wordsworth: Chosen and Edited by Matthew Arnold* [1903] London: Macmillan & Co.).

That year was the start of Wordsworth's most creative decade, and the poem was written five years after his earlier visit, at the age of 23, to the same location. The poem is a long one and begins with the line: "*Five years have past.*" It continues with the lines: "*For nature then (The coarser pleasures of my boyish days, And their glad animal movements all gone by) To me was all in all*". For reasons of space, we will only be studying the following short section from that long poem.

For I have learned to look on nature, not as in the hour
Of thoughtless youth; but hearing often-times,   (90)
The still, sad music of humanity,
Nor harsh nor grating, though of ample power

The complex pleasure of the sublime   61

To chasten and subdue. And I have felt
A presence that disturbs me with the joy
Of elevated thoughts; *a sense sublime*   (95)
Of something far more deeply interfused
Whose dwelling is the light of setting suns
And the *round ocean and the living air,*
And the blue sky, and in the mind of man:
A motion and a spirit, that impels   (100)
All thinking things, all objects of all thought,
And rolls through all things.
                    (A Few Lines Composed Above Tintern Abbey)

"Therefore nature is here called sublime merely because it elevates the Imagination" (Kant, 2005, p. 75). The Romantics were drawn to Kant's *Mathematical* and *Dynamic sublime* – the latter directing attention to that which is greater than anything found in nature, viz., the imagination. In addition, the terror and awe in the face of the dynamic turbulence to be found in nature reflected the unsettled political and cultural climate of that time. In Wordsworth's lines just quoted, one can see at work the impact of Kant's concept of the *Dynamically Sublime*. In uniting this with Kant's transcendental idealism, Wordsworth postulates that all perception results from the observing subject melding sensory data with the *a priori* mental and experiencing apparatus that culminates in the shaping of *all* subjective consciousness. It is to this end that the word "all" is repeated several times in the poem signalling that outside of Kant's model there is nothing else that constitutes subjectivity. The dynamism of the English Romantic poets was inspired by Kant's notion of the *Dynamically Sublime*, the movement of which Wordsworth emphasizes in the poem in the use of extended metaphor such as "round ocean", "living air", and "rolls through all things". In this way, Wordsworth created a new "sense sublime", his work being the purest expression of Kantian thought in poetry.

Conclusion

This chapter has argued that Jung's borrowings from the epistemological content of Kant's thinking were less than satisfactory and that he would have been better served by focusing on Kant's third *Critique* on the *Dynamically Sublime*. In the past, Bishop and Giegerich have pointed out that Jung's often-quoted response to the question about the existence of God: "I do not believe, I know", goes against Kant's categorical denial that anything could enter consciousness without being pre-organized by the mind (Jung, 1959, pp. 525–526). The difficulty here lies with Jung's use of the word "know". Whilst Kant, on the one hand, claimed that knowledge needed to be annulled in order to make room for faith; Jung, instead, abolished faith and replaced it with knowledge of the psychologized symbol. I am at one with Bishop's conclusion that Jung's position is clearly not a *transcendental* one about the conditions for experience but a *transcendent* one that goes beyond experience.

62   Ann Casement

On the other hand, one can see from the last pages of the *Critique of Judgment* how reluctant Kant is to state categorically that there is a God because it is impossible for humankind to vindicate such a concept objectively, as it rests upon subjective conditions alone that allow only a limited formula, as follows: "Theology . . . shall determine the concept of God adequately for the highest practical use of Reason, but it cannot develop this and base it satisfactorily on its proofs" (Kant, 2005, p. 253).

I have gone on to suggest that Wordsworth's poem is a coherent attempt to incorporate Kant's transcendental idealism into his work. In this way, Wordsworth personified the *sublime* and unified two different languages – philosophy and poetry. With regard to poetry, Kant stated the following: "Of all the arts *poetry* . . . maintains the first rank. . . . It strengthens the mind by making it feel its faculty – free, spontaneous and independent of natural determination – of considering and judging nature as a phenomenon . . . and as a sort of schema for the supersensible" (Kant, *Critique of Judgment*, p. 128).

The *sublime* exists as a potential in all forms of life where there is a mind, and where there is also a latent dynamic ingredient that one sees illustrated in Wordsworth's poem wherein the landscape is unchanged but he himself is not the same as at his first sighting of it. The dialectic between the external impressions of nature on the thoughtlessness of the youth has interacted with the internal ordering of those impressions by the intellectual growth of the adult Wordsworth resulting in the production of this sublime piece of poetry.

Furthermore, Kant's thinking on *genius* was a precursor of that of the English Romantics, viz., a faculty that contributes to the production of all art unalloyed by learning or craft. Original genius inspired by muses or a *voice* comes from beyond the poet and is a subjectivity beyond the merely subjective. The subject is the medium or vehicle for a discourse that comes from the *Other*. Poetry appears instantaneously from that source which is hidden from the poet as an ultimate expression of the *sublime*.

Addendum

In June 2018, the Neo-Kleinian Ron Britton gave a presentation at the Freud Museum in London entitled "I saw the Spring Return: on Wordsworth and Loss", in which he spoke about the work and personalities of the poets William Wordsworth and Rainer Maria Rilke. The latter was diagnosed as *narcissistic* and being stuck at the *paranoid-schizoid position*; on the other hand, it was suggested that Wordsworth had progressed to the *depressive position*. Britton went on to say that Samuel Taylor Coleridge had tried unsuccessfully to persuade Wordsworth to incorporate Kantian ideas into the latter's poetry, which I have endeavoured to demonstrate in my chapter is exactly what happened, transforming not only Wordsworth's poetry but that of the English Romantics in general.

References

Burke, E. (1990). *A Philosophical Enquiry into the Origin of our Ideas of the Sublime and Beautiful (1990)*. Oxford: Oxford University Press.

Casement, A. (1998). *Post-Jungians Today: Key Papers in Contemporary Analytical Psychology*. London and New York: Routledge.

Casement, A. (2011, September). Reflections on Wolfgang Giegerich. *The Journal of Analytical Psychology*, 56(4): 532–549.

Doran, R. (2015). *The Theory of the Sublime: From Longinus to Kant*. Cambridge: Cambridge University Press.

Jung, C.G. (1953). *Psychology and Alchemy*. London: Routledge & Kegan Paul.

Jung, C.G. (1954). *The Practice of Psychotherapy: Essays on the Psychology of the Transference and Other Subjects*. London: Routledge & Kegan Paul.

Jung, C.G. (1959). *The Face to Face Interview in C.G. Jung Speaking: Interviews and Encounters* (pp. 525–526). Princeton, NJ: Bollingen Paperbacks.

Jung, C.G. (1960). *The Structure and Dynamics of the Psyche*. London: Routledge & Kegan Paul.

Jung, C.G. (1971). *Psychological Types*. London: Routledge & Kegan Paul.

Jung, C.G. (1973). *Answer to Job*. Princeton, NJ: Princeton University Press.

Jung, C.G. (2009). *The Red Book: Liber Novus*, Ed. Sonu Shamdasani, Trans. John Peck, Mark Kyburz and Sonu Shamdasani. New York: W.W. Norton & Company.

Kant, I. (2005). *Critique of Judgment*, Trans. J.H. Bernard. Mineola, NY: Dover Publications, Inc.

Kant, I. (2007). *Critique of Pure Reason*. London: Penguin Classics.

Otto, R. (1958). *The Idea of the Holy: An Inquiry into the Non-rational Factor in the Idea of the Divine and its Relation to the Rational*. Oxford: Oxford University Press.

Proust, M. (1992). *In Search of Lost Time. IV. Sodom and Gomorrah*, Trans. C.G. Scott Moncrieff and Terence Kilmartin. London: Chatto & Windus.

Rhys Roberts, W. (1899). *Longinus on the Sublime*. Cambridge: Cambridge University Press.

Shamdasani, S. (2011). *C.G. Jung: A Biography in Books*. London and New York: W.W. Norton & Company.

Wordsworth, W. (1903). Lines, Composed a Few Miles above Tintern Abbey, on Revisiting the Banks of the Wye During a Tour. In Matthew Arnold (Ed.), *Poems of Wordsworth*. London: Macmillan and Co., Limited.

FOUR

Jung, the sublime and apophatic mysticism in psyche and art

John Dourley

Summary

The mystics to whom Jung was most attracted were members of the apophatic tradition. The thirteenth-century Beguines (Mechthild of Magdeburg), Meister Eckhart (d 1328), and Jacob Boehme (d 1624) underwent an experiential dissolution into a nothingness which they understood as a moment of identity beyond difference with the divine. Jung equates this experience with the deepest regression of the ego into the unconscious and into a moment of "identity" with God. In a Jungian context, the sublime could thus be understood as the experience, in varying degrees, of the study of consciousness with its unconscious origin within Jung's immensely deepened and extended boundaries of the psyche.

Contemporary scholarship has shown the metaphysical import of this experience especially in the affinity of Jung's psychology with nineteenth-century German Romanticism and Idealism and their roots in the earlier German mystical tradition (McGrath, 2012). But Jung's perspective here also has profound aesthetic implications. The sublime would be revisioned as alive in any art form expressive of that dimension of psyche where divine and human coincided. Recent criticism has shown nineteenth- and twentieth-century expressionist/abstract art was in conscious continuity with the mysticism and theosophy of Boehme and other mystics.

This is particularly true of the work of Kandinsky and Arp. A Jungian aesthetic would make of this art an effort to give whatever kind of form can be given to the formless matrix of all form. It would be an attempt to express the inexpressible depths of the human spirit beyond all formalism in non-representational art. This artistic enterprise lay behind Jung's identification of expressionism as a then-current attempted retrieval of the truly spiritual. Such art would bring a deepening and more inclusive conscious empathy to individual and society currently pathologically removed from the single life-giving source of both personal and communal life.

Preamble

My chapter is frankly somewhat circuitous. It contends that a Jungian understanding of the sublime and its attendant aesthetic rests upon the conscious experience and expression of the archetypal unconscious. Such experience is common to all domains of enduring creativity and so to mystic and artist alike. The chapter goes on to present the radical apophatic experience of those mystics to whom Jung was most drawn and then links this tradition to key members of the early abstractionist school.

The sublime

Jung appreciated Freud's understanding of the sublime as sublimation but distinguished it from his own understanding of the sublime. He understood Freudian sublimation classically as the transformation of sexual energy into creative expressions supposedly more acceptable and of greater value to society (Jung, 1961, para. 286). Jung criticized Freud's understanding of sublimation because, he thought, it gave far too much to the power of the ego and its faculties of mind and will over against the might of instinctual forces (Jung, 1966a, paras. 71–73). Rather than have the ego grasp and transform the energies of the sublime, Jung would have the sublime grasp and transform the ego. He writes: "It [sublimation] is not a *voluntary* and *forcible* channelling of instinct into a spurious field of application, but an *alchymical transformation* for which *fire* and the black *prima materia* are needed" (Jung, 1934a, p. 171). The sublime would thus demand the ego's cooperation in being ushered into consciousness (Jung, 1934b, p. 173, 1966a, paras. 156–158). This conception of sublimity engages the total psyche, conscious and unconscious, as well as the individual and the collective. It not only implicates the importance of the bearer of the sublime acting as a spokesperson for powers greater than the individual but more than suggests that the sublime, through the individuals blessed and burdened with its urgencies, creates history (Jung, 1966b, paras. 130, 131). For with Jung the archetypal powers manifest in the sublime fund the flow of the passing epochs, their cultures and last but hardly least, the religions on which all the cultures rest consciously or unconsciously (Jung, 1964, fn 21, p. 320). In effect, the sublime for Jung entails a philosophy of history which is also a history of religion. The sublime elevates the meaning of history to that of the sequential appearances of the divinities, religious political and cultural, in humanity's inescapable drive to make the ultimate conscious in itself. As Jung and the abstractionists imply, the ongoing revelation of the sublime into consciousness moves history toward its completion as wholly transparent to its originating depth. As such, this process loosely describes a foundational teleology of individual and species variously described by philosophy, depth psychology, the social sciences, the arts and religion. Writes Jung, "All one can say is that things happen as if there were a fixed final aim" (Jung, 1966c, p. 295, fn 19). The philosophy of history and the histories of religion and of philosophy become the history of the sublime made visible in whatever guise it assumes, none more dramatic than in religion and the arts.

This greatly extended understanding of the sublime derives directly from Jung's contention that the ultimate meaning of individual and collective life lies in the processes of the unconscious origin of human consciousness becoming progressively conscious in its child, the conscious life of the ego. In terms of an aesthetic, Jung would imply that beauty is to be found in the expression of the archetypal in the individual, and through those individuals it touches most deeply, in the making of culture and history. Such an aesthetic would also be profoundly religious since Jung would locate the psychogenesis of all religions in the power of the archetypal compensating any given culture toward the totality it lacks and so demands (Jung, 1966b, paras. 130, 131). All beauty becomes a religious beauty, not in the sense of anything foreign to humanity being imposed on it by a transcendent, discontinuous Other, but in the sense that the truly beautiful arises from archetypal depths wholly within an infinitely expanded psyche. In this sense, the artist as mediator of the archetypal is a priest and a prophet to the society the artist addresses. The artist is a priest whose art transmits the experience of the holy as transpersonal and transfixing yet whose matrix lies wholly within the psyche. The artist is a prophet whose iconoclasm smashes the idolatry of the status quo in the service of the kairos in whose genius he or she works in the name of the new bursting into and transforming the temporal (Jung, 1964, para. 585). The art itself becomes sacramental as a visible sign of a future and yet already present sense of a revitalized sense of the ultimate and of humanity's still tentative intimacy with what form it will take.

The apophatic sensitivity

For Jung, religious experience was inescapable because "an authentic religious function" was native to the psyche (Jung, 1969, para. 3). The interplay of humanity with divinity becomes, in the last analysis, the commerce between consciousness as the sole locus in which the unconscious as the creator of consciousness could itself become conscious. In this interchange Jung privileged mystical experience as an unmediated experience of archetypal energies (Jung, 1979, paras. 218–221). In a certain sense, such experience was the ur religion in all eras and behind all religious collectivities. However, on closer examination Jung's preferred mystics, at least in the Christian West, had undergone a radical apophatic experience. This experience is one in which the agencies of mind and will were simply extinguished. At its height, the experience lies beyond all objectification of the true and good as something to be known or willed as distinct from the knowing and willing subject. Forsaking the ability to differentiate, the person undergoing apophatic experience sinks into a moment of identity with an originary nothingness. Such identity defeats the notion of a mutual knowing and willing between the divine and the human. Current scholarship calls such identity a *unitas indistictionis*, a unity beyond all distinction as opposed to a *unitas disitncionis*, a unity in which some distance from the divine is maintained throughout the relationship with it (McGinn, 1998, pp. 217–218, 261–265). As suggested with Jung, the sublime can well be understood as the experience and expression of the archetypal dimension of the psyche common to artist and mystic alike. But the apophatic mystic may sound a depth of the unconscious even beyond the archetypal because the apophatic experience carries with it no immediate need to communicate or to act, whereas archetypal experience is driven by the drive of the archetypes to find formal expression in consciousness and its consequent activity. It is here suggested that the inward flow of libido with the apophatic mystic attains a momentary inhesion in the formless source of all form, the unimaginable origin of all imagery, the silence preceding all word or sound, the nothing behind all that is something (Bowlt, 1986, p. 174). Such experience might well appeal to the abstractionists to forgo representational art in the interests of capturing a domain of spirit simply beyond representational depiction. To appreciate this possibility, a little more must be said of these mystics to whom Jung was drawn.

The historical sequence of the apophatic tradition Jung engages traces its origin to the Beguines in the thirteenth century, runs through Meister Eckhart in the fourteenth and reaches a certain culmination in Jacob Boehme in the sixteenth and seventeenth centuries. The latter is among the most frequently cited mystics in Jung's work. Boehme's experience contributed to such foundational Jungian themes as that of the divinely based polarities seeking their resolution in historical human consciousness in a process at once redemptive of the divine and the human (Dourley, 2014, pp. 118–120). It is interesting, then, that significant individuals among the late nineteenth and early twentieth century expressionists and abstractionists, in particular, Wassily Kandinsky and Jean Arp, found in Boehme's mystical sensitivities the basis of a contemporary sustaining spirituality toward whose recovery their work was into some large degree dedicated. Such a radical turn inward parallels Jung's own sustained efforts to reroot his age and ours in the spirit of the depths maimed or ignored by Enlightenment reason and a scientism severed from the totality of the human cognitive and affective capacity (Jung, 2009, pp. 229, 230, 237, 239). To make these connections between the sublime, a mystical aesthetic and Jung's psychology some time must be given to the mystics of the apophatic who drew Jung's attention.

The mystics

Mechthild of Magdeburg (1208–1282) was a member of a Beguine community. Such communities were a new phenomenon in the late twelfth and early thirteenth centuries. They were made up of women committed to good works who chose neither marriage nor traditional convent life. Ecclesial reaction was mixed. It ranged from occasional qualified approval, to suspicion, to outright opposition (Dourley, 2014, pp. 37–40). Certain of the early Beguines

68   John Dourley

embraced a spirituality based on images of sexual intercourse with a youthful Christ figure opening onto an absorption in divinity so total as to defeat any distinction between the lovers. This psycho-religious dynamic is most dramatically expressed in the imagination of Mechthild of Magdeburg and her fellow Beguine, Hadewijch of Antwerp. Jung was deeply impressed by Mechthild's "Christ-eroticism" and its union of the sexual and spiritual (Jung, 1971, para. 392). Central to her work is a tryst between her soul and a youthful Christ figure in the trope of courtly love. Christ as courtier approaches from a distance and begins a courtship that moves through a dance of love into a recognition that lover and beloved share a common nature demanding their union. Though Mechthild prepares for her lover by clothing herself in virtue in the end she rejects many virtues proffered by the timid senses as a substitute for total identification with her beloved. In the climax, she strips herself of all virtuous endeavour as preliminary and ultimately disappointing to stand naked before her divine lover and brother. In the mutual dissolution of sexual satiation the moment of divine/human identity is consummated (Mechthild, 1955, pp. 20–25). Hadewijch of Antwerp is even more explicit. In one of her major visions she sees Christ as a child offering her sacramental communion. The child transforms into a fully grown adult Christ at the age of 33. They go on to an embrace of total intimacy prior to a state of identity without difference. She writes of this moment, "Then it was to me as if we were one without difference" (Hadewijch, 1980, p. 281). Another Beguine, Marguerite Porete, burnt by the Inquisition in Paris in 1310, endorsed the imagery of "the annihilated soul" (Porete, 1993, pp. 135, 153). As with Mechthild, this state lay beyond virtuous achievement and beyond intellect and will. Paradoxically for Marguerite, dissolution of the soul in the nothingness carried with it a universal relatedness. She writes, "Now this soul has fallen from Love into nothingness, and without such nothingness she cannot be All" (Ibid., p. 193). Jung, borrowing from Goethe, repeats such paradoxical absence as a universal presence. In his search for an authentic spirituality for the modern who can no longer honestly go home to religious traditions, Jung writes that such a seeker "stands before the Nothing out of which the All may rise" (CW 10, p. 75).

Meister Eckhart, dearly appreciated by Jung, died at his own trial for heresy at Avignon in 1328. He is known to have dialogued with religious women, perhaps Beguines, along the Rhine after his second teaching period at Paris. While in Paris, he lived for a time with Marguerite's inquisitor and executioner, John of Paris, a fellow Dominican priest. Through John, Eckhart probably knew Marguerite's writing. His version of the apophatic experience is best expressed in his famous sermon, "Blessed are the poor". In this sermon, he twice prays to God to rid him of God. Within his theology, the prayer would be directed to the Godhead, who precedes the Trinity whose compulsive creation removed the creature from its primordial identity, the Godhead. Jung quotes Eckhart's statement that in coming forth from God, every creature proclaimed God, but as its origin from which it was alienated in creation. Creation and alienation become two sides of the same movement. Salvation would consist in the recovery of a moment of identity with the Godhead beyond the Trinity as creator and so beyond all definition. Such a moment would also be beyond all knowing and loving and action on behalf of or toward a God as other than the creature. Furthermore, this natural point of coincidence would remain with the mystic as the source of the mystic's typical energetic engagement with the world on return from the experience of identity with its origin. Nor is Jung ambivalent that such regression is a wholly psychological reality culminating in identity with the divine releasing new life in the human. He writes of Eckhart's experience, "As the result of this retrograde process the original state of identity with God is re-established and a new potential is produced" (CW 6, p. 255). Dissolution in the nothing becomes the font of energy for engaging the world as nothingness expressed beyond itself.

Jacob Boehme (1575–1624) brings this mystical sequence to a certain height and turns it back to human history. Like Eckhart, Boehme had also experienced some kind of identity with the One and what he calls the *ungrund*, or primal ground. In this, his experience may be deemed apophatic. But his experience of this primordial power turns Boehme back to humanity and history with an emphasis not to be found in Eckhart and with a profusion of imagery more reminiscent of Blake. For Boehme's experience is that the polarities of the Trinity have not been resolved in eternity, as the symbol of the Trinity would have it, but seek their resolution in human consciousness and history necessarily created for that purpose. Jung appreciated Boehme for one of his drawings called *The Philosophical Sphere or the Wondrous Eye of Eternity* and included it in his own work (CW 9ii, p. 291). In this drawing, a circle of totality encompasses two upright semicircles facing backward to each other. The semicircles depict the opposites of the darkness of the Father and the light of the Spirit. They touch in the centre of the circle in the form of a heart through which runs a vertical line to heaven above and the earth below. The sketch succinctly suggests that the Father and Spirit come together in Christ or the human and effect the union of heaven and earth or even of Blake's heaven and hell. Jung's late *Answer to Job* makes these themes even more explicit. In this work, the archetypal unconscious becomes the functional reality of God compelled to manifest in consciousness as conflicting opposites. In this cosmology, humanity is vested with the vocation of bringing the archetypally based opposites together in individual and history with the help and at the demand of its originating power. To the extent such unity takes place, both humanity and divinity are redeemed in the same process. The case can be made that the early expressionists and abstractionists were self-consciously engaged in just such an effort through their art.

Abstract art and the recovery of the spiritual

Wassily Kandinsky (1886–1944)

Contemporary art criticism thoroughly documents the confluence of mysticism, the occult, theosophy, alchemy and other peripheral traditions in early expressionism and the movement toward purely abstract non-representational art (Tuchman, 1986, pp. 18–49). The artists of these schools, like Jung, sought to reconnect their age with "the spirit of the depth" in the face of a materialism "infected with the despair of unbelief, of lack of purpose and ideal" (K. p. 2). They, with Jung, spoke of a need for the recovery of a wholeness, a human totality, whose absence in art and culture dismayed them. Jung himself recognized in this art the culture-wide longing for a depth that wholly evaded materialism. He writes, "Expressionism in art prophetically anticipated this subjective development, for all art intuitively apprehends coming changes in the collective unconscious" (Jung, 1928, para. 167). Jung was uneasy with and critical of these winds of change but read closely, he ultimately was approving. He saw in such change, for instance in Joyce and Picasso, the destruction of a too complacent and pleasing superficiality in art and literature while at the same time identifying their radical iconoclasm as a kairos ushering in a far more strident and realistic appreciation of truth and beauty. The abstractionist turn sought to express the purity of the inward spirit and its unfathomable realms in art that defied representation. Their experiential intimacy with the abyssal domain of the spiritual attracted them to mystics like Eckhart and Boehme and moved them to manifest such profundity to their culture in their art. One critic writes of this attraction to mysticism that caused Wassily Kandinsky to begin "the equation of abstraction, Expressionism and mysticism in the minds of critics and the public" (Long, 1986, p. 202).

In 1911 Kandinsky wrote his mandate to the artistic community, *Concerning the Spiritual in Art*. In it he tasked the contemporary artist with the vocation of living out of the depths of the artist's being expressed in an art that would engage the depths of the viewer. The inner life and light of the artist transparent in the art would awaken the light and life of one who gazed upon it. This would be a life and light so profound that its concretion in art would be maimed or lost in recognizable objective depiction. In this work Kandinsky uses two striking images to describe this artistic sensitivity, its expression and impact on the viewer, as well as its hoped-for effect on the future. The first image is that of the piano, the second that of a moving triangle. With his image of the piano Kandinsky imagines the soul as a piano whose keys are the colours the artist uses in the music of the art. The artist faithful to the pulsations of his own soul thus plays through the colours on the soul of the beholder. Writes Kandinsky "The artist is the hand which plays, touching one key or another, to cause vibrations in the soul" (Kandinsky, 1914/1977, pp. 25, 29). The artist's expression of personal soul to the soul of the other must then avoid an art which could be called literal or photographic, divested of the spiritual and so expressive of a much coarser soul and shallower experience. The piano image implies a certain synaesthesia. The colours pulsate and can be heard like the music of the spheres (T). Without the inner sound played on the canvas of the soul by the colours, the art is empty like a glove without a hand (K). There is room for form. Without the form the colours give to the art it is incoherent, but the form is never of an object. The abstractionist hangs between an objective art devoid of depth and the risk of unintelligibility in expressing the abyss of soul. Kandinsky himself was to wonder in print whether he, his contemporary artists and the wider art world were currently up to the demands of non-representational painting and to the purity abstractionist art sought and demanded.

The second image in Kandinsky's mandate would suggests that the profound interiority demanded by abstract art on artist and viewer alike would grow with both in the future. The image is of a triangle moving forward to the future and upward to a heightened consciousness. Across the triangle close to its top, Kandinsky places a horizontal line so that very few would approach the apex and the majority below the line would be further removed from it. But in his vision, as the triangle moves upward and forward, the horizontal line is lowered so that much more space is gained in the apex and fewer are removed from it. The meaning of the image is that in the future many more artists would express the depths of the soul defiant of depiction and fewer in the collective would remain immune to its expression. This hope is evident in Kandinsky's formulation of the aesthetic rising from his art, "That is beautiful which is produced by the inner need, which springs from the soul" (p. 55).

This aesthetic engages the themes of the history of consciousness and the role of necessity in it, themes that have a prominent place in Boehme's mysticism and in Jung's psychology. In his aesthetic, Kandinsky places a certain need or necessity in the abstractionist's urgency to create reminiscent of Boehme's central theme that divinity must create to become conscious in its finite creature through the unity in time of its opposites unreconciled in eternity. For Kandinsky, the "inner need" of the artist is the need of the eternal to find concretion in time. The need is that of the human spirit to lend eternal substance to all enduring art in and through the ephemeral cultural conditioning in which the art appears. Kandinsky's example is Egyptian art, through whose transient, long abandoned cultural forms the core of its imperishable beauty still prevails. In this the artist is again priest, prophet and mystic in returning to the originary nothingness, the source of the sacred, and making it incarnate through art in the vagaries of his or her current culture. Jung understood the ingression of the *Self* into consciousness as the residual meaning of incarnation. The abstractionist's vocation, as Kandinsky would see it, is to work this same incarnation through art expressive of the drive of the ultimate to become real in the art and through it in those who gaze upon it.

Jean (Hans) Arp (1886–1966)

Kandinsky's sympathy with Boehme is largely thematic, not literary. This is not the case with Jean Arp, Kandinsky's contemporary and colleague. Arp knew textual Boehme from his youth and was also well read in other members of the German mystical and esoteric tradition, including Eckhart. Two major images stand out in Arp's art, with reverberations in Boehme and Jung. Arp also was struck by Boehme's sketch already mentioned of a

72   John Dourley

divinity divided and united in a heart both human and divine against the background of an all-encompassing monistic unity. The divine duality of opposites was more impressive to Arp than the unifying heart at the centre. He was struck by the two centres in the drawing. The theme appeared in Arp's fascination with the "fluid oval" or ellipse in repeated paintings and sketches. The ellipse or oval would have two centres. Written large, the fluid oval would express the idea of two foci emanating from a common all-containing and creative origin. His fluid ovals imply that opposites share a common origin and might well move to a unity in a kind of cosmic teleology, though Arp was reluctant to give such a teleology too sharp a delineation lest it become too defined and vulnerable to narrower religious and philosophical appropriation.

A second image Arp was fond of was that of the amphora. The vessel is characterized by a long narrow neck stemming from a copious body. Arp related the form of the amphora to a generous if not unlimited energy of the heart seeking definition through the narrower stem of consciousness. The copious body suggests a fontal plenitude of energy and potential creative expression. Such endless wealth becomes finite through the narrow neck of the vessel. The implication is that the artist brings definition through the art to the infinity with whom the artist and the art are connected or even continuous. Again, the vision comes back to the artist creating out of a personal experience of spiritual profundity awakening such profundity in the other and so contributing both to contemporary culture and to the movement of spirit in history. In such art, spirit calls out to spirit in the recovery of a more total humanity.

Conclusion

Jung, the abstractionists and the mystics who inspired them sought to reconnect consciousness with the sublime as the divine native to the psyche. In one of his more hopeful moods, Jung suggests that the enterprise common to all three has already borne some fruit when he writes of the evolution of religious consciousness, "It was only quite late that we realized (or rather are beginning to realize) that God is reality itself and therefore – last but not least man. This realization is a millennial process" (CW 11, p. 402). Should Jung's insight that this is the way history moves be correct, his own psychology, the abstractionists and the mystics of the nothing to whom both Jung and the abstractionists turn may be seen as significant contributors to a more universal concord that what *is* is sacred and that what should be embraced is a compassion without boundaries.

References

Bowlt, J.E. (1986). Esoteric Culture and Russian Society. In E. Weisberger (Ed.), *The Spiritual in Art: Abstract Painting 1890–1985*. New York: Abbeville Publishing Group.

Jung, the sublime and apophatic mysticism   73

Dourley, J. (2014). *Jung and His Mystics: In the End it all Comes to Nothing*. London and New York: Routledge.

Hadewijch (1980). *Hadewijch, The Complete Works*, Trans. O.S.B. Mother Columbus Hart. New York: Paulist Press.

Jung, C.G. (1928). The Spiritual Problem of Modern Man." CW 10.

Jung, C.G. (1934a). Letter to Herman Hesse, September 18, 1934. In G. Adler and A. Jaffe (Eds.), *C.G. Jung Letters, Volume I, 1906–1950*. Princeton, NJ: Princeton University Press, 1975.

Jung, C.G. (1934b). Letter to Herman Hesse, October 1, 1934. In G. Adler and A. Jaffe (Eds.), *C.G. Jung Letters, Volume I, 1906–1950*. Princeton, NJ: Princeton University Press, 1975.

Jung, C.G. (1961). The Theory of Psychoanalysis. CW 4.

Jung, C.G. (1964). The Undiscovered Self. CW 10.3.

Jung, C.G. (1966a). Psychology and Literature. CW 15.

Jung, C.G. (1966b). On the Relation of Analytical Psychology to Poetry. CW 15.

Jung, C.G. (1966c). The Relations between the Ego and the Unconscious. CW 7.

Jung, C.G. (1969). Psychology and Religion. CW 11.

Jung, C.G. (1971). Psychological Types. CW 6.

Jung, C.G. (1979). The Tavistock Lectures. CW 18.

Jung, C.G. (2009). *The Red Book*, Ed. S. Shamdasani, Trans. M. Kyburz and J. Peck. London and New York: Norton.

Kandinsky, W. (2006). Concerning The Spiritual in Art. London:Tate.

Long, C. (1986). Expressionism, abstraction, and the search for Utopia in Germany. In *The Spiritual in Art: Abstract Painting 1890–1985*. New York: Abbeville.

McGinn, B. (1998). *The Flowering of Mysticism; Men and Women in the New Mysticism 1200–1350*. New York: Crossroads.

McGrath, S. J. (2012). *The Dark Ground of Sprit—Schelling and the Unconscious*. London: Routledge.

Menzies, L. (trans.) (1955). "The Revelations of Mechthild of Magdeburg (1210–1297) or The Flowing Light of the Godhead," *Scottish Journal of Theology*, 8(2), pp. 221–222.

Porete, M. (1993). *Marguerite Porete. The Mirror of Simple Souls*, Trans. E.L. Babinsky. New York: Paulist Press.

Tuchman, M. (1986). *The Spiritual in Art: Abstract Painting 1890-1985*. Los Angeles, CA: Los Angeles County Museum of Art/Abbeville Press.

Obituary

Fr. John Dourley, 1936–2018

John P. Dourley died on June 22, 2018, at the age of 82. He had been in declining health in recent years but was still in practice, and his death was unexpected.

John was a Roman Catholic priest, a member of the Oblates of Mary Immaculate. He was ordained in June 1964. He held Licentiates in Philosophy and Theology from St Paul University in Ottawa, a Masters in Theology from Ottawa University and an MA from St Michael's College, University of Toronto. In 1971 he obtained his PhD in Theology from Fordham University, New York. His doctoral thesis was on Paul Tillich and Bonaventure, which led to an interest in Jungian psychology. In 1980 he graduated with the Diploma in Analytical Psychology from the C.G. Jung Institut in Zürich.

John taught at Carleton University until 2001, when he retired from academic teaching, which left him freer to reflect and write on Jung and to expand his private practice. He was known to many throughout the world because of his writing on Jung and religion. He was interested in the relation of the human psyche and psychology to religious experience and religions. He wrote books with intriguing titles such as *The Illness That We Are; On Behalf of the Mystical Fool; The Goddess Mother of the Trinity; Love, Celibacy and the Inner Marriage*, to name only a few. The books were attractive to many and challenging to others, radical as they were in the face of patriarchy and conventional theology. Like Jung, John felt compelled to write, to communicate his understanding of Jung's message to the world. "I'm bitten by this", he said, "and I have to keep on writing". He was writing to the day he died.

John Dourley also lectured widely in Jungian and academic circles, addressing the plenary sessions of the International Association for Analytical Psychology in Barcelona 2004, Cape Town 2007, Montreal 2010 and Copenhagen 2013. He presented at the University of Cambridge, at Yale University and at many other meetings in many other countries.

John had a private practice as a Jungian analyst in Ottawa, Ontario, and was one of the founding analysts of the first Canadian training program for Jungian analysts, the Analyst Training Programme of the Ontario Association of Jungian Analysts (OAJA). His analysands spoke of his compassion, wisdom and presence. He was always there, open and ready and focused, one said. Candidates spoke of his sensitivity and felt privileged to work with him. John was one of the outstanding practitioners in the Jungian world, yet he was a humble person who took care to respect others.

On a more personal note, John Dourley enjoyed good conversation and meals with friends and colleagues. He joined local analysts in Ottawa for dinner every month and, when in Toronto for OAJA meetings, would dine with good friends such as Daryl Sharp of Inner City Books. They had known each other in adolescence and met again during training in Zürich. John also enjoyed outdoor sports. In winter during the week he went skating on the Rideau canal. Weekends he drove "up the Gatineau" to ski. On Fridays, he often met up with Carleton University students for afternoon and evening skiing. Later, retired from teaching, when sports activities were curtailed by health, John took long walks in the city he grew up in. His childhood neighbourhood was Sandy Hill, and the family summered at the cottage at Britannia Beach. There was a photo of him about eight years old with three other little boys sitting on the grass laughing for the camera.

In summer John loved to go fishing. His favourite watering hole was at a lake in the Gatineau Hills on land owned by his cousins. He spoke warmly of his summer fishing weekends. In a framed photo on his wall we see John Dourley wearing a jacket and hat, sitting alone in a row boat on the lake fishing on a summer's day. This was, quite possibly, his favourite spot in the whole world, a place where he could relax, reflect and gather himself in tranquillity.

Finally, one last thing. John liked cats and cats like John. No matter at whose house, the resident cat, no matter how shy, would come to John to be stroked, and spoken to and generally worshiped. He had a favourite photo of an orange tabby, a neighbourhood cat, he adopted and fed whenever it came round.

John Dourley was a brilliant thinker, author and theologian – a respected and valued Jungian analyst and a dear friend to many. In Ottawa we were planning to have another analyst lunch soon. His dying was unexpected, but I think he might have preferred a swift exit, seated in his analyst chair, and I wish him Godspeed.

Rosemary Murray-Lapachelle, RP,
Jungian Analyst (OAJA)

The Editors of the current book express their sense of loss at John Dourley's death, which is well commemorated in this obituary. They would also like to thank Father Richard C. Kelly, Rosemary Murray-Lachapelle and Cameron Martin for their great help in getting John's erudite chapter, which they found on his computer following his death, to the Editors in order for it to appear in this book.

FIVE

The subjective sublime: "like a diamond"?

Phil Goss

Introduction: sublime otherness

Taking its cue from William Wordsworth (1770–1850), who took nature as his "teacher" (Hebron, 2008) and used poetry to facilitate contact with feelings and sensations which lie somewhere between the ordinary and the sublime, this chapter explores the dynamics of profound experiential contact with something "other" in the natural and built environments. The presence of "otherness" as sublime in the physical environment can be seen in various ways, but principally as either a mysterious natural phenomenon (Schiller, 2005) or as a subjectively projected experience of something in ourselves which is unfamiliar or disturbed, or a combination of these.

In attempting to identify how "sublime experiences" constellate, I need to first clarify the way I am deploying the term *sublime*. This term can refer to historical definitions, from the Platonic (Shaw, 2006) notion of the sublime as generating profound responses to beauty, to Burke's (1990) emphasis on how ugliness and terror can be equally "sublime" to beauty. More recently there are also valuable angles on the sublime: post-Kantian ideas about how the sublime can come to stand, amongst other things, for our emotional response to the aesthetic quality of a material thing itself (Newman, 1990), the dynamic generated by how or whether the sublime gets boundaried (Derrida, 1987), or what impacts on us due to how it is embedded in language (Lyotard, 1988). A plasticity of theorizing has evolved over time about this notion, while the essential unknowability of sublime experiences, especially where we may experience a sense of something overwhelmingly mysterious or "other", remains – however able we are to apply our reasoning to them.

However, I posit that it is possible to identify characteristics of these experiences as part of the human condition and to think about what generates them in ways which are tentatively useful. It is "sublime experience" that I am interested in and this exploration will draw on Jungian thinking with comparative reference to Lacanian concepts as a corollary to an attempt to formulate a set of overarching propositions for what I postulate as the constellation and workings of the *subjective sublime*, my own version of which I term the *diamond sublime*.

The latter formulations propose the sublime has aspects which can provide a kind of *psychological balm*, *nourishment*, even *inspiration*, sometimes in a compensatory way in the face of trauma or loss.

However, it can also manifest as *shock*, *terror* or *disorientation*: a spur to heightened but disturbed consciousness. Either way, such experiences imply an encounter with something out of the ordinary, something unfamiliar and "other". Here "otherness" in a general sense refers to the phenomenological presence of something unfamiliar or strange, which surprises, captivates or disquiets (possibly frightens) us as we inhabit or move through built and natural environments. This phenomenological application of the term "otherness" stands tangentially to established post-Jungian applications of the notion of "the other". These shed light on conscious and intertwinements of the cultural, political, social and personal and challenge conventional ideas of what is "other", thereby valuing the transformational potential of "otherness" in interpersonal spheres (Samuels et al., 2018). Likewise, the Lacanian deployment of "ego as other", where the imaginary inevitably colours how we perceive other people also stands as a more intersubjective deployment of otherness. However, in his use of the capitalised Other, especially in relation to the Real as an unfathomable alterity, we do get helpfully closer to a "naming" of unnameable experience, albeit with its roots in a preverbal void (Chiesa, 2007).

Moments of contact with, and perception of, otherness associated not with the intersubjective "I" but with encounter with external environmental features will be illustrated by reference to a few lines from Wordsworth's *Ode* and also via a fictionalized vignette which acts as a composite reflector of a range of experiences reported by others in the author's professional and personal life (as well as from his own experience). Fictionalized analytic reportage is only one influence amongst many others in this mix.

More broadly, such moments may include: heightened awareness of features within a landscape, or of a building, or a felt or intuited sense of a greater depth or unfamiliarity present in the spatial field – such as in a moment of thorough stillness, or possibly even a fleeting sense of being outside "ordinary" time and space. One example poetic, the other more prosaic, but both seeming to describe a sense of ordinary life being opened up or disrupted by something behind familiar reality.

As well as exploring the ways experiences such as these may touch us unexpectedly, there will also be an attempt at "why" and "how" they happen – principally utilizing the depth psychological lenses provided by Lacan and Jung. There is also an argument made for the value of subjectivity in formulating frames of reference for describing how the sublime may operate, as modelled by the application of my own. Such postulation is offered in a spirit of cautious but critical curiosity, knowing how full and varied are the ways the human mind can trick itself, fed by its yearning for encounter with the mysterious.

Subjectivity, image and the sublime

In this vein, a term to metaphorically represent "where" sublime otherness may "emanate from" is coined: the *diamond sublime*. This term is entirely subjective on my part but aims to denote the idea of a "field" which draws its influence from the *pleroma* (an idea Jung adopted from Gnostic traditions – an unconscious layer of reality which is full of paradox and potential, containing "everything and nothing" and holding possibilities which show themselves only when it is disturbed or spontaneously irrupts – a dimension of reality which is invisible, inscrutable, but which may generate encounter with "sublime otherness"). As will be explicated, the term *diamond sublime* is a subjectively ascribed one from my own frame of reference, offered in the spirit of valuing the *individuality* of sublime encounter and the possibility of anyone finding their own terminology (or other ways of symbolizing) for what are usually intensely personal experiences.

In this respect, the subjectivity of sublime experience echoes the well-established philosophical tradition stretching back to Descartes and Kant (Howard, 2000) which places self-consciousness at the heart of human knowing and being and underpins the Western emphasis on the individual in practices which aim to enhance self-awareness, such as counselling and psychotherapy. While later philosophical positions on subjectivity inevitably diverge (such as Sartre's (2003), existential emphasis on the ego as seat of subjectivity in contrast to Merleau-Ponty's identification of the body and perceptual capacities as being fundamentally influential on our experiencing of reality (Carmen, 2008)), the subjectivity of the Westernized psyche is generally taken as a given.

Beyond the notion of subjectivity also lie well-established concepts to describe connection with *another* such as Buber's "I-Thou" (1958) with its emphasis on the profound value of genuine meeting between *Self* and other. Intersubjectivity, according to Stern (2000) refers to the sharing of affective states, attention and intention as established in early development, while projective identification (Klein, 1946) describes how one person unconsciously projects aspects of *Self* into another person, often with powerful and disturbing results. The relevance to this discussion of these references around subjectivity is to situate the *subject*, who is experiencing the *object/other* of *sublime* otherness, within a relational context. This also has implications I will come back to when referring to relational trauma, including loss, later in this chapter). These ideas also reinforce the value of subjectivity (deployed with critical reflexivity), including the draw on image, words and other symbolizations of the sublime by the individual who has had a sublime encounter with *otherness*.

One Lacanian way of situating this discussion is to describe the encounter with otherness as something Real, a sensed and felt experience which bursts through "the wall of language" (Lacan, 2007a). This renders reception of undistorted discourse from another unavailable, guarded by the Symbolic order we unconsciously adhere to due to powerful oedipal (phallic), familial and social forces as well as the Imaginary order which led us away from the unbearable loss of fusion with mother.

As mentioned earlier, the portraying of the "location" of sublime otherness through the image of a diamond shape is subjective and informed by experiences in my own life, plus those of others I have had contact with, and my ruminations on them. I am writing only of an *idea* + *image*, not something tangibly "real", but in Lacanian terms possibly an attempt to *imagine and/or symbolise the* Real. This is something which Lacan posited was not possible as the Real is that which eludes the grasp of the Symbolic (most obviously where trauma has rendered *symbolization* in thought or language impossible).

Therefore, the Real also cannot be ascribed a meaning and thus cannot be represented by an *image* (Lacan, 1988). In this sense, any attempt to try to figuratively locate an experience of otherness as Real could be doomed to failure.

However, although the notion of the Real as speaking to the absence of a capacity to "name" or "imagine" sublime experiencing points to the profound difficulty in satisfactorily describing its manifestations; the value of this perspective is counterbalanced – and complemented – when set alongside a Jungian emphasis on the archetypal image-making capacity of the psyche (Jung, 1968a). Here, image arises out of instinct and offers a range of possible forms within the continuum between archetypal polarities present in the *pleroma* (or it could be described in terms of the collective unconscious where according to Jung all human experiences and possibilities are deposited – good/evil, fascinated/terrified, awed/bored *et al.*). This reflects how archetypal forces are by their nature collective and ubiquitous, awaiting activation in the personal unconscious and how some of these get incorporated into images available to the conscious mind, triggered by a combination of past influences, embedded personality features and current lived experience.

In the latter regard, the images produced are thus triggered into awareness by sensory experience, and to use the philosopher and orientalist Henri Corbin's (1964) terminology, converted into a meaningful image generated by the *Mundus Imaginalis* (Imaginal World) in the individual human psyche. We are then able, through our cognitive powers and awareness to: firstly, notice the image, respond to and reflect on it and its possible, metaphorical meanings; secondly, we can then try to differentiate which of these images arise from within our powerfully subjective influences and which have been "placed in front of us" by nature; thirdly, we can then play with possible meanings of these and their implications. These principles correlate with Jung's framework for *active imagination* (Chodorow, 1997).

As indicated, the types of experiences this discussion refers to can include a heightened sense of contact with life, an overwhelming feeling of awe or terror, or a more subtle intimation of mysterious "otherness". In some cases, a sense of being privy to something bewildering but important is present, even if the person cannot put their finger on what that "is". Such moments, a fleeting awareness of, or even a sense of contact with, *otherness* – present in the air, over the hill, around a building – provides an inkling of something present which is "more than" what we would expect to be present "normally" or "naturally" in the environment.

80 Phil Goss

Poetic sublime subjectivity

This is where the example from Wordsworth's poetry comes in. A few lines from his famous *Ode to Intimations of Immortality* (2008, Lines 144–148) speak to more than just the impact on him of the environment around him (the English Lake District with its vivid landscape of high peaks and lush valleys) but how the assault on his senses of his surroundings triggers a heightened and cognitive awareness of his inner life which seemingly connects him to a presence of something truly "other", as he writes of his gratitude:

> for those obstinate questionings
> Of sense and outward things,
> Fallings from us, vanishings;
> Blank misgivings of a Creature
> Moving about in worlds not realized

So how might we make sense of Wordsworth's intimation not just of hidden worlds, but of a "Creature", with its sublime implications of something awesome, strange, possibly terrifying?

Jacques Lacan identified the key relationship between *desire* and *lack* inherent in the human condition.

As Lemaire puts it (1977, pp. 162–163):

> [L]ack is the void, the zero, that which lies before the instinct . . . desire is the successor to the essential lack lived by the child separated from its mother.

As we live our lives in the shadow of unredeemable loss of the maternal object, there will always be lack and by looking for, or imagining we have had, an inexplicable encounter with something mysterious, we may just be tricking ourselves about what is really unattainable: the *Thing* (Lacan, 1992) behind our desire, which cannot be had. This formulation implies the evocation of such a *Thing* in Wordsworth's "Creature", a manifestation of profound otherness which is really the ever-unavailable object of our desire, a ghostly product of the mind's failed attempt to reach the source of its unfulfilled erotic excitation or *jouissance* (Bailly, 2009) towards it.

Another psychological reading of this focuses on the dynamics of such experiences. However, influenced by our projective tendencies, we usually experience them, in the moment of their impact, as happening *to* us. We do not, cannot, consciously make them happen. There is consonance here with one of Jung's notable ideas: the *Self* is a fundamental "centre" of who we are and has a kind of autonomous capacity to reveal itself or make things happen (1968b); a deeper intelligence in us than the conscious ego. This *logos* of the unconscious (Adler, 1980) sometimes surprises us with events or developments we have no choice but to deal with (not unlike the impact of the Real) and to integrate the experience of these into our psychic development. This, I propose takes us closer to the phenomenological impact on the poetic subject (Wordsworth as ego) as he reports a sublime intimation of something mysterious activated by the *Self*.

Imagining the sublime as a "diamond field"

I propose four main dimensions to the activity and experiencing of the sublime, bearing in mind I am applying shorthand terminology to the ultimately unknowable. I do this with reference to Jung's (1966) emphasis on "four-ness" i.e. the quaternity as collectively representing completion/the complete picture of something, which can also be seen to be "of the *Self*" in the phenomenological way Jung describes it happening to us. This four-ness is applied lightly; there can never be any more than an *attempt* at completeness, bearing in mind the (archetypal?) ubiquity of *lack* (Lemaire, 1977). However, a classical Jungian stance on individuation would say it is always worth the attempt.

These four influences are suggested as *numinosity, inscrutability, otherness* and *synchronicity*, imagining each of them as a metaphorical pole corner of the diamond shape, generating a "fifth" – the subtle, invisible but influential *sublime* energy in the "empty space" at the centre of the diamond shape. In this regard, the "fifth-ness" of manifestations of the sublime speaks to the way it "transcends" completion as well as "deconstructs" or even "subverts" it.

The first "corner" of the *diamond sublime* shape (as subjectively imagined by me) is *numinosity*, where the idea of the *numinous* refers to: "something like 'awesome' and refers to the emotional quality of religious experiences. . . (although). . . . It has gained currency in the postmodern world and even materialists and atheists are able to affirm a numinous quality in nature and human experience" (Casement and Tacey, 2006, p. xvi). This, one could say, is the prime energic source which infuses sublime experience with a powerful "charge" which can inspire, disturb or even terrify and refers to the links made by Otto between the sublime and the *numinous* (Otto, 1959). *Inscrutability*, as the word implies, refers to a second corner which renders the source of the sublime experience unavailable and unknowable. I may be having an experience, but I do not know why, or where it comes from. In this regard, the very purpose of the *inscrutability* is, in fact, inscrutable. Here, the sublime, like the *pleroma* is "everything and nothing" rather than a "something". Here, what Culp (2015, p. 33) terms "Advancing towards Nothing" in broader cultural terms – in relation to his critique of the holistic emphasis of Deleuze and Guattari (1987) on connectivity, which could also be applied as a critique of theories of *Emergence* (e.g. Clarke, 2013) – implies the pull towards "nothingness" as an important aspect of the sublime. The third corner, *otherness*, has already been referred to as crucial to the sense of mystery and unfamiliarity which comes from a sublime encounter. Finally, *synchronicity* – the fourth corner of the diamond, provides the acausal quality of sublime experience. Our presence in a physical space and (with prior unknowing) our availability for the experience, coincides with the manifestation of the sublime – one does not cause the other, nor does a third influence generate this. A "meaningful coincidence" (Jung, 1970) occurs, where person/location/object or view "coincide".

So the combination of the four influences just mentioned constellate within the diamond into experience of the sublime. To stress again, I am not proposing the impossible; i.e. a reified description of the sublime, but rather a way of trying to locate our experiencing and dim understanding of its nature. Another symbol for this might be a black hole in reverse – an infinitely dense, inaccessible and unknowable concentrate of reality which occasionally throws out its "dark matter" (Tucker, 2017) for us to experience, possibly portrayed as a tiny black diamond to connect this idea to the suggested symbol of an imagined diamond.

In this regard, I propose "diamond" as an imagined container of the sublime for two cultural-symbolic reasons: The first refers to the way a real diamond was formed, from deep in the earth and the legacy of the mantle created below the surface from hundreds of millions of years of volcanic activity. The extreme heat and pressure combined gradually modified graphite into the triangular influence on the shape of what we now know as diamonds. Sayings such as "the diamond in the rough" or Victor Hugo's adaptation of this in *Les Misérables*: "Diamonds are to be found only in the darkness of the earth, and truth in the darkness of the mind." (Hugo, 1976, p. 231) imply the presence of a diamond as a psychological resource that is often shrouded in *Shadow* (Jung, 1968c

In this respect, it works as a representation of the appearance of – and to take the volcanic metaphor, the *eruption* of – a phenomena into conscious awareness from previously obscured, unconscious territory.

In my own musings around "location" or "container" of the sublime, this image has come forward for me I think partly because of the way the shadier and more unnerving connotations of the sublime imply, in Jungian terms, the presence of some kind of alchemical process at work. Here the messy but creative process of soul-making (Hillman, 1992) seeks something of value that has enduring solidity, which a diamond emerging from the underground darkness certainly does. The second is a broader move to recognize the fading of Christian symbolism and influence over the interpretation of mysterious events we cannot rationally explain within the Westernized mind. Here I acknowledge the specificity of this connection which does not apply to other world faiths or non-Westernized traditions, but which I can link to my own cultural heritage as a faded but fundamental influence on my psychic development and therefore on the seeding of the *diamond* image in my own mind as metaphor for the workings of the *sublime*.

The diamond, when drawn with an emphasis on the vertical plane and particularly when with a smaller top half compared to lower half (though this does not have to be the case), represents the joining of the four points of the Christian cross: top, right, bottom and left *but without the cross itself in the centre*.

This is an idea I have played with before (Goss, 2010), and I propose that it is particularly useful in describing a post-Christian "forcefield" which suggests other possibilities, other reveals, of what is happening in the Westernized unconscious (taking care not to overgeneralize), individually and collectively, whilst respecting the equally important religious and cultural legacy of other Abrahamic religious traditions in this regard. Likewise, I cannot speak with confidence – nor would it be appropriate – about what evolved symbols might reflect how less Westernized religious and cultural traditions might represent "the field of the sublime". However, Christianity – which I am not an adherent of, but the psychological imprint of which still looms large in my psyche – is, like the imprints of other religious traditions, "still with us", however unhelpfully disconnected with lived reality this may be for some. So there are roots and influences in me which lead to my imagining and playing with the generation and "location" (in the broadest sense) of the sublime. Others would have their own unique way of *imagining* or *imaging* a transmitter of, or container for, the sublime.

Urban sublime subjectivity

Now let's consider the second example based on a fictionalized amalgam of reported experiences. A person is walking through the streets of a city with the sounds of traffic and an aeroplane overhead in their ears.

They turn a corner onto a residential road they have not walked down before. As they turn the corner they stop in their tracks as they experience a momentary sense of profound stillness, as if time has stood still. They can hear no sounds in this moment. The wind is still blowing gently through the trees which line the pavements in front of the terraced houses, the features of which seem to stand out vividly, almost luminously; every feature is sharply enunciated – window frames, cornices, even squat brick walls and gates at the front which are so high-definition they seem to move towards the observer in this moment – a stunning vision in an ordinary suburban city street of the aesthetic sublime.

The leaves move, but in what seems like slow motion. The person is aware of their mouth and eyes opening wide, their chest seems to fill with feeling, and they hear their breath intake sharply in the silence. A kind of spatial dissonance leads to a momentary sensation in their fingers of physical contact with the enunciated brickwork of the houses a few hundred yards away. But with a further step, all is as before. Then the moment passes, the sounds return, and the person resumes walking, but with a deep sense of disorientation, as well as wonder.

These sorts of experiences are clearly open to all sorts of interpretation and speculation, including whether this is a kind of altered mental state associated with conditions such as epilepsy or synaesthesia (Ramachandran,

84   Phil Goss

2010) or tendencies which can be triggered by certain atmospheric or environmental influences such as intense sunlight or any other sudden change in the visual, auditory or otherwise sensorial field. In terms of the distortion of reality described, it might also be read as a psychotic episode even if the person had no history of this. Alternatively, Freud (2004) may well have bracketed the experience described under that of *oceanic feeling*: a return to an undifferentiated state of consciousness from the very earliest phase of life before ego emerges under the aegis of maternal preoccupation (Winnicott, 2016). One could speculate within this reading that the experience of the acuteness of the aesthetic encounter with building features is a recapitulation of the "moment" of ego's emergence from the undifferentiated state.

A Lacanian reading of the episode described could again imply a psyche suddenly caught out by a breaking through of the Real as language and imagination fail to catch up with a sudden change in sensory experience and cannot symbolize it (Lacan, 1988). On the other hand, time "stopping" is a kind of *lacuna* – a gap, like a moment where the *lack* "shows itself" in a flash (this is an example of my difficulty in expressing how a "lack" is revealed, emphasizing its contradictory and elusive nature), and then as quickly recedes from consciousness. Here, "something has happened" – however strange – which is noticed as "time has stopped" – i.e. it has been symbolized in language. The odd sensation of touching the distant brickwork and the observer cognitively noting this also suggests a primitive symbolization (though still something of a disruption of the *Symbolic* and *Imaginary* orders), as the meanings and images associated with familiar reality about "house/home" and their connotations are concertinaed in front of the observer, a manifestation of the creaking edges of their defences against the Real breaking through traumatically.

Comparing this to a Jungian take on these moments, we need to consider Jung's ideas about how psychological phenomena can irrupt into conscious awareness, including the role of complexes and synchronicity. *Complexes* as highly charged, emotionally toned influences, according to Jung (1969), form and take root in the human psyche and when activated can deeply and consistently inform felt and behavioural responses to events and other people. A characteristic of a complex at work is where a person is overwhelmed by affect (e.g. anger, desire, sorrow) – "the complex having the person" rather than the other way around. A complex is formed, according to Jung, via a combination of formative unconscious influences, constitutional personality traits and present factors which act as a trigger for the complex to be activated, exerting its pull on us like the moon on the ocean tides. Finally, this combination attracts a powerful archetypal charge from the depths of the unconscious which provides the energic power that can overwhelm. It is also possible to describe the phenomena portrayed as emanating from "beyond a complex' – something which has no connection with the just described influences but which breaks unexpectedly into our awareness like a meteor flaring into view in the sky.

In the fictionalized example given, the "overwhelm" is a kind of sensory overload combined with disorientation, as the observer is impacted by the visual and auditory strangeness of a high-definition urban aesthetic combined with sounds ceasing and then the street seeming to expand and contract.

One could speculatively describe the affective overload as a complex which may have a "parental"/"familial" root, but perhaps we could term a *home complex*, in the way the vision of lots of homes together seems to assail the individual. Clearly one would need a properly detailed case analysis of the individual concerned to unpick and clinically verify what this might be about. Where the notion of *synchronicity* becomes relevant is in Jung's (1970) observation of the apparently acausal nature of meaningful coincidence. In this case, the person involved has encountered a sublime moment which is deeply affecting and which may have activated a powerful but otherwise dormant complex. Jung's description of synchronicity is of a "rupture of time" (Main, 2014). Here, two apparently unrelated factors – the presentation of a vivid urban view and the dormant complex meet in a moment where time ruptures and aesthetic power fires like an arrow into the heart of the observer; it is an encounter with the *Self*, within the *diamond* field of the sublime, which seems to carry meaning even if the person cannot put their finger on exactly why.

For this person, I suggest what matters is not so much the "reason" for it happening but rather how this encounter offers something of enduring value within their lived experience. This value is precisely because we cannot determine or manufacture such encounters, thus giving us a real experience of something which is "other" or "more" than us and adding genuine value to our lives because it frees us from the responsibility to "make meaning" and instead provides a sense of the presence of something meaningful which, though incomprehensible, crucially we experience as "not of us". In turn, this can offer a point of reference – through the counterpoint of its very inscrutability – for us to look more closely at our own existential, possibly spiritual, questions and priorities. Models such as the Gestalt *Cycle of Awareness* (Finlay, 2015), which describes how we wrestle with creative and destructive forces within us to deal with satisfying needs and processing experience, can help provide a framework for reflecting on how we manage these. More than this, sublime encounters can create a psychological atmosphere, even a "jolt", from which arises a spur to notice, or reframe, what really matters to us.

If anything can be said about a subjective attitude which is sensitive to the possibility of sublime experience, then perhaps this would be an approach which waits on its potential without looking too hard. Environments we find ourselves in – say, a footpath, gallery, beach or street – may be familiar to us as ones we have visited or even lived in before, or they may be unfamiliar new ones which seem to evoke certain unexpected reactions in us. In either case, inhabiting any environment implies possibilities for the generation of curiosity, satisfaction, fear, discomfort, yearning and what at times could be experienced as ways of experiencing kinds of emotional and psychological nourishment. This also links to the possibility, as Dowd (2019, p. 245) puts it, of "the necessity of a felt sense of a 'place to put experience' " for the maintenance of psychic health. She writes of the crucial role of the locale, the physical place, in which our lives and sense of self are established and how traumatic being wrenched from a familiar place (e.g. because of war) can be for our sense of self. I suggest psyche can try to heal this kind of rupture through seeking of meaning in whatever environments they go on to live in – either the same or a different place. Encounter with the sublime can offer such healing through providing an experience which is "other" or "overwhelming': meeting the psychic need *to be overwhelmed by something mysterious*. To borrow from Buber (1958), "I – Thou" becomes "I – That" where "That" denotes the unknowable "other" which may help a person meet the "face" of the inscrutability of the card life has dealt them.

The experiences just alluded to suggest the value of exploring and acknowledging the presence of "otherness" as part of the human condition and narrative, but also the possibility such experiences can have therapeutic, healing potential as well as possible spiritually nourishing qualities (where the term "spiritual" is held as holding its own individual meaning for each person and could be substituted with other terms such as "meaningful", "existential", "religious" etc.): operating as a genuinely felt version of meaning-making rather than being prone to the risk of becoming another consumer-related activity for the twenty-first century (Heelas, 2008).

More broadly, such phenomena and experiences relate to an idea of the unconscious being present in some way in the external, as well as inner, environment. Jung, in his considerations about synchronicity (1970) implied there may be, somewhere in between the positivist assertion of observable, provable scientific fact, on the one hand, and the deconstruction of objectivity via postmodernism on the other, a field of "quiet activity" around us which we do not understand but can experience on occasion via synchronistic events. I suggest this can include accessing a sense of "deeper than", "further than", "more than" the here and now (or even "less than" where the experience is one of unusual "emptiness').

Romanticism and the notion of the sublime

As implied, I advocate drawing on recapitulations of the phenomenological heart of Romanticism. Put broadly, this could be portrayed as experiences, or the striving for experiences, of connection with *depth* in nature or the built environment, as a balm to compensate for the daily grind of life and some kind of loss of spirit in the secularization of Western culture, or as an inspiration for living more fully. My deployment of the *subjective sublime*, alongside the notion of the *pleroma* adopted by Jung as an "implicate order" of reality (Bohm, 1980) from which acausal activity can emerge to generate sublime experiences, corresponds with this Romantic sensibility.

This approach also applies a necessary level of criticality which both supports the notion of "the sublime as a drama of subject-formulation" (Vine, 2014, p. 4) and recognizes the importance of situating this within post-Romantic emphases on the Impersonal, pluralistic and historicized contexts of modern and postmodern cultural developments. To reinsert the individual possibilities for self-knowledge, even quiet reinvention via the *subjective sublime* at the centre of these developments argues for a different kind of post-Romanticism which allows for the subjective to also subtly inform something more collective, though this dimension merits its own separate discussion beyond the central remit of this chapter.

Taking this in conjunction with more recent angles such as Derrida's (1987) use of *sublime*, and the question as to whether it can in any sense be "boundaried", points us towards the possibilities of recognizing the *spatial* dynamics of the sublime as enabling contact with otherness. These enter and activate our field of perceptual capacity to notice what is experientially *containable*, even for just a fleeting moment in our awareness and to intuit this in terms of *proximity* – what is *near* and what is *far* (rather than in a concrete "measurable" way).

Freud and Jung: mourning as "emptying out" and glimpses of "life in death" as archetypal

Key concepts drawn from the founder of psychoanalysis and its derivative, but philosophically contrasting offspring, analytical psychology, help provide a theoretical and clinical foundation for the notion of subjectivity as exemplified in my own use of the *diamond sublime*. When combined, or perhaps more accurately, set alongside one another, these founding concepts provide the pillars for a bridge which allows for the deterministic but mythologically informed thinking of Freud and the archetypal emphasis of Jung's approach to support fresh readings of human encounters with otherness in the natural or built landscape.

Freud posited from his clinical observations that "in mourning it is the world which has become poor and empty" (1915/1984, p. 254), as opposed to depression or "melancholia" being a dwindling, even a voiding, of life from the person's inner world. The loss creates an experience of emptiness and void which is located outside the person where the lost loved one used to be, an unconscious projection of the "hole" created within because of what has been lost – i.e. the previously relied upon attachment to the reliable presence of the loved person.

I have previously suggested this could provide an accurate description of the conditions which may sometimes enable encounters with "otherness" to happen (Goss, 2012). I posited a powerful awareness of the "emptiness" of the space around us often arises because of the painful absence of the lost loved one who can no longer be seen, touched or found, however much we may search for them in the outer environment (for example, the home we might have shared with them or another space we associate with that person). A kind of pronounced sensory, emotional and psychological sensitivity to what may be "out there" develops from our reaching out (conscious or unconscious) and evolves into a "radar" which allows the individual who has lost their loved "object" to experience a *compensatory otherness* or a *compensatory sublime*. The example of Wordsworth, losing both his father and mother by the age of 13, and his capacity to generate the most intense descriptions of sublime encounters in nature, seems to support this theory.

Here Jung's idea, derived from influences which include Kant and Hegel, that the opposite is always present, supplies a valuable complementary contribution to Freud's observations. For Jung, paradox and transformation are deemed as archetypal – i.e. present, either in reality, or *in potential*. This formulation is taken by Jung (Beebe, 1989), borrowing from Heraclitus's notion of *enantiodromia*, which refers to the proposition that everything always turns into its opposite. The apparently absent opposite of a presenting phenomena is inherently, nascently present within it. An example which is directly relevant to our discussion is the presence of death in life as something there, waiting to happen.

With respect to the other way around, the argument I am deploying here is not just a familiar one about the "cycle of death – life – death – life" (and so on) in nature, whether that is in relation to a farmer's field which has been allowed to go fallow providing a good environment for growing a new crop or the way a generation of people dies after procreating the next generation. Rather, the implication of this idea is that in some way *life is bound to emerge from death* phenomenologically because of the archetypal principle of compensation, which in Jungian language is about how nature seeks out *homeostasis* or a systemic balance within the psychophysiological being of all living material and creatures, including us, and which applies to the function of dreams (Jung, 2011). Sublime encounters, I suggest, can sometimes serve this life-giving purpose in supplying a bereaved, traumatized or emotionally wounded person a kind of balm, comfort or sense of meaning which helps to ameliorate the sense of loss or emptiness they usually experience. This is not to say, though, that one has to have encountered trauma or loss to "qualify" for encounter with sublime otherness.

Referring back to Dowd's paper (Ibid), she draws on findings from neuroscience which show the hippocampal memory acts to establish patterned responses which attach us to familiar places and create what she terms "place maps" ':

> It is into these "place maps" that our emotional experiencing in relation to our total environment, human and non-human, becomes embedded or encoded as 'organised spatial stories. It is these processes that give rise to the spatial, temporal and relational links . . . essential to a sense of self-cohesion, self-continuity and belonging.
>
> *(Dowd, 2019, p. 252)*

In this respect, encounter with the sublime is facilitated unconsciously out of connections such memory processes make with a place (or a building or object) – either familiar or unfamiliar, associated unconsciously with the neurologically and affectively formed "place map" of the individual – or in my own terminology – the *diamond sublime* field, in a compensatory way.

Fundamentals of the "the diamond sublime" at work

A fundamental proposition arising from this discussion is: when the unconscious is seen as operating as a dynamic *field*, not just a repository or reflector of unprocessed instinctual responses, or interlocutor with our inter- and intra-relational nature, then we can propose the unconscious has its own spatial characteristics in the sense it can come into and across physical space(s) and influence our experiencing of the natural and built environment. It is an unconscious complement to the rational nature of spatial cognition where "spatial properties . . . include location, size, distance, direction, separation and connection, shape, pattern, and movement" (Timmermans, 2001, p. 14771).

In terms of evolutionary development, spatial cognition arose with the image-making capacity needed to notice and remember where places of danger, safety and nourishment within the environment a human or animal inhabited were located, in the interests of survival (Damasio, 2018). Inevitably, an unconscious dimension to something so elemental must have arisen, too.

This unconscious spatial life has more to do with subjective, felt experience of the landscape, natural objects, buildings and specific items and features in the area concerned which may activate memories, associations or complexes. It is possible to play with this in relation to Levy-Bruhl's (1926) concept of *participation mystique* – while taking care not to apply this not-unproblematic anthropological term too readily to something as opaque as the *sublime*. Jung (1971) drew on this concept to highlight the psyche's tendency to unconsciously identify and psychologically intermingle with another person. Here it could be played with in relation to place, natural or made object, or in terms of the considerations about loss mentioned earlier, in relation to an empty space. This unconscious propensity to project self and to seek attachment not just to another person but to the environment we find ourselves in can facilitate the *subjective sublime* constellation of a sense of presence, otherness, depth, emptiness or change in the *proximity-distance* dynamic.

The experience of the often-unbearable emotions associated with grief creates a wound in the face of the death of a loved one at any stage of life may be one way in which a mourner seeks out such experiences. As already speculated, trauma hallmarked by loss may be unconsciously compensated for by the filling of the space created, enabling capacities to experience phenomena which would otherwise be on the other side of the edge of "ordinary" consciousness. Grossman's (2014) novel, which strikingly conveys the "spatial" quality of relationship within altered states associated with loss, is a vivid example of this.

Conclusion: the subjective sublime

To recapitulate my speculative formulation for the possibly "healing"/reparative workings of the *subjective sublime*, here are five working propositions:

- There is an *in potentia* presence of sublime otherness in both natural and built environments, where "otherness" refers to what is unfathomable and thoroughly "not–I", or to adapt Buber's formulation for the "I–Thou" relationship (Ibid): "I–That". Where this kind of experiencing constellates, the individual may experience a sense of something subtly but powerfully mysterious, something disturbing but meaningful.
- This presupposes the unconscious has a spatial ("out there") as well as intra- ("in here") and inter-("between us") presence. In particular, it can manifest as the "otherness" described in the preceding paragraph, and this may be seen as a mysteriously objective phenomenon or as a subjectively projected experience of something unfamiliar in ourselves, or both. This experience of otherness may be said to be "sublime", in that it takes us up to, and over, the "limit" of ordinary conscious experience.
- The human psyche has a capacity to detect and experience "otherness" in the natural or built environment. This can take various forms, e.g. heightened awareness of the natural features within a landscape, or of buildings, or of a felt or intuited sense of a greater depth present in the spatial field (the idea of the *diamond sublime* is my own way to describe this inscrutable "field", but others may have their own ways of conceptualizing or envisaging this).
- Where a person has experienced trauma, particularly loss of a loved one, the wound, or "hole" created in the psyche creates a space through which the presence of otherness can come into awareness in a compensatory way. Where this applies, experiences of the sublime, including ones which are terrifying or shocking, can trigger a compensatory awareness and emotional process (sometimes healing).
- This capacity is probably inherent in every person. However, the nature of the experience of, and responses to, the presence of sublime otherness, is specific to each person and their own frame of reference for making sense of reality. On this basis, the *subjective sublime* offers the individual possibilities to play with and "actively imagine" (Chodorow, Ibid) sublime experience, thus exploring their relationship to reality and possibly gaining psychological or spiritual nourishment via a heightened sense of contact and relationship with the environment.

As Siskin (2018) points out, Edmund Burke's efforts to build "an entire system of human nature and experience through the extension of the binary . . . distinction between categories of pain (sublime) and pleasure (beauty)" laid the foundations for poetic efforts which at times took this system to a point of literalization of Burke's topic: "sub" ("up to") plus "lintel" ("limit"), that is "over the top" (Siskin, 2018, p.115).

This wry critique of where the aesthetic sublime can get over-rationalized contrasts with poets and other writers and artists who have let the weird, the wonderful and the dark break through the "limit" of heightened senses, such as Wordsworth's description of the "Creature". Such action entails reporting individual experience of the sublime by finding or allowing a way, however partial, to express what is beyond the imaginary and the symbolic; to break through "the wall of language" (Lacan, 2007b) via the image-making capacity of the psyche. In this way, the *subjective sublime* can become a living gift to self and others, and its hidden influence can reverberate across time, space and human experience.

References

Adler, G. (1980). *Dynamics of the Self*. London: Coventure.

Bailly, L. (2009). *Lacan: A Beginner's Guide*. Oxford: Oneworld, Chapter 13.

Beebe, J. (ed.). (1989). *Aspects of the Masculine*. Princeton: Princeton University Press, Introduction.

Bohm, D. (1980). *Wholeness and the Implicate Order*. London: Routledge.

Buber, M. (1958). *I and Thou*. New York. Charles Scribner's Sons.

Burke, E. (1990). *A Philosophical Enquiry into the Origin of Our Ideas of the Sublime and Beautiful*. Oxford: Oxford University Press.

Carmen, T. (2008). *Merleau-Ponty*. Abingdon: Routledge.

Casement, A. and Tacey, D. (2006). *The Idea of the Numinous*. Hove: Routledge.

Chiesa, L. (2007). *Subjectivity and Otherness: A Philosophical Reading of Lacan*. Cambridge, MA: Massachusetts Institute of Technology Publications.

Chodorow, N. (Ed.) (1997). *Jung on Active Imagination*. London: Routledge.

Clarke, J. (2013). *The Self-Creating Universe: The Making of a Worldview*. Bloomington, IN: Xlibris.

Corbin, H. (1964). *Cahiers internationaux de symbolisme* 6 (pp. 3–26). Brussels. (Translated into English in *Spring* (Zurich, 1972) as "Mundus Imaginalis or The Imaginal and the Imaginal").

Culp, A. (2015). *Dark Deleuze*. Minneapolis: University of Minneapolis Press.

Damasio A. (2018). *The Strange Order of Things: Life, Feeling, and the Making of Cultures*. New York: Pantheon.

Deleuze, G. and Guattari, F. (1987). *A Thousand Plataeus*. Minneapolis: University of Minnesota Press.

Derrida, J. (1987). *The Truth in Painting*. Chicago: The University of Chicago Press.

Dowd, A. (2019). Uprooted Minds: Displacement, Trauma and Dissociation. *Journal of Analytical Psychology*, 64(2), 244–269. London: SAP Publications.

Finlay, L. (2015). *Relational Integrative Psychotherapy: Process and Theory in Practice*. Chichester: Wiley, Chapter 13.

Freud, S. (1915/1984). *Mourning and Melancholia*. In *The Pelican Freud Library Vol. III: On Metapsychology*. London: Penguin Books, pp. 245–268.

Freud, S. (2004). *Civilization and its Discontents*. London: Penguin Classics.

Goss, P. (2010). *Men, Women and Relationships, A Post-Jungian Approach: Gender Electrics and Magic Beans*. Hove: Routledge, Chapter 8.

Goss, P. (2012). Wordsworth, Loss and the Numinous. *The Wordsworth Circle*, 43(3).

Grossman, D. (2014). *Falling Out of Time*, Trans. J. Cohen. London: Johnathan Cape.

Hebron, S. (2008). *William Wordsworth Selected Poems With an Illustrated Biography*. Grasmere: Wordsworth Trust.

Heelas, P. (2008). *Spiritualities of Life: New Age Romanticism and Consumptive Capitalism*. Oxford: Blackwell.

Hillman, J. (1992). *Re-Visioning Psychology*. New York: Harper Collins.

Howard, A. (2000). *Philosophy for Counselling and Psychotherapy: Pythagoras to Postmodernism*. Basingstoke: MacMillan.

Hugo, V. (1976). *Les Miserables*, Trans. N. Denny. London: Penguin Classics.

Jung, C.G. *The Collected Works*, 20 vols, Eds. H. Read, M. Fordham and G. Adler, Trans. R. F. C. Hull. London: Routledge & Kegan Paul.

Jung, C.G. (1966). The Psychology of the Transference. In *The Practice of Psychotherapy*, CW 16.

Jung, C.G. (1969). A Review of the Complex Theory. In *The Structure and Dynamics of the Psyche*, CW 8.

Jung, C.G. (1968a). Archetypes of the Collective Unconscious. In *The Archetypes and the Collective Unconscious*, CW 9i.

Jung, C.G. (1968b). The Self. In *Aion*, CW 9ii.

Jung, C.G. (1968c). The Shadow. In *Aion*, CW 9ii.

Jung, C.G. (1970). Synchronicity: An Acausal Connecting Principle. In *The Structure and Dynamics of the Psyche*, CW 8.

Jung, C.G. (1971). Psychological Types. CW 6.

Jung, C.G. (2011). *The Undiscovered Self: With Symbols and the Interpretation of Dreams*. Oxford: Princeton University Press.

Klein, M. (1946). Notes on Some Schizoid Mechanisms. In *The Writings of Melanie Klein*, vol. 3 (pp. 1–24). New York: Free Press.

Lacan, J. (1977). *Seminar XI: The Four Fundamental Concepts of Psychoanalysis*, Trans. A. Sheridan. London: Hogarth Press & Institute of Psycho-Analysis.

Lacan, J. (1988). *The Seminar of Jacques Lacan. Book 2: The ego in Freud's Theory and in the Technique of Psychoanalysis, 1954–1955*, Trans. S. Tomaselli. New York: W.W. Norton & Company. (First Published 1978).

Lacan, J. (1992). *The Seminar. Book VII. The Ethics of Psychoanalysis, 1959–60*, Trans. D. Porter. London: Routledge.

Lacan, L. (2007a). *Ecrits*. New York: W.W. Norton & Company.

Lacan, J. (2007b). *The Ethics of Psychoanalysis: The Seminar of Jacques Lacan: Book VII: Part 1*. Abingdon: Routledge Classics.

Lemaire, A. (1977). *Jacques Lacan*, Trans. David Macey. London: Routledge.

Lévy-Bruhl, L. (1926[1912]). *How Natives Think*, Trans. L. A. Clare. Eastford, CT: Martino Fine.

Lyotard, J. (1988). *The Differend: Phases in Dispute*. Manchester: Manchester University Press.

Main, R. (2014). *The Rupture of Time*. London: Routledge.

Newman, B. (1990). *Selected Writings and Interviews*. New York: Alfred A. Knopf.

Otto, R. (1959). *The Idea of the Holy: An Inquiry into the Non-rational Factor in the Idea of the Divine and its Relation to the Rational*. London: Penguin Classics.

Ramachandran (2010). *The Tell-Tale Brain: A Neuroscientist's Quest for What Makes Us Human*. London: Windmill.

Samuels, A., Hauke, C., Papadopoulos, R., Brooke, R., Brewster, F. and Beebe, J. (2018). *Jung and the Other: Encounters in Depth Psychology*. London: IAJS & Routledge.

Sartre, J. (2003). *Being and Nothingness: An Essay on Phenomenological Ontology*. Abingdon: Routledge Classics.

The subjective sublime   93

Schiller, F. (2005). On the Sublime, Concerning the Sublime. In W. Hinderer and D.O. Dahlstrom (Eds.), *Essays* (pp. 22–44 and 70–85). New York: Continuum.

Shaw, P. (2006). *The Sublime*. Abingdon: Routledge.

Siskin, C. (2018). Renewing Wordsworth. In *The Wordsworth Circle* (pp. 113–122). Chicago: The University of Chicago Press.

Stern, D. (2000). *The Interpersonal World of the Infant: A View from Psychoanalysis and Developmental Psychology: A View from Psychoanalysis and Development Psychology*. New York: Basic Books.

Timmermans, H. (2001). Social Cognition. In *International Encyclopedia of the Social and Behavioural Sciences* (pp. 14471–14475). Oxford: Pergamon Press.

Tucker, W. (2017). *Chandra's Cosmos: Dark Matter, Black Holes, and Other Wonders Revealed by Nasa's Premier X-Ray Observatory*. Washington: Smithsonian Books.

Vine, S. (2014). *Reinventing the Sublime*. Eastbourne: Sussex Academic Press.

Winnicott, D. (2016). *The Collected Works of D. W. Winnicott: Volume 5, 1955–1959*, Eds. L. Caldwell and H. Taylor Robinson. Oxford: Oxford University Press.

SIX

The sublime: opportunity for the integration of otherness

Nami Lee

Background

The experience of the sublime is made up of complex phenomena, which may span the biological, metaphysical and spiritual realms. In this chapter, an interdisciplinary approach to the sublime will be presented in order to comprehend the multiple facets of this elusive concept. The earliest mention of the sublime was by Longinus (or pseudo-Longinus, or unknown first-century author), who described it as something beyond language and experienced only in silence (Longinus, 1899, p. IX; Dorsch, 1981). In classical Latin, *sublimis* was described as something "elevated, aspiring, and noble" (Oxford English Dictionary). In order to anchor our modern understanding of the sublime, I begin my investigation with a brief history of its conceptualization.

Critics and philosophers have contrasted an experience of the sublime with an experience of the beautiful, the latter being more common and easier to apprehend. In the modern era, British philosopher and political commentator Edmund Burke (1730–1797) recast Longinus's initial philosophical concept of the sublime. Burke believed that our aesthetic experiences are mainly grounded in physiology, not in intellect. He emphasized the empirical aspects of our responses to beauty and described the sublime as human feeling "dwarfed and solitary in front of the vast and unknowable outside" (Burke, 1756, p. 91). He described the sources of the sublime as originating in and related to the dark, confusion and terrible obscurity. Furthermore, Burke claimed that the beautiful is aesthetically pleasing, but in contrast the sublime often compels and scares us by its indication of infinity (Burke, 2015). While Burke explained the sublime mainly as an emotional and physiological response to an outer stimulus, Kant considered the sublime to be an intuitive and sensible aesthetic judgment beyond cognitive and physiological reaction. Defining beauty as the concept of disinterestedness and formalism, purpose without definite purpose and universal communicability, he argued that the sublime is something beyond human sensibility regarding aesthetic measurements. Kant believed that "true virtue, that is, understanding of an object" belongs to the sublime in aesthetics, while wit and sympathy towards an object belongs to beauty (Kant, 1965, pp. 47–50). Following Kant, Schopenhauer explained that the object induces a sublime mood without any private relation to it and "moves along eternally foreign to earthly life." He argued that human will vanishes from consciousness and individual differences and that the will toward the sublime object is extinguished (Schopenhauer, 1958). In experiencing the sublime, we do not, or cannot, exactly know how our response has been made, since we come to lose the free will and consciousness which would enable us to understand and interpret the sublime beauty.

German idealist Hegel defined the sublime as an attempt to express the infinite outside the domain of physical phenomena. In contrast, beauty is the subject's personal transpiercing of external reality with content and form. To Hegel, the sublime carries the absolute and sacred significance relating to spiritual exaltation. No image is adequate to represent the divine sublime (Saxena, 1974). John Kedney, a professor of divinity, wrote *Hegel's Aesthetic: A Critical Exposition*, in which he focused on the emotional aspect of an encounter with the sublime. He explained the difference between beauty and the sublime: if the mathematical and dynamical force for the emotion were "exceeding the magnitudes we are accustomed to deal with", the event or object could be considered to be sublime. But if an object or an event became familiar from the repetition of its presentation, imagination or feeling could not go further to the sublime, losing "transcending comprehension" of the other. Since the emotion of the sublime is so tense or possessive, he said, "our imaginative souls, becoming weary, often escape to something more familiar and lose contact with the sublime" (Kedney, 1880, pp 50–80).

Later, Lyotard (1924–1998), a prolific postmodern philosopher, mentioned the problem of the sublime in capitalistic society. For example, avant-garde artists are not free from trying to keep balance between "the surprising" and "comforting" of the taste of the public (Lyotard, 1991). He explained sublime feeling as the incommensurability of imagination and reason, and said that our efforts toward achieving the sublime are often hindered by the power of the marketplace. (Lyotard, 1994). While Kant focused on the limitations of reason in exploring the sublime beauty in nature, Lyotard took a larger vista into account in his definition. He related the sublime to the border between a human being's imagination and auditory-visual representation, which extends beyond reason and morality. His definition of the sublime, as an experience which sometimes may lead a vulnerable ego to become insane or powerless beyond reason and morality, touches on psychological status rather than Kantian philosophical debates.

Burnham, another modern philosopher, says that the experience of the sublime is rapid alteration between the fear and the peculiar pleasure of seeing the overwhelming (Burnham, 2000). Upon encountering the sublime, one's familiar daily routines seem to be disturbed and destabilized. Before the sublime, a person who has been confined by habit, ground down by routine and driven by his or her ego-complex may become fearful of losing one's coherence, consistence and ordinary attitude. Despite the diversity in philosophers' conceptions of the sublime since Burke, the common thread focuses on the humbling experience of the observer before the sublime.

The sublime and in-depth psychology

While philosophers have tried to elucidate the sublime from metaphysical perspectives, psychologists have tended to approach the experience of the sublime from their clinical experiences. William James theorized "the Sublime Reservoir", in which our consciousness survives physical death and remains. In his work, he tried to overcome reductive mind–body dualism and absolute idealism by studying the realm of the supernatural trance and spiritual phenomena. His pragmatism and empiricism, partly originating in his "common sense philosophy", emphasized substantial experiences, including encounters of the sublime (Krueger, 2015). Holistic pluralism regarding aesthetic experience includes a view and analysis of both physical and spiritual encounters, as well as individual and collective ones. James presented the third way beyond the oppositional categories of natural versus supernatural. His third way opened a much broader scope, including subliminal consciousness, uncertainties and religiosity as well as experimental and biological aspects (Knapp, 2017).

After James, Abraham Maslow, another American psychologist, conceptualized the peak experience. James and Maslow, as clinical practitioners, focused on patients' elated mood brought on by mystical (or transcendental core–religious) experiences. This stands in contrast to the aforementioned philosophers, who had been interested in abstract theory on the aesthetical meaning of the sublime. Maslow's peak experience is in certain aspects similar to the sublime, as both describe a transient yet highly meaningful state of elation. While Maslow's peak experience includes a feeling of mystic spontaneity and power (Privette, 1983), the sublime emphasizes the dialectical and transcendental interaction between the "vulnerable" ego and the "overwhelming" other, from aesthetical perspectives. Before the sublime, human beings realize how small and transient they are, while the peak experience may lead them to be inflated. Only a few spiritual geniuses have overcome such danger and re-stabilized their once-aggrandized ego. Some people may be trapped by peak experience and fall into madness, while the sublime actually deflates the inflated ego.

After James and Maslow, Carl Jung addressed the psychological meanings of the sublime relating to the unconscious. He emphasized the mystical aspect of sublimation, especially relating to the alchemical process. His concept is more similar to the sublime of other philosophers previously mentioned, in contrast to Freud's well-known theory of sublimation, which relates to the function of repression and higher social relation as a more mature social defence mechanism. Jung used the term *sublimatio* to denote an important conscious step toward totality of psyche, which requires recognizing the limited nature of ego after encountering the unknown and the unexplainable (Jung, 1959). In the alchemical process, *sublimatio* occurs when the ego feels something alien and suffers. Such an encounter with the unknown other thus leads to intrapsychic spiritual transformation. He presented a young theological student's dream, explaining the sublime feeling:

> He was standing in the presence of a sublime hieratic figure called the white magician, who was nevertheless clad in a long black robe. . . . Then the door suddenly opened and another old man came in, the black magician, who however was dressed in a white robe. He too looked noble and sublime. The black magician evidently wanted to speak with the white, but hesitated to do so in the front of the dreamer. The white magician said, pointing to the dreamer, *Speak, he is innocent.* So the black magician began to relate a strange story of how he had found the lost keys of paradise and did not know how to use them.
>
> *(Jung, 1974, pp. 117–118)*

In this dream, the black and white magicians may be the embodiment of the sublime. In front of the sublime, we may feel innocent like this dreamer. The sublime, which induces mysterious and numinous feeling, could help us to open the lost keys of a paradise-like psychic space, but yet we do not know "how to use them".

Jung describes another sublime dream of a young patient which shows the significant danger possible in a sublime experience:

> I am climbing a high mountain, over steep snow-covered slopes. I climb higher and higher and it is marvellous weather. The higher I climb the better I feel. I think "If only I could go on climbing like this forever!" When I reach the summit my happiness and elation are so great that I feel I could mount right up into the space. And I discover that I can actually do so. I mount upwards on empty air, and awake in sheer ecstasy.
>
> *(Jung, 1966, pp. 150–151)*

Instead of psychological interpretation of symbols in his dream, Jung cautiously warned the patient not to go alone mountaineering since this dream might directly tell the danger of climbing. But the patient did not listen to Jung's advice, possessed by his sublime memory. Three months later, while mountaineering, he stepped off the slope out into the air. Jung called it "ecstasy with a vengeance" (Jung, 1966). The climber's fear of dying may have been lighter than his adoration of the sublime. He may have denied the danger of death, while his unconscious energy toward sublime beauty may have enticed and drawn him to the top of the mountain. For the unconscious is "interspersed with spots of brightness of a quasi-consciousness", which may be described as "luminosities or sparks" (Jaffe, 1999). If we are possessed by the spark of the sublime and concretely misinterpret it as our own conscious will and choice, we may become the victims and thus be devoured as in the case of this dreamer.

Although Jung warned the dangers of sublime experiences, he also focused on the positive aspect of the sublime aesthetical moment as related to glorious artistic achievement.

> "Sublime", pregnant with meaning, yet chilling the blood with its strange-ness, it arises from timeless depths: glamorous, daemonic, and grotesque, it bursts asunder our human standards of value and aesthetic form, a terrifying tangle of eternal chaos, a *crimen laesae majestatis humanae*. On the other hand, it can be revelation whose heights and depths are beyond our fathoming, or a vision of beauty which we can never put into words.
>
> *(Jung, 1971)*

Jung's description of the sublime does not vastly differ from Kant's or Lyotard's in terms of touching on the scope beyond clichéd routines or rationalistic ego structure. Like Lyotard, who mentioned the dilemma between "shocking" and "purchasable" of avant-garde artists, Jung seem to have related the sublime feeling to oscillation between sensible meaning and chaotic strangeness.

Neuro-physiological understanding of the sublime

Unlike psychoanalysis, cognitive psychology explains aesthetic experience with a phenomenal model. Leder claimed that aesthetic judgment and emotion are composed of the following aspects from scientific points of view: "1. Perceptual analyses of complexity, contrast, symmetry, order, and grouping; 2. Implicit memory integration; 3. Explicit classification of style and content; 4. Cognitive mastering of art-specific interpretation and self-related interpretation; 5. Evaluation and understanding ambiguity and affective state satisfaction" (Leder et al., 2004). Temporal information-processing models have been discussed for empirical research on the perception of aesthetic experiences (Leder, 2013). Cognitive psychology, which is the bridge between clinical psychology and scientifically tested neuroscience, opened the experimental methods exploring the phenomena of the sublime for the neuroscientists that followed. Neuro-aesthetics in the twenty-first century has delved into how perception, creation and experience of beauty happen within the brain, although the sublime and beauty were not clearly defined (Kawabata and Zeki, 2004). The subjective experience of the sublime, as opposed to primitive hedonic reactions, cannot be objectively and mathematically rated. In contrast to common pleasure-provoking objects, which elicit wanting and liking, the sublime produces ambivalent feelings: wanting, but fearful. A simple pleasure-reward system may not be activated regularly and routinely.

Thus, we can assume the role of neurotransmitters[1] are as messengers of the sublime, but aesthetic feeling toward the sublime has yet to be further clarified. Experiencing the sublime is often a mixture of being elated and daunted, so that excitatory and inhibitory neurotransmitters may function all together. For instance, neuropeptides such as endorphins, enkephalin, oxytocin and neuropeptide-Y regulate pain, pleasure and reward systems. Thus, these may be activated in a sublime experience (Cozolino, 2010). Dopamine regulates motivation and the capacity for joy. Adrenalin may be secreted with the excitement of tasting the sublime. Endorphins surge with their accompanying happiness and thrill. Noradrenalin may provoke fear. Serotonin is excreted and removed, when the exciting or atypical experience is over. Acetylcholine may be involved: remembering the unforgettable. Lastly, melatonin may be involved with exhaustion after the sublime moment (Kabasawa, 2018).

Neural change related to aesthetic experiences may help us understand the sublime experience as well (Zeki, 2001). Responses to representational paintings and abstract paintings were compared, and it was concluded that the left frontal lobe and bilateral temporal lobe were more activated by representational painting. Although researchers have tried to elucidate the difference between the representational and the abstract (Lenger et al., 2007), they could not clearly differentiate between the beautiful and the sublime. It is not conclusive yet how the actual microscopic neuronal change happens with art. The medial orbito-frontal cortex (mOFC) is related to the experience of musical and visual beauty (Ishizu and Zeki, 2011). The sense of responding to beauty of visual art is possibly controlled by insula, amygdala and prefrontal cortex (Flavell and Lee, 2012). The anterior cingulate, the function of which is related to emotional states, and left parietal cortex, related to spatial attention, were prominent in the contrast of "beautiful versus neutral". In order to survive, human beings may genetically have developed to avoid the aversive objects (often subjectively perceiving as "ugly") by the activated anterior cingulate and to approach toward the likable, which may be interpreted as beauty, by the parietal cortex, the motor neuron of the brain.

The anterior NAc (Nucleus accumbens), the reward structure within the subcortical limbic brain (Berridge and Kringelbach, 2013), is possibly an opioid hedonic hot spot and the posterior suppressive cold spot (Berridge and Kringelbach, 2015). This NAc, arranged rostro-caudally (from head to the tail of NAc), can generate intense desire (in the rostral part) and/or caudally strong dread (Richard and Berridge, 2011). Mixed reactions of admiration and fear in the sublime experience may explain the dual pleasure system of NAc. With these lab findings that experiencing beauty and fear happens within a single part of the brain, the dual pleasure system of NAc, we may imagine that our emotions regarding the sublime and fear are strongly interconnected within this specific part of the brain.

Because the sublime feeling is very short-lived and difficult to set up in the lab, so far, we may conceive of our neuro-imaging results regarding beauty as possible neural changes also related to the sublime experience.

The blazing sublime in mystic experiences

While neuroscientists studied substantial manifestations in the brain related to the sublime, some clinicians have focused on sublime moments in near-death experience (NDE), which can occur in cardiac arrest, intoxication, traumatic situations and other brain sicknesses. At the current time, NDEs are becoming more common as a result of "fast developing resuscitation techniques", so the importance of this area of study is increasing (von Lommel et al., 2001). The contents of NDE and the effects on patients, across all cultures and times, are much alike, although the vocabularies to describe and interpret the experience are somewhat different (Ring, 1980). The Near Death Experience Research foundations summarized a common pattern: out of body experiences, separation (mostly elevation) of consciousness from the physical body, heightened sensation or generally positive emotion, passing into or through a tunnel, encountering a mystical or bright light or deceased family members, a sense of alteration of time and space, encountering unworldly realms or learning special knowledge and returning to the body (Long and Perry, 2010).

Often, a NDE will result in a person's attitude being altered and may cause them to reassess their relationship to the afterlife. Having been transformed into loving, empathic, spiritual people and believing in life after death, NDErs report being able to come to understand the true meaning of life (von Lommel et al., 2001). Such change mainly originates from being helpless in the actual dying process of the body. In comparison, within the sublime experience, ego is symbolically dying.

Deathbed visions are similar to near-death experiences, in that they consist of elation, ecstasy, tranquillity, being overwhelmed by meeting the mysterious other and finally letting go of the ego position. Fenwick and Fenwick presented various clinical examples of such deathbed visions, some of which are described as follows:

> [o]n the afternoon of her last day. . . . She suddenly woke up, sat up in bed and held her arms out toward someone, with an ecstatic look of happiness on her face. She then sank back onto her pillow and relapsed into unconsciousness and remained there until her death.
>
> My grandfather quietly said to my father, "Don't worry. I am all right. I can see and hear the most beautiful things." And he quietly died, lucid to the end.
>
> Suddenly she looked up at the window and seemed to stare intently up at it . . . and said, "Don't ever be afraid of dying. I have seen a beautiful light and I was going towards it. . . . I'm not worried about tomorrow and you mustn't be."
>
> *(Fenwick and Fenwick, 2008, pp. 36–43)*

The person experiencing a vision or glimpsing death may be able to see this world of the living and the other all at once. When they are peacefully receptive to the sublime moment, their end time looks more peaceful and calm.

Images dealing with dying in religion are also similar to NDE and deathbed visions. In Buddhist tradition, transcendental experience in the Bardo (literally meaning gap) – the gap between death and living – is similar to NDE and deathbed visions. From the ego position, we may be terrified, anxious, frustrated, saddened and desperate in the face of death. But from the Buddha's perspective, experiences in crossing the Bardo help us to become enlightened. In the Bardo, forgetfulness, confusion, insanity and even annihilation of existence may occur (Padmasambhava, circa the eighth century, reprinted and translated in 2010). Our ego is derided and belittled. But true learning of the Buddha's teachings and achieving the dharma state give us transcendental joy and allow us to overcome the fear of death. The sublime may be a living version of Bardo, accessible to the blessed few. Being aware of the vulnerable psychic reality of the sublime, however, we must be cautious not to be devoured by the supreme and mystic moment of the sublime. Pseudo-enlightenment, mimicking the sublime, may lead us to be spiritually imprisoned in isolation, concrete negation and alienation.

Christian tradition also contains descriptions similar to the sublime. In a well-known biblical story, Moses hid his face, overwhelmed by the fear of God, when God directly called him from the burning bush. God commanded, "Do not come any closer" (Exodus 3: 5). It could be a sacred warning signal to be careful of the blazing sublime. Religious visions carry the sublime images. For instance, paintings of medieval mystic Hildegard von Bingen can be understood in the context of sublime beauty. She experienced the loss of consciousness in her visions of the divine, after which she thoroughly detailed these ecstatic moods in her paintings (Dronke, 1984). Her visionary theology concludes with the symphony of Heaven and her following musical morality play depicted a grotesque purgatory, where each soul would have to cleanse their sins (Newman, 1993). It touched the possible integration between light and dark, ego and the other, enchantment and fear and life and death. Although the sublime moment visits and leaves us like sweeping winds, as von Bingen described, the mystery of the *coincidentia oppositorum* may be concretely actualized within the sublime beauty. Hildegard von Bingen wrote:

> Then I saw that by the diverse quality of the winds, and of the atmosphere as they in turn sweep through it, the humours in man are agitated and altered. For in each of the superior elements there is a breath of corresponding quality by which, through the power of the winds, the corresponding element (below) is forced to revolve in the atmosphere and in no other way is it moved. And by one of those winds, with the agency of sun, moon and stars, the atmosphere which tempers the world is breathed forth.
> *(von Bingen, quoted in Singer, 1928, p. 68)*

Another well-known mystic and philosopher, Emmanuel Swedenborg (1688–1772), wrote of his own visionary experiences, which are comparable to the sublime experience. Although his description of the visionary experiences in a new heavenly city sounds similar to the near-death experience and Bardo, he does not present the fearful aspect touching the divine realm, unlike from Hildegard von Bingen. Swedenborg was more prophetic and spiritual, while von Bingen was more earthly as a suffering and isolated nun. Swedenborg emphasized that "only the interior eye", as distinct from mundane reasoning perspectives, could see the beauty of these visions – visions possibly beyond the death of our living form:

> The souls . . . being introduced into heaven are carried . . . to the *paradisal* regions . . . the celestial and spiritual things. Those who belong to the province of the interior eye are there . . . a little way up . . . the whole atmosphere is made up of such flashes of light . . . from the celestial and spiritual things . . . illuminating and pouring in a light of shining whiteness as cannot be described.
>
> Cities . . . with magnificent palaces, [are] beyond all the art of the architect. . . . These things cannot be credited . . . by reason . . . and yet they are most true. . . [being] seen so frequently by the saints.
>
> *(Benz, 1972)*

> Swedenborg described a conjunction between two components, such as the Divine love and wisdom, the Creator and the created, good and truth, charity and faith duality, charity and faith, husband and wife and God and the Church. The integration of these dual components are not truly *coincidentia oppositorum*, not truly oppositions, but conjoining pairs, in contrast to the Heaven and Hell in the visions of Hildegard. In the Quran, mystical moments similar to the sublime are described. Allah's solemn and divine design on nature could arouse the sublime feeling:
>
> *(Saheeh International, 1997. p. 342)*

The sublime moment, beyond ordinary life, may take away full consciousness as well as the eyesight. Sublime images of the divine, such as Buddha, Christ and Allah, cannot be completely perceived or understood by language or representation. Therefore, we must fill the gap through inference. Experiences of the sublime are similar. The sublime beauty of nature, like luminosities or sparks, brighter than the brightest, may be dangerous since it is too strong to be handled by ego. It may have to present as something not visible, not audible, or not palpable in order to protect us. Those special circumstances cannot be expected or planned with our cognition or reason, as our vulnerable egos are perplexed and disoriented. Each religious tradition mentioned indicates that sublime images, "being ineffable, leading to newer insight, transient and timeless", make the ego small and humble (Happold, 1963).

Sublime beauty therefore often touches the horrifying world which evokes anxiety, discomfort and fear. The sublime is not always tolerable and presentable, but sometimes touches the taboos and the forbidden, such as in the work of Lucian Freud, Francis Bacon, Damien Hirst, Marcel Duchamp, Claes Oldenburg and many artists who betray conventional criteria for beauty. Besides the arts, some extraordinary experiences bring fear and anxiety far more than aesthetic satisfaction. For instance, astronauts walking on the moon could be described as sublime, rather than ordinarily beautiful. Leaving the Earth and watching it from a spaceship may be perceived as something transcendental, deadly and infinite. Such trans-mundane experiences, beyond reason and ego, can be explained with the unconscious process because the unconscious contains the transcendental realm, which often appears to be alien and perplexing, just as the sublime is divergent from ordinary life. Body and soul cannot get used to the sublime. Before the sublime, the earthly entities, including daily routines and ordinary relationships, do not seem to matter, and our reason cannot explain why we are overwhelmed by the sublime.

However, an experience of ecstasy is popularly confused with a sublime one. In this vein, people impulsively partake in drugs, indulge in sex and alcohol and explore the dangerous edges of life, as these are often understood to be extensions of or shortcuts to the sublime. Similarly, religious trance may include bewilderment and weakness of alert consciousness, but it is not particularly related to aesthetical experience. The sublime is more connected to the higher and deeper universal exterior, while ecstasy or trance occur within one's own psyche and body. The magnificence of fully experiencing an aesthetical "other-ness" is not necessarily requisite in ecstasy, as usually the observer or experiencer of trance or ecstasy is trapped within the ego position. It often creates only insatiable thirst. Meanwhile, an experience of the sublime often heals the pathological desire to be great or possess something, as the observer is humbled by awareness of the bigger universe. If sublime experiences lead us to discard the old and small ego and encounter the new and expansive universe, mysterious religious moments similarly teach us and guide us to receive the splendid divine through the painful passage of encountering the Unknown.

Conclusion

Delving into the sublime with language may be an impossible quest, since the definition of the sublime is fundamentally beyond words. Most abstract and idealistic explanations of the sublime need to be supported by tangible experience. The Jungian individuation of the *Self* must similarly be processed through the tangible experience of life. Likewise, Kashmir Saivism, one of the most important Tantric movements in India, teaches that "experiences of (religious) pleasure and aesthetic (sublime) delight can be a means to experiencing the Self" (Mahaffey, 2008, p. 65). However, the cultural image of the divine and the sublime which could empower and maturate the limited ego structure have been sadly smudged and degenerated by the rapid development of modern technology. People often abuse the symbols of life and death in cyberspace where meaningless and ugly violent images are created endlessly. Clichéd horrific figures and scenes in the mass media desensitize us and cause us to lose our awe toward life and death. Instead of experiencing the sublime beauty in art itself, we are enticed to spend in a materialized and commercialized art industry instead of experiencing the sublime beauty itself, as Lyotard mentions. Furthermore, modern city dwellers have less chance of encountering the sublime in nature. In the age of the spaceship, we are less overwhelmed even by the vastness of the cosmos than our ancestors. Among these rueful contemporary situations, the sublime, in images of or during the dying process beyond ordinary life may paradoxically facilitate human beings "to work in a moral or ethical vein against arrogance, self-importance, and egoism" (Mooney, 2009). Through the glimpse of the sublime, we may become aware of the unknown and infinite. An experience of the sublime is an illuminating channel in which our ego is not confined within the conscious and reason, but connected to "the Other-ness".

The encounter with the unknown and infinite sublime beauty of otherness may visit us even in the most tragic and frustrating moments. For instance, in the winter of 1941, the French composer Olivier Messiaen, who became a prisoner of war in a camp east of the River Neisse in Poland, was ordered to perform a piece of music for the enemy guards. Being played in the cold air, his quartet poignantly touched the hearts of dying, wounded and hopeless captives in the camp as well the guards and officers of the camp (Dingle, 2007; Rischin, 2003). Despite the fear of impending death, the sublime beauty of his music could heal the spirits of the soldiers no matter where they had come from and help them to keep hope for their lives and humanity itself.

As Messiaen's score is mixture of life and death, Vladmir Kush's painting "Flight of the Sun" presents an explicit image of the beauty and fear. Kush's painting depicting a mystical sublime moment alludes to several questions: What would happen to the people who sit on the falling part, while they are overwhelmed by the sublime beauty of the sun? Would their eyes be burnt blind by the sun's rays? Would their bodies be eventually dismembered and scattered through the fall? After being destroyed, can they be reborn and resuscitated? Can the sublime be the salvation of our drained and lifeless souls, preserving our hope for transcendence and rebirth?

The sublime is not always and exclusively achieved by encountering something deadening or blazing, or glorious, however. We do not have to reach the sun for the sake of experiencing the sublime. Encountering small, plain and nameless objects in nature could be the best way to see, taste, smell and consume the hidden sublime beauty of the universe. It can also be experienced for ourselves as simple and even humorous. Many enlightened Zen masters have left varieties of poignant yet concise jokes on life and death before they die. Their enigmatic short poems may describe the sublime moment beyond life and death. The senseless and plan-less sublime beauty of monochrome paintings, as well as the avant-garde arts full of mysterious and complicated symbolic images, can lead us to let go of our ego-possession and embrace the grandness of the universe. If the sublime moments free our ego, the tragedies of life and death may be transformed into a divine comedy composed of various meaningful and beautiful moments. The blazing sublime, full of awe and wonder, beyond ego and language, finally enables us to revisit the vastness of our inner psyche and the untouched universe.

Acknowledgement

I'd like to express my appreciation to Hillary Hansen, who gave me thoughtful and insightful comments on my chapter. Thanks to her thorough reviews of my chapter, I could clarify, elaborate and enlarge my ideas on the sublime.

Notes

1 They are categorized into the inhibitory (GABA: gamma amino butyric acid, and Serotonin) and the excitatory (Dopamine, Norepinephrine, Epinephrine, Glutamate, Histamine, and PEA) Endorphins are increased during physical exertion, sexual intercourse and orgasm. Dopamine controls reward-driven and pleasure-seeking behaviour. (Bergland, 2012)

References

Benz, E. (1972). *Color In Christian Visionary Experience in Color Symbolism: Six Excerpts from the Eranos Yearbook*, Trans. J. Stoner (pp. 109–111). Zurich: Spring Publications.

Bergland, C. (2012, November). The Neurochemicals of Happiness: 7 Brain Molecules that Make you Feel Great. *Psychology Today.*

Berridge, J.C. and Kringelbach, M.L. (2013, June). Neuroscience of Affect: Brain Mechanism of Pleasure and Displeasure. *Current Opinion in Neurobiology,* 23(3): 294–303.

Berridge, J.C. and Kringelbach, M.L. (2015, May). Pleasure Systems in the Brain. *Neuron,* 86(6): 646–664.

Burke, E. (1906[1756]). *A Philosophical Inquiry into the Origin of Our Ideas of the Sublime and Beautiful: With an Introductory Discourse Concerning Taste and Several Other Additions.* (World's Classics edition, reprinted in 1925). London: Oxford University Press.

Burke, E. (2015). *A Philosophical Enquiry into the Sublime and Beautiful* (pp. ix and 47–71). Oxford: Oxford University Press.

Burnham, D. (2000). *An Introduction to Kant's Critique of Judgment* (pp. 88–102). Edinburgh: Edinburgh University Press.

Cozolino, L.J. (2010). *The Neuroscience of Psychotherapy* (pp. 61–62). London and New York: Norton.

Dingle, C. (2007). *The Life of Messiaen* (pp. 68–70). Cambridge: Cambridge University Press.

Dorsch, T.S. (1981). *Classical Literature Criticism: Aristotle: On the Art of Poetry, Horace: On the Art of Poetry, Longinus: On the Sublime*, Trans. with an Intro. T.S. Dorsch (pp. 97–157). Middlesex and New York: Penguin Classics.

Dronke, P. (1984). *Women Writers of the Middle Ages* (pp. 162–163). Cambridge: Cambridge University Press. Retrieved from https://cn.wikipedia.org/wiki/Hildegard_of_Bingen#Visions.

Encyclopedia Britannica. Retrieved from https://www.britannica.com.

Fenwick, P. and Fenwick, E. (2008). *Art of Dying: A Journey to Elsewhere* (pp. 36–43). London and New York: Continuum.

Flavell, C.R. and Lee, J.L.C. (2012). Post-training Unilateral Amygdala Lesions Selectively Impair Contextual Fear Memories. *Learning and Memory*, 19(6): 256–263.

Happold, F.C. (1963). *Mysticism: A Study and an Anthology* (pp. 45–47). Harmondsworth: Penguin Classics.

Homer (1997). *Iliad*, Trans. R. Fagles (p. 468). New York: Penguin Putnam Books.

Ishizu, T. and Zeki, S. (2011). Toward a Brain-Based Theory of Beauty. *PloS*, 6(7): e21852.

Jaffe, A. (1999). *An Archetypal Approach to Death Dreams and Ghosts* (p. 145). Zurich: Daimon Verlag.

James, W. (1982). *The Varieties of Religious Experience*. New York: Penguin Classics.

Jung, C.G. (1959). *Aion*, CW 9ii. Bollingen Series XX (pp. 259–260). New York: Princeton University Press.

Jung, C.G. (1966). *The Practices of Psychotherapy* (pp. 150–151). CW 16.

Jung, C.G. (1971). *The Spirit in Man : Art and Literature* (p. 90). CW 15.

Jung, C.G. (1974). *The Development of Personality* (pp. 117–118). CW 17.

Kabasawa, S. (2018). *Nou wo saitekika Sureba nouryoku wa* (Your Brain Needs Optimal Status), Trans. S.Y. Oh. Seoul: Sam and Parkers. (In Korean).

Kant, I. (1965). *Observation on the Feeling of the Beautiful and Sublime*, Trans. J. T. Goldthwait (pp. 45–50). Berkeley, CA: The University of California Press.

Kawabata, H. and Zeki, S. (2004). Neural Correlates of Beauty. *Journal of Neurophysiology*, 91(4): 1699–1705.

Kedney, J.S. (1880). *The Beautiful and the Sublime; An Analysis of these Emotions and a Determination of the Objectivity of Beauty* (pp. 50–53). New York: G.P. Putnam's Sons.

Knapp, K.D. (2017). *William James: Psychical Research and the Challenge of Modernity*. Chapel Hill: The University of North Carolina.

Krueger, J.W. (2015). *The Varieties of Pure Experience: William James and Kitaro Nishida on Consciousness and Embodiment*. Retrieved from https://philpapers.org/archive/KRUTVO.pdf.

Leder, H. (2013). Next Steps in Neuro-aesthetics: Which Processes and Processing Stages to Study? *Psychology of Aesthetics, Creativity, and the Arts*, 7(1), 27–37.

Leder, H., Belke, B., Oeberst, A. and Augustin, D. (2004). A Model of Aesthetic Appreciation and Aesthetic Judgments. *British Journal of Psychology*, 95: 489–508.

Lenger, P.G., Fischmeister, F.P.S., Leder, H. and Bauer, H. (2007, July). Functional Neuroanatomy of the Perception of Modern Art: A DC – EEG Study on the Influence of Stylistic Information on Aesthetic Experience. *Brain Research*, 1158: 93–102.

Long, J. and Perry, P. (2010). *Evidence of the After-life: The Science of Near-Death Experiences* (pp. 91–92). New York: Harper Collins.

Longinus (1899). *Longinus on the Sublime*, Ed. and Trans. W. Rhys Roberts. Cambridge: Cambridge University Press.

Lyotard, J.F. (1991). *"The Sublime and the Avant Garde." The Inhuman: Reflections on Time* (pp. 93–97). Stanford: Stanford University Press.

Lyotard, J.F. (1994). *Lessons on the Analytic of the Sublime*, Trans. E. Rottenberg (pp. 6–7). Stanford: Stanford University Press.

Mahaffey, R. (2008). The Heart of Hindu Mythos: Yogic Perspectives on Self-Realization. In D.P. Slattery and G. Slater (Eds.), *Varieties of Mythic Experience: Essays on Religion, Psyche and Culture*. Einsiedeln, Switzerland: Daimon Verlag.

Maslow, A.H. (1964). *Religions, Values, and Peak Experiences*. London: Penguin Classics.

Mooney, E.F. (2009, Winter). Meditations on Death and the Sublime: Henry Bugbee's in Demonstration of the spirit. *Journal for Cultural and Religious Theory*, 10(1): 42–63.

Newman, B (1993). Hildegard of Bingen and the Birth of Purgatory. *Mystics Quarterly*, 19: 90–97.

Oxford English Dictionary. Retrieved from www.oed.com.

Padmasambhava (2010). *The Tibetan Book of the Dead*, Trans. Joong-Am. Seoul: Jeong-U Publishing Company. (in Korean).

Phillips, A. (1990). Introductory Notes in Burke, E. (1990). In *A Philosophical Enquiry into the Origin of our Ideas of the Sublime and Beautiful*, Ed. with an Intro. and Notes by Adam Phillips. Oxford: Oxford University Press.

Privette, G. (1983). Peak Experience, Peak Performance, and Flow: A Comparative Analysis of Positive Human Experiences. *Journal of Personality and Social Psychology*, 45(6): 1361–1368.

Richard, J.M. and Berridge, K.C. (2011). Nucleus Accumbens Dopamine/Glutamate Interaction Switches Modes to Generate Desire Versus Dread: D(1) and D(2) Together for Fear. *The Journal of Neuroscience*, 31: 12866–12879.

Ring, K. (1980). *Life at Death: A Scientific Investigation of the Near-Death Experience*. New York: Coward McCann & Geoghenan.

Rischin (2003). *For the End of Time: The Story of the Messiaen Quartet* (pp. 34–62). Ithaca: Cornell University Press.

Saheeh International (Trans. Revised and Ed.) (1997). *The Quran. English Meanings* (p. 342). London: Abul Quasim Publishing House.

Saxena, S.K. (1974). Hegel on the Sublime. *Religious Studies*, 10(2): 153–172.

Schopenhauer, A. (1958). *The World as Will and Representation*, vol. II, Trans. E.F.J. Payne (pp. 374–375). New York: Dover Publication.

Singer, Charles (1928). *From Magic To Science: Essays on the Scientific Twilight*. London: Ernest Benn. Reprinted in *Yale Journal of Biology and Medicine*, 78 (2005), 57–82.

Van Lommel, P. et al. (2001, December 15). Near Death Experience in Survivors of Cardiac Arrest: A Prospective Study in the Netherlands. *Lancet*, 358: 2039–2045.

von Bingen, H. (1928). *Wisse die Wege, Scivias, ubertragen und bearbeitet von Maura Bockeler* (p. 17ff). Berlin: Buch II Visio 5. Retrieved from www.isi.edu/~lerman/music/Hildegard.html.

Zeki, S. (2001). Artistic Creativity and the Brain. *Science*, 293(5527): 51–52.

SEVEN

The hermetic subtle body and the sublime in Jung and Lacan

Albert Morell

Show light to the birds of the night-time,
And you hide their light; it is the light
Which binds them and for them light
Is darker than darkness.
Éliphas Lévi (1970[1898], p. 29)

I am the mirror where your image moves,
Neat and obedient twin, until one day
It moves before you move, and it is you
Who have to ape its moods and motions, who
Must now obey.
A.S.J. Tessimond (1985, p. 38)

The sublime, blazing or otherwise, does not readily conjure up images of the abyss, or hell for that matter. The sublime seems rather to suggest that it is a noumenal Good, a reflection of the moral and aesthetic triumph of the human spirit, which is a hallmark of nineteenth-century romanticism, with centuries-old precedents in religious and philosophical traditions. Although these traditions often make allowances for darkness and destruction, they rarely privilege perspectives that celebrate the sublime as dehiscence, depravity, decay, degradation, violence and war, which may have their own transcendent capacities for effulgence. That said, the sublimity of *das Ding* is often associated with evil in traditional systems, as exemplified by the Gnostic demiurge (Hoeller, 2002, p. 40), because it is the Thing that resists symbolization. The meaning of the sublime remains open to interpretation, but Kant's observation that the sublime engenders a struggle between imagination and reason may be the one point on which everyone agrees (Kant, 2007[1790], p. 14).

Cohn and Miles make an instructive etymological distinction between sublimation and the subliminal:

> [In the] lexicon of psychoanalytic terms. . . *sublimation* . . . like the word *sublime* – has something to do

The hermetic subtle body and the sublime   109

> with "up", and. . . *subliminal*, oddly, has something to
> do with "down" – unlike the word *sublime*. *Sublima-*
> *tion*. . . [denotes] either elevation to a higher state or rank,
> or transmutation into a higher or purer condition; similar
> meanings attach to *sublime:* that which is lofty or elevated.
> *Subliminal*, on the other hand, was introduced into English
> in the late nineteenth century [to mean] below the thresh-
> old (of consciousness) . . . [as opposed to sublimation], the
> Latin roots give us "up to the lintel" [i.e. above the slime
> or mud].
>
> *(Cohn and Miles, 1977, p. 289)*

Cohn and Miles go on to explain that the word "sublime" entered the English language in the late medieval period, with the translation of alchemical works from Latin into the vernacular, and that it substantively described the alchemical action of "subliming" or purifying. As such, it was used in both

> scientific terminology. . . [and in] the connection of *subli-*
> *mation* with related alchemical terms and operations: fire,
> violence, and pure essence; these terms and attributes will
> develop most fully in the metaphorical application of *sub-*
> *lime*. . . . Derivatives of *sublime* moved gradually out of the
> province of alchemy into other developing sciences . . . In
> the late nineteenth and twentieth centuries, the newest sci-
> ence, psychoanalysis, adopted the word *sublimation* for its
> own uses and added the neologism *subliminal*. . . . But the
> modern meanings of *sublime* developed . . . from its more
> spiritual and metaphysical sense, as used in the seventeenth
> century. From the alchemical meanings of purification and
> from the idea, again from alchemy, of elevation, came reli-
> gious and secular meanings of purity and loftiness.
>
> *(Cohn and Miles, 1977, pp. 294–295)*

Hermeticism in its varied guises, inclusive of alchemy, formed the basis for religious, philosophical and scientific pursuits for millennia; its influences are rhizomatic in the extreme. Once one starts digging, it is astonishing to find how many Western luminaries in wide-ranging fields were hermetic practitioners, from ancient Greece, through the Middle Ages, the Renaissance, the Enlightenment, the Romantic movement and into the twentieth century, inclusive of Freud and his psychoanalytic circle. Crockett writes: "The Kantian sublime thus passes into the Freudian unconscious, and reappears, most explicitly and powerfully in the sense of the uncanny that disturbs conscious thinking from the inside" (Crockett, 2007, p. 35).

It should also come as no surprise, then, that hermeticism's nineteenth-century international revival had a profound influence on the founding of psychoanalysis. It sheds light on Freud's motivation for writing *The*

Interpretation of Dreams (Freud, 1958[1900*a*]), especially given his long-standing immersion in parapsychological research and spiritism, not to mention his thwarted wish to wed psychoanalysis to parapsychology. In "Dreams and Occultism", Freud posited that telepathy exists in the form of "thought-transference", concluding that what "lies between these two mental acts may easily be a physical process into which the mental one is transformed at one end and which is transformed back once more into the same mental one at the other end" (Freud, 1960[1933*a*], p. 55). Freud became convinced that psychoanalysis and telepathy are inextricably linked: "[B]y inserting the unconscious between what is physical and what was previously called 'psychical', [psychoanalysis] has paved the way for the assumption of such processes as telepathy. If only one accustoms oneself to the idea of telepathy, one can accomplish a great deal with it" (Ibid., p. 55). Freud's firm belief in telepathy, both in dreams and in the transference, even led him to write, in a 1921 letter to Hereward Carrington, a renowned British-American parapsychologist: "If I were at the beginning rather than at the end of a scientific career, as I am today, I might possibly choose just this field of research [the study of so-called occult psychic phenomena], in spite of all difficulties" (E.L. Freud, 1960, p. 334). Hence, Derrida's observation that it is difficult "to imagine a theory of what they still call the unconscious without a theory of telepathy. They can be neither confused nor dissociated" (Derrida, 2007[1981], p. 237). Nonetheless, on the surface, like many Western hermeticists before him, Freud's scientific argument for the existence of the unconscious purported to limit itself to the scientific and medical models of the day.

It is instructive to note that almost all shamanic and non-monotheistic cultures associate the phenomenon of the individual spirit with a subtle or etheric body, which is thought to coexist with the physical body during life, and to separate permanently from it at its death. In tribal traditions, from the Mongolian steppes to the North American mesas, a mandatory qualification for becoming a shaman is the ability to travel out of the body. Mircea Eliade cited well-known data showing that the shamans' capacity to fly out of the body was a requirement of the shamanic initiatory rite. His conclusion was more liberal than that of Ellenberger, who deemed it a "creative illness" (Ellenberger, 1970, p. 889). For Eliade, such flights expressed "an intelligent understanding of secret things" and "metaphysical truths" (Eliade, 2004[1964], p. 479). The subtle body has been fundamental to most sophisticated, non-monotheistic religions and philosophies, including the Greek, Buddhist and Vedic traditions. The Egyptians, most notably, built the pyramids to facilitate the journey of the pharaonic subtle body, the "ka", into the afterlife.

In the West, which tends to favour metaphysical universals, the singular concept of the subtle body has been for the most part dismissed as superstition. The early Church condemned it, and replaced it with the more abstract, non-material concept of the soul, because it associated the former with Dionysian, Eleusinian and other pagan fertility rites (Turner, 1903; Moss, 1998; Mead, 2015[1919]). Hence, there is the "tomb-is-empty" insistence on the resurrected body of Christ, as his mystically transfigured physical body, which is a promise of eternal life to come. Ten centuries later, ecclesiastical suppression resurfaced with a vengeance following the crusades, when Greek and other pagan philosophies came back into the West through monastic centres of learning from Arabic and Persian translations. The medieval Church adapted many pagan philosophical concepts to Church ideology but retained the historical ecclesiastical association of the subtle body with sorcery and demonology. Hence, the burning of witches "flying on broomsticks", invariably en route to satanic orgies.

Western hermetic and alchemical practitioners called the subtle body the "philosopher's stone", because they regarded it as the foundation for spiritual and curative knowledge and as the natural, innate human link between physical and other-dimensional realms of the sublime based on subjective experience, rather than Church teaching. Arnaldus de Villa Nova, a thirteenth-century Spanish physician to Pope Clement V, who was exiled for his alchemical practices, remarked that for the uninitiated the subtle body is the stone the mason throws out into the street as having no value, which is something that Freud, who was a closet Freemason, may have understood.

This brings us to the influences of hermeticism and alchemy in the analytic and psychoanalytic theories of Carl Gustav Jung and Jacques Lacan, whose perspectives on the sublime present themselves at opposite poles. Simply put, one may interpret Jung's perspective as a product of modernist optimism in its emphases on creation, universality, the One, archetype, Self, wholeness, pleroma (as fullness of Being), the mandala, verticality, depth, image, metaphor, the imaginal, the symbol as sign, maternal imago, individuation, *conjunctio* (the union of sexual opposites), the collective unconscious and the *anima mundi*. One may interpret Lacan's obverse approach as a product of postmodernist pessimism in its emphases on destruction, particularity, the many, object *a*, the subject, fragmentation, the void (emptiness of Being), horizontality, the Möbius strip, surface, word, metonymy, the Imaginary, the signifier, the Name-of-the-Father, the sinthome, the Real, *separatio* (there is no sexual rapport) and the Borromean knot.

Even the geometric icons Jung and Lacan used in their respective theories reinforce these oppositions. Jung adopted the mandalic sphere as a transpersonal symbol for wholeness (Jung, 1963, pp. 220–222). Lacan adopted the Möbius strip, a ribbon twisted into a figure eight, as "the basis of a sort of essential inscription at the origin, in the knot which constitutes the subject," whereby "the sphere, that old symbol of totality, is unsuitable", because the sphere is impervious to the cut, and hence to diversity (Lacan, 1972[1966], pp. 192–193). The Möbius surface is continuous, but for Lacan the cut or gap where it folds under and becomes "invisible" implies an inherent division that forecloses the subject's realization of the Jungian self-individuation and unity, as symbolized by the mandala. Jung and Lacan are also opposed in their attempts to define the universalized *Ding* as the source of the sublime. For Jung, it is the *anima mundi* or gnostic "Sophia", a beneficent feminine force that seeks to modulate the creative and destructive polarities inherent in nature and the collective unconscious. For Lacan, it is the Real, the monstrous Thing behind the veil of appearances, the "lamella" writ large, which expresses nature's automatic, driven and senseless functioning (Lacan, 1992[1986], p. 112, 2006[1964], pp. 717–718). What Jung and Lacan do have in common is their uncanny descriptions of corporeality and embodiment, not physical bodies exactly, nor entirely epistemic constructions. They often seem to describe something in-between, like the alchemical middle third – the subtle body – which is a term they both use.

Jung speaks of the subtle body as a less developed form of the diamond body in Eastern systems:

> And you know I believe in science. . . . Science is the highest power of man. . . . You see, there are plenty of secrets. . . . And you can touch one with your hands in this question of the subtle body. . . . At times, it seems to be used as a synonym for the diamond body. Isn't the other, more primitive meaning of "subtle body" a kind of ghost-like body, like a framework, halfway between spirit and matter, which everyone possesses and in which the various centers are located? . . . Well, the diamond body is the equivalent of the concept of the self. . . . In the language of medieval alchemy, it would have been the philosopher's stone.
>
> *(Jung, 1988[1934–'39], p. 444)*

Jung effectively decentres and marginalizes the subtle body and realigns it to fit his transmutative analytic theory by making the "nobler" diamond body the symbol for the higher *Self*. He evades addressing the ontology of the subtle body itself by relegating subtle bodies, ghost bodies and related parapsychological phenomena to what he called the "necrotic" unconscious, as unfit for psychological investigation other than as manifestations of the collective unconscious (Jung, 1982[1920], p. 145). However, one may question the logic of asserting that the radically unempirical diamond body is fit for psychological investigation, whereas the subtle body is not.

Jung's disciple Marie-Louise von Franz followed suit. As she neared the end of her life and her long-term exploration of the subtle body, she addressed the transformative function of the death process by analyzing the dreams of dying subjects. She elaborated on the necessity in life of transforming the subtle body into a sublime glorification body for the afterlife. She associated this eternal body with *spintherismos*, the "scintillating" or "lightning" body, which like the diamond body is a loftier corporeal entity than the subtle body. In the following, von Franz describes the lower functioning out-of-body experience of a friend who finds herself "fully awake" and walking through closed doors:

> [It] is the subtle body in a parapsychological form, the ghost of the dead already capable of walking through shut doors. These reports have to be taken as they are, we cannot discuss them psychologically. We can believe them or not;

The hermetic subtle body and the sublime   113

we cannot make a point out of such things because they
are reports of unique situations – but probably from such
experiences has arisen the generally widespread idea that
the ghost of the dead, the surviving soul, can walk through
material objects, something believed in all countries where
they believe in ghosts. That was and is looked on as proof
of the immaterial, immortal aspect of the psyche.

(von Franz, 1980, p. 237)

Von Franz then goes on to interpret the experience analytically, which may
strike one as something of a stretch, if not altogether implausible:

If we take this, not as an experience of the death process,
but as the experience of a living being, it could be the
influence of the unconscious on the surroundings – not
an intentional one, but because one is in connection with
the Self, the Self begins to have a certain effect on other
people. . . . *If one is connected with the Self inwardly, then
one can penetrate all life situations.* Inasmuch as one is not
caught in them, one walks through them; that means there
is an innermost nucleus of the personality which remains
detached.

(Ibid., p. 237)

The Jungian analyst Nathan Schwartz-Salant followed Jung and von Franz
in his assessment of the alchemist's limitations:

The alchemist's understanding of and transformation of
matter were surely far inferior to what has been accomplished by modern science. His lack of interest in quantita-
tive measurements contributed to this, as did his conceiving
material processes in terms of their purpose or final cause.

(Schwartz-Salant, 1995, p. 3)

Schwartz-Salant conceives the subtle body instead as a transformational
third, conjured up in the clinical temenos (sacred space) as a kind of alchemical homunculus that is created in the interactive field between the analyst
and the analysand (Schwartz-Salant, 1998, p. 25).

Jung makes correspondences between the stages of transmutation in met-
allurgic alchemy and those in his process of individuation, using the archetypes as his lodestone. He concludes: "What the symbolism of alchemy
expresses is the whole problem of the evolution of personality. . . , the
so-called individuation process" (Jung, 1953[1935], p. 35). The alchemical integration of opposites, which is the key to the integration of the *Self*,
approaches at its highest level the *Mysterium coniunctionis* and an expression of the sublime reminiscent of theological mysticism. In effect, Jung
and his followers compromised the ontological integrity of the alchemical

schema by translating it into a symbolic model for transformative self-improvement. Jung began his alchemical investigations with optimism:

> [A]lchemy affords us a veritable treasure house of symbols, knowledge of which is extremely helpful for an understanding of neurotic and psychotic processes. This, in turn, allows us to apply the psychology of the unconscious to those regions in the history of the human mind which are concerned with symbolism. It is just here that questions arise whose urgency and vital intensity are even greater than the question of therapeutic application.
>
> *(Jung, 1963[1955–'56], pp. xviii–xix)*

He speaks of the alchemical "double" (the inner man) as the "Anthropos", and describes it as follows:

> Kinsman and stranger at once, it [the individual ego] recognizes and yet does not recognize that unknown brother who steps towards it, intangible yet real. . . . Here we must feel our way with Paracelsus into a question that was never openly asked before in our culture, and was never clearly put, partly from sheer unconsciousness, partly from holy dread. Moreover, the secret doctrine of the Anthropos was dangerous because it had nothing to do with the teachings of the Church, since from that point of view Christ was a reflection – and only a reflection – of the inner Anthropos. Hence there were a hundred good reasons for disguising this figure in indecipherable secret names.
>
> *(Jung, 1967[1942], p. 171)*

Jung initially believed that he had discovered in the alchemical system a historic precedent for his analytic science. Yet during the mid-1950s he began a dramatic about-face by associating the Anthropos with the shadow:

> We would have to conclude that the alchemists had discovered the psychological existence of a shadow, which opposes and compensates the conscious, positive figure. For them the shadow was in no sense a *privatio lucis*; it was so real they even thought they could discern its material density, and this concretism led them to attribute to it the dignity of being the matrix of an incorruptible and eternal substance.
>
> *(Jung, 1963[1955–'56], p. 125).*

He ended by condemning the alchemists in the manner of a medieval inquisitor for engaging in devilry and conspiring with dark forces. As such, he pathologized his patients' proximate subtle-body experiences:

> With certain patients, I have been able to establish the existence of subjectively experienced levitations in moments of extreme derangement. Lying in bed, the patients felt that they were floating horizontally in the air a few feet above their bodies. This is a suggestive reminder of the phenomenon called the "witch's trance", and also of the parapsychic levitations reported of many saints.
>
> *(Jung, 1954[1946], p. 268)*

The specific cause of Jung's break with the alchemists seems to have been a re-evaluation of the work of Paracelsus, his sixteenth-century fellow countryman, medical scientist and alchemist, with whom Jung identified to the point of speculating that he was Paracelsus's reincarnation. Paracelsus's singular contribution lay in giving both the exoteric and esoteric practice of alchemy an etiological purpose. He thereby sought to extract the virtue inherent in inorganic substances, specifically in chemicals and metals, rather than in herbal and homeopathic treatments. Paracelsus effectively laid the foundation for the science of modern chemotherapy. It was Paracelsus's insistence on the experiential ontology of the subtle body that led Jung to renounce the alchemists as ignorant and superstitious, even allying himself with the Church in its condemnation of the subtle body operation as sorcerous. Jung's bias is clear from his interpretation of the *Tabula Smaragdina*, the famous Hermes Trismegistus tablet, about which he wrote:

> The alchemical mystery is a "lower" equivalent of the higher mysteries, a sacrament not of the "paternal" mind but of "maternal" matter. . . . Whereas the Christian figures are the product of spirit, light and good, the alchemical figures are creatures of night, darkness, poison and evil [expressing] the immaturity of the alchemist's mind, which is not sufficiently developed to equip him for the difficulties of his task. He was underdeveloped in two senses: first, he did not understand the real nature of chemical combinations; and, secondly, he knew nothing about the psychological problem of projection and the unconscious. The growth of natural science has filled the first gap, and the psychology of the unconscious is endeavoring to fill the second.
>
> *(Jung, 1996[1946], p. 211)*

Jung's high-handed commentary has more to do with the fact that if the alchemical opus is, in fact, an ontological operation of *separatio*, and not *conjunctio*, it radically reframes, if not negates, the foundational premise of his analytic psychology, which ironically situates Lacanian theory closer to the alchemical mark. As we shall see, Lacan's connection to the alchemical system and the subtle body tradition only initially appears to be erratic and more occluded than Jung's.

116 Albert Morell

None of this, however, prevented Jung from adopting the spirit-communication techniques of the American psychic Betty White to formulate his method of active imagination (a corollary of Freud's free-association technique), which Jung kept a secret for over 30 years. It is well known, in this respect, that after having suffered a heart attack in his eighties, Jung had an out-of-body experience that greatly impressed him as real. He reported flying high above the earth and described in great detail the layout and coloration of the continents, and the accuracy was allegedly confirmed decades later when astronauts went into space. Jung initially believed that the alchemical mysteries resolved his analytic psychology and, in circular fashion, he believed that his analytic psychology resolved the alchemical mysteries. Hence, we are no nearer to understanding the source of the sublime from a Jungian perspective. As the post-Jungian Wolfgang Giegerich observed about analytic psychology: "We are not any closer to the truth. Rather, we have replaced one set of symbols (that both express and conceal the "truth') by another set of (equally revealing and concealing) symbols" (Giegerich, 1999, p. 158).

In *The Sublime Object of Ideology*, Slavoj Žižek states:

> [T]he Sublime is no longer an (empirical) object indicating through its very inadequacy the dimension of a transcendent Thing-in-itself (Idea) but an object which occupies the place, replaces, fills out the empty place of the Thing as the void, as the pure Nothing of absolute negativity – the Sublime is an object whose positive body is just an embodiment of Nothing.
>
> *(Žižek, 1989, p. 206)*

Welcome to the postmodernist world of the corporeal sublime, where the Real transcendental Thing-in-itself finds its empty reflection in Lacan's singular object *a*, a through-the-glass-darkly version of the medieval *speculum mundi*, which in Lacan's case paradoxically supports the alchemical adage, "as above, so below", despite the Lacanian postmodernist preference for prepositional imperatives that favour horizontality over verticality, such as the planar Borromean knot, the Escher-like signifying chain and the Möbius strip – what Fredric Jameson has referred to as "contrived depthlessness", the postmodern fascination with surfaces, mirrors and appearances (Harvey, 1990, p. 58; Jameson, 1991, p. 12).

Lacan's connection to the alchemical system and the subtle-body tradition seems, on the face of it, more tenuous than Jung's. As to Lacan's sublimitive uses of corporeality, Adrian Johnston writes:

> Despite the convincing nature of his account of embodiment in psychoanalytic metapsychology, Lacan risks overstepping his own rules in apparently speculating that the substantial substratum of a bodily Real underlies the subject's libidinal economy (speculations that become more

The hermetic subtle body and the sublime 117

> and more frequent in his later seminars). . . . Does he avoid this risk by relegating the body to the Real? Kant, for instance, gets caught between an ontologization of the noumenal subject as a *Ding an sich* beyond the limits of possible experience and a de-ontologization of this same subject considered as a regulative idea of reason with no constitutive function. Likewise, Lacan's maintenance of a bodily Real *an sich* potentially veers into an erroneous constitution of an ineffable yet existent substratum.
>
> *(Johnston, 2005, p. 216)*

Elsewhere, he adds: "And yet, the error of the vast majority of exegetical analyses of the bodily Real is to equate this notion with the image of an amorphous, unstructured, fleshy mass" (Ibid., p. 265). The Lacanian "signifying organ" is similarly conceived as a "floating" corporeal thing, a meaningless lump of flesh, taken in isolation from its endowed Imaginary and Symbolic functions (Ibid. p. 264). The resultant "simulacra", or corporeal semblances, thus in turn give form to the "in-itself" of object *a*. Johnston further attempts to refine his discernment of the Lacanian corpo-Real: "Understanding the body's organs as Real signifiers avoids the typical conception of the Lacanian Real *à la* corporeality. When interpreters of Lacan generally designate the body as Real, they generally refer to the 'pre-Symbolic' body, that is, the inert, undifferentiated *Stoff* prior to the divisions and demarcations instituted by the big Other" (Ibid., p. 265). Hence, from a sliding-scale perspective, the sublimity of the Lacanian Real ranges from an inert, shapeless mass like the alchemical "lump of lead", to a noumenal Void in a realm beyond representation and human experience. Crockett sums up the ambiguous ontological duality of the subtle body, along the lines of Lacan's lamella, when he writes that "subjectivity is constituted in the process of one's body – which is perceived as sublime – and this externalized body encountered as substance provokes horror and sublimity (Crockett, 2007, pp. 26–27).

Lacan seems to have had an intuitive affinity for hermeticism, as evinced by his convoluted and abstruse language, his emphases on textual exegesis, glyphs, graphs, mathemes, algebraic equations, mathematical models and metaphysical constructions. However, it appears that he did not come to alchemy from a direct familiarity with the subterranean workings of medieval scholasticism, or the "Church-within-the-Church" hermeticism, as Jung did with Herbert Silberer. He seems rather to have come to it indirectly through his immersion in surrealism, with its "double'-fixation, and his focus on the uncanny relationship between the specular and spectral image, which André Breton had expropriated from the alchemical tradition and exploited as a portal to the sublime in both its marvelous and horrific guises.

Lacan made his reputation by forging unlikely connections between psychoanalysis and other disciplines, from Saussure's structural linguistics, to Lévi-Strauss's anthropology, to mathematics and topology and finally to poetry. Lacan's attachment of psychoanalysis to structural linguistics was an early attempt to refashion the Freudian "scientific" template by severing the concept of the unconscious from any physical, psychical or mytho-metaphoric links. Lacan claimed instead that the *a priori* linguistic structure mirrors the structure of the Freudian unconscious. Hence, the Lacanian aphorism that "the unconscious is structured as a language" (Lacan, 1972[1966], p. 188). When Lacan stated that "language is not immaterial. It is a subtle body, but body it is" (Lacan, 2006[1953], p. 248), he was mimicking the alchemical schema, in that he was using language as an *a priori* subtle body link to the unconscious and the Real. It was his attempt to solve the scientific problem inherent in finding a comprehensible and convincing link between the empirical-sensible and the speculative-conceptual, without conveniently eliminating inherently opposed propositions, or conflating them. Structural linguistics turned out not to be the scientific solution Lacan had hoped for, which is why he later conceded that it was a mistake (Lacan, 1998[1975], pp. 15–16) and moved on to mathemes, topology, set-theory, knot-theory and all the rest. Lacan's inverted placement of the signifier over the signified, which forecloses any fixity, also followed the spirit of surrealism, which was not to reveal some metaphysical reality but to tear away the perceptual quotidian that occludes the often bizarre and uncanny marvelous of the sublime in the mercurial metonymic Real.

The problem of running to ground the source of the sublime is inherent in the non-alchemical Freudian concept of sublimation which, in Lacanian terms, lies within the register of the Real. Lacanian sublimation is defined by the concept of *das Ding* (Lacan, 1992[1986], pp. 43–70). However, unlike the alchemists, Lacan conceived it as a non-existent abstract notion that defines the human condition. He later identified it as the object *a*. It is the hole or vacuum one endeavours to fill with objects, in order to plug the gap in psychical needs. The same problem persists at the level of the mirror stage (Lacan, 2006[1949]), where the gap between the ego-ideal and the ideal-ego renders illusory any intimations of the sublime. However, if one suspends Lacan's unconvincing premise for the mirror stage, it accurately models the split-and-separation "doubling" of the alchemic opus. Lacan's privileging of the gaze over the other senses also endows the mirror stage with almost metaphysical attributes, similar to those he earlier gave to language. Lacan asserted that the gaze precedes perception, and that the "eye is only the metaphor of something that I would prefer to call the seer's "shoot" (*pousse*) – something prior to his eye. . . [which] is the pre-existence of a gaze" (Lacan, 1994[1973], p. 72). He claimed that the gaze endures for life, because it represents a fundamental aspect of the structure of subjectivity that is prelinguistic and unsymbolizable.

Lacan associated the gaze with the object *a* at the event horizon of the Imaginary and the Real, which also accurately describes the exteriorization process of the alchemical operation, in which the subtle body is the object *a* and vision has true ontological primacy. As such, the hermetic opus supports Lacan's statement that the object *a* marks "the primal nature of the essence of the gaze" (Ibid., p. 76). Thus, the ontology of the

The hermetic subtle body and the sublime   119

gaze, which transcends the "symbolic matrix" and the act of seeing, belies materialistic reductionism. It is not surprising, then, that our "natural" and "preternatural" experiences of the sublime are most associated with the scopic drive.

Lacan's conception of the *agalma* is related to the object *a*, and it is even more closely allied with the subtle body. Lacan turned the meaning of the *agalma* on its head, much as he did with the Saussurean sign. He transmogrified the Hellenic *agalma*, from its significance as the philosopher's stone that contains the treasure of "divine" knowledge within it, into an empty vessel and fool's gold pursuit. As Lacan interpreted it, the underlying dynamic of Alcibiades's seduction of Socrates in Plato's *Symposium*, for extracting the secret "treasure" that he believed Socrates was withholding from him, was not one of transference and illusion, but one of transmission instead (much as Freud's "telepathy in the transference" was one of thought transmission) (Lacan, 2015[2001], pp. 135–163). This *agalmatic* transmission originated in Dionysian mystery rites, where sacral inner knowledge and truth were conveyed non-verbally from one eidolonic subtle body to another in coitus, a far cry from the "transference fantasy" of secrets shared in post-coital pillow talk between two physical bodies. And then there is the odd circumstance of shared diminutive qualifiers given to Lacanian "subtle-body" conceptions. Lacan observed that "in the *Symposium* [Alcibiades compares Socrates] to statues representing a satyr or a silenus on the outside, and inside of which something was lodged, as in Russian dolls. We don't really know what was inside, but they were assuredly precious objects" (Ibid., pp. 37–38). The silenus was associated with Dionysian rites (Bremmer, 2013, p. 7), which is why the subtle body, also called the "body of desire" in hermetic and Eastern spiritual traditions, became associated with satanic seduction and sexual practices in the Middle Ages and the Renaissance. Lacan's other corpo-Real concepts – the *agalma* (cast as a tiny votary image), the object *a* and the lamella-like "*hommelette*" (Lacan, 2006[1964], p. 717) – are all eidolonic analogues of the alchemical "homunculus". For Lacan, they are "mutilating" simulacra of the uncanny sublime in both its seductive and horrific guises.

Jung and Lacan devoted their lives to finding the "truth", and in the end both concluded that their theories had failed them. The last words in *Memories, Dreams, Reflections* of Jung, guru of the alchemical individuation process, were: "[I]t seems to me as if that alienation which so long separated me from the world has become transferred into my own inner world, and has revealed to me an unexpected unfamiliarity with myself" (Jung, 1963, p. 392). Giegerich's previously mentioned observation about analytic psychology is worth repeating here: "We are not any closer to the truth. Rather, we have replaced one set of symbols (that both express and conceal the 'truth') by another set of (equally revealing and concealing) symbols" (Giegerich, 1999, p. 158). Lacan effectively came to the same conclusion about his own psychoanalytic theories in the end. Confusion around "separation" persisted even here, in that Lacan realized that his linguistic and topological attempts to separate psychoanalytic subjectivity from philosophical ontology had failed. One may conclude, then, that the entire enterprise was wrongheaded, not only in its execution but also in its conceptual premises. Lacan remarked that in its relationship to the "vanishing point" of the Real, which is crucial to psychoanalytic practice, "psychoanalysis was looking like a swindle", and he concluded that anything not founded on matter is a fraud (Lacan, 1981[1977], p. 5). This is the crux. One may envision that the experiential, quasi-material "middle realm" of the subtle body as "sensible" alternative, when taken to encompass all levels of nature and all levels of human consciousness in a vast (almost limitless) expanse with no vanishing point is, in fact, the source of all our experiences of the sublime. In conclusion, one may say that by rejecting the ontology of the subtle body, Jungian and Lacanian theorists are left with substitutive insufficiencies that they have yet to redress if, as the surrealist poet Philip Lamantia suggests: "Man is a false window/through which his double walks to the truth" (Lamantia, 2013, p. 9).

Acknowledgements

Material excerpted by Eliphas Levi on p. 108 is from *Transcendental Magic*, first American edition published in 1972 by Samuel Weiser, Inc. Originally published in 1896 by Rider & Co., England, used with permission from Red Wheel Weiser, LLC Newburyport, MA www.redwheelweiser.com

The quote from the Collected Poems of A.S.J. Tessimond (Bloodaxe Books 2010) on p. 108 is reproduced with permission from Bloodaxe Books.

References

Bremmer, J.N. (2013). The Agency of Greek and Roman Statues: From Homer to Constantine. *Opuscula: Annual of the Swedish Institutes of Athens and Rome*, 6: 7–21.

Cohn, J. and Miles, T.H. (1977). The Sublime: In Alchemy, Aesthetics and Psychoanalysis. *Modern Philology*, 74(3): 289–304.

Crockett, C. (2007). *Interstices of the Sublime: Theology and Psychoanalytic Theory*. New York: Fordham University Press.

Derrida, J. (2007[1981]). Telepathy. In N. Royle (Trans.), *Psyche: Inventions of the Other*, vol. 1 (pp. 226–261). Stanford, CA: Stanford University Press.

Eliade, M. (2004[1964]). *Shamanism: Archaic Techniques of Ecstasy*. Princeton, NJ: Princeton University Press.

Ellenberger, H.F. (1970). *The Discovery of the Unconscious: The History and Evolution of Dynamic Psychiatry*. New York: Basic Books.

Freud, E.L. (Ed.) (1960). *Letters of Sigmund Freud*, Trans. T. J. Stern. New York: Basic Books.

Freud, S. (1958[1900a]). The Interpretation of Dreams. In J. Strachey (Ed.), *The Standard Edition of the Complete Psychological Works of Sigmund Freud*, vols. 4/5. London: The Hogarth Press and the Institute of Psycho-Analysis.

Freud, S. (1960[1933a]). New Introductory Lectures on Psychoanalysis. In J. Strachey (Ed.), *The Standard Edition of the Complete Psychological Works of*

Sigmund Freud, vol. 22 (pp. 1–182). London: The Hogarth Press and the Institute of Psycho-Analysis.

Giegerich, W. (1999). *The Soul's Logical Life: Towards a Rigorous Notion of Psychology*. Frankfurt am Main: Peter Lang.

Harvey, D. (1990). *The Condition of Postmodernity: An Enquiry into the Origins of Cultural Change*. Cambridge: Blackwell.

Hoeller, S.A. (2002). *Gnosticism: New Light on the Ancient Tradition of Inner Knowing*. Wheaton, IL: Quest Books.

Jameson, F. (1991). *Postmodernism, or The Cultural Logic of Late Capitalism*. Durham, NC and London: Duke University Press.

Johnston, A. (2005). *Time Driven: Metapsychology and the Splitting of the Drive*. Evanston, IL: Northwestern University Press.

Jung, C.G. (1953[1935]). Introduction to the Religious and Psychological Problems of Alchemy. In R.F.C. Hull (Trans.), *The Collected Works*, vol. 12 (pp. 1–38). Princeton, NJ: Princeton University Press.

Jung, C.G. (1954[1946]). Psychology of the Transference. In R.F.C. Hull (Trans.), *The Collected Works*, vol. 16 (pp. 163–326). Princeton, NJ: Princeton University Press.

Jung, C.G. (1963). *Memories, Dreams, Reflections*, Ed. A. Jaffé, Trans. R. C. Winston. London: Collins and Routledge & Kegan Paul.

Jung, C.G. (1963[1955-'56]). Mysterium Coniunctionis. In R.F.C. Hull (Trans.), *The Collected Works*, vol. 14. Princeton, NJ: Princeton University Press.

Jung, C.G. (1967[1942]). Paracelsus as a Spiritual Phenomenon. In R.F.C. Hull (Trans.), *The Collected Works*, vol. 13 (pp. 109–190). Princeton, NJ: Princeton University Press.

Jung, C.G. (1982[1920]). The Psychological Foundations of Belief in Spirits. In *Psychology and the Occult* (pp. 128–149). London: Routledge.

Jung, C.G. (1988[1934-'39]). *Nietzsche's Zarathustra: Notes of the Seminar given in 1934–1939*, Ed. J.L. Jarrett. Princeton, NJ: Princeton University Press.

Jung, C.G. (1996[1946]). Alchemy and Psychotherapy. In N. Schwartz-Salant (Ed.), *Jung on Alchemy* (pp. 180–221). Princeton, NJ: Princeton University Press.

Kant, I. (2007[1790]). *Critique of Judgement*, Ed. N. Walker, Trans. J. Creed Meredith. Oxford: Oxford University Press.

Lacan, J. (1972[1966]). Of Structure as an Inmixing of an Otherness Prerequisite to Any Subject Whatever. In R. Macksey and E. Donato (Eds.), *The Structuralist Controversy: The Languages of Criticism and the Sciences of Man* (pp. 186–200). Baltimore, MD: The Johns Hopkins University Press.

Lacan, J. (1981[1977]). Propos sur l'hystérie. *Quarto*, 2: 5–10.

Lacan, J. (1992[1986]). *The Seminar. Book VII: The Ethics of Psychoanalysis (1959-'60)*, Ed. J.-A. Miller, Trans. D. Porter. New York: W. W. Norton & Company.

Lacan, J. (1994[1973]). *The Seminar. Book XI: The Four Fundamental Concepts of Psychoanalysis (1964)*, Ed. J.-A. Miller, Trans. A. Sheridan. Harmondsworth: Penguin Classics.

Lacan, J. (1998[1975]). *The Seminar. Book XX: On Feminine Sexuality, the Limits of Love and Knowledge (Encore) (1972-'73)*, Ed. J.-A. Miller, Trans. B. Fink. New York: W. W. Norton & Company.

Lacan, J. (2006[1949]). The Mirror Stage as Formative of the I Function as Revealed in Psychoanalytic Experience. In B. Fink (Trans.), *Écrits* (pp. 75–81). New York: W. W. Norton & Company.

Lacan, J. (2006[1953]). The Function and Field of Speech and Language in Psychoanalysis. In B. Fink (Trans.), *Écrits* (pp. 197–268). New York: W. W. Norton & Company.

Lacan, J. (2006[1964]). Position of the Unconscious. In B. Fink (Trans.), *Écrits* (pp. 703–721). New York: W. W. Norton & Company.

Lacan, J. (2015[2001]). *The Seminar. Book VIII: Transference (1960-'61)*, Ed. J.-A. Miller, Trans. B. Fink. Cambridge and Malden, MA: Polity Press.

Lamantia, P. (2013). Man is in Pain. In G. Caples, A. Joron and N. Joyce Peters (Eds.), *The Collected Poems of Philip Lamantia* (pp. 90–91). Berkeley, CA and London: University of California Press.

Lévi, É. (1970[1898]). *Transcendental Magic: Its Doctrine and Ritual*, Trans. A. E. Waite. New York: Samuel Weiser, Inc.

Mead, G.R.S. (2015[1919]). *The Doctrine of the Subtle Body in Western Tradition*. New York: Cosimo, Inc.

Moss, R. (1998). *Dreamgates: Exploring the Worlds of Soul, Imagination, and Life Beyond Death*. Novato, CA: New World Library.

Schwartz-Salant, N. (Ed.) (1995). *Jung on Alchemy*. Princeton, NJ: Princeton University Press.

Schwartz-Salant, N. (1998). *The Mystery of Human Relationship: Alchemy and the Transformation of the Self*. London and New York: Routledge.

Tessimond, A.S.J. (2010). *Collected Poems*, Ed. H. Nicholson. London: Bloodaxe Books.

Turner, W. (1903). *History of Philosophy*. Boston: Athenaeum Press.

von Franz, M.-L. (1980). *Alchemy: An Introduction to the Symbolism and the Psychology*, Trans. E. Kennedy-Xypolitas. Toronto: Inner City Books.

Žižek, S. (1989). *The Sublime Object of Ideology*. London and New York: Verso.

EIGHT

Lacan's clinical artistry: on sublimation, sublation and the sublime

Dany Nobus

Introduction

Sometime during the Spring of 1934, Mária Thomán, an acclaimed concert violinist who was the daughter of István Thomán, distinguished Professor of Musicology at the Royal Hungarian Academy of Music in Budapest (Slonimsky, 1984, p. 891), wrote a letter to Sigmund Freud. Since the original has never been found, we do not know its exact content, nor Thomán's specific reason for writing. Was she interested in starting an analysis with Freud, either for personal reasons or because she wanted to train as a psychoanalyst herself? Did she want Freud's advice because she herself, or one of her musical friends, had already started analysis in Hungary, and there had been some concern over how it might impact upon the artistic inspiration? Or did she simply want to ask "Herr Professor" about a troubling issue, hoping to extract some precious wisdom from him or, better still, alerting him to an unresolved matter in his psychoanalytic explorations of art and culture? We can only speculate about what prompted Thomán to seek Freud's counsel, yet Freud himself must have been sufficiently charmed and captivated by the young woman's letter, since he wrote back to her on 27 June 1934 with the following words:

> It is not out of the question that an analysis results in its being impossible to continue an artistic activity. Then, however, it is not the fault of the analysis; it would have happened in any case and it is only an advantage to learn that in good time. When, on the other hand, the artistic impulse [*der Trieb zur Kunst*] is stronger than the internal resistances, analysis will heighten, not diminish, the capacity for achievement [*so wird die Leistungsfähigkeit durch die Analyse nur gesteigert, nie erniedrigt*].
> *(cited in Jones, 1957, p. 416)[1]*

Freud's statement here has always intrigued me, although I simultaneously feel that I have never fully fathomed its precise meaning and its concrete implications. Freud's biographer Ernest Jones quoted the letter at the very end of a chapter devoted to Freud's attitude towards art, with a view to emphasizing the liberating effects of a psychoanalytic treatment process on the artistic inspiration, yet I have never been convinced by the purportedly uplifting tone of Freud's response to Thomán. For one, Freud seems to be insinuating that a psychoanalytic process is unable to turn someone into an artist if the artistic, creative impulse is not already present from the start, and in a sufficiently powerful capacity to oppose and conquer the forces operating against it. However, psychoanalysis may very well contribute to the fuller expression of this creative impulse, because it can help destroy, or at least soften up, the pockets of resistance that preclude its full deployment. Yet if psychoanalysis may enhance a strong artistic drive that is already present – stimulating, we may assume, the artist to become more productive, or to become better at producing works of art – following Freud it is nonetheless incapable of protecting this drive against its own extinction. If the flame of inspiration is withering, there is nothing psychoanalysis can do to prevent it from dying out altogether. As such, psychoanalysis would seem doomed to follow – in the sense of "being merely responsive to" – the self-sufficient, autonomous mechanism of the creative impulse. If ever an amateur artist were elated by the alluring prospect of his or her craftsmanship being purified and elevated at the hands of a psychoanalyst, I do not think Freud's words would sound very encouraging. And if ever a highbrow creative genius were to think that she or he could find new inspiration in the psychoanalytic exploration of the darkest recesses of the mind, Freud's words would probably not come as a great relief either.

Perhaps Freud's little note to Thomán is highly overdetermined, given that it was written at a moment when he himself was afflicted by one of the most pessimistic moods in his entire career. Ominous sociopolitical circumstances, fuelled by Hitler's unstoppable rise to power in Germany, had followed upon painful professional crises (Sándor Ferenczi, a close personal friend and a highly valued member of Freud's inner circle, had recently died of pernicious anemia, after progressively taking his distance from the established psychoanalytic approach) and had made devastating personal ailments (Freud's cancer of the jaw was advancing rapidly) all the more tangible and intractable.[2] Even then, the pessimistic overtones of Freud's letter to Thomán may have also reflected a deeper intellectual scepticism as to the use of psychoanalysis for the enhancement of the creative impulse, or even for the installation of any kind of mental equilibrium that would bring emotional tranquillity and lasting peace of mind. As Freud had already suggested in *Civilization and Its Discontents*, as a theory psychoanalysis may shed some light on how the "sublimation of the instincts" [*Sublimierung der Triebe*] – i.e. "shifting the instinctual aims in such a way that they cannot come up against frustration from the external world", and thus induce "finer and higher" satisfactions – can help assuage the multifarious sources of human suffering, yet the psychoanalytic treatment process has little or nothing to contribute when it comes to initiating, consolidating or sustaining these particular displacements of the libido" (Freud, 1964[1930a], pp. 79–80). And as he would later admit in the posthumously published expository text *An Outline of Psycho-Analysis*, "God is on the side of the big battalions" but by no means always on the side of psychoanalysis, at least not when it is engaged in the treatment of neurotic conflicts. Of the three factors that might help the psychoanalyst win the war – the patient's "capacity for sublimating his instincts", his "capacity for rising above the crude life of the instincts" and "the relative power of his intellectual functions" – none are directly receptive or amenable to psychoanalytic intervention (Freud, 1964[1940*a*], pp. 181–182). If anyone was ever expecting something sublime to occur at the end of a psychoanalytic treatment process, then it was not just the outcome, but even the process of sublimation leading up to it that was beyond Freud's control, since the latter was allegedly rooted in a particular disposition which, much like the creative impulse itself, obstinately followed its own solipsistic path.[3]

In this chapter, I want to critically re-examine the dual tension that runs through Freud's conception of the creative process in order to interrogate Lacan's prolonged engagement with the questions of sublimation and the sublime during his 1959–1960 seminar on the ethics of psychoanalysis (Lacan, 1992[1986], pp. 85–164) and some related texts. In doing so, I intend to arrive at a conclusion with a fresh reading of the nature and place of the sublime, both in relation to the conceptual status of sublimation, whose qualitative transformation of the sexual drive into a desexualized, higher sociocultural object continues to puzzle scholars and practitioners of psychoanalysis, and in relation to the dynamic interface between the artistic and the psychoanalytic creative process.

The first tension stages the ostensible disparity between Freud's mechanism of sublimation, which he generally presented as the purification and redirection (elevation) of libidinal energy towards a "higher" sociocultural aim (Freud, 1957[1910*a*], pp. 53–54), and the profoundly ambiguous status of its outcome.[4] Irrespective of largely unresolved debates pertaining to the exact nature of Freud's proto-Jungian vision of a desexualized libido, not to mention the contentious convergence between sublimation, repression and reaction-formation, sublimation lies at the heart of the Freudian creative process. Yet whilst sublimation is held responsible for "our highest cultural successes" (Freud, 1957[1910*a*], p. 54), the latter are consistently held to contain very little, almost nothing truly innovative or inventive. Culturally successful or artistically sublime as the results of the redirection of the libidinal energy towards a desexualized aim and object may be, they would always conceal the Nietzschean cycle of eternal recurrence under their appealing mask of creativity. In other words, the first tension puts the great creative force of sublimation fundamentally at odds with the invariably derivative character of its products – sublimely successful as they may appear. What is the meaning of creative sublimation, then, if it only ever leads to a repetition of the same? How can anything still be called sublime if it only ever constitutes a disguised permutation of the subliminal?

If this first tension may easily come across, and could even be dismissed as purely conceptual, meta-psychological or transcendental, the second tension should take away any doubt as to the practical, empirical significance of Freud's intermittent disquisitions on the creative process. Whether dispensing advice to young musicians, or reflecting upon the rampant discontents in civilization, Freud was not just interested in applying and extrapolating his psychoanalytic knowledge to sociocultural issues. On each and every occasion he invoked the questions of creation and creativity, it was also the clinical effectiveness of the psychoanalytic treatment paradigm that was at stake. Hence, the second tension concerns the dynamic connection between the act of artistic creation and the creative potential of the psychoanalytic experience. Theoretical problems aside, this may be the principal reason as to why so many psychoanalysts have deplored and continue to expose the painful "lack of a coherent theory of sublimation" in Freud's work (Laplanche and Pontalis, 1973[1967], p. 433).[5] If sublimation is not merely the psychic mechanism underpinning artistic creation, i.e. the driving force behind the emergence of works of art and other cultural objects, but also a key factor in the transformational change that is effectuated by a clinical psychoanalytic intervention, then how should the psychoanalyst operate with or upon this force? What does it mean for a patient to substitute sublimation for repression? How can the endgame of a psychoanalytic treatment process be conceived in terms of the sublime if the patient is not an artist or does not engage in any type of conventional artistic activity? And if the transformational change on the side of the psychoanalytic patient is sublimely artistic, does this imply that the metamorphic labour on the side of the creative artist may also legitimately be conceived as sublimely psychoanalytic?

First tension: sublimation as creative destruction

Quite a few years before he would become the assigned leader of the French surrealist movement, André Breton already expressed great enthusiasm for Freud's discoveries – as early as 1916 in fact, when he was deployed as a young military doctor at the neuropsychiatric centre of Saint-Dizier (Bonnet, 1992). With none of Freud's works being available in French translation yet, and Breton being unable to read German, he was forced to rely on secondary source materials to indulge in his intellectual curiosity, but that did not stop him from sharing copious notes and reflections with his friend Théodore Fraenkel (Rémy, 1991, pp. 5–8). In one of these, he summarized what he had understood about the practice of psychoanalysis, as follows:

> Depending on the case, the doctor calls upon the subject's adult established reason to destroy the effects of an anterior, infantile judgement, and employs the energy of the repressed complex by exchanging it for behavioural motives, or superior non-sexual thoughts (sublimation, *Sublimierung*), or finally allows the subject to freely accept a well understood sexual hygiene.
>
> *(cited in Bonnet, 1992, p. 127)*

Were Freud to have read this sentence, he would probably have disagreed with Breton's rather simplistic depiction of the psychoanalytic treatment process, but it nonetheless shows that, by 1916, the mechanism of sublimation was already sufficiently well known in psychoanalytic circles for it to be commonly regarded as an indispensable cornerstone of the new clinical science.

Deeply imbued with the creative spirit of the Dada movement, yet still intellectually preoccupied with Freud's ingenious method of dream interpretation and the supporting technique of free association, Breton secured a visit to Freud's residence at Berggasse 19 on 10 October 1921 (Scheidhauer, 2010, pp. 33–36; Esman, 2011, p. 174). Undoubtedly expecting a warm welcome, the 26-year-old Frenchman was sat instead amongst Freud's other patients in the waiting room until Herr Professor was ready for him. And when he was finally admitted into the master's chambers, it was not exactly the start of a stimulating dialogue, let alone a close friendship. Desperately trying to pique his host's interest by lacing the conversation with the names of the great French clinicians, Breton was soon back in the local café with nothing but vague compliments, a small collection of theoretical generalities, and a bitter sense of disappointment (Breton, 1990[1922]; Polizzotti, 2009, p. 146). Throughout the 1920s, Freud's theory continued to have a major impact on the surrealist practice of automatic writing, and many of its key proponents in a wide range of artistic idioms drew inspiration from it (Alexandrian, 1974; Lomas, 2000). But the *Sublimierung* Breton had originally highlighted as an essential psychoanalytic tool eventually became a major obstacle. In *Les Vases Communicants*, Breton called Freud "a relatively unlearned philosophic mind" and he reproached him "for having sacrificed all that he could have drawn from this [the importance of sexuality in unconscious life] . . . to commonplace self-interested motives" (Breton, 1997[1932], p. 22). When, in December 1932, Breton sent Freud a copy of his little volume, he received no fewer than three written responses, Freud first promising his interlocutor that he would read the book carefully, then defending himself against the accusation that he had omitted an important source in *The Interpretation of Dreams* (Freud, 1953[1900a]), and finally finishing off the exchange with a peculiar admission: "Although I receive so much evidence of the interest which you and your friends show toward my research, for myself I am not in the position to explain what Surrealism is and what it is after. It could be that I am not in any way made to understand it; I am at such a distant position from art" (cited in Davis, 1973, p. 131).[6]

As an excuse or a disclaimer, the final sentence cannot but strike as emphatically disingenuous, if only because Freud was known to invest vast amounts of money in his ever-expanding collection of Graeco-Roman and Egyptian statuettes, a small selection of which occupies a prominent place on his desk (Gamwell and Wells, 1989; Armstrong, 2005; Burke, 2006).[7] He may have kept his distance from modern art, yet he kept himself as close as he could to his beloved antiquities. In addition, by the early 1930s Freud had publicly professed the greatest admiration for the sublime artistic

128 Dany Nobus

achievements of Michelangelo, Leonardo da Vinci, Shakespeare, Goethe and Dostoevsky. If he felt rather underwhelmed by the surrealists' confident embrace of psychoanalysis as a perfect technique for releasing the creative spirit, it was no doubt less because of his distance from and insensitivity to art, but due to his fundamental disbelief in the creative potential of psycho-analysis itself, and by extension in the creative potential of the human mind in general, *pace* the mechanism of sublimation.

Numerous examples can be advanced of how Freud time and again reduced the ostensible emergence of the new to the surreptitious return of the old. In Freud's view, the appearance of something previously unseen or unheard was always no more than a cunning simulacrum, concealing the recurrence of something thought to be lost and forgotten. For instance, towards the end of his *Three Essays on the Theory of Sexuality*, he claimed that the finding of an object, which can be used here as a generic phrase for what is conventionally designated as "dating" and "mating", is always but the repetition of an anterior phenomenon: "The finding of an object is in fact a refinding of it [*Die Objektfindung is eigentlich eine Wiederfind-ung*]" (Freud, 1953[1905d], p. 222). Although it commonly presents itself in the form of something entirely new, the object either reinforces templates from early childhood (*frühinfantilen Vorbilder*), or constitutes in narcissis-tic fashion an avatar of the subject's own ego.[8] Outside the realm of sexual-ity, Freud adopted the same modus operandi, of substituting the old for the new, in order to dispute Gustave Le Bon's claim that groups are capable of eliciting new behaviours in their members:

> [I]n a group the individual is brought under conditions which allow him to throw off the repressions of his uncon-scious instinctual impulses [*Triebregungen*]. The *appar-ently new characteristics* which he then displays are in fact the manifestations of this unconscious, in which all that is evil in the human mind is contained as a predisposition.
>
> *(Freud, 1955[1921c], p. 74; emphasis added)*

Most significant for the issues of sublimation and the sublime is Freud's recourse to a virtually identical strategy in his 1919 essay "The "Uncanny"", in which he refuted the idea – adduced previously by the German psychia-trist Ernst Jentsch – that the subjective experience of the uncanny is rooted in persistent psychic uncertainty and a human being's visceral misoneism (Freud, 1955[1919h], pp. 226–233; Jentsch, 1997[1906]).[9] For Freud, the uncanny has nothing to do with any kind of anxiety that may be felt as a result of mental indecision or vacillation, or owing to an ineluctable expo-sure to the new, but epitomizes instead the anxiety experienced in confronta-tion with what "ought to have remained secret and hidden but has come to light", most notably the infantile castration complex (Freud, 1955[1919h], pp. 225, 230–231). Why is this relevant for our understanding of sublima-tion and the sublime? Jentsch's concept of "intellectual uncertainty", which he employed to account for the subjective sensation of uncanniness, clearly

Lacan's clinical artistry 129

echoes Kant's explanation of the sublime (*das Erhabene*), as a struggle between reason and imagination, as what frustrates rational orientation, and as a disruption of judgement by what exceeds the boundaries of comprehension (Kant, 2002[1793], pp. 128–159).[10] Freud's contemporary, the German theologian Rudolf Otto, accordingly averred that *das Erhabene*, which he preferred to render as the "numinous", embodies exactly the same *sui generis* conjunction of mystery and fascination as the uncanny (Otto, 1958[1917], p. 40), an idea that would subsequently be recuperated by Carl Gustav Jung, Mircea Eliade, C. S. Lewis, Aldous Huxley and many others.[11] The close affinity between the uncanny and the sublime (or the numinous) subsequently prompted scholars to argue that the uncanny is nothing but the secular sublime (Prawer, 1963), or the post-Enlightenment, literary "negative" sublime (Bloom, 1982, pp. 101, 108). Owing to this historical, phenomenological and philological confluence between the uncanny and the sublime, Harold Bloom even went so far as to say that Freud's essay on the uncanny is "the only major contribution that the twentieth century has made to the aesthetics of the Sublime" (Ibid., p. 101).[12]

By contrast with Otto's conception, the Freudian uncanny (and its sensuo-spiritual counterpart of the sublime) is not at all *sui generis*. If there is one thing that stands out from Freud's essay, it is his obstinate refusal to accept that the uncanny is *de facto* unrepresentable, unknowable and inexplicable, both in its emergence as a subjective sensation and in terms of the object to which it is attached.[13] As Derrida has suggested, in a characteristically inspired note to his 1970 essay "The Double Session": in "The Uncanny", Freud's relentless objections to undecidable ambivalence (as conveyed, for instance, by Jentsch's intellectual uncertainty) invariably give way to "the process of interminable substitution", one after the other (literary) figuration of the uncanny being "explained" as a (fictional) replacement for an old, and supposedly forgotten, unconscious (psychic) conflict (Derrida, 1981[1970], p. 268, note 67). As I pointed out in the introduction to this chapter, Freud's assiduous urge to locate and identify the archaic sources of cultural products – be it those that appear with the affective quality, or under the guise of the uncanny and the sublime – forcibly minimizes the creative power of sublimation, as the combined diversion of the object and the aim of the sexual drive towards "higher" sociocultural accomplishments. Freud's proposed antagonism between sublimation and direct sexual satisfaction, here, is not distinctly problematic just because it assumes that artists have somehow "learnt" how to postpone direct sexual gratification (or to exchange sex for something more culturally respected), or because it encapsulates a surreptitious value judgement on the advantages of sexual abstinence – in a sagacious amalgamation of the Stoic *sustine et abstine*, the Protestant work ethic, and the good old Communist principle of переключение (switching) (Zalkind, 2001[1929]) – but because the outcome of the libidinal transformation is constantly shown to fail at the very point of its allegedly higher, new creative value. For all Freud's emphasis on the transformational power of sublimation, in his unmitigated appreciation of its inherently repetitive outcomes (from the uncanny to the sublime) he consistently demonstrated his fervent espousal of what can deservedly be termed a "catastrophe theory of creativity" (Bloom, 1982), which not only reduces the (artistic) quality of the newly created object and its associated (sociocultural) goal but also radically destabilizes the psychic process leading up to it, whereby the latter becomes a troublesome contest between the "pull of the new" and the "push of the old" – a "secular psychomachia" as Jack Spector once called it (Spector, 1972, p. 145).

How did Lacan address this first major tension in Freud's work?[14] When returning to the questions of sublimation and the sublime in his 1959–1960 seminar *The Ethics of Psychoanalysis*, Lacan first implicitly reminded his audience of how, at the very end of his previous seminar, on *Desire and its Interpretation*, he had outlined the dialectical relationship between the social system, as predicated upon a symbolic law, and cultural achievements, which are simultaneously within the system and exceeding its boundaries (Lacan, 2019[2013], p. 483).[15] For Lacan, a subject who identifies with and abides by the rules and regulations of the social fabric in which she or he is embedded may simultaneously protest against the various restrictions imposed by the symbolic system, by virtue of opening up of a realm of activity beyond their sphere of influence. It is precisely this subjective act of concurrent compliance with and radical transcendence of the socio-symbolic limits that Lacan initially designated as sublimation (Ibid., p. 484). In *Seminar VII*, he elaborated on this idea, arguing that the most general formula of sublimation is that "it raises an object . . . to the dignity of the Thing [*elle élève un objet. . . à la dignité de la Chose*]" (Lacan, 1992[1986], p. 112). In typically Lacanian fashion, this formula defies easy understanding, yet it is immediately clear that whereas Freud had defined sublimation, in his *Three Essays on the Theory of Sexuality* and elsewhere, as a psychic process through which the sexual goal of the drive is exchanged for a "higher", non-sexual goal (Freud, 1953[1905d], pp. 238–239, 1964[1930a], p. 79), Lacan recalibrated sublimation by situating it primarily with reference to the object. Furthermore, whereas Freud had argued that sublimation entails a diversion, or a redirection of sexual energy away from its "natural" course (as leading to the realization of the sexual goal) – which also explains his intermittent designation of sublimation as a means of fixating "preliminary" sexual goals, such as looking and touching – Lacan, for his part, did not regard sublimation as a process which bars access to the (sexual) object, but saw it, on the contrary, clearing the path for its being refashioned into something else. In other words, the mechanism of sublimation and its projected object of the sublime are collapsed here into a single transformational process. In Freud's take on the matter, the object is displaced as a result of the sublimatory diversion of the drive's goal; in Lacan's reworking, the transformation of the object coincides with the alteration of the goal.

Whilst Lacan did not directly refer to Hegel's dialectic when he articulated the most general formula of sublimation in *Seminar VII*, the term "elevation" (raising) should undoubtedly be acknowledged here in its Hegelian connotations of *Aufhebung*: a process through which something is being lifted onto a higher level and thereby simultaneously annihilated and preserved (Hegel, 2018[1807]).[16] Looking at Lacan's formula through a Hegelian lens, and taking account of the standard English translation of *Aufhebung* as "sublation", one could thus posit that, in Lacan's reading, sublimation sublates the object onto the dignity of the Thing, whereby the object is at once destroyed (in its previous, original state) and lifted up onto a higher level of functioning.[17] Drawing on a different idiom, one might say that sublimation emerges here as the psychoanalytic equivalent of Schumpeter's gale (1976[1942]): it is the mechanism of creative destruction by which an object is simultaneously abolished and maintained. This conception clearly alleviates the first major tension emanating from Freud's theory of sublimation, because the underlying process is no longer conceived or interpreted as strictly creative, and its anticipated outcome is unequivocally ascertained as partially destructive.

How are we to understand the difference, then, between what Lacan termed "an object", underscoring the *in*definite article, and "the Thing", as distinctively presented with the definite article? Merely based on the way in which Lacan constructed his formula of sublimation, it can already be inferred that the main difference between "an object" and "the Thing" is a difference in value, since Lacan proclaimed that sublimation elevates an object to the "dignity" of the Thing. Of course, Freud too had argued that the diversion of sexual energy in the direction of an artistic or intellectual goal (rather than a sexual one) constituted a "superior" achievement, compared to the "inferior" sexual act. Yet it remains unclear whether Lacan's term "dignity" should really be taken at face value. It might very well be ironic, especially in light of the fact that, just before he pronounced the phrase "the dignity of the Thing" (*la dignité de la Chose*), he told his audience that, in finishing his formula, he would have recourse to some wordplay: "I don't mind the suggestion of a play on words in the term I use [*Je ne me refuserai pas aux résonances de calembour qu'il peut y avoir dans l'usage du terme que je vais amener*]" (Lacan, 1992[1986], p. 112). The amusing resonances are effectively twofold. First, during the early stages of the seminar, Lacan had spent two sessions on the observation that, unlike the French (and the English), the German language has two words for "thing", "*das Ding*" and "*die Sache*" (Ibid., pp. 43–70), whereby he had associated "*das Ding*" with an inaccessible, unknowable emptiness, in an implicit reformulation of Kant's transcendental "*Ding an Sich*" (thing-in-itself), i.e. a noumenon which can enter reason, and which is therefore thinkable, but which cannot be empirically experienced, let alone known (Kant, 1997[1788], pp. 47–49).[18] In referring to the dignity of the Thing, he thus first of all played on the near-homophony between dignity and "*Ding*". Second, the French word "*la Chose*" (the Thing) also sounds exactly like "*l'a-chose*" (the un-thing, or the no-thing), and later in his work Lacan would often write "*la Chose*" precisely as "*l'a-chose*" or "*l'achose*" (Lacan, 2001[1970], p. 404; 2006, p. 77; 2013[1971], p. 331). More importantly, the French word "*la Chose*" is routinely used to designate trivial nondescript things, comparable to how in English people would refer to an insignificant, forgotten or forgettable thing with words such as "thingumajig", "thingamabob", or even "whatnot". Given these connotations of *"la Chose"*, Lacan's term "dignity" acquires a rather different tone, then, which might indicate that the dignity in question has nothing to do with the inherent quality of "the thing". "The thing" may very well be an abject, useless "piece of shit" – more of a non-object than an object in and of itself. Put differently, on the surface there might not be any difference whatsoever between "an object" and "the Thing", yet what makes "the Thing" different from "an object" is the fact that the former has passed through a process of subl(im)ation, and therefore occupies a certain liminal place vis-à-vis the socio-symbolic structures in which it is immersed. Perhaps creative artists will already begin to recognize certain elements here of how objects come to be appreciated (or despised) as sublime works of art: what constitutes sublime art has nothing to do with the intrinsic quality (the natural beauty, the underlying craftsmanship, or the moral-ideological value) of an object. Instead, it has everything to do with the transformational work that has given rise to its emergence, its fundamental negation of any kind of use-value that would have been attached to the object and its particular place within and vis-à-vis the socio-symbolic networks and narratives surrounding it.[19]

An object operates strictly within the confines of the symbolic order, the realm of socially established discursive practices of language and the law. In this order, it is born, evolves, is being exchanged and transmitted, may become lost and subsequently be found back – not unlike Freud's aforementioned comment on the object as something that is always already re-found. The Thing, on the other hand, exceeds the limits of the symbolic order; it defies the socially sanctioned norms and values with a view to opening up a "real" space, to which the accepted rules and regulations no longer apply. Whereas the circuit of objects operates in conformity with the regulatory mechanisms that are endorsed and imposed by a given discourse, the Thing is radically nonconformist and situates itself as the antipode of symbolic compliance with an ideological code.

We can now understand how sublimation, in the Lacanian sense, may contribute to the production of (sublime) works of art. What characterizes a work of art is that it interrogates and potentially undermines the normative models of reasoning that keep the hegemonic symbolic structures alive. The work of art is therefore by definition "transgressive", because it refuses to abide by the moral and legal principles maintaining the social fabric. As "the Thing", the work of art is also intrinsically "uncanny", and therefore always already containing within itself the potentiality of the sublime, precisely because it confronts us with the instability of our most cherished worldviews and offers us an opportunity to escape the symbolic constraints that simultaneously make possible and delineate our mental operations and social interactions. The work of art shows us the threshold of liberty and gives us a view of the edge, and this potentiality is simultaneously fascinating, mysterious and terrifying, in the Jungian sense of the alchemical *mysterium coniunctionis* (Jung, 1970[1963]).

As Lacan proposed in *Seminar VII*, this process (of the synthesis of the opposites) takes place as a sublation of an object, or a set of objects, that

Lacan's clinical artistry   133

is available within the socio-symbolic landscape, but the "artistic" quality of the product of this subl(im)ation concerns the process rather than the outcome. Some artists have gone very far in trying to demonstrate how art has nothing to do with the nature of the object but crucially relies on this underlying transformational mechanism. I could refer here to Marcel Duchamp's famous urinal, Jackson Pollock's "Number 26A, Black and White", or Mark Rothko's "Reds". The classic philistine response to these objects – "This is unacceptable, stupid and offensive" – is in a sense precisely what "the Thing" is designed to provoke. It is unacceptable from within the boundaries of an accepted social discourse. It offends those who cherish the norms and values of a socially sanctioned ideology. Yet it only has these effects, because an object (a urinal, the intercourse of black and white, shades of red) has been taken outside these ideological boundaries and placed within a supra- or trans-ideological space of artistic freedom.

In this way, the work of art simultaneously attaches itself to the hegemonic social strategies (by operating with and upon objects that exist within them) and transcends these strategies in the act of subl(im)ation. Or to look at it from the perspective of the artist, when sublating an object to the dignity of the Thing, the artist operates within a given socio-symbolic code, selects an object within this code and subsequently transcends the code by sublating the codified objects and placing them as "the Thing" within a transgressive sphere. With these Lacanian developments, we can also solve the persistent Freudian problem of the distinction between sublimation and repression.[20] By situating sublimation as a process involving the transgression of the symbolic law, Lacan implicitly clarified how it needs to be distinguished from repression, which epitomizes a radical compliance with the symbolic law. For Lacan, the Freudian mechanism of repression coincides with the subject's assimilation of the symbolic rules of language and the law; it follows the subject's identification with the signifiers of the Other. Subl(im)ation, however, is rooted in an act of protest against the identificatory mechanisms that maintain subjective compliance. In an act of subl(im) ation, the subject ventures to escape from the alienating clutches of the assimilated social contract and endeavours to separate itself from the Other by opening up a new space of artistic, creative freedom.

When Lacan first broached the issue of sublimation, at the end of his seminar *Desire and its Interpretation*, he did not hesitate to associate it with perversion and criminality, because "the pervert" also entertains a dialectical relationship with the law – complying with it in order to manipulate it, control it and "pervert" it (Lacan, 2019[2013], pp. 482–485). However, in *The Ethics of Psychoanalysis*, Lacan suggested a distinction between sublimation and perversion/criminality on the basis of a structural criterion that involves the relationship between the subject and the object. In short, Lacan argued that the difference between sublimation and perversion/criminality relates to what comes to occupy the place beyond the symbolic order. In an act of sublimation, this place "beyond the law" is occupied by the object or, to put it more precisely, by the elevated, sublated and "Thingified" object, in which we can indeed recognize the work of art. But the subject remains firmly situated "on the side" of the law; it is from a position within the symbolic order that the artist manages to carve out a space beyond it for "the Thing" that is his or her work of art. When the perverse criminal transgresses the symbolic order, the place beyond the law is occupied by the subject him- or herself, from which she or he then attempts to transform the subjects "on the side" of the law into the new object of his or her "perverse" law. Whereas the subl(im)ating artist lets his or her object "challenge" the law whilst maintaining a law-abiding position as subject, the perverse criminal (or criminal pervert) challenges the law *qua* subject, thus employing it from a position of presumed mastery, as a tool for objectifying indiscriminately all those who continue to function within its radius.

Lacan illustrated the latter principle with the celebrated 1957 novel by Roger Vailland entitled *La loi* (Vailland, 2008[1957]; Lacan, 1992[1986], p. 73). The story is set in a village in Southern Italy where it is no longer possible to distinguish between the "legal law" and the "illegal law", insofar as "enforcing the law" has become the standard phrase used by organized criminals to terrorize and subdue the local population. The inextricable mixture of the social order and criminal practices has even led to the development of a game, appropriately called "the law", in which the winner is allowed to "enforce the law" and tell the losers to do whatever he or she believes is necessary, which eventually comes down to telling them when and how to speak. For Lacan, this fictional narrative exemplifies how the perverse criminal follows an alternative law, starting from a subjective position outside the "legal law". The subl(im)ating artist, by contrast, only goes so far as allowing this "illegal" or "illegitimate" position to be occupied by the artistic object.

Second tension: the sublime and psychoanalytic creativity

With Lacan's outlook on sublimation as a process of creative destruction leading to the uncanny sublimity of the conceivable yet unknowable Thing, we are thus able to separate sublimation from repression and offer a structural distinction between sublimation and perversion. The latter differentiation is important, because Freud too struggled with the issue. Witness the following passage, again from the *Three Essays on the Theory of Sexuality*:

> It is perhaps in connection precisely with the most repulsive perversions that the mental factor must be regarded as playing its largest part in the transformation of the sexual instinct. It is impossible to deny that in their case a piece of mental work has been performed which, in spite of its horrifying result, is the equivalent of *an idealization of the instinct* [*den Wert einer Idealisierung des Triebes nicht absprechen kann*].
> *(Freud, 1953[1905d], p. 161; italics added)*

Freud is unequivocally referring here to the intrinsic creative aspect of the perverse psychic mechanism, which was subsequently taken up again by post-Freudian psychoanalysts such as Joyce McDougall (1995) and Janine Chasseguet-Smirgel (1985), who both argued that perversion incorporates a dimension of radical creativity.

Nonetheless, despite its advantages over Freud's account of sublimation, Lacan's theory still does not explain the vexed relationship – which I have designated in my introduction as the "second tension" – between the artistic impulse, sublimation and the psychoanalytic treatment process, although he himself was very much aware of it. For example, in 1971, when alluding to the fact that James Joyce had at one point been instructed by his patron Edith Rockefeller to commence an analysis with Jung (Ellmann, 1983, p. 466), Lacan averred: "One will recall that a lady 'Maecenas' [*messe-haine*], in wanting to help him [Joyce], offered him a psychoanalysis, as one might offer someone a shower. And with Jung of all people. . . . In the game I am alluding to [Lacan referred to Joyce's project of 'littering' the letter], he would have gained nothing there, going straight in it to the best one may expect from psychoanalysis at its end" (Lacan, 2013[1971], p. 327). Lacan himself thus entertained the idea that the composition of a work of art, in this case the book entitled *Finnegans Wake* (Joyce, 1939), may epitomize the "best one may expect" from a psychoanalytic treatment process. However, much like Freud in his response to Thomán, he did not elaborate on his statement and also failed to explain how exactly the two processes might be linked. The other extant problem with Lacan's theory of sublimation is that it somehow appears to desexualize the entire mechanism. For Freud, sublimation is essentially linked to a diversion of sexual energy away from the realisation of the "normal" sexual goal. Yet when Lacan argued that the most general formula of sublimation is the sublation of an object to the dignity of the Thing, one feels entitled to wonder, despite Lacan's endorsement of all the connotations associated with the notion of "Thing", what has happened to the sexual dimension highlighted by Freud. Moreover, Lacan can hardly be accused, like Jung at one point was, of desexualizing Freudian theory in favour of a pseudo-mystical system of trans-historical and cross-generational archetypes. The answer to both questions – the relationship between the artistic impulse and the psychoanalytic process, and the sexual dimension of sublimation – is to be found, I believe, in the operative mechanism of the fantasy, which Lacan, quite surprisingly, did not reintroduce when discussing the issue of sublimation, even though within his theory the fantasy is the primary psychic factor that modulates the relation between the subject and the object.

The fantasy intermittently surfaced in Freud's discussions of sublimation, yet it is seldom clear which precise role Freud attributed to it. In the final paragraph of his twenty-third introductory lecture on psychoanalysis, which notably deals with the paths to symptom formation, Freud alerted his audience to what he described as "a side of the life of phantasy [*sic*] which deserves the most general interest" (Freud, 1963[1916–'17], p. 375). The side Freud had in mind "leads back from phantasy [*sic*] to reality" and

136   Dany Nobus

concerns "the path of art" (Ibid., pp. 375–376). After conceding that the artist may suffer from neurotic inhibitions as much as any other "unsatisfied" individual, and may consequently turn his back on reality in order to indulge in the "wishful constructions" of phantasy life, Freud detailed how artists may still succeed in solving the conflict between their "instinctual needs" and their neurotic failure to find satisfaction in life. Rather than summarizing or paraphrasing Freud's words, I prefer to quote them at length:

> Their [the artists'] constitution probably includes a strong capacity for sublimation and a certain degree of laxity in the repressions which are decisive for a conflict. An artist, however, finds a path back to reality in the following manner. To be sure, he is not the only one who leads a life of phantasy. Access to the half-way region of phantasy is permitted by the universal assent of mankind, and everyone suffering from privation [*jeder Entbehrende*] expects to derive alleviation and consolation from it. But for those who are not artists the yield of pleasure [*Lustgewinn*] to be derived from the sources of phantasy is very limited. The ruthlessness of their repressions forces them to be content with such meagre day-dreams as are allowed to become conscious. A man who is a true artist has more at his disposal. In the first place, he understands how to work over his day-dreams in such a way as to make them lose what is too personal about them and repels strangers, and to make it possible for others to share in the enjoyment [*mitgenießbar*] of them. He understands, too, how to tone them down so that they do not easily betray their origin from proscribed sources. Furthermore, he possesses the mysterious power of shaping some particular material until it has become a faithful image of his phantasy; and he knows, moreover, how to link so large a yield of pleasure [*Lustgewinn*] to this representation of his unconscious phantasy that, for the time being at least, repressions are outweighed and lifted by it [*aufgehoben werden*]. If he is able to accomplish all this, he makes it possible for other people once more to derive consolation and alleviation from their own sources of pleasure in their unconscious which have become inaccessible to them; he earns their gratitude and admiration and he has thus achieved *through* his phantasy what originally he had achieved only *in* his phantasy – honour, power and the love of women.
>
> *(Ibid., pp. 376–377)*[21]

Irrespective of Freud's rather condescending description of what artists desire, his explanation of their idiosyncratic strategy for avoiding the neurotic solution to internal conflicts deserves closer attention, if only because it includes an additional gloss on the mechanism of sublimation. First, Freud argued that artists, unlike "mainstream" neurotic people, manage to accord some kind of universal value to their daydreams, so that they lose their self-centred particularities and may start to command universal appreciation. Second, artists know how to transform their daydreams in such a way that they can generate uncensored pleasure. In other words, artists can enjoy their daydreams with impunity, similar to how the dreamer fulfils his or her unconscious wishes through the transformation of the forbidden (latent) dream thoughts into a more acceptable (manifest) dream content. Third, and perhaps most crucially, artists know how to create objects that constitute a crystallisation of their fantasy or, to reiterate Freud's own words: artists possess "the mysterious power of shaping some particular material until it has become a faithful image" of their phantasy (Ibid., p. 377). Each of these three points undoubtedly warrants detailed investigation, yet within the context of this chapter, and my current examination of the "second tension", I merely wish to draw attention to how Freud linked sublimation and the creative process here to an activity that essentially takes place at the level of the fantasy (and its derivatives, the conscious daydreams).

Apart from this passage, which is no more than an addendum to a lecture which effectively deals with something else (the pathways to symptom formation), there is at least one other text by Freud in which the connection between the fantasy and the artistic/creative impulse is made, i.e. the short essay "Creative Writers and Day-Dreaming" (Freud, 1959[1908e]). As Freud mentioned in the very first sentence of this paper, the main issue he intended to address in it concerns the question as to where, from which source, artists (in this case, creative writers) obtain their materials. All creative activity, Freud argued, needs to be situated in children's play, which serves the purpose of structuring and mastering reality.[22] Unlike the child, adolescents and adults relinquish recourse to the structures of reality, and seek to satisfy their (unsatisfied, and largely unsatisfiable) wishes by indulging in fantasies. Apart from the fact that adults tend to be much more ashamed and embarrassed by their fantasies than children about their play, there are several other characteristics of fantasizing which Freud highlighted here. First, a fantasy is a type of wish-fulfilment, especially of ambitious (emulative) and erotic wishes. Second, a fantasy connects the present, the past and the future in one continuous sequence: it takes advantage of an event in the present to rekindle an event in the past during which the wish was fulfilled, with a view to creating an event in the future which also displays the fulfilment of the wish.

How do creative writers use fantasies, then, as a basis for their creations? Freud's answer was remarkably simple: the protagonist-hero of the novel is an avatar of the ego, which always occupies the spotlight in the fantasy. As in the concluding paragraph of his twenty-third lecture, Freud eventually also broached the issue as to how the creative writer succeeds in giving pleasure to his readership by indulging in the expression of his own fantasies. And Freud's answer was almost identical to that which he offered in his

138   Dany Nobus

introductory lectures: creative writers tone down the egotistical qualities of their daydreams, and the aesthetic expression of their artwork functions as an incentive-bonus (*Verlockungsprämie*) or a type of fore-pleasure (*Vorlust*) – an aesthetic "yield of pleasure" (*ästhetischen Lustgewinn*) that is capable of triggering larger quantities of unconscious pleasure in the reader, who can then enjoy this newfound pleasure without shame or self-reproach.[23]

By integrating the notion of the fantasy into the theory of subl(im)ation and the creative process, we can both preserve the sexual element in the act of subl(im)ation, and enhance our understanding of the relationship between the subject and the object (including the specific position of "the Thing') in Lacan's theory of sublimation. From a Lacanian perspective, the fantasy epitomizes the formal mechanism of desire, so much so that Lacan even went so far as to define the fantasy as "desire for/of" (*désir de*) (Lacan, 2006[1962], p. 653; 2014[2004], p. 100; 2015[2001], p. 315) and as the structure which modulates every "object-relation" (Lacan, 2019[2013], p. 366). As such, the fantasy is not only the place where the subject finds his or her objects of desire, that is to say, where his or her desires are being fulfilled, but also the point at which the subject maintains his or her desire, precisely because the fantasy represents desire as "un-realized", as something which has not found its realisation in reality (just yet). As a structure which modulates and fluctuates between the subject and the object, the fantasy should not be regarded as something which is controlled and monitored by the subject. The subject does not assimilate the fantasy in order to use it subsequently as a template for (re)finding certain objects. This is where the Lacanian perspective differs from the Freudian viewpoint. Freud remained convinced that the fantasy is the most basic template from which other activities, and especially the creative process, proceed. For Freud, the artist's work is a secondary formation which originates in the primary structure of the fantasy. For Lacan, by contrast, the fantasy is a specific relationship between the subject and the object that follows its autonomous path, which is neither controlled by the subject nor the object.

How does the fantasy affect the transformational act, process or mechanism of subl(im)ation? In Lacan's most general formula of sublimation – the sublation of an object to the dignity of the Thing – the Thing is situated beyond the boundaries of the symbolic order, in a sublime, transcendental, transgressive space. I believe that this act of protest, which lies at the root of the creative impulse, and which constitutes a form of creative destruction, effectively puts the object in a highly privileged position – hence the term "dignity" – from which it acquires unprecedented power over the symbolic order buttressing and underpinning the fantasy. It seems to me, here, that in its subl(im)ation to the level of "the Thing", the object not only challenges the cherished principles of the symbolic order but also serves the (re)construction of the fantasy as such. To put it more provocatively, in the process of subl(im)ation that leads to the emergence of a (potentially sublime) work of art, it is not the fantasy that constructs the work of art, *pace* Freud, but the work of art that constructs the fantasy. And this may in turn explain, then, why artists are incapable of revealing the source and origin of their work. The work of art is in itself the source and origin of a creative act, which contributes to the (re)construction of the fundamental fantasy.

However, the key issue permeating the "second tension" concerns the relationship between the creative act and the psychoanalytic treatment process. And so the question remains as to how all of the aforementioned considerations may be applied to psychoanalytic clinical practice. As Lacan pointed out towards the very end of his *Seminar XI*, on *The Four Fundamental Concepts of Psychoanalysis*, the construction (and subsequent traversal) of the fantasy, which involves a prolonged labour of "working-through" (Freud, 1958[1914g]) on the side of the patient, can be regarded as the most advanced goal of a psychoanalytic process (Lacan, 1994[1973], pp. 273–274). Art and psychoanalysis thus share the same teleological principle, that of the construction and traversal of the fantasy.[24] This, it seems to me, is precisely why Lacan could say that Joyce would not have gained anything from his analytic treatment with Jung that he had not already achieved in his writing, even before the publication of *Finnegans Wake*. This is also, I believe, why Freud, in his letter to Thomán, refused to situate psychoanalysis beyond the artistic impulse, as some kind of meta-artistic discourse that might be capable of releasing and/or taming the vicissitudes of creative power. Rather than a discourse which might be able to master the mainspring of fine art, psychoanalysis is rather to be conceived as a fine art in itself. However, its fine art would not consist of explaining away the creative impulse – as Freud pointed out to Thomán, psychoanalysis can neither prevent the artistic impulse from dying out, nor its being expressed more vehemently, if it does not already have a power of its own – but of mapping out its terrain as a highly delicate, clinical process of subl(im)ation, which is simultaneously transformational, transgressive and traversive. Away from the analytic couch, artists may achieve subl(im)ation and the installation of the sublime "Thing" via the intense process of making, re-making and un-making objects, doing, re-doing and un-doing letters, notes, paint and clay; within the clinical setting, the patient arrives at the symbolic equivalent of "the Thing", which Lacan also designated as $S(\not{A})$, via an arduous working and re-working, a laborious locating and dis-locating of the signifier.[25]

Conclusion

For Freud, there is no such thing as *creatio ex nihilo*. The product of a creative process is never irreducible, since it can always be traced back to a constellation of anterior factors presiding over its realisation, such as the materials derived from creative writers' daydreams. It should not come as a surprise, then, that Freud was rather pessimistic concerning the creative potential of psychoanalysis, all the more so as his life's work developed and his working life entered its final stages. As he suggested in "Analysis Terminable and Interminable", psychoanalysis cannot completely overrule, cancel out or disable unconscious mental processes (Freud, 1964[1937c]). At best, it can reorganize these processes in such a way that the subject is less "subjected" to them or feels less troubled by their intractable pressures. Or, as he already put it during the mid-1890s, in the final paragraph of the *Studies on Hysteria*, psychoanalysis can probably do no more than transform hysterical misery into the unhappiness of everyday life (Breuer and Freud, 1955[1895d], p. 305).

Freud did not believe in "creationism" – as the production of something out of nothing, the emergence of a new fullness from an empty nothingness – and it is precisely because he did not believe in it that he believed he could offer an explanatory framework for it. In this respect, he generally avoided employing the term "creation" altogether – the German nouns "*Schöpfung*" or "*Schaffung*" do not even feature in the index to his complete works – and preferred to talk about "productive processes", or the "capacity for achievement" (*Leistungsfähigkeit*), as he did in his 1934 letter to Mária Thomán. The fundamental question then is: how are we to conceive psychoanalytically of these processes, and of the works (of art) that they generate? Starting from Freud's letter to Thomán, I have supplemented this foundational question with a series of others invoking the relationship between sublimation and the sublime, and inscribing the interface between the "artistic/creative impulse", the realisation of the work of art and the process and goals of a psychoanalytic treatment. How does the artistic impulse lead to the crystallization of an artwork? Does the mechanism operate beyond the boundaries of language and rationality, or is it strictly controlled by a symbolic machinery? And if a psychoanalytic process can only "follow" the artistic impulse in its autonomous, self-regulatory functioning, without being able to affect it directly, what does this parallelism reveal about the operative mechanisms within the treatment?

Returning to the letter of Freud's statements on sublimation, I have endeavoured to answer these questions by identifying two constitutive tensions running through his work. The first, a largely theoretical tension, concerns the antinomy between the ostensibly creative power of sublimation and the invariably derivative nature of the sublime to which it gives rise. The second, a distinctly clinical tension, questions the practical significance of sublimation within the psychoanalytic treatment as a key transformational process that lies at the heart of analytic (or therapeutic) effectiveness. Without wanting to go so far as to say that Lacan's explorations of sublimation (and the sublime) in his seminar on *The Ethics of Psychoanalysis* encapsulate the only possible operation to alleviate these tensions and resolve the aforementioned questions, I have demonstrated how Lacan's reconsideration of sublimation as the sublation of an object to the level (and the dignity) of the Thing presents sublimation as a process of creative destruction. Insofar as the Hegelian dialectical operator of sublation (*Aufhebung*) involves both a cancelling out and a preservation of the object on a new, higher level of functioning, it indeed allows us to think of sublimation as a process that is not unequivocally creative and to consider the sublime as an outcome that is not strictly derivative. Inasmuch as Lacan defined the (sublime) outcome as the dignity of the Thing, we may also acquire a new understanding of how sublimation generates another type of object, which is conceivable without being fully knowable and which has lost its practical use-value on account of its positioning outside the socio-symbolic rules and regulations of an established order.

With regard to the second tension, I have argued that the conceptual bridge between the artistic work of sublimation and its clinical equivalent in the psychoanalytic treatment is to be found in the psychic structure of the fantasy, which represents a space of desire, and which modulates the relationship between subject and object. However, when inserting this term in the equation between sublimation, sublation and the sublime, it is important to acknowledge that the fantasy does not (re-)construct the Thing but that the Thing (re-)constructs the fantasy. Lacan's assertion that the end of analysis coincides with a traversal of the fantasy is therefore crucially predicated upon the articulation, location and identification of the Thing. At this point, I have drawn a parallel between the sublimatory work of the artist, which may be ascertained in the writer's littering of the letter, or the painter's pasting of the paint, and the sublimatory working-through of the psychoanalytic patient, which may be acknowledged in his or her protracted shedding of the signifier.

We may never know what Thomán's concrete request to Freud was, when she wrote her letter to him in the Spring of 1934. Yet despite the inconsistencies and infelicities of his response, he was undoubtedly right when he resisted the temptation to recommend to her that she start an analysis with him, or with one of his colleagues. For as an acclaimed violinist, she was already deeply immersed, and probably on a daily basis, in the working and re-working of notes, chords, keys and scales. She would not become the Anne-Sophie Mutter of her generation, yet (paraphrasing Lacan) in the game I am alluding to, she would have gained nothing from a psychoanalytic treatment with Freud or anyone else, going straight in it to the best one may expect from psychoanalysis at its end.

Notes

1 Freud's original letter to Thomán is preserved in the Sigmund Freud Papers at the Library of Congress in Washington, DC, and can now also be accessed online via the Library's website: www.loc.gov. Full transcriptions of the letter can be found in Rauchfleisch (1990, p. 1124) and Widmaier-Haag (1999, p. 34).

2 After his appointment as Chancellor of Germany, at the end of January 1933, Hitler gradually tightened his political grip, culminating in the infamous "Night of the Long Knives" of 30 June 1934, i.e. three days after Freud's letter to Thomán. Sándor Ferenczi had died on 22 May 1933, at the age of 59. In his obituary, Freud had written: "From unexhausted springs of emotion the conviction was borne in upon him that one could effect far more with one's patients if one gave them enough of the love which they had longed for as children. . . . Wherever it may have been that the road he had started along would have led him, he could not pursue it to the end. . . . It is impossible to believe that the history of our science will ever forget him" (Freud, 1960[1933c], p. 229). As to

142 Dany Nobus

Freud's deteriorating health, a letter to Marie Bonaparte of 2 May 1934 contained the following admission: "I am not writing anything. For this one does need a certain measure of physical well-being which I can no longer muster up, and also a friendlier attitude to the world than it is possible to have at this time" (cited in Schur, 1972, p. 454). For an excellent discussion of the impact of Hitler's rise to power and the Nazi annexation of Austria on Freud and psychoanalysis, see Edmundson (2007).

3   It goes without saying that I am not suggesting here that all theories of the sublime *de facto* presuppose a psychic mechanism of sublimation, even in the most general sense of the term – as a particular transformation of matter, form or energy. In fact, apart from Nietzsche and (to a lesser extent) Schopenhauer (2017[1851]), none of the most important pre-Freudian scholars and theorists of the sublime, such as Longinus (1995), Boileau (1965[1674]), Silvain (1732), Burke (2015[1757]), Mendelssohn (1997[1761]), Kant (2002[1793], 2011[1764]), Schiller (1998[1793]) and Hegel (1998[1835]), consider its occurrence relative to a specific psychic mechanism called sublimation. Even Freud himself may not have interpreted all instances of the sublime as the result of a psychic process of sublimation, although whenever the issue of sublimation arose, he habitually described its outcome in terms of "higher" artistic, moral or sociocultural aims (see, for example, Freud, 1953[1905*d*], p. 157, 1964[1930*a*], p. 79). Purely with reference to Freud, we thus already need to guard ourselves against the fallacy of the *non distributio medii*: if all sublimation gives rise to a form of the sublime, all forms of the sublime may not necessarily be due to sublimation. For excellent general surveys of the notion of the sublime, see Russo (1987) and Saint Girons (1993, 2005).

4   In their definitive philological account of sublimation, the subliminal and the sublime, Cohn and Miles posited that Freud had borrowed the term sublimation (*Sublimierung*) from "a chemical-scientific vocabulary", although they also noted how Freud consistently wrote the word in *Sperrschrift*, which was the German publishers' equivalent of the current practice of italicization, generally suggesting either a specific emphasis or the use of a neologism (Cohn and Miles, 1977, p. 301). However, in a letter to Jung of 10 January 1912, Freud commented on an essay by Lou Andreas-Salomé as follows: "We ought not in principle to decline [the paper's publication], provided she contents herself with sublimation [*Sublimierung*] and leaves sublimates [*Sublimation*] to the chemists" (McGuire, 1974, p. 480). In other words, Freud was (understandably) fully conversant with the chemical-scientific vocabulary of his era, but explicitly distanced himself from it in opting to designate his newly coined psychic mechanism as *Sublimierung* instead of *Sublimation*. Of course, this does not solve the question as to whether Freud had silently "borrowed" the term from Nietzsche, who uses *Sublimirung* [*sic*] or its cognates regularly in *Human, All Too Human* (1996[1878]), *Daybreak* (1997[1881]), and occasionally in *Beyond Good and Evil* (Nietzsche, 2002[1886], p. 79) and *On the Genealogy of Morals* (Nietzsche, 1998[1887], p. 49). For a painstakingly detailed, historical and semantic analysis of sublimation in Freud and Nietzsche, see Gasser (1997, pp. 313–365). For more accessible, critical discussions of the matter, see Kaufmann (2013[1950], pp. 211–256), Lehrer (1995) and Gemes (2009).

5   The numerous lacunae and inconsistencies in Freud's theory of sublimation, which he himself never failed to acknowledge (Freud, 1955[1923*a*], p. 256, 1964[1930*a*], p. 79; Jones, 1957, p. 464), were already highlighted by the early Freudians, and have resulted in countless post-Freudian revisions of the concept and its psychoanalytic significance. For early criticisms of Freud's

ideas on sublimation, see Bernfeld (1922), Sterba (1930), Glover (1931), Deri (1939) and Levey (1939). For critical surveys of the various passages on sublimation in Freud's work, see Flournoy (1967), Laplanche (1980), Gay (1992), Vergote (1997), de Mijolla-Mellor (2012), Goebel (2012[2009], pp. 107–155) and Rath (2019, pp. 19–140). Shortly after the outbreak of World War I, Freud started work on 12 interconnected essays for a book provisionally titled *Zur Vorbereitung der Metapsychologie* (*In Preparation for the Metapsychology*) (Paskauskas, 1993, p. 312), yet the volume never materialized and only five of the essays were ever published as separate texts during Freud's lifetime, the other seven disappearing without a trace, apart from the final one, which was discovered by accident in 1983 in a cache of documents Sándor Ferenczi had left to his Hungarian pupil Michael Bálint (Grubrich-Simitis, 1987). In his editor's introduction to Freud's papers on metapsychology for the *Standard Edition* of Freud's work, James Strachey opined that at least one of the vanished essays dealt with the question of sublimation (Strachey, 1957, p. 106), yet this proposition cannot be supported on the basis of clear textual or other evidence.

6 The whereabouts of Freud's copy of Breton's book remain unknown. In 1938, faced with the dire prospect of imminent emigration, Freud decided to leave part of his substantive personal library in the hands of his friend Paul Sonnenfeld, who in turn sold the books to the antiquarian bookdealer Heinrich Hinterberger. Most of the books in this collection were eventually bought by the New York State Psychiatric Institute and arrived in the United States in September 1939. Among these books was a copy of Breton's *Second manifeste du surréalisme* (Breton, 1930), which is now at Columbia University, and an uncut dedicated copy of Breton and Éluard's *L'immaculée conception* (Breton and Éluard, 1930), which is now held at the Library of Congress. The dedication on the title page of the latter volume reads: "*Exemplaire du Professeur Freud | notre véritable père | André Breton | Paul Éluard*". See Eissler (1979, p. 40).

7 For an illustrated guide to all the art objects Freud kept right in front of him on his desk, see Spankie (2015). For a different reading of Freud's final letters to Breton, see Rabaté (2014, pp. 96–98).

8 Between 1905 and 1925, the *Three Essays* went through six, sometimes extensively revised, editions, yet the quoted sentence was already included in the very first edition and remained unaltered throughout the book's life cycle.

9 The reader will find more detailed discussions of Freud's critique of Jentsch in Nobus (1993), Morlock (1997), Royle (2003, pp. 39–50) and Masschelein (2011).

10 For synthetic expositions of Kant's views on the sublime, see Crowther (1989), Crockett (2001, pp. 9–22), Clewis (2009, pp. 32–145), Doran (2015, pp. 171–285) and Shaw (2017, pp. 93–115).

11 Even though Otto's seminal volume on the holy was published in 1917, i.e. around the time Freud would have been considering the notion of the uncanny, he did not reference it, neither in the essay itself nor in any of his other published works. Cohn and Miles (1977, p. 301) indicated that Freud did use the word *Erhabene* in "The 'Uncanny'", yet this is factually incorrect. Whereas Strachey's English translation of the essay does refer to the sublime (Freud, 1955[1919*h*], p. 219), the original German text has the word *anziehenden*, which could have been more accurately rendered as "the attractive".

12 Other scholars who have since drawn attention to the convergence of the uncanny and the sublime include Lehmann (1989), Ellison (2001, pp. 52–84), González Moreno (2007) and Hertz (2009[1985], pp. 113–134).

13 "Inexplicable" is also the title of a short story by L. G. Moberly, to which Freud alluded in "The 'Uncanny'", without mentioning this title or its author (Freud, 1955[1919*h*], pp. 244–245; Moberly, 1917). In a terrific essay on the way in which Freud's paper on the uncanny was profoundly shaped by the turbulent times of World War I and its traumatic aftermath, John Zilcosky has claimed that Moberly's story has been almost completely neglected in the voluminous scholarship on "The 'Uncanny'" (Zilcosky, 2018, p. 172, note 20). However, back in 1992, I had already published a French translation of this story alongside a detailed critical commentary, which was followed the year after by a Dutch translation of both the story and the commentary. See Moberly (1992[1917], 1993[1917]) and Quackelbeen and Nobus (1992, 1993).

14 Restrictions of space will prevent me from doing justice to each and every aspect of Lacan's theory of sublimation. The secondary literature on the topic is extensive, yet readers wishing to investigate the matter further will benefit from Moyaert (1994), Crockett (2007, pp. 51–67), De Kesel (2009[2001], pp. 163–203, 2019), Porge (2018), Rath (2019, pp. 48–52, 141–152) and various essays in Adams (2003).

15 Curiously, Jacques-Alain Miller, the general editor of Lacan's seminars, has placed the final session of *Seminar VI* under the double heading of "Conclusion and Overture", and "Toward Sublimation" (Lacan, 2019[2013], pp. 469–471). Lacan's decision to devote no fewer than six sessions of his seminar on the ethics of psychoanalysis to a careful unpacking of the problem of sublimation may seem equally strange were it not for the fact that, in a strictly Freudian sense, sublimation already invokes the origin of "higher", moral systems of thought, i.e. Kant's famous "pure practical reason" (Kant, 1997[1788]). In addition, from the very start of his seminar, Lacan also made it clear that he would utilize the phrase "ethics of psychoanalysis" as a generic name for the aims and objectives, the goals and direction of the psychoanalytic treatment, to which sublimation has always been linked.

16 Hegel uses the noun *Aufhebung*, or the verb *aufheben*, in numerous passages of *The Phenomenology of Spirit* as well as in subsequent works, but one of his clearest definitions of it occurs in the second section of the first part of the *Phenomenology*, on consciousness: "The *sublation* [*Das Aufheben*] exhibits its truly doubled meaning, something which we already have seen in the negative; it is now a *negating* [*ein Negieren*] and at the same time a *preserving* [*ein Aufbewahren*]" (Hegel, 2018[1807], p. 69). It should also be noted that in Hegel's *Aesthetics*, instances of the sublime (*das Erhabene*) are consistently attributed to the dialectical movement of *Aufhebung*. See, for example, Hegel (1998[1835], pp. 362–365). In one of his annotations to Lacan's *Seminar XXIII*, Jacques-Alain Miller asserts that the "elevatory means of sublimation as an upward operation was often named by Lacan using the well-known Hegelian term *Aufhebung*", yet there is no solid evidence for this (Lacan, 2016[2005], p. 185).

17 The noun "sublation" and its various cognates were first introduced by the Scottish philosopher James Hutchison Stirling in his hugely influential 1865 volume *The Secret of Hegel* (Stirling, 1972[1865]).

18 Lacan extracted the notion of *das Ding* from Freud's posthumously published *Project for a Scientific Psychology* (Freud, 1966[1950*a*]), yet his theoretical explorations of it were also indebted to Heidegger's eponymous 1950 lecture on the topic (Heidegger, 1954[1950]). This lecture was included in the 1954 collection *Vorträge und Aufsätze* (Heidegger, 1954), from which Lacan had already translated the essay "Logos" for the first issue of "La psychanalyse"

(Heidegger, 1954[1951], 1956[1951]). Of course, Lacan's conception of the Thing also echoes Hegel's definition of the sublime: "The sublime in general is the attempt to express the infinite, without finding in the sphere of phenomena an object which proves adequate for this representation. Precisely because the infinite is set apart from the entire complex of objectivity as explicitly an invisible meaning devoid of shape and is made inner, it remains, in accordance with its infinity, unutterable and sublime above any expression through the finite" (Hegel, 1998[1835], p. 363).

19 "Use-value" must be understood here in the sense of functional or instrumental worth or as serving a practical purpose. Hence, I do not want to go so far as to suggest that art is inherently devoid of uses and effects, yet these artistic powers need to be considered outside the sphere of concrete functionalism, in terms of the transmission or the deconstruction of meaning. For an excellent discussion of the semantic usage of (symbolist) art and its relation to counter-empiricist movements in mathematics and logic, see Pop (2019).

20 Freud never provided a satisfactory answer to the question concerning the difference between sublimation and repression, unless he resolved the issue in one of his lost metapsychological essays. One possible solution to the problem might proceed from a differential appreciation of the outcome. For whenever Freud referred to the result of a process of sublimation, he mentioned intellectual work and works of art, reserving the term "symptom" for more clinically based phenomena such as obsessional ideas, bodily ailments, etc. Yet it seems rather gratuitous to use the status of the outcome as a criterion for assessing and differentiating between the nature of the mechanisms responsible for it. Furthermore, there is no good reason to believe that all intellectual work is by definition non-symptomatic, never driven by an "obsessive" structure, or never reducing the quality of life. Alternatively, were we to add "social value" to the distinction, and say that the products of sublimation are always socially valued whereas those stemming from repression are not, we may run the risk of employing an arbitrary ideological criterion for separating between two distinct psychic mechanisms.

21 The italics appear in Strachey's translation, but do not feature in the original text.

22 Throughout his text, Freud was at great pains to point out that the opposite of play is not "seriousness", because the child takes its play very seriously, but rather "reality", because a child knows how to distinguish between play and reality, and takes the templates for its play from reality.

23 When read in conjunction with the last paragraph of Lecture 23, Freud's text clearly offers additional insights into the origins of the creative process (and, as can be inferred from Lecture 23, Freud later extended his ideas to the artist in general), yet it also seems to contain two major inconsistencies. First, if creative writers derive their material from the activity of their daydreams, why is it, then, that, as Freud himself stated at the beginning of his paper, "the writer himself gives us no explanation, or none that is satisfactory" (Freud, 1959[1908e], p. 143). Second, if the novel's protagonist is modelled after the writer's ego, and this can be justified by virtue of those writers Freud described as "the less pretentious authors of novels, romances and short stories, who nevertheless have the widest and most eager circle of readers of both sexes" (Ibid., p. 149), it seems exceptionally difficult to understand how this aspect of "mimesis" could possibly operate outside the realm of literature – in abstract art and non-representative idioms, such as music. Perhaps these inconsistencies could be

146   Dany Nobus

alleviated by minimizing the impact of conscious daydreams and emphasizing the significance of the formal structure of the fantasy, which not only operates at the level of the unconscious (and thus requires reconstruction, owing to its inaccessibility to consciousness) but which is also quite far removed from direct representations of the fantasizing individual's ego, as Freud demonstrated in "A Child is Being Beaten" (Freud, 1955[1919e]). However, neither in "Creative Writers and Day-Dreaming' nor elsewhere did Freud consider this option.

24 It remains an open question whether this fantasy ought to be reserved for the subject of the artist, or might also be extended to the subject who reads, looks at, or listens to works of art. In addition, when Lacan referred to the traversal (*la traversée*) of the fantasy, what he had in mind was not a reduction, let alone an abolition of the fantasy, but rather a subjective (criss-)crossing of the fantasy, leading to its acquiring more versatile, less petrified characteristics.

25 In "The Subversion of the Subject and the Dialectic of Desire", Lacan defined S(Ⱥ) as "a line that is drawn from its circle without being able to be counted in it. This can be symbolized by the inherence of a (-1) in the set of signifiers. It is, as such, unpronounceable" (Lacan, 2006[1960], p. 694). The difficulty of rendering S(Ⱥ), much like "the Thing", in a meaningful way expresses precisely what the term itself is meant to convey. S(Ⱥ) epitomizes the symbolic representation (S) of a lack in the symbolic order (A); it constitutes, by way of an algebraic notation, the signifier (or better, the trait) for what does not exist as a complete entity, for the place where the Other reaches its limit, for the point where the power of the Other ends. In other words, S(Ⱥ) represents the unrepresentable and accounts for the epistemic point where knowledge meets (and newly becomes) ignorance. This clearly resonates with Hegel's definition of the sublime as "the attempt to express the infinite, without finding in the sphere of phenomena an object which proves adequate for this representation" (Hegel, 1998[1835], p. 362). For a more detailed discussion of how S(Ⱥ) plays out in the analytic discourse and the endgame of psychoanalysis, see Nobus (2017). I have also extended the argument of painting as a labour of creative destruction, in the context of a reconsideration of the artistic practice of Francis Bacon (Nobus, 2019).

References

Adams, P. (Ed.) (2003). *Art: Sublimation or Symptom*. London and New York: Karnac Books.

Alexandrian, S. (1974). *Le surréalisme et le rêve*. Paris: Gallimard.

Armstrong, R.H. (2005). *A Compulsion for Antiquity: Freud and the Ancient World*. Ithaca, NY and London: Cornell University Press.

Bernfeld, S. (1922). Bemerkungen über "Sublimierung". *Imago: Zeitschrift für die Anwendung der Psychoanalyse auf die Geisteswissenschaften*, 8(3): 333–344.

Bloom, H. (1982). Freud and the Sublime: A Catastrophe Theory of Creativity. In *Agon: Towards a Theory of Revisionism* (pp. 91–118). Oxford: Oxford University Press.

Boileau, N. (1965[1674]). Preface to his Translation of Longinus on the Sublime. In E. Dilworth (Ed. and Trans.), *Selected Criticism* (pp. 43–52). Indianapolis, IN: Irvington.

Bonnet, M. (1992). La rencontre d'André Breton avec la folie: Saint-Dizier, août-novembre 1916. In F. Hulak (Ed.), *Folie et psychanalyse dans l'expérience surréaliste* (pp. 115–135). Nice: Z'éditions.

Breton, A. (1930). *Second manifeste du surréalisme*. Paris: Kra.

Breton, A. (1990[1922]). Interview du Professeur Freud. In *Les pas perdus* (pp. 94–95). Paris: Gallimard.

Breton, A. (1997[1932]). *Communicating Vessels*, Trans. M.A. Caws and G.T. Harris. Lincoln, NE and London: University of Nebraska Press.

Breton, A. and Éluard, P. (1930). *L'immaculée conception*. Paris: Éditions surréalistes.

Breuer, J. and Freud, S. (1955[1895d]). Studies on Hysteria. In J. Strachey (Ed.), *The Standard Edition of the Complete Psychological Works of Sigmund Freud*, vol. 2. London: The Hogarth Press and the Institute of Psycho-Analysis.

Burke, E. (2015[1757]). *A Philosophical Enquiry into the Sublime and the Beautiful*. Oxford: Oxford University Press.

Burke, J. (2006). *The Sphinx on the Table: Sigmund Freud's Art Collection and the Development of Psychoanalysis*. New York: Walker & Company.

Chasseguet-Smirgel, J. (1985). *Creativity and Perversion*. New York: W. W. Norton & Company.

Clewis, R.R. (2009). *The Kantian Sublime and the Revelation of Freedom*. Cambridge: Cambridge University Press.

Cohn, J. and Miles, T.H. (1977). The Sublime: In Alchemy, Aesthetics and Psychoanalysis. *Modern Philology*, 74(3): 289–304.

Crockett, C. (2001). *A Theology of the Sublime*. London and New York: Routledge.

Crockett, C. (2007). *Interstices of the Sublime: Theology and Psychoanalytic Theory*. New York: Fordham University Press.

Crowther, P. (1989). *The Kantian Sublime: From Morality to Art*. Oxford and New York: Oxford University Press.

Davis, F. (1973). Three Letters from Sigmund Freud to André Breton. *Journal of the American Psychoanalytic Association*, 21(1): 127–134.

De Kesel, M. (2009[2001]). *Eros and Ethics: Reading Jacques Lacan's Seminar VII*, Trans. S. Jöttkandt. Albany, NY: State University of New York Press.

De Kesel, M. (2019). Sublimatie en perversie. Hoe psychoanalyse onze moderne ethiek heroriënteert. In *Het Münchhausen Paradigma. Waarom Freud en Lacan ertoe doen* (pp. 83–100). Nijmegen: Vantilt.

de Mijolla-Mellor, S. (Ed.) (2012). *Traité de la sublimation*. Paris: Presses Universitaires de France.

Deri, F. (1939). On Sublimation. *The Psychoanalytic Quarterly*, 8(3): 325–334.

Derrida, J. (1981[1970]). The Double Session. In B. Johnson (Trans.), *Dissemination* (pp. 187–316). Chicago and London: The University of Chicago Press.

Doran, R. (2015). *The Theory of the Sublime: From Longinus to Kant*. Cambridge: Cambridge University Press.

Edmundson, M. (2007). *The Death of Sigmund Freud: Fascism, Psychoanalysis and the Rise of Fundamentalism*. London: Bloomsbury.

Eissler, K.R. (1979). Bericht über die sich in den Vereinigten Staaten befindenden Bücher aus S. Freuds Bibliothek. *Jahrbuch der Psychoanalyse: Beiträge zur Theorie und Praxis*, 11: 10–50.

Ellison, D. (2001). *Ethics and Aesthetics in European Modernist Literature: From the Sublime to the Uncanny*. Cambridge: Cambridge University Press.

Ellmann, R. (1983). *James Joyce* (New and Revised ed.). Oxford and New York: Oxford University Press.

Esman, A.H. (2011). Psychoanalysis and Surrealism: André Breton and Sigmund Freud. *Journal of the American Psychoanalytic Association*, 59(1): 173–181.

Flournoy, O. (1967). La sublimation. *Revue française de psychanalyse*, 31(1): 59–93.

148   Dany Nobus

Freud, S. (1953[1900a]). The Interpretation of Dreams. In J. Strachey (Ed.), *The Standard Edition of the Complete Psychological Works of Sigmund Freud*, vols. 4/5. London: The Hogarth Press and the Institute of Psycho-Analysis.

Freud, S. (1953[1905d]). Three Essays on the Theory of Sexuality. In J. Strachey (Ed.), *The Standard Edition of the Complete Psychological Works of Sigmund Freud*, vol. 7 (pp. 123–243). London: The Hogarth Press and the Institute of Psycho-Analysis.

Freud, S. (1955[1919e]). 'A Child Is Being Beaten': A Contribution to the Study of the Origin of Sexual Perversions. In J. Strachey (Ed.), *The Standard Edition of the Complete Psychological Works of Sigmund Freud*, vol. 17 (pp. 175–204). London: The Hogarth Press and the Institute of Psycho-Analysis.

Freud, S. (1955[1919h]). The 'Uncanny'. In J. Strachey (Ed.), *The Standard Edition of the Complete Psychological Works of Sigmund Freud*, vol. 17 (pp. 217–256). London: The Hogarth Press and the Institute of Psycho-Analysis.

Freud, S. (1955[1921c]). Group Psychology and the Analysis of the Ego. In J. Strachey (Ed.), *The Standard Edition of the Complete Psychological Works of Sigmund Freud*, vol. 18 (pp. 65–143). London: The Hogarth Press and the Institute of Psycho-Analysis.

Freud, S. (1955[1923a]). Two Encyclopaedia Articles. In J. Strachey (Ed.), *The Standard Edition of the Complete Psychological Works of Sigmund Freud*, vol. 18 (pp. 233–259). London: The Hogarth Press and the Institute of Psycho-Analysis.

Freud, S. (1957[1910a]). Five Lectures on Psycho-Analysis. In J. Strachey (Ed.), *The Standard Edition of the Complete Psychological Works of Sigmund Freud*, vol. 11 (pp. 7–55). London: The Hogarth Press and the Institute of Psycho-Analysis.

Freud, S. (1958[1914g]). Remembering, Repeating and Working-Through (Further Recommendations on the Technique of Psycho-Analysis II). In J. Strachey (Ed.), *The Standard Edition of the Complete Psychological Works of Sigmund Freud*, vol. 12 (pp. 145–156). London: The Hogarth Press and the Institute of Psycho-Analysis.

Freud, S. (1959[1908e]). Creative Writers and Day-Dreaming. In J. Strachey (Ed.), *The Standard Edition of the Complete Psychological Works of Sigmund Freud*, vol. 9 (pp. 141–153). London: The Hogarth Press and the Institute of Psycho-Analysis.

Freud, S. (1960[1933c]). Sándor Ferenczi. In J. Strachey (Ed.), *The Standard Edition of the Complete Psychological Works of Sigmund Freud*, vol. 22 (pp. 225–229). London: The Hogarth Press and the Institute of Psycho-Analysis.

Freud, S. (1963[1916–'17]). Introductory Lectures on Psycho-Analysis. In J. Strachey (Ed.), *The Standard Edition of the Complete Psychological Works of Sigmund Freud*, vols. 15/16. London: The Hogarth Press and the Institute of Psycho-Analysis.

Freud, S. (1964[1930a]). Civilization and its Discontents. In J. Strachey (Ed.), *The Standard Edition of the Complete Psychological Works of Sigmund Freud*, vol. 21 (pp. 57–145). London: The Hogarth Press and the Institute of Psycho-Analysis.

Freud, S. (1964[1937c]). Analysis Terminable and Interminable. In J. Strachey (Ed.), *The Standard Edition of the Complete Psychological Works of Sigmund Freud*, vol. 23 (pp. 209–253). London: The Hogarth Press and the Institute of Psycho-Analysis.

Freud, S. (1964[1940a]). An Outline of Psycho-Analysis. In J. Strachey (Ed.), *The Standard Edition of the Complete Psychological Works of Sigmund Freud*, vol. 23 (pp. 139–207). London: The Hogarth Press and the Institute of Psycho-Analysis.

Freud, S. (1966[1950a]). Project for a Scientific Psychology. In J. Strachey (Ed.), *The Standard Edition of the Complete Psychological Works of Sigmund Freud*, vol. 1 (pp. 281–397). London: The Hogarth Press and the Institute of Psycho-Analysis.

Gamwell, L. and Wells, R. (Eds.) (1989). *Sigmund Freud and Art: His Personal Collection of Antiquities*. New York: Abrams.

Gasser, R. (1997). *Nietzsche und Freud*. Berlin and New York: Walter de Gruyter.

Gay, V.P. (1992). *Freud on Sublimation: Reconsiderations*. Albany, NY: State University of New York Press.

Gemes, K. (2009). Freud and Nietzsche on Sublimation. *Journal of Nietzsche Studies*, 38(1): 38–59.

Glover, E. (1931). Sublimation, Substitution and Social Anxiety. *The International Journal of Psycho-Analysis*, 12(3): 263–297.

Goebel, E. (2012[2009]). *Beyond Discontent: "Sublimation" from Goethe to Lacan*, Trans. J. C. Wagner. London: Continuum.

González Moreno, B. (2007). *Lo sublime, lo gótico y lo romántico: La experiencia estética en el romanticismo inglés*. Cuenca: Ediciones de la Universidad de Castilla-La Mancha.

Grubrich-Simitis, I. (Ed.) (1987). *Sigmund Freud. A Phylogenetic Fantasy: Overview of the Transference Neuroses*, Trans. A. Hoffer and P.T. Hoffer. Cambridge and London: The Belknap Press of Harvard University Press.

Hegel, G.W.F. (1998[1835]). Symbolism of the Sublime. In *Aesthetics: Lectures on Fine Art*, vol. 1, Trans. T. M. Knox (pp. 362–377). Oxford: Clarendon Press.

Hegel, G.W.F. (2018[1807]). *The Phenomenology of Spirit*, Trans. T. Pinkard. Cambridge: Cambridge University Press.

Heidegger, M. (1954). *Vorträge und Aufsätze*. Pfullingen: Günther Neske.

Heidegger, M. (1954[1950]). Das Ding. In *Vorträge und Aufsätze* (pp. 163–181). Pfullingen: Günther Neske.

Heidegger, M. (1954[1951]). Logos. In *Vorträge und Aufsätze* (pp. 207–229). Pfullingen: Günther Neske.

Heidegger, M. (1956[1951]). Logos. J. Lacan (Trans.). *La psychanalyse*, 1: 59–79.

Hertz, N. (2009[1985]). *The End of the Line: Essays on Psychoanalysis and the Sublime* (2nd expanded ed.). Aurora, CO: The Davies Group Publishers.

Jentsch, E. (1997[1906]). On the Psychology of the Uncanny. R. Sellars (Trans.). *Angelaki: Journal of the Theoretical Humanities*, 2(1): 7–16.

Jones, E. (1957). *The Life and Work of Sigmund Freud. Vol. 3: The Last Phase (1919–1939)*. New York: Basic Books.

Joyce, J. (1939). *Finnegans Wake*. London: Faber & Faber.

Jung, C.G. (1970[1963]). Mysterium Coniunctionis: An Inquiry into the Separation and Synthesis of Psychic Opposites in Alchemy. In G. Adler and R.F.C. Hull (Trans.), *The Collected Works of C. G. Jung*, vol. 14. Princeton, NJ: Princeton University Press.

Kant, I. (1997[1788]). *Critique of Practical Reason*, Trans. M. Gregor. Cambridge: Cambridge University Press.

Kant, I. (2002[1793]). *Critique of the Power of Judgment*, Ed. P. Guyer, Trans. P. Guyer and E. Matthews. Cambridge: Cambridge University Press.

Kant, I. (2011[1764]). *Observations on the Feeling of the Beautiful and Sublime*, Trans. P. Guyer. In P. Frierson and P. Guyer (Eds.), *Observations on the Feeling of the Beautiful and Sublime and Other Writings* (pp. 9–62). Cambridge: Cambridge University Press.

Kaufmann, W. (2013[1950]). *Nietzsche: Philosopher, Psychologist, Antichrist*. Princeton, NJ and Oxford: Princeton University Press.

Lacan, J. (1992[1986]). *The Seminar. Book VII: The Ethics of Psychoanalysis (1959-'60)*, Ed. J.-A. Miller, Trans. D. Porter. London and New York: W. W. Norton & Company.

Lacan, J. (1994[1973]). *The Seminar. Book XI: The Four Fundamental Concepts of Psychoanalysis (1964)*, Ed. J.-A. Miller, Trans. A. Sheridan. Harmondsworth: Penguin.

Lacan, J. (2001[1970]). Radiophonie. In *Autres Écrits* (pp. 404–447). Paris: du Seuil.

Lacan, J. (2006). *Le Séminaire. Livre XVIII: D'un discours qui ne serait pas du semblant (1971)*, Ed. J.-A. Miller. Paris: du Seuil.

Lacan, J. (2006[1960]). The Subversion of the Subject and the Dialectic of Desire in the Freudian Unconscious. In B. Fink (Trans.), *Écrits* (pp. 671–702). London and New York: W. W. Norton & Company.

Lacan, J. (2006[1962]). Kant with Sade. In B. Fink (Trans.), *Écrits* (pp. 645–668). London and New York: W. W. Norton & Company.

Lacan, J. (2013[1971]). Lituraterre. D. Nobus (Trans.). *Continental Philosophy Review*, 46(2): 327–334.

Lacan, J. (2014[2004]). *The Seminar. Book X: Anxiety (1962-'63)*, Ed. J.-A. Miller, Trans. A. R. Price. Cambridge and Malden, MA: Polity Press.

Lacan, J. (2015[2001]). *The Seminar. Book VIII: Transference (1960-'61)*, Ed. J.-A. Miller, Trans. B. Fink. Cambridge and Malden, MA: Polity Press.

Lacan, J. (2016[2005]). *The Seminar. Book XXIII: The Sinthome (1975-'76)*, Ed. J.-A. Miller, Trans. A. R. Price. Cambridge and Malden, MA: Polity Press.

Lacan, J. (2019[2013]). *The Seminar. Book VI: Desire and Its Interpretation (1958-'59)*, Ed. J.-A. Miller, Trans. B. Fink. Cambridge and Medford, MA: Polity Press.

Laplanche, J. (1980). *Problématiques III. La sublimation*. Paris: Presses Universitaires de France.

Laplanche, J. and Pontalis, J.-B. (1973[1967]). *The Language of Psychoanalysis*, Trans. D. Nicholson-Smith. London and New York: W. W. Norton & Company.

Lehmann, H.-T. (1989). Das Erhabene ist das Unheimliche. Zur Theorie einer Kunst des Ereignisses. *Merkur: Deutsche Zeitschrift für europäisches Denken*, 43(487): 751–764.

Lehrer, R. (1995). *Nietzsche's Presence in Freud's Life and Thought: On the Origins of a Psychology of Dynamic Unconscious Mental Functioning*. Albany, NY: State University of New York Press.

Levey, H.B. (1939). A Critique of the Theory of Sublimation. *Psychiatry: Journal for the Study of Interpersonal Processes*, 2(2): 239–270.

Lomas, D. (2000). *The Haunted Self: Surrealism, Psychoanalysis, Subjectivity*. New Haven, CT and London: Yale University Press.

Longinus (1995). On the Sublime. In W.H. Fyfe and D. Russell (Trans.), *Aristotle/Poetics, Longinus/On the Sublime, and Demetrius/On Style* (pp. 159–305). Cambridge: Harvard University Press.

Masschelein, A. (2011). *The Unconcept: The Freudian Uncanny in Late Twentieth-Century Theory*. Albany, NY: State University of New York Press.

McDougall, J. (1995). *The Many Faces of Eros: A Psychoanalytic Exploration of Human Sexuality*. London: Free Association Books.

McGuire, W. (Ed.) (1974). *The Correspondence between Sigmund Freud and C. G. Jung*, Trans. R. Manheim and R.F.C. Hull. Princeton and London: Princeton University Press.

Mendelssohn, M. (1997[1761]). On the Sublime and Naive in the Fine Sciences. In D.O. Dahlstrom (Ed. and Trans.), *Philosophical Writings* (pp. 192–232). Cambridge: Cambridge University Press.

Moberly, L.G. (1917). Inexplicable. *The Strand Magazine: An Illustrated Monthly*, 54(324): 572–581.

Moberly, L.G. (1992[1917]). Inexplicable. J. Quackelbeen and D. Nobus (Trans.). *Quarto*, 48/49: 88–95.

Moberly, L.G. (1993[1917]). Onverklaarbaar. D. Nobus and J. Quackelbeen (Trans.). *Psychoanalytische Perspektieven*, 19/20: 43–53.

Morlock, F. (1997). Doubly Uncanny: An Introduction to "On the Psychology of the Uncanny". *Angelaki: Journal of the Theoretical Humanities*, 2(1): 17–21.

Moyaert, P. (1994). *Ethiek en sublimatie. Over* De ethiek van de psychoanalyse *van Jacques Lacan*. Nijmegen: SUN.

Nietzsche, F. (1996[1878]). *Human, All Too Human: A Book For Free Spirits*, Trans. R. J. Hollingdale. Cambridge: Cambridge University Press.

Nietzsche, F. (1997[1881]). *Daybreak: Thoughts on the Prejudices of Morality*, Eds. M. Clark and B. Leiter, Trans. R. J. Hollingdale. Cambridge: Cambridge University Press.

Nietzsche, F. (1998[1887]). *On the Genealogy of Morals*, Trans. D. Smith. Oxford: Oxford University Press.

Nietzsche, F. (2002[1886]). *Beyond Good and Evil*, Eds. R.-P. Horstmann and J. Norman, Trans. J. Norman. Cambridge: Cambridge University Press.

Nobus, D. (1993). Freud versus Jentsch: Een kruistocht tegen de intellectuele onzekerheid. *Psychoanalytische Perspektieven*, 19/20: 55–65.

Nobus, D. (2017). En rencontrant le gai savoir: La fin de l'analyse comme l'analyse de la fin. *Psychoanalytische Perspectieven*, 35(3): 251–259.

Nobus, D. (2019). From Sense to Sensation: Bacon, Pasting Paint and the Futility of Lacanian Psychoanalysis. In B. Ware (Ed.), *Francis Bacon: Painting, Philosophy, Psychoanalysis* (pp. 95–116). London: Thames & Hudson.

Otto, R. (1958[1917]). *The Idea of the Holy: An Inquiry into the Non-rational Factor in the Idea of the Divine and its Relation to the Rational*, Trans. J. W. Harvey. Oxford: Oxford University Press.

Paskauskas, R.A. (Ed.) (1993). *The Complete Correspondence of Sigmund Freud and Ernest Jones 1908–1939*. Cambridge and London: The Belknap Press of Harvard University Press.

Polizzotti, M. (2009). *Revolution of the Mind: The Life of André Breton* (Revised and updated ed.). Boston: Black Widow Press.

Pop, A. (2019). *A Forest of Symbols: Art, Science, and Truth in the Long Nineteenth Century*. New York: Zone Books.

Porge, É. (2018). *La sublimation, une érotique pour la psychanalyse*. Toulouse: Érès.

Prawer, S.S. (1963). Reflections on the Numinous and the Uncanny in German Poetry. In A. Closs (Ed.), *Reality and Creative Vision in German Lyrical Poetry* (pp. 153–173). London: Butterworths.

Quackelbeen, J. and Nobus, D. (1992). Á propos de l'élucidation d'une référence freudienne: l'Inexplicable de L.G. Moberly. *Quarto*, 48/49: 83–87.

Quackelbeen, J. and Nobus, D. (1993). Over een opgehelderde referentie bij Freud. Het "Inexplicable" van L.G. Moberly. *Psychoanalytische Perspektieven*, 19/20: 35–42.

Rabaté, J.-M. (2014). *The Cambridge Introduction to Literature and Psychoanalysis*. Cambridge: Cambridge University Press.

Rath, C.-D. (2019). *Sublimierung und Gewalt. Elemente einer Psychoanalyse der aktuellen Gesellschaft*. Gießen: Psychosozial-Verlag.

Rauchfleisch, U. (1990). Psychoanalytische Betrachtungen zur musikalischen Kreativität. *Psyche: Zeitschrift für Psychoanalyse*, 44(12): 1113–1140.

Rémy, A.-R. (1991). *Beau comme la rencontre fortuite . . . entre Breton et Freud: La psychiatrie et la psychanalyse dans l'œuvre d'André Breton.* Thèse de médecine. Université Louis Pasteur – Strasbourg.

Royle, N. (2003). *The Uncanny.* Manchester: Manchester University Press.

Russo (Ed.) (1987). *Da Longino a Longino. I luoghi del Sublime.* Palermo: Aesthetica Edizioni.

Saint Girons, B. (1993). *Fiat Lux. Une philosophie du sublime.* Paris: Quai Voltaire.

Saint Girons, B. (2005). *Le Sublime. De l'antiquité à nos jours.* Paris: Desjonquères.

Scheidhauer, M. (2010). *Freud et ses visiteurs Français et Suisses francophones (1920–1930).* Strasbourg: Arcanes.

Schiller, F. (1998[1793]). On the Sublime. In W. Hinderer and D.O. Dahlstrom (Eds.), D.O. Dahlstrom (Trans.), *Essays* (pp. 22–44). London: Continuum.

Schopenhauer, A. (2017[1851]). On Ethics. In A. Del Caro and C. Janaway (Ed. and Trans.), *Parerga and Paralipomena: Short Philosophical Essays,* vol. 2 (pp. 183–216). Cambridge: Cambridge University Press.

Schumpeter, J.A. (1976[1942]). *Capitalism, Socialism and Democracy.* London: Routledge.

Schur, M. (1972). *Freud: Living and Dying.* London: The Hogarth Press.

Shaw, Ph. (2017). *The Sublime.* London and New York: Routledge.

Silvain, M. (1732). *Traité du sublime.* Paris: Pierre Prault.

Slonimsky, N. (Ed.) (1984). *Baker's Biographical Dictionary of Musicians* (7th ed.). New York: Collier MacMillan.

Spankie, R. (2015). *Sigmund Freud's Desk: An Anecdoted Guide.* London: Freud Museum London.

Spector, J.J. (1972). *The Aesthetics of Freud: A Study in Psychoanalysis and Art.* London: Allen Lane.

Sterba, R. (1930). Zur Problematik der Sublimierungslehre. *Internationale Zeitschrift für Psychoanalyse,* 16(3/4): 370–377.

Stirling, J.H. (1972[1865]). *The Secret of Hegel: Being the Hegelian System in Origin, Principle, Form and Matter.* Dubuque, IA: William C. Brown.

Strachey, J. (1957). Papers on Metapsychology: Editor's Introduction. In J. Strachey (Ed.). *The Standard Edition of the Complete Psychological Works of Sigmund Freud,* Vol. 14. (pp. 105–107). London: The Hogarth Press and the Institute of Psycho-Analysis.

Vailland, R. (2008[1957]). *The Law,* Trans. P. Wiles. London: Eland Books.

Vergote, A. (1997). *La psychanalyse à l'épreuve de la sublimation.* Paris: du Cerf.

Widmaier-Haag, S. (1999). *Es War das Lächeln des Narziß: Die Theorien der Psychoanalyse im Spiegel literatur-psychologischen Interpretationen des 'Tod in Venedig'.* Würzburg: Königshausen & Neumann.

Zalkind, A.B. (2001[1929]). ПОЛОВОЕ ВОСПИТАНИЕ ЮНЫХ ПИОНЕРОВ, in Педология: *Утопия и реальность* (pp. 345–362). Moscow: Agraf.

Zilcosky, J. (2018). "The Times in Which We Live": Freud's *The Uncanny,* World War I, and the Trauma of Contagion. *Psychoanalysis and History,* 20(2): 165–190.

NINE

A crumpled note or purloined letter? Sublime and feminine creativity in destruction in Jung and Lacan[1]

Susan Rowland

By looking at C.G. Jung and Jacques Lacan's treatment of two literary texts, I propose that each figures a sublime and feminine creativity in destruction that is comparable, perhaps even equivalent, and yet not quite the same. Taking a lead from Philip Shaw's invaluable study of the sublime in which he defines it as the failure of the mind or language to know or to express something that may or may not exist beyond both mind and language (Shaw, 2006, p. 3), I will show that both psychologists offer a feminine sublime of contiguity that arises in relation to a sublime in the destruction of transcendence. Here "contiguity" is taken from Lacan's depiction of what he calls *jouissance*, a feminine desire not denied to men yet significantly not organized around the phallus (Lacan, 1982, p. 97). *Jouissance* can be sublime when its playfulness in language evokes possibilities beyond the capacity of representation.

> Which is why Dupin will at last turn toward us the medusoid face of the signifier.
>
> *(Lacan, 1988, p. 52)*

> But it is only modern man who has succeeded in creating an art in reverse, a backside of art.
>
> *(Jung, 1932, para. 178)*

> Even so it is creative – a creative destruction.
>
> *(Ibid.: para. 180)*

This chapter focuses on creativity in destruction in Lacan's "Seminar on the Purloined Letter," and Jung's "*Ulysses:* A Monologue" (Lacan, 1988; Jung, 1932). In the former, the misplaced letter comes to materialize the monstrous power of the signifier as "medusoid," having the capacity of the

154   Susan Rowland

angry divinity to turn to stone all who gaze on her (Lacan, 1988, p. 52). For the latter, "a crumpled note" represents the destruction of cultural and psychological structures by a monstrous non-human creature that destroys being (Jung, 1932, para. 190). Out of such devastation both psychologists discern a sublime feminine creativity; although only Jung posits the cooperative contiguity of non-human nature.

Destruction in Lacan's "Seminar on 'The Purloined Letter'"

> If what Freud discovered has a meaning, it is that the displacement of the signifier determines the subjects in their acts, in their destiny . . . and in their fate . . . without regard for character or sex.
>
> *(Lacan, 1988, pp. 43–44)*

> [T]he signifier . . . materializes the agency of death.
>
> *(Ibid.: 38)*

Lacan takes Freud's notion of Oedipal splitting and applies it to the psyche's relation to language, which structures being within its symbolic order of the Law and is haunted by loss. Here words are signifiers as Lacan says, "a unit in its very uniqueness, being by nature symbol only of an absence" (Lacan, 1988, p. 39). What is so fascinating to Lacan in Poe's story of a letter purloined by an opportunist minister from royal apartments, is that it is an instrument of supreme power only while being unknown and unread. So to Lacan, the letter makes visible all that is overwhelming, and at the same time empty, in the potency of the signifier.

Lacan decides early in his essay that the feminine addressee of the letter must be the Queen who is unable to thwart the minister due to the presence of her husband, the King. Poe's story actually begins with detective Dupin at home with an unnamed narrator when both are visited by a near-desperate Prefect of Police. The official forces of the law have been unable to find the Queen's purloined letter in the home of the minister, despite pursuing fantastically detailed searches.

Of course during his second visit, the Prefect will be astonished when Dupin hands over the letter in return for a very large cheque. With many diversions, Dupin then explains how he was able to spot the letter in plain view. It was disguised as a trivial note to the minister.

Lacan's attribution of sovereignty to the bereft woman enables him to stabilize the role of the letter. It is potentially disruptive to the symbolic order in which the King ought to incarnate the Law. As Queen hiding her letter from the King, she is disloyal (Lacan: 42).

Lacan details how glancing knowingly and unknowingly at the letter, and then possessing or not possessing it, shifts gender roles. The minster, so bold as to seize what is not his, is subsequently feminized by being forced into the "Queen's" role of concealing the letter in full view. And astonishingly, the letter comes to stand for the full and empty effects of the signifier as the forever absent lost body of the mother.

> Just so does the purloined letter, like an immense female body, stretch out across the minister's office when Dupin enters.
>
> *(Ibid.: 48)*

The office is not the immense female body, the letter is. So the letter is an immense woman's body because woman is the sign of castration. So if language is so castrating, so immanent in its severing of being, is it an organ of the sublime within the very structuring of consciousness?

Lacan's sublime

Lacan certainly offers a sense of the sublime in his notion of the Real, which is the unpresentable "Thing" that has to be posited for the symbolic order to do its job of (illusory) ordering (Bowie, 1991, pp. 94–95). The Real is only apparent when the symbolic order is ruptured. Arguably Lacan traces the presence of the Real in his description of the signifier as "medusoid," referring to the feminine monster with snakes for hair who turns to stone all who look on her. He says that Dupin enacts this Medusa signifier in the quotation he leaves for the minister to find in place of the purloined letter. The quotation refers to a father forced to drink the blood of his son, the revenge of his brother (Lacan: 52).

The signifier is both the protection from, and the hapless partner of, such terrifying and subject-annihilating sublime. The letter here stands for all signifiers in its ability to mutate gender, shatter the psyche and engender death, "the return of the stone guest I shall be for you" (Lacan: 52). And yet gender and the sublime for Lacan are more ambivalent than might at first appear.

Critic Malcolm Bowie points out an ambiguity in Lacan's writing between his masculinist discourse by which the phallus becomes a transcendental signifier of desire (so suggesting a transcendent sublime). Such a proposition does not fully allow for his two emphases in the structuring of desire itself (Bowie, 1991, pp. 141–142). For along with the phallocentrism, there is his insistence on the neutrality of the subject divided by language, together with the genderless potential of desire in the impossibility of need and demand in the psyche (Ibid.). Given that here the "letter" takes the "phallic" role in assigning gender *as a role*, only to be revealed as like the monstrous feminine Medusa, this seminar additionally indicates another kind of gendering altogether.

Jouissance *and the seminar on the purloined letter*

In questing for origins of desire, Lacan offers what he calls *jouissance* as the energy of feminine sexuality. Importantly this playful energy is not denied to men, yet is to be understood as different from the desire organized around the phallus.

156   Susan Rowland

> Far from its being the case, indeed, that the passivity of the
> act corresponds to this desire, feminine sexuality appears as
> the effort of a *jouissance* wrapped in its own contiguity . . .
> to be *realized in rivalry* with the desire which castration
> releases in the male by giving him its signifier in the phallus.
> *(Lacan, 1982, p. 97)*

Desire is here a fundamental human energy that remains caught up in the
subject's division by language. So *jouissance* is a pleasure in thinking, writing, being-in-language in which there is a kind of release from fixed meanings, finding an enjoyment in playful signifying energy. It is, arguably, a
feminine sublime of contiguity.

> *Jouissance* of the kind Lacan chooses to call feminine is to
> be found in the sinews, in thinking, in writing – wherever
> *significance*, the combined production of meaning and plea-
> sure, occurs. Enjoying oneself and not knowing anything
> about it is "feminine" in a way, but this does not mean that
> men are debarred by their gender from reaching such states.
> *(Bowie, 1991, p. 153)*

I suggest that this feminine *jouissance* of rhetorical play is to be found in
two modes in Lacan's essay on "The Purloined Letter." It is hinted at in his
depiction of the Queen while being superbly displayed by Lacan himself in
the position he takes towards knowing as explored by Jane Gallop later in
the volume *The Purloined Poe* (Gallop, 1985).

Before looking further at Lacan's *jouissance* in his essay on "The Purloined
Letter," it is worth noting that he also depicts desire as more than human,
as animal. The minister needs a "lynx eye" to see through the Queen's play
acting (Lacan, 1988, p. 30). Later, driven by the signifier, he is "a beast of
prey ready to spring" (Ibid.: 48).

Lacan suggests that the non-human is collaborator with the "medusoid"
signifier is making a person simply a vehicle for its annihilating power. But
what if nature was actually considered to be contiguous in a sense of having patterns and powers of its own that in certain circumstances could collaborate creatively or playfully with the human? What if non-human nature
was a partner in *jouissance*? Then one would find a feminine sublime like
women writers in Romanticism, according to critic Ann Mellor, quoted by
Shaw on the sublime. They found in nature a co-creative partner in desire
and pleasure in signifying without mastery:

> [The sublime is] an ecstatic experience of co-participation
> in nature . . . explicitly gender[ed] as female. For [these
> woman writers] this female nature is not an overwhelming
> power; nor even an all bountiful mother. Instead nature is
> a female friend.
> *(Mellor, in Shaw, 2006, p. 109)*

Sublime and Feminine creativity in destruction   157

It is time to return to Gallop's diagnosis of Lacan as masquerading or simulating, like his Queen, in his essay on "The Purloined Letter." While the Queen's impersonation of mastery is short-lived because castrated by the stealing of the letter (which reveals her as already castrated), Lacan himself plays at mastery of signifying throughout his text.

> Lacan plays a certain imaginary of the analyst to the hilt; he plays "the subject presumed to know," the great oracle, interpreter of enigmas. To fall for the illusion of Lacan's mastery is to be trapped in the imaginary of the text.
>
> *(Gallop, 1988, p. 281)*

Here Gallop is making a crucial point about reading, consciousness and theory. To identify writer Lacan as *authoritative* Lacan in his "The Purloined Letter" essay is to remain mired in the imaginary gazing at Lacan as idealized analyst, "the one presumed to know." Gallop argues that Lacan's ethical imperative is to get beyond the analyst as mirror (providing ego certainties of knowing) and to see the mirror in the analyst merely as a mirror. She says this must similarly apply to Lacan's writing on Poe (Gallop, 1988, pp. 271–272). Lacan playing the one presumed to know is not providing the mirror. Rather the true analytical mirror function is to be found in the unnamed narrator.

Of course, in any comparison of Jung and Lacan, one can prefer either psychologist by using his ideas to "explain" the other. Each move constructs their individual theories as a symbolic order imperfectly penetrated by the other, so making the subordinate views imaginary. And yet as Gallop points out, such a simple opposing of two kinds of writing remains itself imaginary. While not expecting to escape this trap, my project is to seek out the sublime feminine haunting both writers as they consider that unreliable source of psychological truth: literature. By tweaking out a feminine sublime in Lacan on Poe and Jung on Joyce, might the combined efforts of four male writers provide something "other?"

Jung on Ulysses

> Thus I read to page 135 with despair in my heart, falling asleep twice on the way.
>
> *(Jung, 1932, para. 165)*

The essay begins with Jung as established as the one who does *not* know. Not only his intellect, but even his body resists the book. If ever someone was invited to see the inert mirror as mirror rather than as the one presumed to know, it is Jung's reader embarking with him on a voyage into what is presented as unknowable.

> Joyce's Ulysses . . . is a passive, merely perceiving consciousness . . . to the roaring, chaotic, lunatic cataract of

psychic and physical happenings, and registering all this with almost photographic accuracy.

(Ibid.: para. 163)

Here indeed is the mirror as mirror, as the narrator is deemed to be little more than a recording device. At this moment, Jung as hapless reader is fatefully exposed to the chaotic Real with only the thin membrane of the mirror/passive perceiving consciousness to protect him. Yet in a move that is like and crucially unlike Lacan, Jung has recourse to the non-human. Where Lacan in "The Purloined Letter" sees animal desire in the Minister as both opposed to and constituting the symbolic order in its relation to the letter as signifier, Jung sees animality as part of the body's capacity to be *productively* involved in the psyche. Jung finds an image of the book as sense-less worm.

From a Lacanian point of view, Jung generates an imago, a pre-symbolic image, in the worm that eventually engenders the sublime as subjectivity traverses the imaginary into first destroying and then reconstituting the symbolic order. From a Jungian point of view, the stuck reader, Jung, performs active imagination with his worm image that serves to weave body and psyche anew.

Furthermore, the resourceful worm shows itself to be a tapeworm, an unpleasant parasite rather like the effect of the book on Jung's stupefied body. Such a creature is both internal and yet foreign, other. So it is a fitting teacher of how internal and external can comingle, even to the extent of a hideous transcendence.

Objective and subjective, outer and inner, are so constantly intermingled that one wonders whether one is dealing with a physical or transcendental tapeworm (Ibid.: para. 166).

Themes are unavoidable

At last, Jung decides to resort to Lacan's overall tactic in "The Purloined Letter" essay, impersonating the one presumed to know. Unlike Lacan, he explicitly takes on the role of the analyst in order to import structures of meaning or "themes."

A therapist like myself is always practicising therapy – even on himself.

(Jung: para. 168)

Nevertheless, themes are unavoidable, they are the scaffolding for all psychic happenings.

(Ibid.: para. 169)

Fascinatingly, Jung identifies themes as "scaffolding," something added to repair, repaint or maintain. He has to make a deliberate and well-rehearsed

Sublime and Feminine creativity in destruction   159

shift from abject unknowing reader to knowing analyst while admitting the artificial nature of this assumed role. As therapist, what he first sees is sublime destruction of art.

> But it is only modern man who has succeeded in creating
> an art in reverse, a backside of art.
>
> *(Jung: para. 178)*

Ulysses also manages to undo Jung's own conceptual schema to the extent of failing to be archetypal (showing the influence of inherited potentials for images and meaning) and symbolic (producing images that connect ego to unconscious) in the ways he would expect.

What *works* for Jung the therapist is his realization of the creativity in the sublime destructiveness of *Ulysses*. Coherence is a destination in the reader rather than a quality of the novel itself. Here Jung, the therapist does indeed put his faith in psyche rather than art, but it is a psyche both destroyed and re-created by art. Not only does the author find a unity in the disruption of the book, but Jung the therapist of culture discerns a collective process of sublime creativity and renewal.

> Such manifestations of the collective psyche disclose their
> meaning only when they are considered teleologically as an
> anticipation of something new.
>
> *(Jung: para. 175)*

In terms of the sublime, Jung needs to import his "scaffold" of the teleological and compensatory properties of the collective psyche and art in order to contain, to limit, what he finds impossible to stomach in the novel. The worm, the image of abject psyche that was both inside as tapeworm and outside as transcendent, is defeated by the assumption of the position of cultural therapist.

The worm is also the abject reader because the book destroyed all clean and proper boundaries of the subject. It can be seen in terms of Julia Kristeva's notion of abject as pre-subjective and terrifyingly destructive of necessary boundaries for being (Kristeva, 1982). This worm is not sublime because the sublime needs a boundary unless it is to be a mere figure for undoing, unmeaning, rather than a defeat of or a "beyond" of meaning. Only by assuming the role of cultural therapist is Jung, the reader, able to figure the sublime. The novel is a backside of art and its same fissile nature is now understood as a necessary function of creativity.

An age corrupted by sentimentality requires "drastic purgatives," (para. 179). Jung demonstrates that the sublime may be immanent to the psyche and yet requires some structuring beyond the individual psyche, such as the teleology of psyche and art. Otherwise what is left is the worm, appearing here as endless procreation without creation, without any possibility of something new. Signifying, even the signifying of the blockage of signifying, needs something from outside itself in order to *work*.

From creativity in destruction to the crumpled note

At last Jung finds his symbol, which for him is the image that joins ego to unconscious and so provides a gateway to transformation. Time swallowed by reading can become symbolic, which suggests that the novel's mobilization of the abject psyche in the tapeworm can give way to a *reforming* of being.

Repeatedly in the essay Jung comes to the "detachment" he discerns in the narrative voice, a separation from body, the deep psyche and world that is answered by Jung in the active imagination of the monstrously embedded tapeworm. Detachment has "Homeric image[s]" including a crushed piece of paper, an advertisement known as a "throwaway" (Jung: para. 186).

As an image of a detached consciousness, the crumpled throwaway is superbly weightless and valueless. "Throwaway" is also the name of a horse that unexpectedly wins a race. Leopold Bloom, the wandering Jew of Dublin is regarded as of no account, a "throwaway" hero. Here Jung makes a leap in taking this figurative detachment as an invocation of the Self, that notion of being in psyche that is conceptually boundless, sublime. The *Self* is both a centring archetype and also a word for totality, which cannot be fully known or mapped because it is rooted in the unconscious.

> The ego of the creator of these figures is not to be found . . . all and everything . . . is Joyce himself . . . not the ego but the self.
>
> *(Jung: para. 188)*

From detachment and a crumpled scrap of paper to the Self is a transition made possible by Jung's abjection in the worm coming to recognize a crucial aspect of the immanence of the Joycean sublime. *Ulysses* is a novel in which the purgation of modernity does have aesthetic precedents in medieval Catholic art of the suffering Christ. Again, finding an external structure in the history of art makes abjection into the sublime by giving a limit to its destruction both of knowing and of aesthetics.

Jung's own way of putting it is that by making the time of reading symbolic, the novel remakes the psyche as Self. Reading the novel becomes a process of enduring the destructive sublime through the abject worm, becoming so detached as to experience the worthlessness of a throwaway note and yet, in these very processes of undoing and un-being finding a transcendence, a sublime of creativity in destruction. Here again the empty signifier is not quite empty because it mobilizes transformation.

Just as for Lacan the letter in "The Purloined Letter" is powerful by virtue of its unknown contents and therefore structures and destroys being, so too does Jung regard the crumpled throwaway note as an emerging image of the symbolic properties of the novel as psychic processing of time. Throwaway is recurrent on the current of the book. It is a figure for the scatological erasing of eschatology, dirty waste paper for a sublime epic book, and also images that abject becoming immanent sublime in revealing the writer as

Self. Then it is revealed in relation to a transcendent (masculine) sublime as Joyce's false Elijah invokes numinous Elijah.

> The "light crumpled throwaway" drifts towards the East. Three times this crumpled note turns up in *Ulysses*, each time mysteriously connected with Elijah. Twice we are told: "Elijah is coming".
>
> *(Jung: para. 190)*

Eros Sublime, the feminine and nature

Shaw in his book *The Sublime* (2006) quotes the philosopher J. Milbank on Eros as love in immanence; the specific located thing or person can also release the sublime from immanence as a restriction. Love, however bounded and particular, is connected to desire as potentially unbounded and endless. Such experience offers "contiguity" to an infinite sublime. Therefore, the persistence of desire may release us from the melancholia of the transcendent sublime as loss.

> For as soon as *Eros*, conceived here as the love of the particular, is added to the sublime it becomes possible, once again, to conceive of the infinite as "in analogical continuity with what lies within the finite".
>
> *(Milbank, 2004, p. 229, italics in original)*

Desire expands being beyond the immanence of our physical senses, in ways anticipated (somewhat differently) by both Jung and Lacan. Milbank's "analogical contiguity" resembles Lacan's *jouissance* "wrapped in its own contiguity" (Bowie, 1991, p. 148). In addition, we might recall Shaw citing Mellor on women Romantic writers positing a "sisterly" or continuous relationship to nature.

In concluding, it is useful to return again to the crumpled note, its comparison to Lacan's "purloined letter" and the "medusoid signifier". Jung too has his monstrosity in signification in his reading of *Ulysses*.

> Try to imagine a being who is not a mere colourless conglomerate soul composed of an indefinite number of ill-assorted and antagonistic individual souls, but consists also of houses, street-processions, churches, the Liffey, several brothels, and a crumpled note on its way to the sea.
>
> *(Jung: para. 198)*

In its ruthless apportion of psyche, gender and destiny, the purloined letter, according to Lacan, materializes the signifier as death. It is medusoid, freezing being into stone for all those who try to look on her/the letter. For Jung, the crumpled note is a stage in the formation of the novel as Self, a

162   Susan Rowland

monstrous being of psyche that encompasses matter, humans, place, time and non-human nature. The crumpled note images the necessary crumbling of ego in the formation of sublime and "beyond" human being of the Jungian Self. Indeed the crumpled note is the image for, and means of, shattering psychic identity such as gender and all meaningful connections in the ego. In this sense the crumpled note is Jung's purloined letter. By converting Homeric heroism to abject throwaway paper, the crumpled note similarly depletes being.

However, in the comparison to Lacan, Jung takes two roles in his essay. He begins as the one who does not know, who is subjected to the signifier's materialization of death in annihilating meaning and almost defeating the psyche as creative of being – Jung falls asleep and finds mere reproduction without production (of meaning). Jung the hapless reader does achieve a Lacanian trope in perceiving the mirror as mirror; the nothingness in the book; its "truth" as the throwaway note.

Secondly, Jung adopts the role as the "one presumed to know" in overtly importing themes in his assumed position as therapist. Fascinatingly, this one presumed to know initially finds his own theory of little use. Yet not unlike Lacan, he exposes his theory's validity in pointing to the literary work's capacity for psychological transformation.

At this point a difference emerges between the two depth psychologists. For Lacan, the "lynx eye" and the "beast of prey" seem to collaborate in the capacity of desire to undo human identity. Animals stand for loss of the symbolic order. Such at first appears to be the case with Jung's worm. At the beginning it is the book; it is undifferentiated in Lacan's imaginary, then a parasite making abject the reader as subjectivity is undone. And yet the worm is an immanence that achieves transcendence when the unmaking of meaning and psyche gives way to the discovery of an ordering principle foreign to the ego. Put another way, the animal offers a way to meaning-making potential in bodily mobilization of psyche through time.

More so than Lacan, Jung suggests a bodily and animal strata to human being that is productive of re-forming subjectivity. He calls it finding the Self in a new relation to creativity and history. We *all* become citizens of Catholic Ireland in reading *Ulysses* because its ability to evoke abjection remakes our sense of transcendence as a possibility for the psyche.

Here we remember that in Jung's inherited archetype, this psychic potential has a bodily root that neither determines, nor is separate from, its imaginative properties. In Jung's essay we witness both body and psyche failing to cope with the novel when Jung falls asleep twice. At this moment the reader is failing to "symbolize" in *both* the Lacanian and Jungian senses. The book drags the psyche from the symbolic order, while right now it cannot inspire or inspirit the Jungian archetypal psyche with a symbol. A symbol in Jung's psychology always, as an archetypal image, possesses a bodily aspect.

And yet, the final move of the masculine Self in the novel, according to Jung, is to become feminine receptivity in Molly Bloom's end thoughts on the beginning of her sexual life with the man she marries, Leopold Bloom, the "throwaway" hero. Put another way, the crumpled note is not only the signifier for a monster like Lacan's medusoid purloined letter. It does more.

Sublime and Feminine creativity in destruction   163

For the crumpled note drifts on the waters of the Liffey. As a throwaway it is vulnerable to the "backside" elements of the city in disposing of waste. Yet it also encounters the natural forces of the river, which are used by the signifying symbolic order but not reducible to them. We are told the note drifts like boats used by Odysseus. The crumpled note on the river is both throwaway waste (from the symbolic order) and also liberated from that condition. It has *jouissance*, a playfulness in signifying on the waves without being controlled by the signifier. Jung, far more than Lacan, adopts the notion of animals and natural forces such as rivers as *productive* mirrors to psyche.

To summarize, we have in Jung's crumpled note and Lacan's purloined letter a realization of a sublime creativity in destruction of aesthetics. Also in both Lacan and Jung there is a feminine sublime in contiguity, a *jouissance*. I argue that Jung more clearly supports this sublime feminine by perceiving ordering principles in nature that can collaborate with human *jouissance* as playfulness in bodily pleasure and signifying, not subjection to them. Such a feminine sublime is not wholly immanent for its contiguity to the other (whether nature or not) still offers an external structuring influence. Similarly the transcendent sublime of creativity in destruction is far from wholly transcendent in its reliance on the backside of art (Jung: para. 195).

So Jung and Lacan each find in literature processes of psychological undoing and remaking. Both explore how narrative simultaneously relies upon and exposes the gap in what Lacan calls the symbolic order and what Jung sees as a problematic yet necessary relation in signifying between body and psyche. Ultimately both find gender more complex than can be adequately accounted for by merely relating to Elijah, or to the phallus. In evoking creativity in sublime destruction they discover two gendered and mutually related conditions of the sublime.

Note

1 Material from this chapter first appears in chapter 6 of *Remembering Dionysus: Revisioning Psychology and Literature in C. G. Jung and James Hillman*, Routledge, 2017. Except where a different publication is noted, all references are, by volume and paragraph number, to the edition of Jung, C. G. *The Collected Works of C.G. Jung* (CW), edited by Sir Herbert Read, Dr Michael Fordham and Dr Gerhard Adler, translated by R.F.C. Hull (1953–91). London: Routledge; Princeton, NJ: Princeton University Press.

References

Bowie, M. (1991). *Lacan*. Fontana Modern Masters. London: HarperCollins.
Gallop, J. (1988). The American Other. In J.P. Muller and W.J. Richardson (Eds.), *The Purloined Poe* (pp. 28–54). Baltimore, MD: The Johns Hopkins University Press.
Joyce, J. (1992[1922]). *Ulysses*. Harmondsworh: Penguin Classics.

164 Susan Rowland

Jung, C.G. (1932). "Ulysses": A Monologue. In *Collected Works, Volume 15: The Spirit in Man, Art and Literature* (pp. 127–154). London: Routledge; Princeton, NJ: Princeton University Press.

Kristeva, J. (1982). *Powers of Horror: An Essay on Abjection (European Perspectives Series)*. New York: Columbia University Press.

Lacan, J. (1982). Guiding Remarks for a Congress on Feminine Sexuality. In J. Mitchell and J. Rose (Eds.), *Feminine Sexuality*. London: Macmillan.

Lacan, J. (1988[1972]). Seminar on "The Purloined Letter". In J.P. Muller and W.J. Richardson (Eds.), *The Purloined Poe* (1988) (pp. 268–282). Baltimore, MD: Johns Hopkins University Press.

Milbank, J. (2004). Sublimity: The Modern Transcendent. In Regina Schwartz (Ed.), *Transcendence: Philosophy, Literature, and Theology Approach the Beyond*. London and New York: Routledge.

Mitchell, J. and Rose, J. (Eds.) (1982). *Feminine Sexuality; Jacques Lacan and the École Freudienne*. London: Macmillan.

Muller, J.P. and Richardson, W.J. (Eds.) (1988). *The Purloined Poe: Lacan, Derrida and Psychoanalytic Reading*. Baltimore, MD: The Johns Hopkins University Press.

Poe, E.A. (1844). The Purloined Letter. In J.P. Muller and W.J. Richardson (Eds.), *The Purloined Poe* (1988) (pp. 6–27). Baltimore, MD: The Johns Hopkins University Press.

Shaw, P. (2006). *The Sublime*. Abingdon and New York: Routledge.

PART II
CULTURE

TEN

The object of
Victor Frankenstein's desire

Lionel Bailly

If sublimation disguises sexuality and presents its effects in the form of socially valued activities such as artistic creation and intellectual inquiry, the sublime results are not without ambiguity. The word itself suggests "what lies under the threshold", the entrance (*sub limen*), or "what cannot be faced directly" and has to be addressed obliquely (*sub limus*) (see Online Etymology Dictionary). Chemists may only have seen in sublimation the change of a substance from a solid to a gas without ever passing through a liquid phase, but the alchemists did not miss its metaphoric value, which they associated with the spiritualization of the body and the embodiment of the spirit (Ripley, 1591), processes highly relevant to the story of Victor Frankenstein (Shelley, 1999[1831]).

There is little doubt that Mary Shelley's story *Frankenstein, or The Modern Prometheus* has become a modern myth. Almost everybody on the planet knows of the monster, even if it is mostly through its cinematic shape. This creature they also call Frankenstein. This, in itself, is an interesting fact, because Shelley never called "it" this. He was the "monster", the "demoniacal corpse", the "filthy daemon", yet over time the public asserted the monster's right to a patronym. Victor Frankenstein was its father, and it should therefore rightfully inherit his name. Moreover, many studies of the story have focused on the monster and not on his creator. The fascination for his transgressive nature, embarrassing physicality and uncontrollable violence seems to have distracted commentators from the fact that these attributes are the direct consequences of the way he was created. This essay will therefore focus on Victor Frankenstein's motives in creating the creature.

It is commonly accepted that one of the functions of myths is to validate and maintain a certain social system, a shared set of rights and wrongs, proprieties or improprieties, on which a particular social unit depends for its existence. According to anthropologists, the story of Oedipus, in its connection with the incest prohibition, lies at the heart of mankind's move from nature to culture. The Oedipus story itself contains a few monsters: in the background, there is the chthonian dragon killed by Kadmos in order for mankind to be born from the earth, and obviously there is the Sphinx, a monster unwilling to permit men to live. Claude Lévi-Strauss suggests that myths have to do with "the inability, for a culture which holds the belief

The object of Victor Frankenstein's desire   167

that mankind is autochthonous, to find a satisfactory transition between this theory and the knowledge that human beings are actually born from the union of man and woman" (Lévi-Strauss, 1955, p. 434). In mythology, autochthones are those mortals who have sprung from the soil, rocks and trees. They are rooted in and belong to the land eternally.

Born from the union of man and woman – how do we know? How are human beings born? Freud pointed out that this type of questioning appears to have been a human preoccupation since time immemorial: "We seem to hear the echoes of this first riddle [Where do babies come from?] in innumerable riddles of myth and legend" (Freud, 1959[1908c], p. 213). Children try to answer this question, and one example of the theories they produce is given by Freud in his case presentation of the Wolf man: "So far he had had no reason for supposing that children only came from women. On the contrary, his Nanya had given him to believe that he was his father's child, while his sister was his mother's . . . and this closer connection with his father had been very precious to him. He now heard that Mary was called the Mother of God. So all children came from women, and what his Nanya had said to him was no longer tenable" (Freud, 1955[1918b], p. 65). Freud took the development of children's sexual theories to be the prototype of the individual's abstract thinking, both in what brings it on – the subject is confronted with dangerous information (the primal scene, the impending arrival of a new baby) – and in how the threat is dealt with, i.e. by the formation of a hypothesis. The theory is therefore the result of a defensive process, and Freud felt that its effectiveness lies in giving the subject an illusion of possible control over reality, "as though thinking were entrusted with the task of preventing the recurrence of such dreaded events" (Freud, 1959[1908c], p. 213). Not only is the sexual theory an independent creation of the child but it "goes on operating as a self-sustained instinct for research [*als selbständiger Forschungstrieb weiter arbeitet*]" (Ibid., p. 213).

During this research, the child first realizes the crucial role of the mother, and in particular how to monopolize her. This is well described by Lacan's version of the Oedipus complex. It involves a young child and focuses in a first phase on the dealings between the mother and the child. The child is aware that the mother is coming and going. This awareness comes from the fact that when she is present, the world of the child changes, and it changes again when she leaves, something that the baby senses even before being able to fully symbolize it. This leads, Lacan suggests, to a theoretical reflection on the mother's coming and going, and in particular on what causes it: "What does she want? I would really like it to be me that she wants, but it's very clear that it's not just me that she wants. There are other things at work in her" (Lacan, 2017[1998], p. 159). Lacan continues: "What is at work in her is the x, the signified. And the signified of the mother's comings and goings is the phallus" (Ibid., p. 159).

With the first symbolization of the mother, something is instituted which is subjectified at a primitive level: "This subjectification consists simply in posing the mother as the primordial being who may be there or not" (Ibid.,

p. 165). The first symbolization of the mother leads the child to separate its dependence on her desire from the living experience of that dependence. More importantly, what the subject desires, is "not simply a matter of appetition for the mother's care, contact or even her presence, but of appetition for her desire" (Ibid., pp. 165–166). What the child seeks is to be able to satisfy his mother's desire and to be the object of the mother's desire, and to do so it will identify with this object that is the satisfying object for the mother.

Lacan is then moving away from a literal interpretation of the role of the father in the Oedipus complex, by stating that in the Oedipus complex the father is not a real object, even though he must intervene as a real object to embody castration. The father is symbolic. More precisely, says Lacan, the father is a metaphor: "The father's function in the Oedipus complex is to be a signifier substituted for the first signifier introduced into symbolization, the maternal signifier" (Ibid., p. 159). The mother being the first object to be symbolized, she is at the centre of the baby's preoccupations, and the need to "secure" her is paramount.

However, as we have just seen, in the dialectic of presence/absence the child has to think about what keeps her away and thus faces the question of the mother's desire. Having been able to symbolize its first object, it is logical for the child to postulate an object that the mother is after, even though from the child's point of view "it should be me that she wants". This imagined object, something the mother desires more than anything else, is what Lacan calls the phallus. The Oedipal drama, in its first phase, rests on an impossible exchange. "Prove to me, by your behaviour, that I have it", is the child's demand. "How can I tell him/her that he/she's not everything for me?" underlines the mother's non-response. The mother anticipates that the whole truth would be devastating in its raw form: you don't have it, you can't fully please me and I will leave you because of this. Or worse: you have it, and I don't need anything or anyone else and we will stay forever enmeshed. A subterfuge is in the best interest of both the baby and the mother's libidinal investments. This disguising of the truth will be made possible by the metaphoric process, which precisely substitutes and hides signifiers.

However, this process implies the submission of the child to it. There are numerous ways of refusing, avoiding, rebelling against this necessity to submit. All of these have consequences. There can be individual consequences for the psyche of the subject – for example, the famous foreclosure of the Name-of-the-Father and the creation of a psychotic structure (Lacan, 2006[1958]) – but there could also be consequences at a social level. I have mentioned, in this respect, the social role of the incest prohibition described by anthropologists. Lévi-Strauss points out that this incest prohibition is less a rule prohibiting marriage with the mother, sister or daughter than a rule obliging the mother, sister or daughter to be given to others. Incest is prohibited "not because [of] a biological danger . . . but because exogamous marriage results in a social benefit" and "provides the fundamental and immutable rule ensuring the existence of the group as a group" (Lévi-Strauss, 1969[1949], pp. 480–481).

The object of Victor Frankenstein's desire 169

As a child, Victor Frankenstein opted out of the Oedipal confrontation. Let us examine his background: "I am by birth a Genevese, and my family is one of the most distinguished of that republic. My ancestors had been for many years counsellors and syndics, and my father had filled several public situations with honour and reputation" (Shelley, 1999[1831], p. 29). In other words, a famous family, a filiation one can be proud of, but also a father who is a mighty rival. This powerful father marries a woman whose position is at least fantasmatically incestuous, for she is the very young daughter of a deceased friend: "after the internment of his friend, he conducted her to Geneva, and placed her under the protection of a relation. Two years after this event Caroline became his wife" (Ibid., p. 31). Young Victor's life is described as blissful, but marked by his conviction of having a special status:

> There was a considerable difference between the ages of my parents. . . . My mother's tender caresses, and my father's smile of benevolent pleasure while regarding me, are my first recollections. I was their plaything and their idol, and something better – their child, the innocent and helpless creature bestowed on them by Heaven.
>
> *(Ibid., p. 31)*

The family's tendency to transgress rules and their fascination for the sublime qualities of certain beings continues with the adoption of a girl met by chance. Their infatuation for the girl derives from their immediate imaginary fantasies about her looks and qualities:

> Her hair was the brightest living gold, and, despite the poverty of her clothing, seemed to set a crown of distinction on her head. Her brow was clear and ample, her blue eyes cloudless, and her lips and the moulding of her face so expressive of sensibility and sweetness, that none could behold her without looking on her as of a distinct species, a being heaven-sent, and bearing a celestial stamp in all her features.
>
> *(Ibid., p. 33)*

Next on the list of transgressions is the mother's confusing statement for the development of Victor's sexual theories:

> On the evening previous to her being brought to my home, my mother had said playfully, "I have a pretty present for my Victor – to-morrow he shall have it." And when, on the morrow, she presented Elizabeth to me as her promised gift, I, with childish seriousness, interpreted her words literally, and looked upon Elizabeth as mine – mine to protect, love, and cherish.
>
> *(Ibid., p. 35)*

170   Lionel Bailly

Elizabeth, incarnation of the feminine, is sublime in body and mind and thriving in the equally sublime landscape:

> She busied herself with following the aerial creations of the poets; and in the majestic and wondrous scenes which surrounded our Swiss home – the sublime shapes of the mountains; the changes of the seasons; tempest and calm; the silence of winter, and the life and turbulence of our Alpine summers.
>
> *(Ibid., p. 36)*

However, Victor becomes engaged in a different pursuit:

> While my companion contemplated with a serious and satisfied spirit the magnificent appearances of things, I delighted in investigating their causes. The world was to me a secret which I desired to divine. Curiosity, earnest research to learn the hidden laws of nature, gladness akin to rapture, as they were unfolded to me, are among the earliest sensations I can remember.
>
> *(Ibid., p. 36)*

His research will be influenced by a particular event:

> When I was about fifteen years old we had retired to our house near Belrive, when we witnessed a most violent and terrible thunder-storm . . . on a sudden I beheld a stream of fire issue from an old and beautiful oak, which stood about twenty yards from our house; and so soon as the dazzling light vanished, the oak had disappeared, and nothing remained but a blasted stump . . . I never beheld any thing so utterly destroyed.
>
> *(Ibid., p. 43)*

What is so powerful that the mighty oak can be "utterly destroyed"? Victor reflects: "The catastrophe of this tree excited my extreme astonishment; and I eagerly inquired of my father the nature and origin of thunder and lightning. He replied, 'Electricity'" (Ibid., p. 43). The aim of Victor's subsequent research would be the mastery of this amazing power, and he could have become a scientist, yet:

> I chanced to find a volume of the works of Cornelius Agrippa. . . . A new light seemed to dawn upon my mind; and, bounding with joy, I communicated my discovery to my father. . . . My father looked carelessly at the titlepage of my book, and said, "Ah! Cornelius Agrippa! My dear Victor, do not waste your time upon this; it is sad trash".
>
> *(Ibid., p. 40)*

The signifiers used by his father unfortunately produced the opposite effect he had intended. The "sad trash" sparked an irresistible attraction. Victor would then teach himself to rely on a knowledge his father did not have:

> [W]hile I followed the routine of education in the schools of Geneva, I was, to a great degree, self taught with regard to my favourite studies. My father was not scientific, and I was left to struggle with a child's blindness, added to a student's thirst for knowledge. Under the guidance of my new preceptors, I entered with the greatest diligence into the search of the philosopher's stone and the elixir of life.
>
> *(Ibid., p. 41)*

His intentions and fantasies are very clear: "I will pioneer a new way, explore unknown powers, and unfold to the world the deepest mysteries of creation" (Ibid., p. 53). Victor wonders:

> Whence, I often asked myself, did the principle of life proceed? It was a bold question, and one which has ever been considered as a mystery. . . . I succeeded in discovering the cause of generation and life; nay, more, I became myself capable of bestowing animation upon lifeless matter. The astonishment which I had at first experienced on this discovery soon gave place to delight and rapture.
>
> *(Ibid., p. 59)*

Victor then embarks upon the course of giving birth outside the laws of procreation; his creation would be made from dead parts, buried bodies – the earth (autochthonous). He would become the founder of a new "species": "A new species would bless me as its creator and source; many happy and excellent natures would owe their being to me" (Ibid., p. 61).

Not only does Victor avoid any Oedipal rivalry with his father and the risk of castration, but he will have sons who will not be in a position to rival him: "No father could claim the gratitude of his child so completely as I should deserve theirs" (Ibid., p. 62). However, the story warns of the impossibility of such a project, and the product of the procreation is a disappointment: "[B]y the glimmer of the half-extinguished light, I saw the dull yellow eye of the creature open; it breathed hard, and a convulsive motion agitated its limbs" (Ibid., p. 66). This child is not good enough, and once the tension of the process of making a baby has gone, it is disgust that Victor experiences:

> I had worked hard for nearly two years, for the sole purpose of infusing life into an inanimate body. For this I had deprived myself of rest and health. I had desired it with an ardour that far exceeded moderation; but now that I had finished, the beauty of the dream vanished, and breathless horror and disgust filled my heart.
>
> *(Ibid., p. 67)*

172   Lionel Bailly

In a cowardly way, Victor runs away from his responsibility:

> His jaws opened, and he muttered some inarticulate sounds, while a grin wrinkled his cheeks. He might have spoken, but I did not hear; one hand was stretched out, seemingly to detain me, but I escaped and rushed down stairs.
>
> *(Ibid., p. 68)*

The reader then witnesses the collapse of Victor's family and in some ways of society. The creature murders Victor's brother William, his friend Clerval and his then-wife Elizabeth. Justine, William's nanny, is hanged for the murder of William, whereas Victor himself is imprisoned for the murder of his friend and he suffers a mental breakdown in prison. These plagues are the punishment for having tried to be outside humanity, which is defined by the fundamental law of procreation, and for having refused both his responsibility for and any attempt at humanizing the creature: teaching it to speak, showing love, or giving him a bride, so that maybe they can reintegrate the human family.

As a child, Victor did not compete to bear, or to possess the phallus but revelled in the sublime enjoyment of nature, his adopted sister's beauty and his mother's ability to provide serenity and comfort. Whilst enjoying nature, he also noticed its overwhelming and dangerous force, and decided that this was what he wanted to control. Outside the expertise of his forefathers, Victor studied, and he decided to embark on the adventure of giving birth outside sexuality, making himself the catalyst of a process in which nature (electricity) self-fecundates the earth, the dead flesh of bodies. The return to the pre-Oedipal world of the Greek autochthons could not be anything for mankind other than a catastrophe. Victor's way did not involve castration and the confirmation of human fundamental taboos. His lawless creation and the lawlessness of his position led to death, not simply the punishment of the transgressive perpetrator, but death in his family as a warning about social cohesion. The story also illustrates the unshakable character of the curse Frankenstein brought onto himself. The transgression was his choice and was therefore part of him. As the fruit of this process, the monster had to be where Victor was. Wherever he travelled, whatever precautions he took, the monster still appeared and had the power to destroy.

There is something of the Lacanian Real in this creature that is born outside the symbolic realm. In his "Response to Jean Hyppolite's Commentary on Freud's 'Verneinung'", Lacan states that *what did not come to light in the symbolic appears in the real*" (Lacan, 2006[1956], p. 324). And elsewhere: "For the real, whatever upheaval we subject it to, is always and in every case in its place; it carries its place stuck to the sole of its shoe, there being nothing that can exile it from it" (Lacan, 2006[1957], p. 17). Victor Frankenstein and his creature travel to the North Pole as one, until the death of one implies the end of the other. Faced with the body of his creator, the creature declared: "That is also my victim!"; "[I]n his murder my crimes are consummated; the miserable series of my being is wound to its close!"

(Shelley, 1999[1831], p. 297). His last revendication of kinship takes the form of a desperate act of identification with his creator, and the mirroring of Victor's megalomania, as he masochistically announces: "I shall ascend my funeral pyre triumphantly, and exult in the agony of the torturing flames" (Ibid., p. 303). At the beginning of the story the dazzling flames of lightning destroyed a mighty oak; at the end, the flames of the funeral pyre destroy what the myths teach us should have never been created.

Victor's fascination for the laws of nature illustrates the problematic elaboration of sexual theories for a boy growing up in a quite transgressive family with a father who does not hesitate to marry the child of his best friend, parents who acquire another child because she is beautiful and helpless and a mother who gives this girl to her son as a future sexual partner. Victor tries to escape the curse of such a background – the curse being the stunting of true creativity that results from the non-integration of the paternal metaphor – through sublimation, but his solution is hysterical: he will not compete with his father for the phallus but will find an object of desire unknown to his parents. Alchemists provide an imaginary filiation whose potency is revealed by the destructive power of lightning. Electricity is the signifier Victor Frankenstein substitutes for the phallus in the paternal metaphor. This opens a field of non-phallic sexuality where he can give birth without a woman. Victor has truly become an alchemist, and he enjoys immensely, like them, playing with the embodiment of the spirit. However, the real of his creation exposes the futility of his whole attempt. The creature was the living proof of his limited potency. Where the children born of sex were beautiful, lively and loving, his creature was dull and inarticulate. The creature, having been the cause of desire, was once obtained found wanting and discarded. The drama of Victor Frankenstein was written from the moment he failed to consider the knowledge of his father and invested in the imaginary scenario of his alchemist hero. Outside the paternal metaphor his path led, quite sublimely, to destruction.

References

Freud, S. (1955[1918*b*]). From the History of an Infantile Neurosis. In J. Strachey (Ed.), *The Standard Edition of the Complete Psychological Works of Sigmund Freud*, vol. 17 (pp. 1–124). London: The Hogarth Press and the Institute of Psycho-Analysis.

Freud, S. (1959[1908*c*]). On the Sexual Theories of Children. In J. Strachey (Ed.), *The Standard Edition of the Complete Psychological Works of Sigmund Freud*, vol. 9 (pp. 205–226). London: The Hogarth Press and the Institute of Psycho-Analysis.

Lacan, J. (2006[1956]). Response to Jean Hyppolite's Commentary on Freud's "Verneinung". In B. Fink (Trans.), *Écrits* (pp. 318–333). New York: W. W. Norton & Company.

Lacan, J. (2006[1957]). Seminar on "The Purloined Letter". In B. Fink (Trans.), *Écrits* (pp. 6–48). New York: W. W. Norton & Company.

Lacan, J. (2006[1958]). On a Question Prior to Any Possible Treatment of Psychosis. In B. Fink (Trans.), *Écrits* (pp. 445–488). New York: W. W. Norton & Company.

Lacan, J. (2017[1998]). *The Seminar. Book V: Formations of the Unconscious (1957-'58)*, Ed. J.-A. Miller, Trans. R. Grigg. Cambridge and Malden, MA: Polity Press.

Lévi-Strauss, C. (1955). The Structural Study of Myth. *Journal of American Folklore*, 78(270): 428–444.

Lévi-Strauss, C. (1969[1949]). *The Elementary Structures of Kinship*, Ed. R. Needham, Trans. J. Harle Bell and J.R. von Sturmer. London: Eyre & Spottiswoode.

Online Etymology Dictionary. Retrieved from www.etymonline.com.

Ripley, G. (1591). *The Compound of Alchymy*, Ed. R. Rabbards. London: Thomas Orwin.

Shelley, M. (1999[1831]). *Frankenstein; or, The Modern Prometheus*. New York: The Modern Library.

ELEVEN

The Soviet Antigones: the poets versus the state

Helena Bassil-Morozow

The Soviet citizen has always been a source of fear and mystery to the West. Resilient yet creative, strong yet passionate, switching between the high state of heroism and the greyness and banality of everyday existence (or *byt*), "homo soveticus" was asked to develop an impossible constellation of character traits which would combine being happy, productive, creative and inspired with very limited individual (and indeed, creative) freedom.

Soviet poets, authors, theatre directors, filmmakers and composers were expected to trade their creative identity and unique vision for state support by choosing to work with state-approved forms of art, genres, styles and narratives. Some, however, rebelled and were duly punished (killed, silenced, expelled) for daring to defy the collective. This chapter will examine the fates of three Soviet authors – Osip Mandelstam, Mikhail Bulgakov and Joseph Brodsky using a combination of Lacanian and Jungian ideas. It will consider in particular Lacan's analysis of individual autonomy in Sophocles's *Antigone* (441 BC) and the concept of the trickster (mainly in its Jungian version, but also going beyond Jung's vision of it).

All three authors can be considered martyrs, as they opposed the Soviet system and preferred death, suffering and stigma to physical comfort and physical survival. Lacan's interpretation of *Antigone* juxtaposes martyrdom and death to the pleasure principle and conformity. Antigone's ethical choice is beautiful precisely because it is a form of self-sacrifice in defiance of the system.

Similar ethical choices have been made by many authors throughout the history of the Soviet Union. The poet Joseph Mandelstam (1891–1938) died in prison for writing a "blasphemous" poem about Stalin, the novelist Mikhail Bulgakov (1891–1940) was not allowed to publish his works, and Joseph Brodsky (1940–1996) went through every harassment imaginable organized by the state but still refused to conform to the style of "socialist realism" – a representational mechanism whose aim was authentic rendition of the everyday life of the common people. Representatives of the so-called "creative intelligentsia" were treated in the Soviet Union as dangerous tricksters. The regime had a range of ways of keeping the hazardous trickster in check. They included harassment, censorship, persecution, imprisonment (including in mental health institutions) and exile.

The Jungian/anthropological idea of the trickster (as an anti-systemic element, an individuating force and an agent of change) complements Lacan's analysis of the individual taking control over her or his life and death via the "tragic transgression". Both Jung and Lacan have attempted to grasp (rather than define) the moment of tension between the civilized order, the careful arrangements of the system, and transition with its threat of chaos. In his description of the trickster archetype, Jung maintains that the individual should not forget the unconscious, should not forget "how things looked yesterday" (CW 9/I: para: 480), and Lacan outlines the state of being human as "the process of splitting apart", as "moving along the joint between the imaginary and the symbolic", as "the gap between nature and culture" (Lacan, 2008, p. 337).

Lacan draws attention to the famous song by the Chorus of Theban Elders in *Antigone* which starts off with the praise to the greatness and splendour of man, the wonder that is civilization with its language and its technology and then declares that the man is "full of tricks" (Lacan's translation, 2008, p. 337), cunning in his endless creativity and inventiveness and, finally, ends with the advice "to observe law" and to "tread the righteous path" (Sophocles, 1998, p. 14). Both Jung and Lacan capture the trickster's (and the individual taking on the role of the trickster in society) core qualities – the willingness to ask uncomfortable questions when everyone else is keen to comply. What they also capture is the pain and marginalization that inevitably accompanies martyrdom, for no "normal" citizen will ever doubt the system and its rules.

The trickster: an overview

Most trickster narratives (mythological, literary or cinematic) share a number of stock themes and motifs that serve as the backbone for the plot. Usually, a trickster narrative starts with the cunning creature being or feeling restricted (often physically), goes on to describe the trickster's escape and its adventures, and ends with the dissolution/transformation of the trickster. The most common structural elements of trickster narratives are being trapped, boundary-breaking, licentious behaviour, scatological humour, immense (and messy) creativity, bodily transformations, the presence of animals (which I prefer to call "the animal connection"), naming issues, loss of control over one's body and mind and the trickster's dissolution/death/transformation at the end of the story. Not all of the elements can be present in one story, film or myth, and their place in the narrative sequence is certainly not fixed.

Being trapped

Physical entrapment in narratives is an allegory of control and order. It symbolizes the structure's desire for being in charge. The trickster that is not controlled is a menace, because unrestrained and therefore unpredictable, it can damage or even destroy the system. Neither the systemic control nor the trickster's actions aimed at blocking it are intrinsically good or bad. In fact, the "being trapped" motif foregrounds the balance between stability and change. Tricksters can be trapped at any stage throughout the narrative, and when they are locked up, this is usually as a punishment for some misbehaviour such as theft, lying or murder. When a narrative starts with the trickster freeing itself from his prison, the rest of the narrative is devoted to the characters' efforts to regain control over the situation and to recapture or tame him.

Restrained tricksters can be presented as suffering and heroic, malevolent and dangerous or playful and stupid – but their task is always to defy and dupe the system. Translated into the relationship between the state and the creative artist, this element designates the ideology's power to silence the individual, to physically imprison them or to force them to confine themselves to an existing discourse.

Boundary-breaking

Tricksters are notorious boundary-breakers. In myth, folk tales and literary and cinematic narratives, they cross all kinds of boundaries, from physical (such as property borders) to metaphysical (for instance, sacred cultural values and taboos). Metaphorically, this means that the trickster has no respect for the structural aspect of the social. Neither does he respect the structuring function of the system. He does not accept "the way things are" and keeps attempting to redraw the map. Civilization is born with the emergence of boundaries, physical as well as psychological: rules of decency and propriety, property borders, psychological boundaries, etc. Boundaries separate the unconscious, pre-civilized man (or child) from an adult member of community, conscious of his actions and prepared to take responsibility for them. It is these boundaries that the trickster keeps challenging and disregarding. In political terms, by refusing to conform to the official discourse, the creative artist challenges the state and its discursive practices.

Shamelessness

Shamelessness designates existence before the system, and, essentially, pre-social, pre-civilized consciousness. Shame is also used by cultural frameworks to mould the individual into a certain kind of human being – standardized, normalized and knowing his limitations. It is thus a boundary-making tool whose task is to delimit the individual's sense of omnipotence in order to create a "social being". Seen in this light, structures use shame to tame dissenting and rebellious impulses in their subjects. Adults comply with the rules and regulations out of fear of being marginalized and shamed, out of fear of being "the odd one out". It therefore requires a certain amount of bravery (which is regarded by the system as insolence and shamelessness) to go against an accepted political discourse.

Creativity and creationism

Tricksters tend to be madly, unstoppably creative. Often their creative activities are linked to the birth of the world. Their creativity is not human – not directed, conscious and framed – but spontaneous, wild and random. It is the opposite of the system in that it is free and unframed. Like their endless tricks, it is part of their playful attitude towards the world. They are capable of rearranging their surroundings and adapting them to suit themselves. The new order is born out of mischief and play.

Creativity can be a dangerous weapon, and it is managed differently by different kinds of political systems. It was tightly controlled in the Soviet Union, whereas capitalism uses it to fuel innovation, change, to create more consumer choice and to speed up the production–consumption cycle.

Loss of control

On the one hand, the trickster's psyche and body are so fluid that it does not always have control over them. On the other hand, it can play tricks with human beings and cause them to lose control over their minds and bodies. The "loss of control" metaphor renders the idea of the interdependence of consciousness and the unconscious. The under-civilized trickster is silly and childlike and therefore can be easily deceived, but the very adult-like "consciousness" can become so confident in its over-inflated "wisdom" and "maturity" that its vision becomes dangerously narrow. A stagnant vision and loss of perspective makes consciousness vulnerable for the traps set up by the unconscious.

The artist is seen as a threat by the system because they can challenge its rules and processes, thus causing chaos and loss of control. There is no space for a creative impulse in a structure that is founded on rigid rules. It is in fear of losing control over its processes and is therefore unlikely to welcome any change, particularly a sudden or a disruptive one.

Dissolution

In many trickster tales – and this is particularly noticeable in large cycles containing a series of trickster transformations – the trickster spirit is dissolved at the end of the narrative. After the creative, chaotic unconscious energy has been woken up for the purpose of disrupting the stale (personal or social) order, it must go back to its dark wellspring. The trickster impulse does not die but is absorbed by various parts of the structure, its energy still alive underneath the surface of the social order.

Ultimately, systems attempt to stifle or "dissolve" tricksters. Metaphorically, the idea is to destroy the energy of change and defiance. Metonymically, and translated into the Soviet political context, the state's relationship with rebellious creatives invariably ended in death, exile, imprisonment or forced mental health treatment for the dissenting individual.

The Soviet state and the creative rebel

Creative expression was famously state-managed in the Soviet Union because it was seen as a big threat to the uniformity of its mass thinking. Various ways of limiting the creative impulse were invented, while the remaining creative elements were tightly controlled and significantly curbed. For instance, all Soviet art was to be done in the style of "socialist realism" – a representational mechanism whose aim was authentic rendition of the everyday life of the common people. Its rules applied to both literature and the arts and incorporated a range of stylistic and ideological elements. In order to "reflect the truth of life" (in contrast to the inflated artificiality and pretentiousness of the bourgeois art), a painting or a work of fiction was only allowed to use basic stylistic tools and had to eschew any complexity or excessive adornment in its depiction of workers and peasants. The works of the writers Maxim Gorky, Alexander Fadeev and Alexander Sholokhov, and sculptors like Vera Mukhina (1889–1953) (author of the famous statue "The Worker and the Kolkhoz Woman" were shining examples of the Socialist Realism genre. These authors cooperated with the frame-workers and managed the trickster in accordance with the current ideology.

Meanwhile, socialist realism was a very narrow framework, and inside it the trickster was almost stifled to death. Artists who did not wish to comply with the rules, or only accepted them partially, had trouble finding funding and audience for their work – even after Stalin's death and during the so-called "thaw" (Nikita Khrushchev's rule, 1953–1964) and "stagnation" (Leonid Brezhnev's rule, 1964–1982) periods when Soviet ideological and cultural restrictions were relaxed.

Representatives of the so-called "creative intelligentsia" were treated in the Soviet Union as dangerous tricksters. In fact, the intelligentsia was regarded with suspicion both in pre-and post-revolutionary Russia as a motley group of people united by one common trait: independent thinking and desire for change. Their fate was often far more violent than limited exposure or shortage of funding. Prior and during the Stalin years, many representatives of the "creative intelligentsia" died in prison camps or were executed, including the poets Nikolai Gumilev (1886–1921) and Osip Mandelstam (1891–1938); the novelist Isaak Babel (1894–1938); and the theatre director Vsevolod Meyerhold (1874–1940). Some – like the authors Aleksander Solzhenitsin (1918–2008) and Varlam Shalamov (1907–1982) and the historian Lev Gumilev (1912–1992), the son of the poet Anna Akhmatova, were lucky enough to survive the horrors of labour camps.

The role of the "creative intelligentsia" in the Soviet (also, now Russian) society corresponds to the martyr aspect of the trickster impulse emphasized by Jung. Taking on a structure – and particularly a large-scale ideological monster – is bound to be a painful experience. In foregrounding their role as tricksters and "tellers of truth", Soviet (and Russian) writers and artists have often forgot that they were also human beings – fragile and mortal. Without much regard for their own physical well-being or psychological comfort, they expressed, and keep expressing, their disdain for the stupidity, cruelty and shallowness of the structure.

Osip Mandelstam

In November 1933 – during the first wave of Stalinist purges – Mandelstam (Mandel'shtam) composed a poem which has become known as "the Stalin Epigram". The poem was read out loud to a small group of friends, one of whom must have reported Mandelstam to the authorities. In May 1934 the poet was arrested and exiled; later he was sent to a prison camp in Siberia where he died in 1938. The epigram is a dark satire, ruthless in its depiction of the distortion which the individual's existence and human relations underwent under Stalin's rule.

In an attempt to ease his suffering in exile, Mandelstam composed an *Ode to Stalin*, its tone the complete opposite of the *Epigram*, and a true testament to the poet's broken spirit. This U-turn did not help to avert the tragedy – presumably, because Stalin did not trust Mandelstam. The creative rebel, the trickster who has clearly crossed a line was first marginalized, then trapped and finally dissolved. Mandelstam dared to speak when millions of others were silently awaiting their fate or denouncing others in the hope to save themselves. The poet's bravery must have looked like stupidity and recklessness to an ordinary Soviet citizen. That was clearly not the kind of political humour Stalin would appreciate – composing a satire in which the country's leader and a prominent revolutionary hero is likened to a giant cockroach, and particularly reciting it to a group of people, meant certain death.

The decision to dissent despite the clear danger ahead could perhaps be explained using Lacan's commentary on *Antigone*. Lacan writes that Antigone "could not bear" the injustice to the extent that it "weighs down on her" (Lacan, 2008, p. 323). The Chorus who calls her "so mad and defiant, so disobedient to a King's decree" (2008, p. 324), are a group of observers rather than "actors" (as most choruses are in Greek tragedies). Lacan calls them "a docile collection of yes-men" (2008, p. 326). To the Chorus, Antigone and her actions are "raw", almost uncivilized; her decision to protest takes her "beyond the limits of the human" (2008, p. 324). The Chorus of Elders is disturbed by the very idea of someone showing disrespect for the law, albeit created by another human being who just happens to be above others in the hierarchy. They are keen to demonstrate their compliance and obedience to Creon:

> You, being sovereign, make what laws you will
> Both for the dead and those of us who live.
> *(Sophocles, 1998, p. 9)*

According to Jung, the trickster – the very metaphor for disobedience and change – is both "subhuman and superhuman, a bestial and divine being, whose chief and most alarming characteristic is his unconsciousness" (CW 9/I: para. 472). The Elders' fascination and criticism of Antigone's "madness"

The Soviet Antigones   181

and lack of civilized behaviour are signs of being institutionalized – of being so ingrained into the system that their grasp of the situation is severely limited. Like Mandelstam, Antigone has done the unthinkable – she has gone beyond the system for no other reason than not being able to bear it anymore (as Lacan puts it) and has become the martyr – one of the noblest incarnations of the trickster principle.

Mikhail Bulgakov

The novelist Mikhail Bulgakov (1891–1940) probably had the most mysterious fate of all Soviet tricksters: although his novels and plays, including *The Master and Margarita* (completed in 1940) and *A Dog's Heart* (completed in 1925) were neither realistic nor ideologically safe to be printed or staged, he was nevertheless inexplicably liked by Joseph Stalin (Curtis, 2012). In Bulgakov's case, Stalin's sadistic "love" did not mean anything good – the writer was locked in a limbo, not being able to either publish or go abroad. He sublimated his frustration into writing plays about creatives being persecuted by tyrants – Moliere, Pushkin – choices simultaneously conformist and dangerous because both were regarded in the Soviet Union as revolutionaries fighting against the aristocracy, and yet were used by the playwright to express his defiance in the face of oppression. Bulgakov stayed in this stifling trickster state up until his death from nephrosclerosis on March 10, 1940.

The curious and oxymoronic relationship between the tyrant and the writer, the system of oppression and the trickster attempting to keep creativity alive, is well documented and was even made into a play – *The Collaborators* (2011) by John Hodge. Stalin certainly knew how to control the country's creative forces: the braver ones were arrested and exiled or shot, some – like the poet Vladimir Mayakovsky (1893–1930) – committed suicide; others were stuck in a limbo of not being able to travel or to publish, but the compliant ones were allowed to go abroad and were given *zhilploshad* or living space (spacious apartments).

Bulgakov belonged to the category of trapped tricksters metaphorically imprisoned in their own country. Throughout the second part of the 1920s, his plays were severely criticized for "anti-Soviet sentiments" and banned. Unable to find work or a stable job, the writer was destitute. Yet, bizarrely, Stalin was a big fan of *The Days of the Turbins* (1926) – Bulgakov's play about the tragic fate of several White Army officers during the Russian Civil War. The story of the Civil War was traditionally depicted as black-and white (or, rather, red-and-white) – no moral ambiguities were allowed, and the enemy was clearly delineated. By contrast, Bulgakov's play portrays the officers as human rather than a grotesque, objectified enemy, and Stalin seemed to appreciate this. No other author, songwriter or painter was allowed to express insolence on this scale. The play was cancelled in 1929 but reinstated in 1932 in Moscow Art Theatre – the only place where it was allowed to run; more or less for Stalin who saw it many times.

On 18 April 1930, three weeks after sending a letter to the government demanding that he is allowed to go abroad, Bulgakov received an unexpected phone call from Stalin. The *vozhd* asked him if he *really* wanted to go abroad, to which the terrified Bulgakov replied that, obviously, a Soviet writer cannot live outside of his homeland (Curtis, 2012, p. 111). Stalin rewarded him with the promise of a job at the Moscow Art Theatre – something Bulgakov was very happy to hear after having previously been rejected. Soon after he became the MAT's assistant director.

Stalin's attention clearly flattered the writer – after all, many of his colleagues and ordinary citizens were imprisoned and shot for lesser "crimes" than writing prose doubting the moral righteousness of the regime, such as the novella *A Dog's Heart* (1925), and he was spared this terrible fate. Yet the limbo proved to be impossible for Bulgakov.

Like Mandelstam, he attempted to appease the tyrant with a flattering play about the young Stalin called *Batum*. Predictably, Stalin did not believe the sincerity of the playwright's intentions and the play was not allowed to be staged. Although not physically imprisoned, but nonetheless trapped and marginalized, he was writing, to use a Russian expression, "into the table" – producing texts without any hope that they would ever see the light of day. To apply Lacan's analysis of Antigone's suffering, to Bulgakov, he crossed

> the entrance to the zone between life and death. . . . [His] punishment will consist in [his] being shut up or suspended in the zone between life and death. And it is from that moment on that [his] complaint begins, [his] lamentation on life.
>
> *(Lacan, 2008, p. 345)*

Bulgakov lived for his art and died writing. Creativity, one of the key trickster attributes, is something that a human mind cannot control, something that is born regardless of the will and wishes of its human carrier – something that grows out of the artist like a tree, as a "force that achieves its end either with tyrannical might or with the subtle cunning of the nature itself, quite regardless of the personal fate of the individual who is its vehicle" (CW15: para. 114). A true writer cannot stop writing, and even when the human form suffers or dies, the force itself lives on and keeps giving. The system will attempt to silence the trickster, but ever the shapeshifter, it will be reborn in a different reincarnation. Creative forces can be trapped and even temporarily squeezed into a box, but eventually they will find a way of escaping. Or, in the words of Woland from *Master and Margarita* (the novel Bulgakov completed shortly before his death) "manuscripts don't burn" (Bulgakov, 1997, p. 406).

Joseph Brodsky

In the 1960s and 1970s, a new trickster phenomenon emerged in the Soviet Union – the "buried alive" trickster force, the dissident movement. Not surprisingly, many members of the movement, including the poet Joseph Brodsky, the writer Sergey Dovlatov (1941–1990) and the musician

Mstislav Rostropovich (1927–2007) were eventually thrown out of the country and settled abroad. The regime had a range of ways of suppressing the intelligentsia and keeping the hazardous trickster in check. They include harassment, censorship, persecution, imprisonment (including in mental health institutions) and exile. The trickster could either be stifled with the help of prisons, psychiatric hospitals and other authoritarian institutions, or – when everything else failed – expelled from the country altogether as a foreign body.

For instance, Joseph Brodsky went through every harassment imaginable organized by the representatives of the system but still refused to conform to the "norm" or to cooperate with them. A gifted poet and translator, he was arrested in 1964 and put on trial for "social parasitism", vagrancy, corruption of youth and distribution of prohibited materials. After the trial he went through the most powerful "trickster silencing" ordeals the system had: psychological and physical torture at two different psychiatric clinics, imprisonment and internal exile with hard labour (Haven, 2002, p. xviii). He was targeted because being a poet (or, at least, a poet not being recognized by the state as such) was not a proper vocation. Brodsky's survival skills matched those of the mythological Prometheus, and his ability to restore himself after a significant trauma could rival those of the North American tricksters Coyote or Wakdjunkaga (Radin, 1956): in these conditions he kept writing poems and learning foreign languages (2002, pp. xviii–xix).

Seeing that all their efforts to crush the trickster failed, and that he still kept writing and being proactive, the Soviet authorities announced their decision to expel Brodsky from the country. True to himself, Brodsky told them that he did not wish to go anywhere, to which the reply was that he would still have to leave because "the coming winter was going to be very cold" (2002, p. xix). In 1972 he travelled to Vienna where he was met by Auden, then to London, and finally to the United State (Volkov, 1992, p. 130).

In his Nobel Prize acceptance speech, Joseph Brodsky describes the relationship between literature and the state in temporal terms as the conflict of the present and the past, between today and yesterday. It is the system that is really impermanent, not the trickster because the system is man-made, and literature draws out of the sublime – the creative impulse. Thus, the poet should avoid being lured by the system, "mesmerized" by its features because they will lose credibility and timelessness:

> Language and, presumably, literature are things that are more ancient and inevitable, more durable than any form of social organization. The revulsion, irony, or indifference often expressed by literature towards the state is essentially a reaction of the permanent – better yet, the infinite – against the temporary, against the finite. To say the least, as long as the state permits itself to interfere with the affairs of literature, literature has the right to interfere with the affairs of the state. A political system, a form of social organization,

as any system in general, is by definition a form of the past tense that aspires to impose itself upon the present (and often on the future as well); and a man whose profession is language is the last one who can afford to forget this. The real danger for a writer is not so much the possibility (and often the certainty) of persecution on the part of the state, as it is the possibility of finding oneself mesmerized by the state's features, which, whether monstrous or undergoing changes for the better, are always temporary.

(Joseph Brodsky – Nobel Lecture)

Lacan writes that in the play by Sophocles, Antigone appears

as αυτόνομος, as a pure and simple relationship of the human being to that of which he miraculously happens to be the bearer, namely, the signifying cut that confers on him the indomitable power of being what he is in the face of everything that opposes him.

(Lacan, 2008, p. 348)

Brodsky managed to remain this αυτόνομος – true to himself and his ideas – in the face of legal and psychiatric torture at the hands of the Soviet authorities.

Creativity is an invaluable element of the social climate. One of its key roles is managing stagnation and providing cultural renewal. It keeps social mechanisms healthy and vibrant while also challenging and questioning the political processes. A society in which the creative trickster is repressed suffers from stagnation, and eventually its elements start dying off. Damage to the trickster equals damage to the freedom of expression. Without the creative impulse, which is responsible for the singularity of each individual, mass thinking may give birth to a monstrous version of systemic narcissism. The trickster foregrounds voices of dissent, whereas the collective shadow emerges from the depths of the national psyche and rolls like a wave, sweeping everything in its path. In the Soviet Union, the revolutionary optimism and elation of 1917 soon transmogrified into a controlling, trickster-bashing nightmare which had lasted for seven decades and finally, devoid of renewing energy, ran out of steam and fell apart like a house of cards.

Note

Material from this chapter first appears in *The Trickster and the System: Identity and Agency in Contemporary Society* (2015).

References

Brodsky, Joseph (1987). Nobel Lecture, NobelPrize.org. Nobel Media AB 2018. Retrieved from www.nobelprize.org/prizes/literature/1987/brodsky/lecture/.

Bulgakov, Mikhail (1997). *The Master and Margarita*, Trans. R. Pevear and L. Volokhonsky. London: Penguin Classics.

Bulgakov, Mikhail (2007). *The Heart of a Dog*, Trans. Michael Glenny. London: Penguin Classics.

Curtis, J.A.E. (2012). *Manuscripts Don't Burn. Mikhail Bulgakov: A Life in Letters and Diaries*. London: Bloomsbury.

Haven, Synthia (Ed.) (2002). *Joseph Brodsky: Conversations*. Jackson, MS: University Press of Mississippi.

Jung, C.G. (2014). *The Collected Works* (CW), edited by G. Adler, M. Fordham, & H. Read and translated by R.F.C. Hull. London: Routledge.

Lacan, Jaques (2008). *The Ethics of Psychoanalysis. The Seminars of Jacques Lacan: Book VII*. London: Routledge.

Mandel'shtam, Osip (1983). *Selected Poems*, Trans. David McDuff. London: Writers and Readers.

Radin, Paul (1956). *The Trickster: A Study in American Indian Mythology*. New York: Schocken Books.

Sophocles (1998). *Antigone, Oedipus the King, Electra*, Trans. H.D.F. Kitto. Oxford: Oxford University Press.

Volkov, Solomon (1997). *Conversations With Joseph Brodsky: A Poet's Journey Through the Twentieth Century*. New York: Simon and Schuster.

TWELVE

Thunder, Perfect Mind: entering the land of the sublime

Isabelle M. DeArmond

Introduction

Jung described images as a gate to the subliminal and as powerful instruments for stirring psychic energy. He said: "These images, ideas, beliefs, or ideals operate through the specific energy of the individual, which he cannot always utilize at will for this purpose, but which seems rather to be drawn out of him by the images" (Jung, 1967b/1952, p. 157). Poetry, with a tapestry of colourful, evocative words, can also convey images and stir the psyche. Attending to the psychic energy these images spark in the reader is a way to explore the psyche. I will here describe my personal relationship to a poetic text, *Thunder, Perfect Mind* from the Nag Hammadi scriptures (Poirier, 2007) and, being attentive to the emerging internal force that engages and responds to the text, how ultimately this relationship is a relationship to the self, the whole psyche, including conscious and unconscious contents. Moreover, being with *Thunder* is an encounter with the sublime, irrational and inhuman, and with the transcendent.

For Jung, individuation consists of an awareness of recessed parts of the psyche and therefore of an increased consciousness. In Jung's representation of the psyche, the self is the totality of the psyche including the ego, the conscious part of the psyche, but also the *shadow* and the personal unconscious. The self, often represented in dreams or active imagination by an *imago dei*, image of the transcendent (Jung, 1969/1958, p. 469), is in direct relationship with the collective unconscious through numerous archetypes, which are patterns of psychic functioning and which are expressed through collectively shared images charged with energy (Jung, 1967c/1952, p. 232). Complexes within the personal unconscious have an archetypal core and are therefore bridging the psyche to the collective unconscious. The self, emanating from the archetypal realm, is not to be confused with Divinity and therefore often not capitalized by contemporary Jungian authors. Stein (2008), commenting on the relationship between the Divinity and the self said:

> If the self is an *imago Dei*, the *Dei* of which it is an image must be greater, a deeper mystery, a more encompassing

reality. If, moreover, there exists some kind of congruence between the structure of the self and the *Dei* of which it is an *imago*, and both can be said to be a coincidence of opposites, a composite of brightest light and densest darkness, they reflect one another.

(Stein, 2008, p. 313)

Moreover, in Fordham's model, in order to avoid the confusion between the self and the experience of the self, the definition of the self is reserved to the psychosomatic entirety of the individual (Urban, 2008, p. 331). In this model, there is a deintegration of the psyche out of an early psychosomatic unity during early development (Urban, 2008, p. 334).

According to Poirier (2007, pp. 367–371), the text of *Thunder, Perfect Mind* dates from the first half of the fourth century and is a Coptic translation of a lost Greek original. The place and date of composition are unknown as well as the exact background. *Thunder, Perfect Mind* comes from a Jewish wisdom tradition but a gnostic background is also possible. *Thunder, Perfect Mind* conveys for me an evocation of the sublime and of the numinous defined by Otto (1958[1923], pp. 12–24) by the added valence of terror and fear to the sublime and by the experience of the *terror tremendum*, a combination of awfulness, surrender and energy. This is not a unique representation of the feminine divine and similar expressions of the divine exist. These include the Great Mother with her positive and negative features (Neumann, 1974, pp. 24–54); the threatening figure of Salome in Jung's *The Red Book* (Jung, 2009, pp. 245–248); Isis, Sophia and the widow of the Kabbalah (Jung, 1963[1955], pp. 20–22) and the dark and beautiful Shulamite of *The Song of Songs* (Bloch and Bloch, 2006, p. 47). All share the same voice and have the power to stir deep layers of the psyche. I focus here on the nature of my relationship to *Thunder* as an *imago dei*, an image of the transcendent and an expression of the sublime and how this relationship is inscribed in the Jungian approach of individuation.

The voice of *Thunder, Perfect Mind*

Thunder first grasps the reader by introducing herself and her purpose. She is a messenger from the beyond and insists to be heard:

I was sent from the power and have come to those who contemplate me and am found among those who seek me. Look at me, you who contemplate me, and you who hear, listen to me. You awaiting me, take me to yourselves. Do not banish me from before your eyes.

(Poirier, 2007, p. 372)

Her self-description becomes more and more vibrant and colourful and uses dramatic opposites defying the rational mind. There is a confusion of active and passive roles:

> I am the first and the last. I am the honored and the scorned. I am the whore and the holy. I am the wife and the virgin. I am the mother and the daughter. I am the limbs of my mother. I am a barren woman who has many children. I have had many weddings and have taken no husband. I am a midwife and a woman who does not give birth. I am the solace of my own birth pains. I am bride and groom, and my husband produced me. I am the mother of my father and the sister of my husband, and he is my offspring. . .
>
> *(Poirier, 2007, pp. 372–373)*

Thunder turns to deeper and deeper opposites urging to stay with her.

> I am silence that is incomprehensible and insight whose memory is great. I am the voice whose sounds are many and the word whose appearances are many. I am the utterance of my own name. . . . For I am knowledge and ignorance. I am shy and bold. I am shameless; I am ashamed. I am tough and I am terror. I am war and peace.
>
> *(Poirier, 2007, p. 373).*

She takes us in a dance with an infernal tempo.

> I am present in all fears, and I am strength in agitation. I am a weak woman, and I am well in a pleasant locale. I am foolish and I am wise. . . . I am the one called life, and you have called me death. I am the one called law, and you have called me lawless. I am the one you pursued, and I am one you seized. I am one you have scattered, and you have gathered me together. I am the one before whom you have been ashamed, and you have been shameless to me. I am a woman who does not celebrate festivals, and I am she whose festivals are many. I, I am godless, and I have many gods. . . . I am the knowledge of my search, the discovery of those who seek me, the command of those who ask of me, the power of powers, through my knowledge, of angelic ambassadors, through my word, of gods among gods, through my counsel, of spirits of all people dwelling with me, of women dwelling within me. I am honored and praised, and scornfully despised. I am peace, and war has come because of me. I am alien and citizen. I am substance and a woman without substance.
>
> *(Poirier, 2007, pp. 374–376).*

The poem ends with an injunction for attention and a promise of eternal life to the ones who listen to her.

Relating to *Thunder, Perfect Mind*

I am in awe, fascinated and deeply moved whenever I read this text; *Thunder* talks with a strong, deep voice. I also wonder what is unique in *Thunder* and why she is touching me so deeply. She seems to know the words to soften my heart. I am transported into a creative and ambiguous space where my rational mind is at rest.

The tapestry of words brings images of strong and colourful opposites, as when she says, "I am the whore and the holy". The liberating constellation of opposites creates space and freedom of being. I feel more and more being thrown into a plastic space with infinite possibilities of being, possibilities evoked by the multiplicity of *Thunder*'s facets. All these opposites, either positive or negative, belong to *Thunder*. I feel free to playfully embody one of *Thunder*'s opposites and then the other, no matter how provocative she could be. I am empowered to be the "honored and the scorned". She is shamelessly breaking the boundaries of what seems acceptable. There is often a confusion of subject and object, as when she says: "I am the solace of my own birth pains". She becomes simultaneously the giver and the receiver. I am *Thunder* and she is I, since there is no longer a subject and an object. In this space, the multitude of beings freely coexist, and the beings no longer exclude each other. I can also espouse the shadowy aspects of the feminine and live the unacceptable through her. I fear *Thunder*'s destructiveness and walks on a narrow bridge, wondering if it is safe to trustfully follow her. The transformation I am subjected to imparts destructiveness, but I trust destructiveness and creativity will bring transformation. She has the power of separating opposites and rearranging them. *Thunder* is not human, and I am fascinated by the impossibility to grasp her and also by her power of foreknowledge. I am reassured by images of birthing, as when she says, "I am the solace of my own birth pains", that something new from the confrontation of opposites will emerge. I also feel empathy for her singularity, her isolation, suffering and rejection. She evokes in me a call for reparation, healing and unification.

Being with *Thunder* is a departure from the rational mind, and *Thunder* is a kingdom of multiplicity, a sacred container of transformation. She allows the paradox to be once irreconcilable opposites, as for example being, "a barren woman who has many children". *Thunder* is defying logic and invites consciousness to rest. She is paradoxical and the discourse is obscure from the perspective of the rational mind, as when she says, "I am silence that is incomprehensible and insight whose memory is great". *Thunder*'s voice defeats my understanding and leaves me vulnerable without the lustre of the usually respected rational mind. I have to separate from my safe rational side and trust the other side of me, free from the burden of the ego. I feel free, with no limitation of time and space; I am out of ego boundaries; I belong to something larger.

Thunder is an injunction to relate. She demands attention and imposes a transpersonal reality. She belongs to a dreamy world but she is the one who awakens me from my uni-dimensional ego life to embrace a larger reality. She is an encouragement to dare and explore through a relationship to her and not through deeds. Eroticism is ever present, as when she says, "I have had many weddings and have taken no husband". *Thunder* is fully using the erotic dimension, body-based and non-verbal, to reach out to the human heart and arouse the emotion of union. The materiality of the body impulses adds a level of concreteness and reality to the bonding experience. Eros is a way to grasp me, connect and unite the opposites in her and in me all together. *Thunder* can be authoritarian and stern in her injunction to receptiveness and in her wrathful predication. She is the authority to remind me to devote all my attention to her and to her imaginal field. Her discourse is an injunction to receptiveness to a broad range of opposites and a widening of consciousness. *Thunder* asserts her expectations no matter what my ego is embedded into. As a biblical prophet, she can be judging, predicating, forcefully leading the way and using fear to enforce her law. I feel surrendered, powerless and moulded by her archetypal force.

In this poem, there is a rhythm created by the successive juxtaposition of two opposites and by the emergence of a third component, the imaginal field of possibilities, in between. The three times tempo is created by one opposite, the other and me dancing in between and identifying with one opposite and then the other. *Thunder* takes me in an exhilarating dance, which leaves me breathless, speechless and resilient to whatever could happen. My body surprisingly knows the steps and I dance this infernal tango with ease. Once again, the psychic change is anchored in the body impulses.

Mapping the journey

I will attempt to retrace the steps of the dance with *Thunder* and with the sublime to better appreciate the imprint of the relationship to the sublime on the psyche. Is *Thunder* an external reality or a projection of my own psyche? If *Thunder* is stirring my psyche, as probably it does to others, what is the nature of the changes and how are these changes inscribed into the conceptual framework of individuation described by Jung?

An encounter with the sublime and the numinous

Thunder is an example of where the sublime and the numinous meet. In the Oxford Dictionary, sublime refers to an experience "of such excellence, grandeur, or beauty as to inspire great admiration or awe." The origin of the word sublime is *sublimis* in Latin, which means high, elevated. The sublime is in the realm of the suprarational. Kant, in his *Analytic of the Sublime* (2005[1790], pp. 61–66), emphasized the energy and the irrational/unpredictable, stormy character of the experience in the definition of the sublime. He differentiated the beautiful from the sublime; "The sublime touches, the beautiful charms" (2011[1764], p. 16). He defined the sublime based on the emotions it triggers. It is not so much the object that is sublime but the state of mind in the estimation of the object. When the feeling of it is accompanied with some dread or melancholy, the sublime is called the terrifying sublime; when the feeling is accompanied with quiet admiration, it is called the noble sublime; and when it is met with a sense of beauty, it is called the magnificent sublime. For example, St Peter's in Rome is magnificent. Its frame is grand and simple. The expansive display of gold and mosaics gives the sentiment of the sublime (Kant, 2011[1764], p. 17). Talking about his intuited emotion of entering St Peter's at Rome, Kant said:

> For there is here a feeling of the inadequacy of his Imagination for presenting the Ideas of a whole, wherein the Imagination reaches its maximum, and, in striving to surpass it, sinks back into itself, by which, however, a kind of emotional satisfaction is produced.
>
> *Kant, 2005[1790], p. 67*

Kant contrasts the sublime and the beautiful in terms of dynamic energy. For Kant, the feeling of the sublime is characterized by a movement of the mind bound up to judge the object, while in case of the beautiful, the mind is in a restful contemplative state (Kant, 2005[1790], p. 70).

For Hegel, the sublime is a synthesis and is met at the ultimate condition defined as one "in which the synthesis is remade, wrong relations reversed, and a perfect correspondence brought about between the ethical, intellectual and physical elements which, in all concrete existence, can never be separated" (Hegel, 2012[1892], p. 175). Hegel includes the negative in his definition of the sublime. He gives as an example the effort of moral heroism, which is always an emotion of the sublime even though moral heroism also includes strength of will in the cause of evil (Hegel, 2012[1892], p. 180).

Therefore, the sublime could be described as an experience including the elements of awe, with positive and negative elements, transcendence, and multiplicity with the concomitant presence of opposites, and a pregnancy of meanings and potentiality. *Thunder* meets this definition of the sublime. She forces respect and fear. She embodies the extremes of the feminine. She is irrational and inhuman. She has multiple faces and constantly defines herself in irreconcilable opposites. She is impossible to grasp and seems to have the power of foreknowledge.

In addition to evocating the sublime, *Thunder* also conveys an experience of the numinous. Rudolf Otto (1958[1923], pp. 8–11) defined the nature of the numinous based on the feelings it is stirring. The numinous adds to the sublime a valence of terror and fear. For Otto, we experience the numinous when we experience a sense of *terror tremendum* and we are drawn to the terror with a strange fascination called *fascinans* (1958[1923], pp. 31–32). The *tremendum* is evocated by the combination of awfulness, "overpoweringness" (*majestas*) and energy.

This energy could express itself in different forms. Otto said: "It clothes itself in symbolical expressions – vitality, passion, emotional temper, will, force, movement, excitement, activity, impetus" (Otto, 1958[1923], p. 23).

192   Isabelle M. DeArmond

The Dionysiac energy and vitality can also express themselves through eros and desire. All of the elements of awfulness, overpoweringness, and energy or vitality contained in an experience of the numinous belong also to the experience of the sublime. However, relatedness to the transcendent and a mysterious irrationality belong more specifically to the numinous. For Otto, a common trend of mysticism is "the *Identification*, in different degrees of completeness, of the personal self with the transcendent Reality" (1958[1923], p. 22, italic in text). For Otto, *Mysterium* stresses the irrational and first means unexplained mystery. In the religious sense, the most striking experience of the *Mysterium* is what is beyond the sphere of the intelligible and fills the mind with wonder and astonishment (1958[1923], p. 26).

In *Thunder* too, the wrathful predication is intended to raise fear. This multiplicity of the expression of a force, or energy, is also present in *Thunder* along with eros. In her monologue, *Thunder* wrestles to establish a connection with the reader and, in turn, I am drawn to identify with her. Elements very representative of a numinous experience, such as an intense relatedness or identification and an emphasis on the irrational are ever-present.

The fertile sublime

Being with *Thunder* is entering the fertile land of the sublime. *Thunder* is close to another interesting archetypal image of the feminine divine, Sophia. In Gnosticism and Kabbalah's myth, Sophia, the spouse of God, had broken the universal vessel of light and was trying to retrieve the sparks of light to repair the broken vessel and restore wholeness and unity (Scholem, 1995[1941], pp. 265–269). Sophia is a redeeming image of wholeness. Here again, in Sophia's myth there is a contrast between coexisting opposites within the same myth: containment and infinity, multiplicity and unity, destruction and repair, darkness and light. Interestingly, the description of Sophia Jung gave could easily be superimposed to *Thunder*. He said, comparing Sophia to the earth and the serpent hidden in the earth:

> [I]t is the moon, the mother of all things, the vessel, it consists of opposites, has a thousand names, is an old woman and a whore, as Mater Alchimia it is wisdom and teaches wisdom, it contains the elixir of life in potentia and is the mother of the Saviour and of the *filius Macrocosmi*, it is the earth and the serpent hidden in the earth, the blackness and the dew and the miraculous water which brings together all that is divided.
> *(Jung, 1963[1955], p. 21, italic in text)*

The relationship to Sophia or to *Thunder* is constellating the formless psyche for transformation. These divine figures contain opposites and are an indefatigable force of unification and repair. *Thunder* as an expression of the self is a challenge to the narrow way of defining oneself through the lens of the ego. In a world giving a one-sided preference to the rational mind's world view, *Thunder* equally asserts the multiple aspects of her personality, and the permanent reality of the transcendent shines through her. *Thunder* may represent an *imago dei* and therefore a representation of the self, including the dark psychic contents. Relating to her brings energy, a reconfiguration of the psyche and an enlargement of consciousness. It is an experience of de-integration or deconstruction and a freedom of being. This deconstruction is critical to allow the full expression of other parts of the personality, which needs to be enlivened for wholeness. The experience of being with *Thunder* is also a widening of the horizons of reality.

Thunder is a companion, a messenger and a guide to another side of reality through the sublime's field. She guides me in the journey to the subliminal and gives me the strength to face this other frightful side of reality. *Thunder* is the *sorror mystica* of the alchemists that is a mystical companion for the alchemical opus. As in analysis, where analyst and analysand are forming a couple, with the analyst holding inaccessible parts of the analysand's psyche, *Thunder* may be here holding the irreplaceable symbolon and the deep recess of the psyche needed in the quest for wholeness.

In the seventh and last sermon to the dead, Jung expressed his concept of man being related to the divine:

> Man is a gateway, from which you pass through the outer worlds of Gods, daimons, and souls, into the inner world, out of the greater into the smaller world. Small and inane is man, already he is behind you, and once again you find yourselves in endless space, in the smaller or inner infinity.
>
> At immeasurable distance a lonely star stands in the zenith. This is the one God of this one man, this is his world, his pleroma, his divinity.
>
> In this world, man is Abraxas, the creator and destroyer of his own world.
>
> *(Jung, 2009, p. 354, quote in text)*

Relating to *Thunder* is a way to make contact with the lonely star, to link ego consciousness with the infinite sky of the unconscious. The infinity of *Thunder* is connecting with my inner world and I become a gateway.

A transformative psychic experience

Jung considered the alchemical procedures very symbolic to individuation. The alchemists projected their psychological and spiritual transformations on matter, and there is an implicit correspondence between spiritual, psychological and concrete material transformations. The action word of sublimation means literally to cause to pass from the solid state to the vapor state by heating and to condense back to a solid form. This is an interesting allusion to some concretization of the sublime. The alchemical stage of sublimation was interpreted by Jung as a stage in the process of individuation (Jung, 1968b[1952], pp. 242–254) and as transference (Jung, 1966b[1954],

194 Isabelle M. DeArmond

pp. 206–207). The first stage of the procedure is the *unio mentalis*, a mental union of spirit and soul, consciousness and unconsciousness. For Jung, the goal of the *unio mentalis* is "the attainment of full knowledge of the heights and depths of one's own character" (1963[1955], p. 474). The *unio mentalis* stage is evocative of the mental union of ego-driven consciousness to the larger unconsciousness, as when relating with ego consciousness to the symbolic imagery of *Thunder*. Becoming aware of the opposites of *Thunder* facilitates the conscious apprehension of the diverse facets of one's personality and facilitates a wider consciousness. According to this paradigm, the sublime experience of relating to *Thunder* is an alchemical experience of sublimation and induces a transformative psychic experience.

Being with *Thunder* is a departure from the dualistic mind. Giving precedence to rational, analytic mind gives a narrow experience of reality and unilaterally develops one part of the psyche. When writing *The Red Book*, Jung (2009) gave free way to active imagination and described his encounter with different archetypal images or splints of his own unconscious psyche. At this time, he was trying to make room for the imaginal in a busy life filled with obligations and dominated by a powerful discriminant mind. In *The Red Book*, Jung described the *prima materia* as the field of undifferentiation and potentiality of being, while consciousness and ego life brings differentiation and the liveliness of one opposite at the expense of the other. He said:

> [H]ow did creation come into being? Creatures came into being, but not creation: since creation is the very quality of the Pleroma, as much as noncreation, eternal death. Creation is ever-present, and so is death. The Pleroma has everything, differentiation and nondifferentiation.
>
> *(Jung, 2009, p. 347)*

While ego consciousness gives liveliness to some parts of the personality, relating to *Thunder*, as probably relating to other expressions of the divine would do, is a gateway to the *prima materia*, the formless matter needed for the alchemical opus and the process of individuation. Because of her insistence that two dramatic opposites all together belong to her personality, and because at times of the cryptic self-description with opposites which exclude each other, relating to *Thunder* is leading to a way of experiencing far from the dualistic and rational mind. *Thunder* is hard to follow without abandoning the safe cushioning of a dualistic, rational approach. There is no longer a subject and an object. Thus, irrational and inhuman, the powerful and beautiful *Thunder* is a gateway and as an archetypal image of the feminine divine, she belongs to the land of the sublime and the transcendent.

Activation of the transcendent function and release of psychic energy

In one's individuation journey, the task is to integrate opposites and contradictory aspects of the personality, including the less accessible dark side of one's personality, called the *shadow* (Jung, 1966a[1953], p. 266). In Jung's

Thunder, Perfect Mind   195

model of wholeness and individuation, individuation is the process whereby psychic contents, including archetypal images, rise to consciousness and make connection to the ego. The transcendent function mediates the union of opposites and results in wholeness (Jung, 1981[1960], pp. 73–74). The transcendent function operates as a mode of understanding through experience mediated by the archetypes (Jung, 1966a[1953], p. 109). Jung defined what is required to activate the transcendent function as unconscious material coming from dreams and fantasies (Jung, 1981[1960], pp. 77–81). The intensity of the emotional disturbance gives energy for an enlargement of consciousness (Jung, 1981[1960], p. 82), maybe through the activation of an archetype of transformation, which Jung defined as "typical situations, places, ways and means, that symbolize the kind of transformation in question" (Jung, 1968a[1959], p. 38). According to this definition, the sublime experience of entering St Peter's at Rome, as described by Kant earlier, would activate the archetype of transformation and release energy for psychic transformation.

Jung noted that individuation "occurs when the analysis has constellated the opposites so powerfully that a union or synthesis of the personality becomes an imperative necessity" (Jung, 1963[1955], p. 494). The release of the control of the psyche by the ego is necessary for individuation and for the experience of the self to occur. For Jung, "_the experience of the self is always a defeat for the_ ego" (Jung, 1963[1955], p. 546, italics in text).

The poetic and lavish profusion of opposites in _Thunder_ may foster a transformation of the psyche through the activation of the transcendent function with deconstruction of the unity and split in opposites within the psyche. _Thunder_'s transformative power may function through reenactment: identification with positive and with negative aspects and being in relationship with each. In this wedding dance of being with _Thunder_, the transcendent function is activated by the polarization of the opposites of _Thunder_'s attributes and the opposites within my psyche by assimilation. The transformative power of _Thunder_ may also occur through an urge to move to a wider place of rest. Ultimately, being with _Thunder_ generates a feeling of harmony and wholeness and has a centring effect. This centring effect may come as a return to equilibrium after a tumultuous storm of emotions or as a result of feeling one with a larger reality, feeling which is impossible to delineate in human terms.

Eros, a force for this transformation, is very present in the Kabbalistic tradition, and one of the expressions of the divine is _yesod_, the male potency which guaranties and consummates the _hieros gamos_, the holy union of male and female power (Scholem, 1996[1960], p. 104). This union has been described by Jung as a powerful image in the process of individuation (Jung, 1963[1955], pp. 534–535). Jung, commenting on the alchemical symbolism of Rex and Regina and on the surrender to the power of the _anima_ as a psychopomp, noted the redeeming effects of the changes of the conscious attitude and said:

> This more exalted attitude raises the status of the anima from that of a temptress to a psychopomp. . . . The coronation, apotheosis, and marriage signalize the equal status

of conscious and unconscious that becomes possible at the
highest level – a *coincidentia oppositorum* with redeeming
effects.

(Jung, 1963[1955], p. 380).

In the case of relating to *Thunder*, attraction and desire are closely related to
transformation. Facing the sublime and numinous *Thunder* may release psychic energy through the transformation induced by changes in libido. Jung
defined libido as "an energy-value, which is able to communicate itself to
any field of activity whatsoever, be it power, hunger, hatred, sexuality, or
religion, without being itself a specific instinct" (1967a[1952], p. 137). Jung
broadly identified "psychic energy" with "libido". For Jung, the canalization
of the libido is a force for psychological growth that is for a change in the
personality and wholeness. For him, "the libido that is forced into regression
by the obstacle always reverts to the possibilities lying dormant in the individual" (1967b[1952], p. 153). Moreover, being attracted to *Thunder* may
be a desire for some aspects of the personality we do not possess, or not possess yet, including the dark aspects of the *shadow*. Lacan (2013[1958–1959],
pp. 555–573) developed the dynamic of desire in the analytical field and
noted that the analytic experience is based on the tension between the object
of desire and the subject. This tension is ever-present in *Thunder*. Also, for
Lacan, in analysis, the desire is the high point, the key to unlock a sequence
of actions, which are the expression of our deep inner truth (2013[1958–59],
pp. 558–559). With this paradigm, the attraction to or desire of *Thunder* is
a way to unlock and develop the expression of the personality from within.

Tantric yoga is a striking example of visualization and eros at the service
of spiritual development with the confrontation, assimilation, love making
to the internal Śakti, the supreme female principle. Zimmer notes:

> [B]oth visualize and experience life and the universe as
> the revelation of that Supreme Divine Force (*śakti*) with
> which he is in love, the all-comprehensive Divine Being in
> its cosmic aspect of playful, aimless display (*līlā*) – which
> precipitates pain as well as joy, but in its bliss transcends
> them both.
>
> *(Zimmer, 1974[1951], p. 571)*

Reciprocally, in the second sermon to the dead of *The Red Book*, Jung said
of the image of the divine Abraxas: "He is the fullness that seeks union with
emptiness" (Jung, 2009, p. 350) and touched on the complementarity of the
divine with creation.

Receiving *Thunder* is receiving an infusion of libido. *Thunder*'s passion
is critical to give energy for change and widening of consciousness. Without this encouragement, it is easy to restrain oneself to one aspect of one's
personality, to stay at the border and be afraid of entering this land of the
sublime. Relating to *Thunder* is following an impulse to receive and assimilate the divine, but the divine may equally be attracted in this relationship.

Thunder is an experience of the sublime, and she escapes a single definition. She is altogether an experience of the *prima materia*, of the collective unconscious, an expression of the self and of the transcendent. She stirs the readers to enlarge their apprehension of reality and awareness through the activation of the transcendent function and psychic libido.

Conclusion

Thunder, Perfect Mind, a poetic text from the Nag Hammadi Scriptures, is a powerful incantation strongly holding the opposites of the feminine transcendent. Being with *Thunder*, probably similarly to being with other feminine divine figures, is an experience where an aesthetic, poetic experience reaches the sublime and the numinous. I used my reflection on the nature of my attraction to *Thunder*, to the sublime, as a way to explore the relationship between sublime and psyche. In the interest of space, I kept a focus on my experience with *Thunder*, but the facets of this experience, depending on the expressions of the feminine divine, on one's own cultural heritage and personal history, the stability of this experience or its fluidity based on one's life stage remain to be studied.

Relating to *Thunder* moulds a plastic place of freedom and awareness of the possibilities of being. *Thunder* is a sacred container of experience. While, the awareness and embodiment of the extremes generates acceptance and empathy, I surrender to her archetypal creative force, being moulded by her hands. *Thunder*, with her sublime and numinous character, represents an *imago dei* and a representation of the self. She escapes and breaks the objective, rational mind. Relating to *Thunder* may very well be entering a field of transformation, with an activation of the transcendent function and a stirring of psychic energy, and the fostering of a relationship to the self with its unfathomable depth. The experience of being with *Thunder*, a powerful archetypal image of the feminine divine, is an experience of actively allowing the psyche to be stirred, an experience of being drawn to the land of the sublime, the land of the collective unconscious, an undifferentiated *prima materia* rich in possibilities. I carry *Thunder* within me.

Note

This chapter was originally written for and presented at the Joint Jung/Lacan Conference organized by Ann Casement and held in Cambridge, England, September 12–14, 2014.

References

Bloch, C. and Bloch, A. (Trans.) (2006). *The Song of Songs*. New York: Random House.

198   Isabelle M. DeArmond

Hegel, G.W.F. (2012[1892]). The Sublime and the Pathetic in Art. In J. Steinfort Kedney and G.W.F Hegel (Eds.), *Aesthetics, a Critical Exposition* (pp. 170–180). Charleston, SC: Forgotten Books.

Jung, C.G. (1963[1955]). Mysterium Coniunctionis: An Inquiry into the Separation and Synthesis of Psychic Opposites in Alchemy. In *Collected Works*, vol. 14. Princeton, NJ: Princeton University Press.

Jung, C.G. (1966a[1953]). Two Essays on Analytical Psychology. In *Collected Works*, vol. 7. Princeton, NJ: Princeton University Press.

Jung, C.G. (1966b[1954]). The Psychology of the Transference. In *Collected Works*, vol. 16. Princeton, NJ: Princeton University Press.

Jung, C.G. (1967a[1952]). The Concept of Libido. In *Collected Works*, vol. 5. Princeton, NJ: Princeton University Press.

Jung, C.G. (1967b[1952]). The Transformation of Libido. In *Collected Works*, vol. 5. Princeton, NJ: Princeton University Press.

Jung, C.G. (1967c[1952]). Symbols of the Mother and Rebirth. In *Collected Works*, vol. 5. Princeton, NJ: Princeton University Press.

Jung, C.G. (1968a[1959]). The Archetypes and the Collective Unconscious. In *Collected Works*, vol. 9. Princeton, NJ: Princeton University Press.

Jung, C.G. (1968b[1952]). The Psychic Nature of the Alchemical Work. In *Collected Works*, vol. 12. Princeton, NJ: Princeton University Press.

Jung, C.G. (1969[1958]). Answer to Job. In *Collected Works*, vol. 11. Princeton, NJ: Princeton University Press.

Jung, C.G. (1981[1960]). The Transcendent Function. In *Collected Works*, vol. 8. Princeton, NJ: Princeton University Press.

Jung, C.G. (2009). *The Red Book: Liber Novus*, Ed. S. Shamdasani. New York: W.W. Norton & Company.

Kant, I. (2005[1790]). Analytic of the Sublime. In I. Kant and J.H. Bernard (Trans.), *Critique of Judgment* (pp. 61–136). New York: Dover Publications.

Kant, I. (2011[1764]). Observations on the Feeling of the Beautiful and Sublime. In P. Frierson and P. Guyer (Eds.), *Observations on the Feeling of the Beautiful and Sublime and other Writings* (pp. 11–62). New York: Cambridge University Press.

Lacan, J. (2013[1958–'59]). *Le Seminaire, livre VI; Le desir et son interpretation* [the Seminar, Book VI; the desire and its interpretation]. Paris: Edition de la Martiniere et le Champ Freudien Editeur.

Neumann, E. (1974). *The Great Mother: An Analysis of the Archetype*, Trans. R. Manheim. Bollingen series XLVII. Princeton, NJ: Princeton University Press.

Otto, R. (1958[1923]). *The Idea of the Holy: An Inquiry into the Non-Rational Factor in the Idea of the Divine and its Relation to the Rational*, Trans. J. W. Harvey. New York: Oxford University Press.

Poirier, P.H. (2007). Thunder, Trans. M. Meyer. In M. Meyer (Ed.), *The Nag Hammadi Scriptures* (The International ed.) (pp. 367–378). New York: HarperCollins.

Scholem, G.S. (1995[1941]). *Major Trends in Jewish Mysticism*. New York: Schocken Books.

Scholem, G.S. (1996[1960]). *On the Kabbalah and its Symbolism*, Trans. R. Manheim. New York: Schocken Books.

Stein, M. (2008). "Divinity Expresses the Self . . ." An investigation. *Journal of Analytical Psychology*, 53: 305–327.

Urban, E. (2008). The "Self" in Analytical Psychology: The Function of the "Central Archetype" within Fordham's Model. *Journal of Analytical Psychology*, 53: 329–350.

Zimmer, H. (1974[1951]). *Philosophies of India*. Bollingen Series XXVI. Princeton, NJ: Princeton University Press.

THIRTEEN

Unconscious processes, instrumental music and the experience of the sublime: an exploration through Messiaen's *Quartet for the End of Time*

Giorgio Giaccardi

Introduction

While I was considering whether the music of the French composer Olivier Messiaen would be a suitable choice to exemplify my ideas on the sublime and the unconscious, I attended a performance of his *Turangalila-Symphonie*, an exuberant meditation on primordial love that has been defined as "a penetration of the barbaric through sophisticated means" (Griffiths, 2008[1985], p. 139). As it often happens when I listen to his music, I found myself in a not-me space, where all I could feel or imagine were not my own personal feelings and ideas but something more archaic and somewhat objective – a point which I will expand on later. It felt like I had been put in touch with anxiety-provoking and bewildering aspects of the mind, for which discursive understanding proves unsuitable. Messiaen's music throws the listeners into an unfamiliar territory, holding on to which requires both concentration and immersion, and yet it stirs and moves – or, as a Messiaen scholar puts it, it ejaculates (Griffith, 2008[1985], p. 138).

I also noticed that many in the audience kept looking at the programme notes, visibly puzzled and in need of some anchorage, however not out of boredom or disengagement (the final applause was enthusiastic), rather as if their usual way of listening were not suitable for the reception of that music.

That night I then had a long dream revolving around a psychotic woman who was taken care of by a team I was part of. It was a vivid dream which seemed to allow me to feel into a psychotic's mind. The only detail I could remember was that I self-assuredly told the team that she identified completely with her behaviour, therefore she was mad. I thought that this female dream figure might have appeared to represent music identified with itself

199

without concern for the ordinary human, hence I took it to be a hint that I was on the right path in choosing Messiaen's music for my exploration of the notion of the sublime.

I will argue that the experience of the sublime engendered by some instrumental music mirrors and connects to archaic and preverbal unconscious processes, hence its perceived character of radical otherness and intense energy.

The choice of instrumental music is key to my argument. Although instrumental music had obviously long existed within the Western tradition, it is only with Romanticism that it began to acquire an independent legitimation. Schopenhauer (1966[1814]) argued that music, being "a copy of the Will itself", deserves priority in the hierarchy of arts because of its unique link with the essence of feelings and the metaphysical realm of the Will. The music critic Hanslick (1854) subsequently claimed that music should be regarded as completely emancipated from anything external to it – including the metaphysical. The subject of a piece of music – Hanslick argues – is entirely within itself, nothing but dynamic sound patterns. According to the musicologist Dalhaus (1978), who has examined in detail this (controversial to some) idea of "absolute" music, such development implies a double movement of dissolution, both from song (language) and from man (empirical reality). He quotes the musicologist Kurth, who envisages the starting point of the former in Beethoven and of the latter in Bach. In Nietzsche's words, the last of Beethoven's quartets "put the entire realm of empirical reality to shame" (*ibidem*, p. 17).

The somewhat paradoxical nature of music is concisely conveyed in the following formulation by Wilson (2015, p. 13): "Music as a mode of organised sound signifies nothing, has no referent other than itself and yet is a mode of symbolization".

Psychoanalysis has taken a long while to begin to explore the peculiar symbolic function of music, and when it does so, it still usually privileges sung music, probably for its closer affinity with the symbolic register of language. However, in line with the increasing attention to prelinguistic forms of symbolization, psychoanalytic reflection would benefit from including the consideration of instrumental music in its attempts at exploring these processes.

In the next section I will briefly review the relation between music and psychoanalysis with a focus on Jung's and post-Jungian approaches to music. I will then look in greater detail into connections between the symbolic value of music and unconscious processes. This will be followed by an appraisal of the importance of music in the experience of the sublime. Finally, I will refer to Messiaen's *Quartet for the End of Time*, in order to exemplify the contribution of a type of instrumental music to the experience of the sublime and its relation to unconscious processes.

Psychoanalysis and music: a weak relation

The substantial lack of appreciation of instrumental music's contribution to psychological understanding marks psychoanalytical thought as a whole, with a few notable exceptions usually by psychoanalysts also trained as musicians (for instance, Heinrich Racker). Both Freud and Lacan remained almost silent on the subject, in what has been referred to as a "non-relation" to music (Regnault, 2010).

In one of his few references to this topic, Freud (1914, p. 211) wrote:

> I am almost incapable of obtaining any pleasure [from music]. . . . Some rationalistic, or perhaps analytic, turn of mind in me rebels against being moved by a thing without knowing why I am thus affected, and what it is that affects me.

In a recent book on psychoanalysis and music, the consequence of Freud's "melophobia" has been summarized by observing that "while musical innovation and psychoanalysis germinated on the same creative socio-cultural soil [Vienna at the turn of century] they subsequently diverged on oral and aural roads to the unconscious" (Nagel, 2013, p. 6). The same author indicates a biographical hypothesis for Freud's disdain of music, consisting of his jealousy of Martha Bernay's relationship with a musician prior to their engagement and of his mother's intention to buy a piano for his younger sister. Such jealousy may have been displaced onto music – and on the piano that Freud prohibited his (musically inclined) mother from allowing into their house.

Jung did not explore either the capacity of music to symbolically represent unconscious processes, which is all the more surprising given the indebtedness of his ideas on the unconscious to Schopenhauer. He reportedly got deeply upset by certain types of music, for instance, Beethoven's late quartets, that "churned him up almost beyond endurance" (as reported by A. Jaffe'), which he therefore avoided listening to. The fact that Jung, who notoriously endured years of immersion in deeply unsettling unconscious processes and creatively engaged with them, would be so strongly defended against music, may have to do precisely with music's inescapable ability "to reach into deep archetypal material". In other words, the Apollonian protection against the Nietzschean "overwhelming drives" afforded to Jung through structured visual symbols such as mandala images was not granted by the kind of music that he found most upsetting. He also stopped short of exploring the wealth of mythological connections between sound and the divine. For instance, in Sufism the soul before its incarnation is sound, as is God the Creator in Indian mythology (Schneider, 2007).

The neglect of music shown by the fathers of psychoanalysis may also be understood, beyond their personal complexes, if we consider the historical marginality and inferior status of music within not just the psychological discourse but also the Western intellectual tradition and the hierarchy of arts until the nineteenth century. Reservations against music may be grouped in two main categories, namely, the Platonic/Augustinian view on the potentially detrimental and manipulative influence of music on society and individuals, and the intellectual, logocentric assumptions about music as an inferior art due to its indeterminacy and lack of content, which one finds variously stated by Aquinas, Kant, Hegel and Kierkegaard among

202   Giorgio Giaccardi

others. Hegel, in his analysis of the historical process of revelation of the Spirit, sees music as inferior to poetry because of its non-conceptual nature (Davies, 2014). Although he recognized that, as a phase of intellectual history, modern music is a process of abstraction consisting of the progressive dissolution of its contents and retreating into "empty inwardness", he didn't ascribe a higher dignity to music, as "he held fast to the tradition that spirit was word", so that the philosophical history of art would end with poetry and that of the world spirit in philosophy (Dalhaus, 1978, p. 96).

Jung, however, did come to acknowledge the importance of music towards the end of his life. In 1956, for instance, he reportedly said that "music . . . reaches the deep archetypal material that we can only sometimes reach in our analytical work with patients" (quoted in Skar, 2002, p. 631). And in a letter, while declining a request to write about music, he argued that "music expresses, in some way, the *movement of feelings* (or emotional values) that cling to the unconscious processes. . . . Music expresses in sounds what fantasies and visions express in visual images. . . . I can only draw your attention to the fact that music represents the movement, development, and transformation of the motifs of the collective unconscious" (*ibidem*, p. 632). Jung's reference to music therefore highlights its inherent capacity to represent psychic dynamism and unconscious processes and is consonant with the subsequent definition of affect given by Andre Green (1999, p. 293) as a "movement in search of a form". In *Mysterium Coniunctionis*, his last book-length work completed when he was 80, Jung gave an important albeit tentative indication for the possibility of practising active imagination through music: "A musical configuration might also be possible, provided that it were really composed and written down"(Jung, 1970[1955], p. 530).

Jung's intuition that music points to a more archaic level of psychological functioning, closer to the *affective* core of the complex, was to be explored by analytical psychology decades later (McGlashan, 1987; Storr, 1992; Romano, 1999; Skar, 2002; Carta, 2009; Ashton and Bloch, 2010; see also Sapen (2012) for an application of Jungian concepts to jazz). The cited authors address this topic both from a developmental perspective, in connection to the primacy of hearing over sight in the womb and in the baby, and from an archetypal one, drawing upon mythological narratives – like Orpheus and Eurydice – that show the petrifying effect of sight and the need for the image to dissolve so that its qualities may be recovered symbolically. After losing Eurydice, clung to and frozen in his gaze, Orpheus regains her in music (Zabriskie, 2000).

Music doesn't feature significantly in Lacan's exploration of the unconscious either, and instrumental music remains fairly neglected by contemporary Lacanian studies. Some of the few references I found, though, seem to confirm, albeit from a different theoretical frame, that music is uniquely capable of reaching primitive areas of experience. Žižek acknowledges the change occurred in the state of music with the rise of Romanticism and Schopenhauer's perspective on it. He summarises the latter by saying that "what music expresses is . . . the underlying 'noumenal' flux of jouissance, beyond linguistic meaningfulness. . . . It is the inexpressible excess which forms the very core of the subject . . . what Hegel called the 'Night of the World', the abyss or radical negativity" (Žižek, 2006, pp. 229–230). From this standpoint, music is viewed as an attempt to reach for and encounter the Real (Wetzler, in Ashton and Bloch, 2010). Although Žižek warns that the music's rendering of emotions may be "a lie" (*ibidem*), this line of thinking has been recently developed by Wilson (2015, p. xvi), a Lacanian-oriented academic, for whom music can be regarded as a "language" of the Real both "as a particular system of essentially meaningless notes that nevertheless provide regularities offering structure and orientation, and as the language of love, a means of mediating jouissance or the agonies and ecstasies that result from the real of sexual difference".

Another way in which sound has been incorporated into Lacanian theory is through the consideration of the voice as "acoustic mirror" (Silverman, 1988). For instance, a Lacan-oriented musicologist (Schwarz, 1997, p. 21) has explored the idea that both the "sonorous envelope" in which human life is contained in its intrauterine stage (at least since the fourth month, when the foetus" hearing develops) and the baby's auditory field, articulated by the mother's voice, represent an acoustic mirroring, preceding the visual mirror stage, through which the baby first recognizes itself in the vocal mirror supplied by the mother. In line with these observations, the psychoanalyst Maiello (1995) explores the role of sound in the development of the foetus's capacity for symbolization, which would be fostered during the intrauterine life by the alternating presence and absence of the mother as registered through the experience of her voice and silence – the latter being the first signifier of maternal absence that the child has to face.

The symbolic function of music

A symbol, from a Jungian perspective, is a container that bounds and channels psychic energy otherwise inaccessible. It is "the psychological machine that transforms energy" (Jung, 1928, p. 50), a gradient that allows the excess of energy that individuals are endowed with to be employed, beyond its conscious use, in a way different from its natural direction. Through the symbol, the ego establishes links with affective, numinous, dynamic aspects of the psyche hitherto inaccessible to consciousness.

Instrumental music is inherently and immediately symbolic, as it does not require – or it does to a lesser extent – the preliminary work of dissolution from the fixed and coherent meaning that words and images have to undergo in order to unlock the underlying unconscious dynamism. As Lévi- Strauss (1994[1964], p. 18) puts it, "[M]usic is the only language with the contradictory attributes of being at once intelligible and untranslatable". Music is the permanent dissolving agent of the alchemical dictum "make volatile what is fixed". It has a great importance in Nietzsche's philosophy, who envisaged in Dionysian music the fundamental and creative – that is, form-dissolving – impulse behind all the arts and philosophy, breaking down the *principium individuationis* (Giaccardi, 2006). Michael Eigen (in Ashton and Bloch, 2010,

p. 166) expresses this by saying that "[music's] power can destroy your usual way of organising experience, destroy your own cliche, or habitual style, a radical revision of the psyche just by hearing a few notes". Alchemically, this process could be seen as one of liberation of sulphur – the element evoking the notion of Soul – from the prison of the complexes in which it first expresses itself and to which it remains wedded (Edinger, 1995, p. 103).

Even music's relation with feelings is less defined and concrete than in any other type of language. The philosopher Langer (1942, Chapter VIII), in her important study of symbolism, argues that music, while having a very powerful, emotional impact, is not derived from affects nor intended for them, rather it is *about* them, as it shares with them the same logical form, and for this reason can reveal the nature of feelings with a detail and truth, as well as ambivalence, that are foreclosed to language. Music "merely sounds the way the mood feels". In this sense, music is an "unconsummated symbol", which "can articulate feelings without being wedded to them". Instances of the parallel morphology of music and feelings given by Langer are crescendo, diminuendo, accelerando, ritardando, interruptions of rhythm, tensions and resolutions, fulfilment, excitation, sudden change.

From a psychoanalytic perspective, music appears closer than other symbolic products to what Freud referred to as the unrepressed unconscious, a concept later abandoned by Freud but subsequently developed in Matte Blanco's theorization of the symmetrical unconscious (Carvalho, 2014). This level of psychic experience is unconscious for structural reasons, not as a result of repression. According to Matte Blanco, in what he defines as the zone of symmetry, everything is undifferentiated and substitutable. Instincts and emotions are not discernible yet, as their identification requires discrete processes. This deeper "stratum" of the unconscious is essentially affective, albeit in an undifferentiated way, and somatic. It is unspeakable but communicable. Civitarese (2018, p. 79) argues that "hearing [compared to seeing] is still further beyond language. It has more to do with sense than meaning. More to do with the body than with the intellect".

Music may allow these "symmetrical" features of the unrepressed, presymbolic unconscious to have a glimpse of themselves and be witnessed by the listener, as a reverie into an original sensory marasmus, a "cauldron full of seething excitations" (Freud, 1933, p. 73). Botella and Botella (in Levine et al., 2013, pp. 108–109) talk about "acoustic figurability" as a possibility of connecting with unrepresented psychic processes, exemplifying such occurrence in the transference with reference to the account of an analyst facing a patient's hostile and prolonged state of silence: "The melody of a tango by Astor Piazzolla, *Adios, Nonino*, in tribute of his deceased father, invaded him during a session . . . and enabled the analyst to find a way of avoiding an impasse in the treatment".

What specifically qualifies music to isomorphically represent deep unconscious processes are two key inherent features: (1) being rooted in the physiology of the body and affects, and (2) its happening in time.

As for the first inherent dimention, music, like a sexual fantasy, is experienced through the body and the emotional mind, which makes its symbolic power more wholly felt and compelling – unbearably so to some. Music uniquely provokes strong autonomic arousals (such as "skin orgasms") occurring in "ancient emotion-generating regions of the mind" (Panksepp, 2011, p. 35) where emotional and bodily pathways of activation are inextricably intertwined. As Panksepp goes on to say, "[A]ffect is the fuel of the cognitive mind, allowing it access to the sublime".

In the Jungian theory of archetypes, the so-called infrared end of the archetypal spectrum, that is, the instinctual polarity involving the vegetative nervous system, provides a physiological foundation – hence energy – to any psychological experience. It is this infrared polarity, coexisting with the ultraviolet, spiritual end of the spectrum, that music specifically allows individuals to integrate in their experience of symbols.

A second inherent dimension of music is the temporal, which also accounts for its isomorphism with inner life. As mentioned earlier, music's happening in time offers a possibility of representation to the inherent property of affects which is movement. However, music can also transfigure physiological and existential time, offering possibilities of evoking "an atemporal dimension of time", as argued by Agamben (quoted in Civitarese, 2018, p. 79), for whom "in a musical piece, although it is somehow in time, we perceive rhythm as something that escapes the incessant flight of instants". For Civitarese, this means that rhythm "takes us out of ourselves, immersed as we are in the unnoticed flow of time, and by making us rediscover this crucial dimension it constitutes us as subjects" (*ibidem*). Lévi-Strauss (1994[1964], pp. 15–16) points out the special nature of the relation of music with time, one which it shares with mythology: "It is as if music and mythology needed time only in order to deny it. Both indeed are instruments for the obliteration of time . . . the act of listening immobilizes passing time . . . by listening to music, and while we are listening to it, we enter into a kind of immortality".

Striving for a synthesis of time-boundedness and timelessness is germane to any creative endeavour, including psychoanalysis, which is shaped by a contrast of temporalities. On one hand, we have the "analyst-master" setting the rules for the administration of time, while on the other hand, various key aspects of the psychoanalytic process point to infinity, such as inherent interminability, repetition, transference, dreamwork, regression to an "oceanic" fusion with the object. I shall illustrate later how Messiaen peculiarly and innovatively pursues such synthesis – a task also pursued by Jung in *Mysterium Coniunctionis*, which in Edinger's description (1995, p. 281) may be viewed as a "symbolic process resulting into a borderline state . . . where time and eternity are united".

The musically sublime

Instrumental music began to acquire an autonomous status at the same time as the notion of the sublime reappeared in philosophy, which was in the second half of the eighteenth century.

In the Burkean and Kantian tradition, the narrative of the sublime is linear in time and revolves around a movement from displeasure and tension (overwhelming impressions, privation of certainty, failure of imagination) to some form of resolution (relief as privation of terror, affirmation of reason) on a superior level (Shaw, 2006).

In music, this narrative was clearly present in the heroical qualities of Beethoven's symphonies, particularly the ninth, as well as in his late piano sonatas and quartets, and it was achieved through the massive and voluminous, roller coaster rides eventually leading to a newly conquered possession of tonality, or a breakthrough to a higher and more complex spiritual level.

A different narrative of the feeling of the sublime subsequently developed, starting in the Romantic period and through to the twentieth century, on which, as the musicologist Wurth (2009) argues, instrumental music played a pivotal role thanks to its inherent indeterminacy. She suggests that this idea of the sublime has to do with liminality, remaining in between two intensities rather than breaking through to another side, inhabiting the space between a longing for the infinite and a sense of loss and nostalgia. Deferral, lingering on a threshold, suspension between desire and mourning and between pleasure and pain are key aspects of a Romantic experience of the sublime. No breakthrough but hesitation.

Instrumental music appeared the natural means to reach into such an uncanny and ambivalent experience of the sublime. In the process, music undertook three orders of change that equipped it to express, produce and sustain this feeling of liminality and undecidability.

First, the Romantic view of music reverses the hierarchy between music and words as a result of which music comes home to itself, fully assuming its status of having everything within itself, never coagulating in any specific form. As Jankelevitch (1983) puts it, music has to do with the ineffable, not the unspeakable, the former being what cannot be explained, as there are infinite things to be said of it, none of which is exhaustive. Music dissolves in the moment it is played and only leaves behind a trace of a glimpse, which can then be repeatedly sought. Romanticism initiates an emptying (or *kenosis*) of music as a process of "obliteration of content by form and then the shattering of form by the sublime . . . for the subject to know itself as autonomous and surpass as infinite" (Chua, 1999, p. 188).

Also, for Jankelevitch music doesn't communicate and doesn't address an audience. From this viewpoint, the audience witnesses music speaking to itself. As he simply puts it, "Someone who talks to nobody is mad. Someone who sings to nobody, as if he were a bird, without addressing anyone, is just happy" (p. 20).

Second, at this point in time the physical quality of the sound produced by the materiality of instruments gained more prominence as an aspect of performing music. The nineteenth-century theorist Arthur Seidl distinguishes sublime in music, obtained through techniques, and sublime of music, inherent in music's very texture, that is, its sound-colour, stretched beyond the conventional use of instruments. Liszt's virtuosism, for instance, "defies aural resolution" (Wurth, 2009). One can almost hear the thing itself – ivory and metal – when listening to the piano. According to Messiaen (quoted in Van Maas, 2009, p. 103), "[T]here is one thing that is true: natural resonance of sonorous bodies". Bodily resonance never stabilizes into repeatable structures, but directly affects physiology as an individual occurrence. The physicality of instruments also affects the performer in a circular movement between matter and music, as exemplified by the Arabic musical system "maqam" that links physicality and musicality by referring at once at "a physical place in the musical scale, the fingers placing on the oud's strings and the melody which expresses this . . . a meditative state" (Faran Ensamble, 2012).

Third, music adopted a range of techniques aimed at emphasising ambivalence through deferrals, suspensions, chromatism, constant harmonic modulation and tonal ambiguity. Although the obvious examples of these techniques can be found in late Romantic composers such as Wagner, Strauss, Mahler or Busoni, Chopin himself wrote some pieces of music with an inherent uncanny character tonal ambivalence. In Jankelevitch's words (1983, p. 58), "[M]usic is the domain where ambiguity holds sway". In such domain, opposites are not played against each other nor mystically fused but are inherently and unresolvedly intertwined, like in the notion of syzygy that for Jung represents the type of *coniunctio oppositorum* pertaining to *anima* and *animus*. Roland Durand (2009[1963]) sees music as germane to what he defines as the third structure of the Imaginary, namely, the synthetic. Whereas the schizomorphic structure separates opposites and the mystical structure merges them, the synthetic is based on the notion of *coincidentia oppositorum*, in which opposites are differentiated but at the same time contained in a structure.

In sum, from the mid-nineteenth century onwards the emersion of absolute, instrumental music as a congenial art for the dissolution of individual identifications corresponds to a transformation in the notion of the sublime. Music increasingly assumes its status of pure form, suitable to attract projections of a desire for infinity and unboundedness and to represent the psychological experience of liminality. Instead of sublimatory compensation to the loss of its previous established forms, music offers now its own inherent properties as an anchorage point in the face of such process of dissolution.

In the next and last section I will describe the way Messiaen further develops music's properties and originally shapes the experience of the sublime and how the latter reflects some properties of archaic unconscious processes.

His music has to be considered in the light of the reaction to emotional expressionism that took place in the twentieth century. Jankelevicth (1983) identifies two main forms of such reaction: impressionism and a search for the inexpressive. He recapitulates the movement from expressionism to the inexpressive as follows: "[T]he expressionist expressed sentiments having to do with sensations; the impressionist takes note of his sensations about things; and inexpressive music allows things themselves to speak, in their primal rawness, without necessitating intermediaries of any kind" (p. 32). This trajectory is brought about by two subsequent negations: impressionism abolishes sentiment; inexpressive music in turn abolishes the ego.

Impressionism was a first step towards retrieving the objective, the world we are in, by freeing it up from the soul's pathos and its sticky attachments. For instance, Jankelevicth (1983, p. 36) suggests that in *La Mer* Debussy "puts a stethoscope to the ocean's chest, to the tide's lungs", as opposed to expressing the feelings evoked by the sea.

The inexpressive, in turn, implies the erasure of the human figure, a mere attention to things for how they present themselves once we have stripped them bare not only of words, but also of personal emotions and sensations. Ravel, Prokofiev, Satic, Bartok, Messiaen, among others, have contributed to this development in music. Lyotard, from a postmodern perspective, says that where the sublime is, the subject is not (Wurth, 2009). The kind of subject implied by this notion of sublime is active and engaged, yet dispassionate and detached, as conveyed by the indication given by Hindemith for the execution of his cello sonata op.25: "lively without any expression". For Langer (1942, p. 223) "the personal character to the relation has been so to speak filtered. It has been cleared of the practical, concrete nature of its appeal", while for Jankelevicth (1983, p. 39) "[O]nly at the moment when one reaches things in themselves, only then does inexpressive music become expressive again; on the verge of losing its actual musical character, extreme realism becomes music again". From this perspective, the sublime moment concerns a movement of loss of oneself not tempered by a heroic reassertion but rewarded by the development of a new kind of receptivity to things. Perhaps Bachelard (1971, p. 73) refers to a similar state of mind when he writes in relation to poetry and reverie about "a sphere of pure sublimation; of a sublimation which sublimates nothing, which is relieved of the burden of passion, and freed from the pressure of desire".

In line with a contemporary Jungian position taken by Wolfgang Giegerich, it seems to me that the search for the "inexpressive" in music represents an attempt at dealing with the problem of the alienation of the soul in the ego. Giegerich (2008, p. 16) in this context defines the ego as "the soul in the form of otherness, externally, and fundamentally alienated from itself". From this perspective, the inexpressive may be seen as an attempt to sublate the ego and allow the soul to come home to itself. The agent of this process is the *animus*, which represents an aspect of the soul alongside *anima* (their union constituting the *syzygy*). *Animus* is the killing agent that violently severs the *anima*'s state of the *unio naturalis*. In a similar vein, Messiaen claims that music must be a bearer of "spiritual violence". Psychologically, this violence is needed to cure neurosis, if neurosis is nothing but "a soul having systematically and deliberately leapt out of itself" (Ibid., p. 24). Giegerich sums up this perspective as follows: "Killing, if it is ritual killing and not killing out of human emotions and for egoic purposes, is the basic form of the *opus contra naturam*" (Ibid., p. 33). *Natura*, once gone through these transformations, is recuperated to itself.

The notion of the sublime from a postmodern approach also has to be mentioned, as it shares some aspects with the approach I will articulate with reference to Messiaen.

Unconscious processes, music, the sublime   209

As Lyotard (1991, p. 126) points out, one key feature of the postmodern sublime is that it is not outside the work, but "in the very matter of the artistic work". The sublime moment is the performance, minimal and barren, of an unexpected if random occurrence. Wurth (2009, p. 129) refers to this scenario as "an emptiness which is suddenly enlightened with energy". John Cage says: "you make a little clearing where the penumbra of an almost-given will be able to enter" (quoted in Wurth, 2009, p. 129). As analysts know, this is the attitude that may allow deeply obscure, energy-laden, pre-symbolic material to find, somehow and sometimes, its way into the consulting room. Lyotard (1993, p. 245) describes the moment of the sublime as a moment of grace, albeit a provisional and incomplete one: "Art, writing, gives grace to the soul condemned to death, but in such a way as to not forget it".

Messiaen: techniques for the sublime

Messiaen's approach to music, which is steeped in the twentieth century music revolution characterized by the rupture of the organic wholeness of form, pitch, rhythm and harmony, is complex and multifaceted. He removes the individual from his/her central position in the world while also strongly appealing to the subjective psycho-physiological response and participation in the musical event he creates. He emphasizes the autonomy of music as an art whose pure form and sound are its essence and yet provides plenty of verbal elucidation to his own works.

Music is regarded by Messiaen as the only art that can convey faith. In this sense, it would be not just isomorphic to the emotional processes, as mentioned earlier, but also suitable to provide a symbolic form for preverbal unconscious processes, some of which are implied in what Jung referred to as a "religious instinct". In a musicologist's definition (Asplund, 1997), his music represents "the actual fabric of eternal existence" (p. 175), which reminds us of "other modes of experience that may be possible" (Messiaen, in Mellers, 2008, p. 220). Griffiths (2008[1985], p. 18), a Messiaen scholar, sees in his music "the presence of the eternal within the temporal, the unmeasurable within the measured, the mysterious within the known". In this sense, Messiaen's music adds an inherently religious quality to the experience of the sublime beyond Romantic melancholic nostalgia and postmodern nihilism. The music critic Alex Ross highlights the difference between Schoenberg and Messiaen as ultimately theological, as the former "believes that God is unrepresentable and that His presence could be indicated only by placing a taboo on the familiar", whereas "Messiaen felt that God was present everywhere and in all sound" (Ross, 2007, p. 488).

Messiaen sought ways to facilitate a living experience of the religious attitude, an attempt certainly in line with Jung's lifetime opus to heal Christianity of its lifelessness and to foster the experience of a link with the infinite. However he is not concerned with exploration of evil, archetypal *shadow* and suffering, which attracted some criticism of one-sidedness. He stated that he had no talent for suffering, that joy is far more difficult to express than pain, and also that in contemporary music "nobody at all represents joy" (quoted in Asplund, 1997, p. 183).

The affirmation of the *sublime* is conceived by Messiaen (1978, p. 4) as a "breakthrough toward the beyond, towards the invisible and unspeakable". The structure of his music, whose techniques I will shortly describe, allows for an experience of inner "dazzlement", an overwhelming of senses or thought, or both. Messiaen adopts new forms and techniques for the hypersaturation of the ear through excess in sound and colour, or through overlapping and highly heterogenous layers of sounds whose simultaneous appearance is perceived as stasis. He compares these experiences to the impression caused by stained-glass windows, whose effects of light and colours may be so strong that pictorial figures cannot be taken in.

van Maas (2009, p. 116) sees in his music the disposition to "typical gestures towards the sublime, such as the sensation of overpowering, the majestic and the unimaginable . . . some of which may be quite violent and repellent to the ear". This requires in the listener a child-like capacity for enthusiasm, fervour, wonder and the miraculous, although this attitude is not one of mere naïveté. As van Maas goes on arguing (*ibidem*, pp. 174–178), what is called upon is a capacity for immediacy, not in the regressive sense of the word "as one that precedes reflection and implies a regression of listening toward a presymbolic wholeness", but rather as immediacy "after, or through the (self-)reflection of conscious perception, breaking through what Kierkegaard would describe as a 'second immediacy' or 'immediacy after reflection'". To exemplify this notion he also refers to the idea of "second naïveté", which Ricoeur (1967, pp. 351–352), in his reflections on the distress of modernity for the loss of the symbolism of the sacred, identifies as a possibility to pursue a return of a new naïveté "in and through criticism . . . it is by interpreting that we can hear again". For van Maas (*ibidem*), this implies "a movement of mediation between faith and understanding, and between understanding and having faith anew". In contemporary Jungian language, this second naïveté may be seen as the result of the dialectic between *anima* and *animus*, which as described earlier co-happens as *syzygy* – adherence and severance, innocence and killing being two modalities inherently intertwined and constantly, mutually implying, like when we reflect on dreams and we try to stay both within and without them.

The singularity and spontaneity of the single, sublime moment is the product of artificial and repeatable techniques, a combination which evokes a parallelism with the psychoanalytic process. I will exemplify some of Messiaen's innovative techniques for the sublime, and their relationship with unconscious processes, by referring to two movements from his best known work, *Quartet for the End of Time*. This piece for piano, violin, cello and clarinet (a chance combination dictated by the availability of instruments) was written by Messiaen while he was detained in a prisoners' camp in Silesia during the Second World War. It was performed in January 1941 together with three inmate musicians to an enchanted audience made both of prisoners and wardens.

Unconscious processes, music, the sublime   211

It consists of eight movements, two of which are based on music composed previously. Although it is accompanied by a reference to the Angel of the Apocalypse, who raises his hand saying "There will be no more time", Messiaen (1942) specified that "[he] did not in any sense want to comment upon the Apocalypse" and that "[his] only wish was to articulate [his] desire for the dissolution of time". Beyond the imaginable, poignant resonance of this notion for prisoners in a war camp, Messiaen did not mean this as a metaphor but as an experience of time dissolved, both existentially and with regard to the conventional time structures in music.

Abolition of time has also to do with detachment from concrete circumstances, which Messiaen (1942) expressed as follows: "The greatest benefit was that in the midst of thirty thousand prisoners, I was the only man who was not one" (quoted in Pople, 1998, p. 15).

I will refer to the first movement, titled "Liturgie du Cristal", and to the last one, titled "Louange a l'Immortalite de Jesus". They frame the *Quatuor* in two very different ways.

The first movement, which opens the *Quatuor*, displays a range of Messiaen's technical innovations. Piano and cello play some repeating sequences, while violin and clarinet superimpose birdsong fragments. On this movement Pople (1998, p. 18) states that "for three minutes or so we are eavesdropping on something everlasting". Messiaen's association to this movement are birds singing in the stillness of the morning around 3:00 and 4:00 a.m.

The impression of eternity is produced through two main rhythmic innovations in the piano and cello parts. The first one is that they are made of isorhythmic patterns. The term isorhythm indicates "a rhythmic sequence overlaid on a melodic shape, each recurring continuously but independent of each other" (Matheson, 2008, p. 238), or "an independent rhythm which constantly repeated itself, without paying heeds to the rhythms which surround it" (Pople, 1998, p. 24). They are complex development of the Bachian pedal. Whereas the latter consisted of a single note extended and eventually resolving, Messiaen's pedals are intricate patterns repeating and never resolving. The point of isorhythms is that they achieve a dissociation of rhythm from melody and harmony, an important antecedent of which may be found in Stravinsky's *Rite of Spring*.

In this movement, both the cello and the piano parts are made of two distinct isorhythmic patterns. The cello plays a five-note melodic line over a rhythm of 15 values, while the piano plays a 29-chord sequence over a rhythm of 17 values. Messiaen's specific innovation was to combine two such isorhythms, which multiplies the range and complexity of patterns occurring before the two instruments return to the starting point, so that we just hear a fragment of what would be an enormous process. The sense of eternity is engendered (albeit unconsciously) by the fact that such return would occur after hours. Instead, the movement is brought to an arbitrary close by the violin-bird.

This musical event is highly evocative of the repetition-compulsion element of a complex, which has its roots in the timelessness of the unrepressed unconscious (Freud, 1933). The musical representation of this trait

212   Giorgio Giaccardi

offers an experiential containment, mediated by the ear and the ensuing physiological-affective response, alternative to compulsive, behavioural enactment of the same. As Scarfone states, "[W]e psychoanalysts work with the implicit belief that what is repeated and discharged in action can eventually be reproduced in the psychical field". (Levine et al., 2013, p. 83). An element of pleasure is involved in both situations, but in the former the ego is removed from mundane pursuits and more directly attuned to this property of the unconscious.

An important aspect of repetition in Messiaen's music is that it doesn't appear as a mechanical, automaton-like phenomenon. Nuances of timbre and colour, complex rhythmic patterns and harmonic context produce distinct events albeit similar, what Messiaen (1956[1944]) calls "varied periodicity", like the periodicity of sea waves in which "each wave is slightly different from another with regard to its volume, its height, its duration, the lengthiness or brevity of its formation, the power of its climax, the prolongation of its fall, of its flow, of its dissipation". For Kierkegaard, repetition is the paradoxical return of the actual-with-a-difference (van Maas, 2009). Jankelevicth (1983, pp. 22–24) highlights the difference between the logos's perspective, whose signification is based on development, for which what is said is not being re-said, from that of music and poetry, for which "what is said remains to be said, and to be said without cessation, inexhaustibly said". Repetition is like "the joy of finding a friend whom one had missed. For the listener and the performer, the reprise is no less a renewal: hearing again, playing again, become modes whereby to discover, interminably, new relationships or subtle correspondences, beauty kept secret or hidden intentions".

Besides isorhythmic patterns, the second rhythmic innovation consists of the so called "non-retrogradable" character of the rhythmic patterns used in the cello and piano parts. This means that they are palindromic, as the order of their values is the same from left to right and right to left and doesn't change if played backwards.

Melodically, this piece is based on the whole-tone scale, which is one of the seven "modes of limited transposition" devised by Messiaen, and also one of the oldest, most archaic types of scale. These modes are characterized by the fact that after just few transpositions of their initial note up a semitone these modes repeat themselves. Also, the series of notes are symmetrical – i.e. they can be divided in two, three or four equal intervals. Messiaen (1942, p. i) describes them as "achieving a kind of tonal ubiquity" and "drawing the listener toward eternity in space or the infinite".

Symmetry, therefore, both rhythmically and melodically, stands out as an important cipher of Messiaen's musical techniques for creating images of the end of time. Symmetry, making the last moment identical with the first, denies the idea of progress. Again, this brings us back to a description of the unrepressed unconscious, whose property of timelessness and symmetry cannot be grasped by the conscious mind. Messiaen (1956[1944], p. 13) sums up his rhythmic and melodic symmetries with the term "charm of impossibilities", which he explains as follows: "This charm, at once voluptuous and contemplative, resides particularly in certain mathematical impossibilities of the modal and rhythmic domains. Modes which cannot be transposed beyond a certain number of transpositions, because one always falls again into the same notes; rhythms which cannot be used in retrograde, because in such case one finds the same order of values again – these are two striking impossibilities".

Harmonically, chords in Messiaen are meant to be blocks of sounds rather than functional harmonizations. Harmony here is totally vertical, without horizontal connections. Fragmentation and discontinuity are typical attributes of the *abaissement du niveau mental* (as described by Janet). Harmonic resolutions are often incorporated in the same chord so there is no dynamism but instead a static quality in which the choice of notes forming the chord is primarily based on colour, that is timbre, acoustic resonance. This technique leads to incorporate opposites in a single event, whose ambivalence and inherent tension is accordingly maximized and remains unresolved. Verticality as a radical event cutting the flow of ordinary experience closely recalls the unconscious disruption brought about by the "symptom" – a word whose Greek etymology denotes a happening, an accident, through which another level of psychic experience is revealed and experienced. This is why Messiaen's music is not meant to accompany religious rituals, which have a dramatized and therefore horizontal narrative structure, but rather to convey theological mysteries (Nativity, Ascension, Transfiguration, etc.), aiming at isomorphically representing the unintelligible dazzlement evoked by "the terrible and the sacred, whose detail cannot be understood, that transports us to a world of light that is too strong for our reason" (Messiaen, quoted in van Maas, 2009, p. 37).

Upon this relentless tapestry woven by piano and cello, violin and clarinet give voice to the birds. For Messiaen (1942, p. i), "[B]irds are the opposite of Time; they are our desire for light, for stars, for rainbows and for joyous songs". They are heard many times in varied forms. The recourse to bird songs in Messiaen represents a meeting point between objectivity and personal. He painstakingly recorded and transcribed their subtlest nuances, lending his highly sophisticated musical skills to translating this language of nature with a spirit of devotion, while also employing his own melodic modes to articulate variations of the bird songs. As Mellers (2008, p. 221) puts it, Messiaen, "rather than asserting man's ego and will, sought release from them at a primitively physiological level".

The second piece I would like to refer to, after the Liturgie du Cristal examined above, is the final movement from the *Quatuor*, titled "Louange a l'Immortalite de Jesus", which is one of the two "Louanges" (eulogies) to Jesus present in the *Quatuor*. Here the endless character of time is conveyed through a more traditional technique, slowness, stretched to a point of loss of contact with temporal reality. The indications by Messiaen on the execution of the eulogies recite: "Sustain implacably the extremely slow speeds of the two eulogies", in an "infinitely slow" way which dissolves time by almost entirely removing the forward motion (quoted in Pople, 1998, p. 8).

There is a difference between the experiences of eternity conveyed by the two movements of *Quartet for the End of Time* I have chosen. Whereas the

"Liturgie" proceeds out of a movement independent of any human agency (ostinato and bird songs) that leaves the listener outside, the unbroken string melody of the "Louange" invites an active participation and offers a more comfortable container for the listening mind. Griffiths (2008[1985]) sums this up by saying that the "Liturgie" expresses the objective eternity and the "Louange" the subjective eternity. Perhaps we could envisage here a parallelism with the Kantian notions of the mathematically and the dynamically sublime.

Finally, the texture of the violin sound, seamlessly unfolding upon a hypnotic and repetitive piano rhythmic cell, gains absolute prominence. One can almost hear the physicality, the matter which strings and bow are made of, increasingly so during the piece. Music becomes fully embodied like the Word made flesh – this eulogy being addressed to "the man Jesus" and its slow ascent towards a spiritual reunion with Father. In the process, music becomes pure, full sound, in a movement of infinite ascent. In Messiaen's words, this leads to "sheer fascinating saturation of the ear" (quoted in van Maas, 2009, p. 108). In this sense, Messiaen has been described as a "sound-alchemist obsessed with the material of sound itself; with the possibility of changing sound-matter through understanding of and identity with its laws; and ultimately with the possibility of man himself being alchemically reborn" (Mellers, 2008, p. 231).

Conclusion

The increasing awareness of music's suitability to carry a symbolic function, in my opinion, calls now for a dialogue with psychology beyond the self-expressiveness of music therapy or the technical descriptiveness of psychoacoustics.

Music's symbolic pregnancy transcends the boundaries of individual expression and uniquely allows pathways into transpersonal, archaic psychic processes. Music's resonance with this level, particularly with regard to the experience of time, physiology and affects, offers an important possibility for a symbolic representation of this psychic area.

Particularly through the music of Messiaen, I have referred to some aspects of the feeling of the sublime as they have evolved from the Burkean and Kantian views through Romanticism, postmodernism and beyond. Such aspects reflect archaic unconscious processes and include notions I have touched on such as liminality, coalescence of opposites, symmetry, repetition, unboundedness, saturation, dazzlement, materiality, lack of development, erasure of the subject and transcendence. They are reflected in and contained by key inherent properties of instrumental music.

Finally, Messiaen's approach to the sublime through music is inscribed in a movement of reconciliation with beauty and Eros. While requiring a detachment of the subject from ego-identifications and a submission to a super-personal area of experience, Messiaen – particularly so in the first half of his creative trajectory – also states the necessity of "refined voluptuous pleasures" as integral to an experience of the sublime. To him, love of

God and love of man coincide. As Johnson (1989[1975], p. 10) points out, while agreeing on the importance to develop music's objectivity in the sense described here, Messiaen also sought "to restore to music a more human and spiritual quality".

In this sense, he overcomes what Milbank (2004, p. 230) identifies as the dualism of sublime and beautiful within critical philosophy, both modern and postmodern, which has de-eroticized the sublime under "either the command of absolute self-sacrificial duty" or of "a delirious necrophiliac narcissism". For Milbank, "[T]ranscendence involves both Agape and Eros, both Sublime and Beauty". Messiaen's way of rendering the sublime calls upon a range of human faculties which also involve an erotic fascination with the deepest creative power of the unconscious.

Note

This chapter is a slightly modified version of an article previously published in the British Journal of Psychotherapy (November 2015, Volume 31, Issue 4). The original article was commended in the Rozsika Parker Prize 2014 (post-qualification path). Permission for reuse has been granted by Wiley.

References

Ashton, W.A. and Bloch, S. (Eds.) (2010). *Music and Psyche: Contemporary Psychoanalytic Explorations*. New Orleans, LA: Spring Journal Books.

Asplund, C. (1997). A Body with Three Organs: Three Approaches – Cage, Bach and Messiaen. *Perspectives of New Music*, 35(2).

Bachelard, G. (1971). *On Poetic Imagination and Reverie*. Dallas: Spring Publications.

Carta, S. (2009). Music in Dreams and the Emergence of the Self. *Journal of Analytical Psychology*, 54: 85–102.

Carvalho, R. (2014). Synchronicity, the Infinite Unrepressed, Dissociation and the Interpersonal. *Journal of Analytical Psychology*, 59: 366–383.

Chua, D. (1999). *Absolute Music and the Construction of Meaning*. Cambridge: Cambridge University Press.

Civitarese, G. (2018). *Sublime Subjects. Aesthetic Experience and Intersubjectivity in Psychoanalysis*. London and New York: Routledge.

Dalhaus, C. (1978). *The Idea of Absolute Music*. Chicago: The University of Chicago Press.

Davies, S. (2014). Analytic Philosophy and Music. In T. Gracyk and A. Kania (Eds.), *The Routledge Companion to Philosophy and Music*. London and New York: Routledge.

Durand, G. (2009[1963]). *Le Strutture Antropologiche dell' Immaginario*. Bari: Edizioni Dedalo.

Edinger, E.F. (1995). *The Mysterium Lectures. A Journey through C.G. Jung's Mysterium Coniunctionis*. Toronto: Inner City Books.

Faran Ensamble (2012). Retrieved from givensound.com/2018/01/24/arabic-music-video-faran-ensemble-dune-2012.

216 Giorgio Giaccardi

Freud, S. (1914). *The Moses of Michelangelo*. Standard Edn Vol XIII. London: Hogarth Press.

Freud, S. (1933). *New Introductory Lectures on Psycho-Analysis*. Standard Edn, vol. XXII. London: Hogarth Press.

Giaccardi, G. (2006). Accessing the Numinous: Apolline and Dionysian Pathways. In A. Casement and D. Tacey (Eds.), *The Idea of the Numinous. Contemporary Jungian and Psychoanalytic Perspectives*. London and New York: Routledge.

Giegerich, W. (2008). *Soul-Violence*. New Orleans, LA: Spring Journal Books.

Green, A. (1999). On Discriminating and Not Discriminating Between Affect and Representation. *International Journal of Psychoanalysis*, 80: 277–316.

Griffiths, P (2008[1985]). *Olivier Messiaen and the Music of Time*. London: Faber and Faber.

Hanslick, E. (1986[1854]). *On the Musically Beautiful*. Indiana: Hackett Publishing.

Jankelevicth, V. (1983). *Music and the Ineffable*. Oxford and Princeton, NJ: Princeton University Press.

Johnson, R. (1989[1975]). *Messiaen*. London: Omnibus Press.

Jung, C.G. (1928). *Contributions to Analytic Psychology*. London: Routledge.

Jung, C.G. (1970[1955]). *Mysterium Coniunctionis*. Princeton, NJ: Princeton University Press.

Langer, S.K. (1942). *Philosophy in a New Key*. Cambridge: Harvard University Press.

Levine, H., Reed, G. and Scarfone, D. (Eds.) (2013). *Unrepresented States and the Construction of Meaning*. London: Karnac.

Lévi-Strauss, C. (1994[1964]). *The Raw and the Cooked*. London: Pimlico.

Lyotard, J.F. (1991). *The Inhuman: Reflections on Time*. Cambridge: Polity Press.

Lyotard, J.F. (1993). *Postmodern Fables*. Minneapolis: University of Minnesota Press.

Maiello, S. (1995). The Sound-Object: A Hypothesis about Prenatal Auditory Experience and Memory. *Journal of Chid Psychotherapy*, 21: 23–41.

Matheson, I. (2008). The End of Time: A Biblical Theme in Messiaen's Quatuor. In P. Hill (Ed.), *The Messiaen Companion*. London: Faber and Faber.

McGlashan, A.R. (1987). Music and the Symbolic Process. *Journal of Analytical Psychology*, 32: 327–344.

Mellers, W. (2008). Mysticism and Theology. In P. Hill (Ed.), *The Messiaen Companion*. London: Faber and Faber.

Messiaen, O. (1942). *Preface to the Score of Quatuor pour la fin du temps*. Paris: Durand.

Messiaen, O. (1956[1944]). *The Technique of my Musical Language*. Paris: Leduc.

Messiaen, O. (1978). *Conference de Notre-Dame*. Paris: Leduc.

Milbank, J. (2004). Sublimity: The Modern Transcendent. In R. Schwartz (Ed.), *Transcendence. Philosophy, Literature, and Theology Approach the Beyond*. London and New York: Routledge.

Nagel, J.J. (2013). *Melodies of the Mind. Connections between Psychoanalysis and Music*. London and New York: Routledge.

Panksepp, J. (2011). Affective Foundations of Creativity, Language and Music and Mental Life: In Search of the Biology of the Soul. In R. Hoffman and I. Boyde Whyte (Eds.), *Beyond the Finite: The Sublime in Arts and Sciences*. Oxford: Oxford University Press.

Pople, A. (1998). *Messiaen. Quartet Pour La Fin Du Temps*. Cambridge: Cambridge University Press.

Regnault, F. (2010). *Psychoanalysis and Music*. Retrieved from lacan.com.

Ricoeur, P. (1967). *The Symbolism of Evil*. New York: Harper & Row.

Romano, A. (1999). *Musica e Psiche*. Turin: Bollati Boringhieri.

Ross, A. (2007). *The Rest is Noise. Listening to the Twentieth Century*. London: Fourth Estate.

Sapen, D. (2012). *Freud's Lost Chord. Discovering Jazz in the Resonant Psyche*. London: Karnac.

Schneider, M. (2007). *Il Significato della Musica*. Milan: SE.

Schopenhauer, A. (1966[1814]). *The World as Will and Representation*. New York: Dover.

Schwarz, D. (1997). *Listening Subjects. Music, Psychoanalysis, Culture*. Durham: Duke University Press.

Shaw, P. (2006). *The Sublime*. London and New York: Routledge.

Silverman, K. (1988). *The Acoustic Mirror*. Bloomington, IN: Indiana Press.

Skar, P. (2002). The Goal as Process: Music and the Search for the Self. *Journal of Analytical Psychology*, 47: 629–638.

Storr, A. (1992). *Music and the Mind*. New York: HarperCollins Publisher.

van Maas, S. (2009). *The Reinvention of Religious Music. Olivier Messiaen's Breakthrough Towards the Beyond*. New York: Fordham University Press.

Wilson, S. (2015). *Stop Making Sense. Music from the Perspective of the Real*. London: Karnac.

Wurth, K.B. (2009). *Musically Sublime. Indeterminacy, Infinity, Irresolvability*. New York: Fordham University Press.

Zabriskie, V. (2000). Orpheus and Eurydice: A Creative Agony. *Journal of Analytical Psychology*, 45: 427–447.

Žižek, S. (2006). *The Parallax View*. Cambridge: The MIT Press.

FOURTEEN

The *Sinthome* and the work of Imre Kertész

Sharon R. Green

Introduction

In 1943 at just 14 years of age, Imre Kertész was deported to Auschwitz together with 7,000 other Hungarian Jews. He was transferred to Buchenwald and liberated from there in 1945. His first novel, *Fatelessness* (2004a), was published in 1975 in Hungary. *Fatelessness* is a first-person account and analysis of life in the concentration camps from the point of view of the 14-year-old narrator. It is chilling in its straightforward, methodical account of the unfolding of events – in the narrator's words everything in the camps happened "step by step" and with each step every person was implicated in their actions – victims and perpetrators alike. *Fatelessness* was initially not well received in Hungary, but Kertész (2002) relentlessly continued to write, and in 2002 he was awarded the Nobel Prize for literature. In the words of the Swedish Academy, he was awarded the prize for writing that "upholds the fragile experience of the individual against the barbaric arbitrariness of history" (Nobel Diploma). In accepting his Nobel Prize, Kertész said:

> I have endeavoured . . . to perform the existential labour that being an Auschwitz-survivor has thrust upon me as a kind of obligation. . . . I have seen the true visage of this dreadful century; I have gazed into the eye of the Gorgon, and have been able to keep on living.
>
> *(Nobel Banquet Speech)*

Kertész's ability to go on living – as well as his Nobel achievement – is linked to a necessary and never-ending process of binding the trauma of his childhood in Auschwitz and Buchenwald and his adult years in a totalitarian regime through his writing. In Lacanian terms, this process reflects Kertész's *sinthome*, which is a neologism that is derived from the archaic spelling of the French word for symptom (symptôme).

Kertész's novels exemplify the capacity to create great literature in the wake of utter evil and catastrophe. His writing insists that we embrace our irreducible, singular subjectivity while recognizing the kernel of monstrousness in all of us. Most importantly, his writing calls us to the ethical dimension of our being – demanding that we accept responsibility for our unique fate and actions even under extreme conditions. This is what Lacan called *identification with the sinthome*, which at the end of his career, Lacan saw as the final goal of analysis. "Identification with the *sinthome*" is not related to any meaningful imaginary identity but refers to a mode of being that remains in touch with the irreducible hard kernel of the Real at the core of our symptoms (Ruti, 2012). This involves the capacity to bear the breakdown of our comfortable social identities while coming into traumatic contact with the void at the core of our subjectivity. When we live our *sinthome*, we recognize that there is no Other who has the final answer or meaning to our lives, no guarantee of safety and security in the promises of the Big Other (Covington, 2012). Most importantly, striving for "identification with the *sinthome*" means that we make a choice to assume full responsibility for our actions and our lives (Verhaeghe and Declercq, 2002, p. 65). This is the basis of ethics and of freedom.

The Sinthome

Lacan's concept of "*le sinthome*" emerged out of his deep study and enjoyment of the writing of James Joyce, which he explicated in his 1975 seminar of the same name (Thurston, 2010). Lacan (2016) recognized that Joyce lacked "the Name of the Father", the paternal function, and so was at risk of falling into psychosis; however, Joyce's innovative style of writing allowed him to create a new language and a singular subjectivity without becoming psychotic.[1] In the same seminar, Lacan extended his work on the Borromean Knot, his late topological structuring of subjectivity. The Knot is described as a chain consisting of three rings or links – the Real, the Symbolic and the Imaginary – interlaced such that if one of the links is broken, the entire chain falls apart. The Borromean Knot is not a thing but a description, which according to Lacan generates a failure of imagination (p. 30). In Lacan's later work, this Borromean triad points to the equal participation of the Real, the Symbolic and the Imaginary in the structuring of subjectivity with the *sinthome* introduced as a mobile fourth ring, interweaving and looping through our signifiers, our imaginary identifications and our relationship with trauma (Ruti, 2012). The *sinthome* is our particular symptomatic way of being in relationship with the hard kernel of the Real – the nucleus of *jouissance* that holds the subject together on the level of the drives (p. 62). Like James Joyce, Kertész's writings became a crucial expression of his *sinthome*. By looping the energies of the Real into his writing, Kertész was able to bind his traumatic madness, thus fashioning his singular subjectivity and his unique style of writing.[2]

It is easy to fall into the trap of reifying the concept of the *sinthome*, because it defies any straightforward phenomenological description. The *sinthome* is in fact linked to negativity, to failure, to impossibility. Rather than any positive attribute or quality, it has been likened to our unique pathological "tic" (Žižek, 1992, p. 138). Roberto Harari (2002a) suggests the *sinthome* is similar to "negative theology" in that it cannot be described;

it is not positive being but instead is expressed in the phrase, "I am all – but not *that*" (pp. 32–33). The *sinthome* points to those existential dimensions of human life related to our constitutional lack – in other words, the lack of any ultimate truth or foundational ground for the meaning of our being – and to the subject's unique response to the never-ending process of trying to make sense of our nonsensical, contingent existence. The *sinthome* reflects the intrinsic messiness of our lives for which there is no diagnosis or cure. Energies of the Real – sometimes called the death drive – unbind our subjectivity so that we are forever at risk of falling apart, coming undone from our imaginary and symbolic constraints (Ruti, 2012). And yet, in order for change to occur, we must fall apart, productively dissociate (Harari, 2002a). When our symbolic and imaginary constraints are loosened, with the *sinthome*, we can knot ourselves back together in a way that is more inclusive of the Real. Although horror is our response to these infusions of the Real, remaining open to this process of unbinding is also the source of our creativity and freedom (Harari, 2002a; Hinton, 2009). The "essence" of the *sinthome* is the little leftover kernel of the Real that resists symbolization; paradoxically, it is not actually substance, but our never-ending *failure* to achieve any positive presence or final closure to our being – while still cohering as a singular subject (Verhaeghe and Declercq, 2002; Ruti, 2012). This coherence is what allows us to assume agency and responsibility for our lives even in the face of our throwness into the world and its "arbitrary history".

The *sinthome* has been called Lacan's "re-invented symptom" (Thurston, 2002). With symptoms, the subject remains in a neurotic relationship with the Other, responding to imagined demands and desires, always asking, "*What does the other want of me?*" The subject as *sinthome* is not "an answer of the Other" but rather "an answer of the Real" (Verhaeghe & Declercq, p. 68). Symptoms can be dissolved when the subject can verbalize the "truth" of its desire in the network of the signifier, and so the symptom has been described as that which *can* "cease being written" through the analytic processes of interpretation (Ruti, 2008, p. 61). Lacan recognized that the *sinthome* is a unique kind of symptom that cannot be resolved through the intervention of the signifier, because it is not an expression of repressed desire. Rather, the *sinthome* is the most fundamental organization of the subject's *jouissance* beyond any processes of symbolization, interpretation or working through (pp. 61 & 116). As one's singularity, the *sinthome* is the *necessary* condition for living one's life and as such must constantly be written and rewritten. In his memoir, *Dossier K*, Kertész (2013) points to his *sinthome* when he responds to a question about why he persists in his writing:

> Out of an existential angst that may have silenced everything else inside me . . . A compulsive psychosis . . . a categorical inner imperative . . . the fulfillment of a task . . . how should I know?
>
> *(p. 135)*

The disruptive energies of the Real of the *sinthome* generate the possibility for new signifiers to emerge from the places of rupture in the symbolic and imaginary orders and keep language from becoming stale, worn out or lifeless (Ruti, 2008). This is experienced as threatening and disruptive to the ego, but is a necessary process for infusing new life into dead signifiers, for bringing the sublime into our lived life in the here and now. As speaking beings, we incline towards the safety and refuge of everyday discourse (Harari, 2002a; Ruti, 2008). We prefer to allow meaning to remain the same and latch on to worn-out understandings of "how things are" or "who I am". Linking the *sinthome* to the body, Lacan calls the *sinthome* the site of "*jouis-sens*" – enjoyment in meaning. It is a word play on *jouissance* that points to our embodied enjoyment of the *process* of creating meaning above and beyond any positive *contents* of meaning. Like a poem, the *sinthome* can enliven language – the house of being – by producing an entire chain of signifiers and untranslatable enigmas that remain opaque and without closure (Hoens and Pluth, 2002, p. 11). This process echoes in Kertész's (2013) words: "I may have written a novel, but I have solved nothing. The riddle of the world has remained just as tormenting a thorn as it was before" (p. 74). We are able to be open to new meaning because we are always already enjoying the structure within which meaning occurs. Kertész has written: "Even if that raw material looks fairly cheerless, the form is able to transform it and turn it into pleasure, because writing can only come from an abundance of energies, from pleasure; writing . . . is heightened life" (p. 58).

Luke Thurston (2002) has written that in the seminar *Le Sinthome*, "Lacan struggles to place something *untranslatable* at the centre of his work, a disruptive excess that no topology can finally reduce or master" (p. xix). Kertész has placed the untranslatable Real of Auschwitz at the centre of his work. Through the irruption of his singular *jouissance* into the symbolic register, Kertész (2013) has created new meanings for the signifier "Auschwitz". He has even gone so far as to say that through his novels he "invented Auschwitz" (p. 9) and that he is the "medium for the spirit of Auschwitz" (p. 183). For Kertész, the enigmatic signifier "Auschwitz" represents a total rupture in Western civilization and the collapse of the ethical culture of Europe (p. 182–183).[3] "Auschwitz" is not in the past, but remains alive as a signifier reminding us of our always present capacity for evil. Because Kertész's writing is infused with the energies of the Real, it resists any coherent narrative of meaningfulness and evokes an intensely visceral response in the reader. Kertész says that it was "his aim to traumatize the reader," because it is impossible to convey anything about his lived experience of the camps with ordinary language (Vasvári, 2005, p. 267).

Although the trauma of the Real of Auschwitz is ultimately *unrepresentable*, in his novel *Kaddish for an Unborn Child*, Kertész's (2004b) alter ego insists that there is nothing *unexplainable* about Auschwitz. Auschwitz existed and was thus not a product of any "incomprehensible" forces: "[T]he explanation for Auschwitz . . . is inherent in individual lives, solely in individual lives; Auschwitz, to my way of thinking, is a rational process"

(p. 37). Kertész insists that evil is neither an accident nor a mistake, but a consequence of rational thinking by individual people, and *actions* that are taken one step at a time (Gustafsson, 2014). Action points to another dimension of the *sinthome*. Lacan said, "To know how to handle, to take care of, to manipulate . . . to know what to do with the symptom, *that is the end of analysis*" (Verhaeghe and Declercq, 2002, p. 65). In other words, identification with the *sinthome* means that one gains a certain "know-how" or "savoir faire" in terms of creative action and invention in the world (Harari, 2002a). Accepting responsibility – even for those actions we do not intend consciously – is in direct contrast with conventional psycho-analytic goals of "insight" or "understanding", which can become defensive ways of refusing responsibility for one's life (Harari, 2002a, pp. 112–113). One of Lacan's many humorous word plays on *sinthome* is the two-word homonym *saint homme* – the saintly man. Even though we are never fully present to ourselves, the saintly man is the singular individual who has come to accept responsibility for the impact of their actions on others and on the world. Questions of action and responsibility become especially vexing in extreme situations. Kertész accepted responsibility for his unique fate and choices without recourse to any socially acceptable identity. Instead he turned to the creative invention of writing to fashion and refashion his subjectivity. Kertész (2013) writes: "Dictatorships make children out of people inasmuch as they do not permit existential choices and thereby deprive one of that wonderful burden of being responsible for oneself" (p. 117).

Singularity is not a state of feeling comfortable, confident or secure. Intense feelings of shame emerge as we extricate ourselves from the gaze of the Other and the longing for the recognition and approval of the Other. In his classic work *Shame and Necessity*, the philosopher Bernard Williams (2008) says that shame is the mortifying affect that alerts us that we are not who we imagine ourselves to be in a world in which we could actually imagine living. We can feel objectified by the shaming gaze, which reveals our vulnerability and our lack. The relationship between shame and writing is a recurrent theme in Kertész's work. Pointing to the link between shame and the *sinthome*, Kertész (2012) writes:

> But in order to survive, he had to formulate his shame deftly and give what he had formulated lasting form. In other words, he had to become a good writer . . . to subjectivize [his] perpetual objectivity . . . to become the name-giver instead of the named.
>
> *(p. 65–67)*

Although shame points to the painful breakdown of our ego's imaginary identifications, shame also opens the possibility for embracing our *sinthome* – that is, embracing the fractured, conflicted fools that we are. Developing the capacity to bear shame and reflect on it, allows us to take responsibility for transforming those aspects of ourselves and our world that we can no longer endure. The task that Lacan calls "identifying with the *sinthome*" points to how we *are* our symptoms and that to psychically survive, we must – like Imre Kertész – find ways to creatively live with these constant processes of turbulence and failure that generate our always-changing subjectivity. One way to do this is to welcome shame as a teacher and an ethical guide for our singular actions and choices (Hinton, 2002).

The *sinthome* is non-relational and heralds a break from the "Big Other". The singular subject achieves freedom from the Other as the cause of our desires, as the one who names us and gives meaning to our lives. Identification with the *sinthome* is the *sine qua non* for living an ethical life, because it implies that the subject is no longer in the grip of the fantasy that any "Big Other" can offer unity, completion, or wholeness – i.e. there is no Sovereign Good awaiting us in this world or any other (Ruti, 2008). Kertész (2013), whose fate was determined by those who gave their minds over to Adolph Hitler, writes: "Our era does not favour the preservation of the individual; it is simpler to surrender ourselves to salvational ideas than stick to our own unique and irreproducible existence, to choose our own truth rather than *the* truth" (p. 77).

In a passage from *Fiasco*, Kertész (2011) depicts the painful struggle of the individual – "his uniqueness which was writhing there, his abandoned, ownerless life" – who chooses to make the fateful jump away from the seductive "twilight happiness of eternal forgetting" and the security of the irresistible, blind tide of the multitude into the depths of his own singular life (pp. 355–356). When we accept ourselves as our symptomatic singularity we are freed from the fantasy that there can be a symmetrical relationship with the Other; then we can acknowledge and recognize our narcissistic fantasies of the actual other person (Bosetti, 2010, p. 377). Paradoxically this allows us to respond to the other in *their* singularity and their absolute alterity (p. 377).

Like Antigone, who refused to give in on her ethical desire despite facing death at the hands of the State, and like the resistance fighters of World War II, the singular subject is ironically often identified as the criminal, the outlaw, the outsider. The need to blindly follow the habitual moral precepts of the Other in order to feel safe and secure can give way to ethical subjectivity. This subjectivity is a never-ending process of falling apart and then creatively regenerating in the face of what actually is happening in the world without the hope that someone knows the ultimate truth. This is the ethics of the *sinthome*, and possibly it is our only safeguard against surrendering to the security of the multitude – or to those who offer us totalizing fantasies of utopian worlds that leave us vulnerable to committing "banal evil".

At the age of 85 and suffering from Parkinson's disease, Kertész gave – what he claimed would be – his last interview with *The Paris Review* (Zieliniski, 2013). In this interview, Kertész places himself along with his spiritual brothers – Paul Celan, Jean Améry and Tadeusz Borowski – in a radical tradition of literature that created new values from the immense suffering of the Holocaust.[4] Kertész notes that most of his "spiritual brothers" perished in this attempt, and he credits his writing with his own psychic and bodily survival. Following Lacan, this is what I have called his *sinthome*. However, I will give Kertész (2004b) the last word on his writing: "[T]he reason I work incessantly is that as long as I keep working, I am, whereas if I didn't work, who knows whether I would be or not" (p. 3).

Jung and Lacan

Since I am a Jungian psychoanalyst, I would like to reflect on my choice to use the late ideas of Lacan rather than Jung for my personal process of coming to grips with the traumatic and transformative work of Imre Kertész.[5]

Lacan's ontology precludes the notion of a Sovereign Good, and by steadfastly looking into the abyss, challenges us to find new modes of consciousness and new forms of ethics appropriate to our postmodern world (Miller, 2002) – a world in which the Holocaust happened and Western cultural values collapsed. Lacan's work rests on the assumption that there is no foundational ground that assures a final fixed meaning to our lives but instead a fundamental incompleteness to reality (Johnston, 2008). Our subjectivity is predicated on lack. Our drives and desires push us endlessly around a void of non-meaning. We create fantasies to bridge the gap between the events of our unrepresentable birth and death. The idea that we can achieve any state of completion, harmony or balance is a fantasy that keeps us slaves to the prevailing master signifiers (Ruti, 2008).

Jung had many profound insights into the human condition and a great lifelong struggle with the problem of evil. Despite this, for me, Jung's thinking is not up to the task of answering the needs of the twenty-first century. Jungian analyst Ladson Hinton (2011) has written that the "constitutive myth" guiding much Jungian thought and practice is Jung's vision of the *Unus Mundus*. The *Unus Mundus* is an experience in which a *spiritus rector*, or inner guide, leads the individual towards the unity of a transcendent, foundational ground. In Jung's theory, this is the core of individuation. The *Unus Mundus* is theorized as timeless and beyond our historical world; it privileges ideals of wholeness and an ultimate ground of Meaningfulness (Jung, 1963; Hinton, 2011). However, any system that promises wholeness or "the" Truth is a totalizing system, which inevitably aligns it with totalitarian ideologies that can lead to genocidal activities. Genocides such as Hitler's Final Solution point to the will to eradicate entire peoples who are perceived as obstacles to the attainment of a group's longed-for Utopia (Žižek, 2009; Hinton, A., 2011). In Lacan's language, these ideologies are based on the fantasy that there is no lack in the Other. Jung saw individuation as the achievement of wholeness and the final goal of analysis. This is in stark contrast to Lacan's thought that the final goal of psychoanalysis is to live our *sinthome* – which is to accept our constitutional negativity and embrace the *im*possibility of any final unity.

Jung often gazed into the abyss of human suffering. However, he then attempted to redeem the horrors that he witnessed with the *Deus ex machina* arrival of a reified, rescuing archetype from a transcendent realm beyond our fractured world (Jung, 1963, p. 524; Brooks, 2011). Wolfgang Giegerich (2007) points out that our modes of consciousness – what he calls the soul's logical life – are constantly being transformed through *real historical processes*, including events such as war, social change, technological development and the challenges of great art (Casement, 2011). Giegerich (2008) charges Jung and certain Jungians with privileging the "there and then" of the premodern mythological world rather than staying in the "here and now" of our historical, modern world. As he points out, this kind of premodern thinking results in grandiose archetypal symbols and theories that allow us to turn away from the reality of our current cultural context and the particularity of the world's suffering (Casement, 2011; Hinton, L., 2011). Jung's disavowal of the everyday here and now world in favour of a noumenal realm may point to his need to bind his own psychosis through his theories (Meredith-Owen, 2011; Tanaka, 2014).

In his paper "Requiem for analytical psychology" Marco Heleno Barreto (2014) boldly and persuasively argues that Jung's project has reached completion and is no longer appropriate to the needs of postmodern consciousness. Viewing Jung's catastrophic visions and dreams through a specific interpretive framework,[6] Barreto argues that "man as such" as the ultimate goal of civilization, the last sacred and highest Western value, has been destroyed. In its place is a "post-human" consciousness where human beings have become replaceable parts serving the goals of the great systems of technology and global economics (p. 75). Kertész (2013) made a strikingly similar observation:

> I don't know when it first occurred to me that there had to be a terrible mistake . . . and that terrible mistake is culture itself, the belief system, the language and the concepts that conceal from you that you have long been a well-oiled component of the machinery that has been set up for your own destruction.
>
> *(p. 67)*

In today's world, genocides continue to be perpetrated, and economic and technological systems transform us into automatons serving global forces – this is *our* "barbaric arbitrariness of history". The question arises – who is "upholding the fragile experience of the individual"? Who can we turn to for help in creating new modes-of-being for *this* post-Auschwitz world? Imre Kertész said that he was able to go on living after gazing into the eye of the Gorgon of the dreadful twentieth century. When looking to our psychoanalytic forebears for help in reflecting on the challenges of the twenty-first century, who among them has truly gazed into the eye of the Gorgon?

Notes

1 Joyce lacked the paternal function "The Name of the Father", leaving him vulnerable to psychosis, but through his writing became "Father to the name" (Thurston, 2010).

226 Sharon R. Green

2 In the novel *Fiasco*, Kertész's (2011) protagonist/alter-ego describes going mad as his only solution to barbaric demands placed on him by the totalitarian regime in post-war Hungary.

3   "[I]f the memory of the Holocaust is to remain then it will remain through culture, which is really the vessel of memory. . . . The holocaust is an absolute turning point in Europe's history, an event in the light of which will be seen everything that happened before and that will happen after. . . . It's not seen simply as an event of history, but rather as an event that casts an entirely different light on all our ideas about ethics and morality".

(Kertész, 2012, pp. 42–43)

4 These great writers were Kertész's literary contemporaries and fellow survivors of the Nazi concentration camps; each of them ended their lives through suicide (Kertész, 2012). In an interview, Kertész explained:

"Writers such as Jean Amery or Tadeusz Borowski conceived their works for people who were already familiar with history and were aware that old values had lost their meaning. What was at stake was the creation of new values from such immense suffering, but most of those writers perished in the attempt. However, what they did bequeath to us is a radical tradition in literature".

(Zielinski, Paris Review, p. 4)

5 This chapter was originally written for and presented at the Joint Jung/Lacan Conference, organized by Ann Casement and held in Cambridge, UK, September 12–14, 2014.
6 Following Giegerich, Barreto uses the methodology of "Psychology as a Discipline of Interiority".

References

Barreto, M.H. (2014). Requiem for Analytical Psychology: A Reflection on Jung's (Anti)Catastrophic Psychology. *Journal of Analytical Psychology*, 59: 60–77.

Bosetti, L. (2010). *From the Criminal to the Sinthome: Lacan's Ethics of Psychoanalysis and Contemporary Life*. PhD thesis, University of Nottingham. Retrieved from http://etheses.nottingham.ac.uk/2768/1/523030.pdf.

Brooks, R.M. (2011). Un-thought out Metaphysics in Analytical Psychology: A Critique of Jung's Epistemological Basis for Psychic Reality. *Journal of Analytical Psychology*, 56: 492–513.

Casement, A. (2011). The Interiorizing Movement of Logical Life: Reflections on Wolfgang Giegerich. *Journal of Analytical Psychology*, 56: 532–549.

Covington, C. (2012). Hannah Arendt, Evil and the Eradication of Thought. *The International Journal of Psychoanalysis*, 93: 1215–1236.

Giegerich, W. (2007). *The Soul's Logical Life: Towards a Rigorous Notion of Psychology* (4th ed.). Frankfurt am Main and New York: Peter Lang GmbH, Internationaler Verlag der Wissenschaften.

Giegerich, W. (2008). *Soul Violence*. New Orleans, LA: Spring Journal, Inc.

Gustafsson, M. (2014). Imre Kertész: A Medium for the Spirit of Auschwitz. *Nobelprize.org*. Nobel Media AB. Retrieved from www.nobelprize.org/nobel_prizes/literature/laureates/2002/kertesz-article.html.

Harari, R. (2002a). *How James Joyce Made His Name: A Reading of the Final Lacan*, Trans. L. Thurston. New York: Other Press.

Hinton, A. (2011). Genocide, Categorical Certainty, and the Truth: Questions from the Khmer Rouge Tribunal. *Journal of Analytical Psychology*, 56: 390–396.

Hinton III, L. (2002). Shame as a Teacher: "Lowly Wisdom" at the Millennium. Retrieved from www.nsanpsy.com/publications/shame-as-a-teacher/.

Hinton III, L. (2009). The Enigmatic Signifier and the Decentred Subject. *Journal of Analytical Psychology*, 54: 637–657.

Hinton III, L. (2011). Introduction: Fragmentation of the *Unus Mundus*. *Journal of Analytical Psychology*, 56: 375–380.

Hoens, D. and Pluth, E. (2002). The *Sinthome*: A New Way of Writing an Old Problem? In L. Thurston (Ed.), *Reinventing the Symptom* (pp. 1–18). New York: Other Press.

Johnston, A. (2008). *Žižek's Ontology: A Transcendental Materialist Theory of Subjectivity* (1st ed.). Evanston, IL: Northwestern University Press.

Jung, C.G. (1963). Mysterium Coniunctionis. CW 14.

Kertész, I. (2002). The Freedom of Self-Definition. In H. Engdahl (Ed.), *Witness Literature: Proceedings of the Nobel Centennial Symposium*. London: World Scientific.

Kertész, I. (2004a). *Fatelessness* (Reprint ed.). New York: Vintage.

Kertész, I. (2004b). *Kaddish for an Unborn Child*. New York: Vintage.

Kertész, I. (2011). *Fiasco*. Brooklyn: Melville House.

Kertész, I. (2012). *The Holocaust as Culture*. London and New York: Seagull Books.

Kertész, I. (2013). *Dossier K: A Memoir*. Brooklyn: Melville House.

Kertész, I. (2014). Banquet Speech. *Nobelprize.org*. Nobel Media AB. Retrieved from www.nobelprize.org/nobel_prizes/literature/laureates/2002/kertesz-speech.html.

Kertész, I. (2014). Nobel Diploma. *Nobelprize.org*. Nobel Media AB. Retrieved from www.nobelprize.org/nobel_prizes/literature/laureates/2002/kertesz-diploma.html.

Lacan, J. (2016). *The Sinthome: The Seminar of Jacques Lacan, Book XXIII (1975–6)*, Ed. J.-A. Miller, Trans. A.R. Price. Cambridge: Polity Press.

Meredith-Owen, W. (2011). Winnicott on Jung: Destruction, Creativity and the Unrepressed Unconscious. *Journal of Analytical Psychology*, 56: 56–75.

Miller, J.-A. (2002, December). Milanese Intuitions. In *Mental Online: The International Journal of Mental Health and Applied Psychoanalysis* (pp. 9–16). Retrieved from www.lacancircle.net/MentalOnline11.pdf.

Ruti, M. (2008). The Fall of Fantasies: A Lacanian Reading of Lack. *Journal of the American Psychoanalytic Association*, 56(2): 483–508.

Ruti, M. (2012). *The Singularity of Being: Lacan and the Immortal Within*. New York: Fordham University Press.

Tanaka, Y. (2014). *Why was Jung Unable to Bring his Forehead Quite Down to the Floor? Jung's Substantial Denial of the "Psychological Difference" in his Psychology*. Presented at the 2nd International Conference for the ISPDI Berlin on July 20, 2014.

Thurston, L. (2002). Introduction' In L. Thurston (Ed.), *Reinventing the Symptom* (pp. xiii–xx). New York: Other Press.

Thurston, L. (2010). *James Joyce and the Problem of Psychoanalysis* (1st ed.). Cambridge: Cambridge University Press.

Vasvári, L. (2005). The nOVELNESS of Imre Kertész's *Sorstalanság (Fatelessness)*. In L. Vasvári and S. de Zepetnek (Eds.), *Imre Kertész and Holocaust Literature* (pp. 258–270). West Lafayette: Purdue University Press.

Verhaeghe, P. and Declercq, F. (2002). Lacan's Analytic Goal: *Le sinthome* or the Feminine Way. In L. Thurston (Ed.), *Reinventing the Symptom* (pp. 59–82). New York: Other Press.

Williams, B. (2008). *Shame and Necessity* (2nd ed.). Berkeley: University of California Press.

Zielinski, L. (2013). Imre Kertész, the Art of Fiction, No. 220. In *The Paris Review*. Retrieved from www.theparisreview.org/interviews/6235/the-art-of-fiction-no-220-imre-kertesz.

Žižek, S. (1992). *Looking Awry: An Introduction to Jacques Lacan through Popular Culture* (Reprint ed.). Cambridge: MIT Press.

Žižek, S. (2009). *The Sublime Object of Ideology* (2nd ed.). London and New York: Verso.

FIFTEEN

Expressing the inexpressible: art as a challenge to its own object

Nihan Kaya

Jung has always insisted that psyche and matter cannot be separated, even if they can be distinguished from each other. "Psyche and matter are two different aspects of one and the same thing" (CW 8, par. 418). I understand this difference Jung mentions syntactically but not semantically. To make things clearer, I will explain reality as composed of two dimensions: the horizontal, which is the mundane, practical, concrete, physical, outer material axis, and the vertical, which names an inner, non-empirical, core reality that is never totally graspable. This chapter aims to show how and why every act of creativity is a third *being* coming out of the union between the horizontal and the vertical, and that the Sublime is an intrinsic part of this process even if it finds its form in the horizontal or the ordinary.

Every condition, sign or object has both a horizontal and a vertical dimension which are two different aspects of one and the same thing. The horizontal realm is the phenomenal and empirical surface that is superficial and dead if it is taken at its face value only. (The horizontal can be thought in line with Hegel's "schein", which, in German means "shine" or "seeming appearance"). To flesh out the meaning that is latent within a horizontal phenomenon, matter or situation, to make the horizontal viable, it is essential to go into its depths, to dig into its material, which is always operated by means of a vertical movement.

The horizontal and the vertical are not opposed to one another but make the other meaningful, expand the other's reality and contain each other. For example, horizontal seeing, which is, seeing by means of sensory perception, leads to a different kind of seeing that is vertical. Vertical seeing leads to more horizontal seeing, and an endless, mutual process of feeding each other is always possible between these two.

Assume that you go to a museum, stand in front of a painting and look at it, which are all actions on the horizontal level. If you see something vertically in the painting, then you are highly likely to stop, which means, to stop on the horizontal level. You stop *horizontally*; because now you have begun to *move vertically*. And how do you move vertically? By seeing more into the painting *horizontally*. Your horizontal being narrows down, but becomes compact and condenses as it finds a vertical channel in the object. It is by means of the horizontal seeing that you begin to see vertically. The horizontal is dead without the vertical, and we experience verticality only through the shared reality of the horizontal. When we find a vertical channel in and *through* the object, we become the least active on the horizontal realm but concentrate on this intersection point where the horizontal meets the vertical.

Rollo May talks about how he is taken by Cézanne's painting of a tree. As in the example I have just given, he becomes least active on the horizontal realm, concentrates on looking at Cézanne's painting, studies the painting from different angles, and keeps looking at the painting for minute after minute, hour after hour, only because he was *vertically seeing* the image as well. May is more inclined to look at the painting horizontally as he sees the painting vertically, and he is more inclined to see the painting vertically as he studies the painting horizontally. So his horizontal experience widens and propagates and strengthens his vertical experience and his vertical experience widens and propagates and strengthens his horizontal experience, and this mutual feeding goes on and on.

Cézanne goes through a similar experience when he is painting the tree. Here is how Rollo May explains this process:

> Cézanne sees a tree. He sees it in a way no one else has ever seen it. He experiences, as he no doubt would have said, "being grasped by the tree." The arching grandeur of the tree, the mothering spread, the delicate balance as the tree grips the earth – all these and many more characteristics of the tree are absorbed into his perception and are felt throughout his nervous structure. These are part of the vision he experiences. This vision involves an omission of some aspects of the scene and a greater emphasis on other aspects and the ensuing rearrangement of the whole; but it is more than the sum of all these. Primarily it is a vision that is now not tree, but Tree; the concrete tree Cézanne looked at is formed into the essence of tree. However original and unrepeatable his vision is, it is still a vision of all trees triggered by his encounter with this particular one.
>
> *(1994, pp. 77–78)*

Rollo May's famous term "encounter" can be read as crucial points when the horizontal meets the vertical.[1] Rollo May's "encounter" is when we encounter a door opening up to the vertical at some point in our horizontal life. Anything horizontal is a possible door to the vertical. Through the objective, horizontal reality of the tree, Cézanne sees into a vertical reality of the tree, and out of this encounter, a literally new, unique and original Tree is issued. And this is exactly why Cézanne's painting is a work of art. Because creativity is "the ability to bring something new into existence", as defined by Frank Barron (1965, p. 3). It is bringing something that did not exist before into the world. If Cézanne's Tree were just a copy of something else that already existed, it would not be a work of art. When a painter depicts a tree in Nature, the portrayed does not display the tree in Nature anymore, but another unique and original Tree beyond that tree. Rollo May writes: "No matter how many times Monet returned to paint the cathedral at Rouen, each canvas was a new painting expressing a new vision"[2] (Ibid., p. 79). As Marcel Proust states, each time we see a painting by Elstir, if we are familiar with the artist's work, we immediately recognize that it is Elstir's: "One feels unmistakably, when one sees side by side ten different portraits of different people painted by Elstir, that they are all, first and foremost, Elstir's." (1929, p. 209). But it is also true that even if Elstir portrays the same person, each painting of this same person is unique, and it must be unique, if we are to call it "art". Each time you write a story, it is a different story even if the plot is the same. As Raymond Aron said, all sorts of writing are indeed rewriting (Ricoeur, 1990, p. 55). Each artist has an authentic signature latent in all his/her works, and this doesn't change the inevitability of each of these works being new and authentic in itself. The created object is new to the world and new to the creator himself/herself.

However, still, the work of art is not only unique, but also universal. Rollo May writes: "I can say without exaggeration that I never really *saw* a tree until I had seen and absorbed Cézanne's paintings of them" (Ibid., p. 78). So, the more Rollo May looks at Cézanne's particular Tree, the more he looks into the essence of all trees in the world beyond that unique Tree. May experiences Cézanne's subjective Tree and an objective reality of all trees through it at one and the same time.

Actually, Cézanne's unique tree contains an essence of all trees in the world *right through* its very particularity. This is, indeed, what art is. It is experienced as a tension between particularity and universality, or, in other words, the Sublime. Through its eachness, art makes connection with infinity, an infinity that is *beneath* the image but not *above*, an infinity that is not "an *otherworldly* infinity" (Giegerich, 2005, p. 164) but "an infinity that belongs to me as finite man and that can be encountered in concrete shapes, such as Zarathustra, Philemon, lapis, totem animal" (Ibid.) and, "the image of that sort is the inner. . . *it has conversely the world and ourselves within itself*" (Ibid., p. 85). As art historian Max Raphael said: "Originality is not the urge to be different from others, to produce the brand-new; it is to grasp the origin, the roots of both ourselves and things" (Read, 1965, p. 11). Art is something happening, and it happens at the point the ordinary meets the Sublime.

The vertical is never above the image, but always beneath it. The vertical movement is always downwards, as the image contains all its verticality within itself. This is what Jung meant when he said "Image is soul", or, when he wrote in a letter to Erich Neumann: "I have to be everywhere *beneath* and not *above*." (*Letters 2*, p. 34, 5 January 1952). Jung was telling us about the ways to seek the vertical beneath the horizontal, just as Lacan, who was talking about the vertical signified within the horizontal signifier. The Sublime is within the horizontal/image/letter; it is a worldly sublime.

I sometimes explain this beneathness with an analogy to a lampshade that is embroidered with very fine details. We may not see the embroidered

232   Nihan Kaya

patterns with the naked eye, but with light coming from the depth of the very same object, we begin to see the details, the colours that were not visible to us in the first place.

According to the aesthetic Collingwood: "We 'see more in' a really good picture of a given subject than we do in the subject itself." (1958, p. 308). Art doesn't take us away from the horizontal object, but by pushing forward its vertical essence and meaning to the surface, it revives the horizontal aspect. It *is* the revival of a horizontal object; image, word or whatever the horizontal object of the work of art is. Art is a manifestation of the Sublime through its substance.

Henri Bergson, who, in my opinion, talks about nothing but horizontal and vertical time, gives examples from the art of music, because the horizontal substance of music is time. Bergson asks: "*Can you shorten the melody without altering its nature?*" (2007, pp. 8–9, italics mine), and replies: "*The inner life is that very melody*" (Ibid., p. 9, italics mine). The vertical essence is in the horizontal reality, which is the duration of the melody in that case. We cannot even think them as separate from each other, just as the Sublime which cannot be thought separately from the ordinary.

Works of art stand at crucial points where the horizontal intersects with the vertical. Art makes connection with the Sublime, or the finite horizontal reality of the art object serves as a medium to probe deeper into the infinite reality of the vertical, which is the Sublime. Works of art retain a physical existence on the horizontal line; they are expressed through the objects of the horizontal, but the reality they refer to is vertical/Sublime.

In fact, this verticality is the essence of art. I suggest that the more vertical potentiality a work contains, the more artistic value it has. Like everything else, the objects that make up the material of the work of art, words, paints, notes, clay, etc., have both horizontal and vertical dimensions. They are ordinary objects within the everyday reality of the horizontal, but through a work of art, they go beyond their horizontal reality. A person is an artist only to the extent that she/he is able to transform the objective reality these objects have on horizontal level. A poet creates a unique, peculiar Language out of the net of the language. On the horizontal level, language/words function for communication. In literature, language serves as a medium to create a Language of its own. What a true work of art conveys is incommunicable, like the Sublime. A work of art cannot be expressed in any way other than itself. Nothing else can explain it or stand for it.

A novel's horizontal reality is its text, and we can summarize the horizontal text; but what a novel is really about is something that is impossible to summarize. The horizontal text serves only as a medium to convey what the novel is actually conveying beneath what it seems to be talking about. We can never summarize a novel, even if we summarize every single part of the chain of events in the horizontal story. Every time we summarize a film or novel out of necessity, we miss the artistic point. It is not the text but the subtext latent within the text of the novel that we judge its art by. *Crime and Punishment* is not a novel that tells the story of a young man who murders and robs an old lady. Literature is about learning to question rather than finding answers.

Novels tell us that things might be much more complicated than they seem to be, and they do this by giving a vertical sense to us, and showing that actions – or things that are horizontal – are only results of the vertical. In this sense, arts are very similar to psychology, in which, symptomatology – the horizontal – is only the result of the vertical. When we read the news "A defenceless, old woman is murdered bloodthirstily in her own house and then robbed" in the newspaper, the span of our assessment of what we are being told by the newspaper may differ radically depending on whether we have read *Crime and Punishment* and to what vertical extent we could read it. Whilst seeming to tell the story of a poor man planning to murder an old, rich woman, we know that the novel is actually revealing something else that is neither observable nor explainable. If Dostoyevski was only documenting the thoughts and feelings of Raskolnikov and what happened, it would not be a novel. Likewise, in Kafka's novel, *The Trial*, we have a vague sense of what K. is accused of, which also happens to be the same vague sense that the novel itself is centred around. But we also sense this "what K. is accused of" as something unnameable, or we are aware that we would lose it the moment we would attempt to name it. The artistic success of *The Trial* is based on this inexpressibility the novel conveys and makes the reader subject to.

The art of a novel is created through words, but it is more than what is expressed through words. Actually, it begins at the point that it goes beyond what it expresses. It is this "beyondness" from its own horizontal material that makes something a work of art. The work of art rests on the vertical depth that it may potentially take a reader to from its horizontal reality. In other words, a work of art rests on the distance between its own horizontal and vertical axis. The criteria to assess the artistic value of an object is this potential distance between its own horizontal and vertical reality. This is why art is a *challenge to its own object*, and why art is the Sublime horizontalized.

Many people mistakenly regard art at its face value and talk *about* its horizontal contents, such as its theme. Talking *about* horizontal elements of a work of art is not the way to relate to art. The story, the chain of events, how you write the story, the language, are all things related to the horizontal text. It is a very common mistake to reduce a work of fiction to its story. The storyline of a novel is, however, its least important element. To give an example, the story of Layla and Macnun was told and written many times before Fuzuli, but it is only Fuzuli's version that became a classic. In terms of creativity, there is not really a distinction between creating the epic *The Iliad* by Homer and a play by Samuel Beckett in which nothing much really happens on thrhorizontal level. It is very wrong to regard literature as an art of self-expression or expression of something; like any other created object, the work of literature expresses itself and itself only[3]. Poetry is not about finding nice expressions. Novels and short-stories are not making up nice stories and trying to find nice, beautiful ways to tell them. Yes, they do that. But such horizontal beauty comes only as a *result* of their inner essence, the Sublime. The initiating point of the arts is never horizontal, although art occurs *through* the horizontal.

In *Psychology and Alchemy* (CW 12), Jung underlines the interesting fact that alchemists usually work with ordinary materials that are extensively available to us in our daily life, such as water, sulphur, salt, vinegar, earth, iron, but they transform the combination of these ordinary substances into something entirely different and extraordinary. Art resembles alchemy, in the sense that it is also done with ordinary materials that are extensively available to us in our daily life, such as words, stones, paints, and, like alchemy, secret of art lies in transforming the combination of these ordinary substances into something entirely different and extraordinary. Like the alchemist, the artist makes "magic" through simple matters we daily encounter, and his transformation is always unique, although we extract a universal knowledge from it. Jung writes that "what [the alchemist] sees in matter, or thinks he can see, is chiefly the data of his own unconscious which he is projecting into it" (Ibid., par. 332). The work of art's truth is latent within this data, which is both highly individualistic and collective, both ordinary and sublime at the same time.

A work of art is always more than the sum of the elements it is composed of. For instance, a novel is more than the plot, the language, the story that it is composed of. It may be considered a bad novel by literary criteria, even if each of these components might be very good standing alone. As David Harned states in *Theology and the Arts*, "What the artist creates is more than the sum of its parts" (1966, p. 141). The piece's artistic energy is charged from the synthesis of all these elements, but goes beyond their combination. Art is not only an energic, but also synergic action. In art, two plus two makes more than four and art begins after four when two plus two is in question. And, the work's art doesn't rest solely on the horizontal or vertical dimension, but within a synergy their combination has transformed.

Max Scheler has written:

> The mission of all true art is not to reproduce what is already given, nor to create something in the pure play of subjective fancy, but to press forward into the whole of the external world and the soul, to see and communicate those objective realities within it which rule and convention have hitherto concealed.
>
> *(1954, p. 253)*

In *The Forms of Things Unknown*, Herbert Read says that he would amend these words of Scheler's only in one detail, "for the objective realities of art are not seen by the artist and then communicated: seeing is creating, and creation is communication: the objective realities come into existence in the act of creation" (1960, p. 28). In other words, "[T]he artist tends to see what he paints rather than to paint what he sees" (1967, p. 69), as Herbert Read repeats in *Art and Alienation*. Creation is actually in this seeing. Seeing and creating – meaning, giving the work of art its form – happen at one and the same time; they naturally blend in together.

Art is nothing but form. The created object reveals a form that could not be otherwise. The created object is complete in itself; it has an independent existence. It begins in its very form, it ends in its very form. It serves as a means to itself, and all its inexpressible essence, Sublime and content is this form itself. In that sense, essence is also nothing but the image. Form and content of a work of art are never two separate things; we are inevitably talking about one of them when we are dealing with the other. It is not only that essence creates form and form creates essence but also creating a form means creating an essence at the same time, and creating an essence means creating a form, and it is neither the form nor the essence but the piece of art that is created as one thing in the end. One of the reasons for why the work of art is an expression of itself only is because creating a new form means creating a new way to see or show something. Each form is an idea. And each form is a *different* idea.

Michel Butor has written that new things will reveal new forms within reality (1991, p. 20). Like most true statements, this is also inadequate. *A new form is a revealment of a new reality itself*. Art means creating a reality *through* a new form. Such a reality is a reality that is intrinsic to the particular work of art itself, but also in relation to the reality of art in general; a reality that is *a* reality, but not *the* reality, although its subjectivity is valuable insofar as it can be linked to an objectivity; a reality that is neither horizontal nor vertical, but, as Giegerich would put it, in a third category. Each art is *a* form in which *the* inexpressible Sublime is expressed.

Whether they are aware of it or not, all artists are aesthetic philosophers. Each novel is an embodied idea of what a novel is. Each novel redefines the art of the novel in its own way whilst being a part of the art of the novel in the general. Herbert Read, who I think was an excellent aesthetician, said that he derived his aesthetic philosophy directly from the works of art themselves, from appreciating them. True appreciation of art is never on a simply emotional, sensational level; it naturally, spontaneously includes contemplating on this appreciation. All great aestheticians, i.e. Herbert Read, Rollo May, Proust, Sartre, Kundera, were also people who were engaged in the creation of some form of art. Nietzsche is known to have said: "One should try to create a work of art before s/he speaks about it." Herbert Read wrote: "No good artist exists who is not, at every point at his career, firstly a good critic. The world of art emerges within a field of critical perceptions" (1938, p. 127). Reading a novel teaches you what a novel is, and as you read novels, you get more and more into the aesthetic theory of the novel. In time, you begin to have, or maybe even create your own theory of the novel, whilst you get a big picture of the theory of the novel. This unique, particular, authentic theory of the novel takes its particularity in its relation to the general theory of the novel. And creating a form of art is creating a theory of a form of art.

French novelist Kléber Haedens in his theoretical book *The Art of the Novel* talks about some people who say "I prefer a sentence that doesn't sound beautiful to the ear, but that makes sense, to a beautiful sentence that is meaningless" (1961, p. 76). Haedens says such an argument is out of the question, because, "*You cannot indicate one sentence that is both beautiful and meaningless. Because, beauty itself, has meaning*" (Ibid., italics mine). And, Haedens says, the beauty and depth of the language of a novel is dependent on the beauty and the depth of its thought, and Balzac writes like Balzac, no matter whether he is writing novels or theories (Ibid.).

The artistic sort of beauty is a call from and a call to the Sublime. As humans, we are naturally drawn to artistic beauty even if we can't appreciate its vertical aspect, which is meaning. Maybe a Picasso painting is ugly from a solely horizontal point of view, but even if we think it is ugly, even if we may not understand why we like it, we are still drawn to a Picasso painting, because we sense the hidden beauty, the hidden meaning in the very horizontal subtance of the image. Picasso may claim to be a rebel, but his paintings are proof themselves that he is trying to make a connection. He communicated with the Sublime through works of art and now he is communicating this Sublime through his own paintings.

As Ernst Kris wrote, "Art, always, consciously or unconsciously, serves the purpose of communication" (1953, p. 61). The need to engage in arts arises when we are very much alone with a truth that is inexpressible, and daily/horizontal means of communication are felt to be insufficient. This sort of inexpressible truth that one feels alone with is always beyond horizontal reality, is related with the Sublime and even if we use objects from horizontal reality as a medium to refer to this vertical truth of the Sublime, these horizontal objects used become valuable insofar as they can go beyond themselves and beyond their daily, practical, horizontal function and face value, in other words, the horizontal material of the art object becomes artistic as far as it is transformed by the artist.

Art is always an experience, and art is always experienced as a *movement*. This is true for all kinds of artistic experiences at all levels. As audience/ reader, we are *moved* by objects of art. And it is with this sort of movement that something vertical *moves* the artist to become objectified in a horizontal vessel. Pre-object, as Michael Balint names it, wants to become an object. Creativity is a tendency from the vertical to the horizontal and it is experienced as a movement; we perceive it as an activity even if it is not always observable or even if it is sometimes blocked. I regard this movement in line with movement of the soul and the soul-*making* that Giegerich talks about. Aesthetic sense and art-making is about psychic energy.

French writer Saint Exupéry said that *truth is not what we discover, but what we create*. Likewise, Herbert Read stated: "Art must be discovered, not received. It must be created, not conferred. It must arise spontaneously in persons and among groups, as an expression of their vitality" (1955, p. 120). Art is the Sublime thinking through the image. Art is making the seemingly frozen image move/think, or, rather, making us move/ think through the image, the *Schein* that "is not a mere semblance, but that appearance from which – even if it is a delusion, something shines forth that gives a radiance to things and a meaning to life – in short, something that brings *soul* to the world" (Giegerich, 2005, p. 152).

Mentioning "the letter killeth while the spirit giveth life" from the Bible, Lacan also questions how the spirit could live without the letter and notes that it is the letter that produces all the effects of truth involving the spirit in man (2004, p. 454). The letter is horizontal, whilst the spirit is vertical. We all share horizontal reality, we are inevitably surrounded by horizontal reality, and horizontal vessels are the only means we have to convey the vertical/Sublime. Any form of creativity is a magical revival of the letter by the spirit. It is the "third" thing, the child, the *being* born out of the magical union of two things, which were never as separate as we thought – although, the "magic" part is new and therefore invaluable. The horizontal is the masculine, whilst the vertical is the feminine. Luce Irigaray, rethinking Lacan in terms of the masculine and the feminine, explained life, in my view, as something resembling the female genital, concealing its roots inside the body whilst showing the flowers attached to its roots on the outside (2014, p. 41). Anything we say about aesthetics is also true for life and psychology, and vice versa. Like Irigaray, Jung likens life to a plant that lives on its rhizome. "The true life is invisible, hidden in the rhizome", he writes, and "the part that appears above ground lasts only a single summer. . . . What we see is the blossom it passes. The rhizome remains" (1995, p. 4).

Being a moralist, Tolstoy first depicted Anna Karenina as an unsympathetic character, because a woman who was having an affair was unacceptable to him personally. If he stuck to his first plan, we would judge Anna Karenina, not be able to relate to her inner conflicts and feel that she got the punishment she deserved when she threw herself under a train at the end of the novel. A person whose pen is not wiser than himself/herself is not a creative writer, whether she/he is writing a novel or something else.[4] Being creative means having *the capacity to be open to change* in accord with the pre-object one is dealing with.[5] Even if Tolstoy's conscious thought was telling him that an adulterous woman is not to be liked, Tolstoy sensed that it was wrong to portray his character as such and changed his initial drafts *in spite of* himself. Learning to write creatively is about learning to give an ear to your novel's own voice, to be able to relate to what your novel wants to become in its own right, and what your novel wants to become is not always in harmony with your present self. Both Rollo May and Cézanne were changed by the Tree, because they let themselves be open to hear what the tree/Tree says about itself. Jung also describes psychic experience of a creative nature as something "whose object is the emergence of a new and yet unknown content" (CW 9, par. 285). Child archetype represents creativity and self-actualization, and as Clarissa Pinkola Estés states, "the deepest urge of all, the urge for new life" (1992, p. 273), because the child is invaluable to the extent that it can have an independent existence, "manifestly separated or even isolated from its background (the mother)" (CW 9, par. 286). Child is something evolving towards independence (Jung and Kerenyi, 1963, p. 87). Metaphorical child stands for any sort of "potential" which is defined as "the inherent capacity or ability for growth, development, or coming into being" by *American Heritage Dictionary*. Each child is born with potentials that are at odds with her parents at their present

238   Nihan Kaya

selves, and we are good parents to the extent that we may support our child to become her own self rather than the child we would like her to be. The same is true for the process between the artist and her pre-object, between the analyst and the analysand and for the process of self-becoming between our present self and our self-to-be or non-self. *It is not only we who create what we create; we are not creating if what we are creating is not also creating us at the same time.* Creativity is the Sublime actualized within the psyche. Just as we are not really parenting if our relationship with our child is not interactive, and we are not allowing ourselves to be changed by our child, and just as we are not really analyzing if we are not regarding our analysand as a separate entity and allow the process to be mutual, we are not creating if we are only imposing our pre-object to become the object our present self would like it to be. Then the result is an object, but not a *created* object – as it would be in the first scenario of Tolstoy – then there would not be a "third" being, a metaphorical "child" in the clinic room, resulting from the relationship between the analyst and the analysand,[6] resulting from the relationship between our present self and our self-to-be. Our non-self is the invisible, vertical aspect of our being, and it is not really a separate entity than who we are at the moment, which is our horizontal current being. The child is precious because it represents the unknown and our capacity to make ourselves available to our own unknown and non-self, which is, again, the Sublime, and our own sublime. Making inner contact with a work of art as a reader/audience is also making inner contact with our own unknown; it is communication on a vertical level or communication with the Sublime.

Creativity proceeds via the tension between – seemingly – opposites such as horizontality and verticality, consciousness and unconsciousness, discipline and inspiration, form and non-form, tradition and novelty, conformity and rebellion[7], matter and mind. Both sides are active during the formation of a "new" being, whether it is a work of art or a part of ourselves that is being created. Creativity is about a part of our unconsciousness wanting to become conscious, about some content wanting to become a form, about something vertical wanting to manifest itself going up on the surface, in other words, to be horizontalised. Creativity is the magical moment when the horizontal and the vertical meet and an entirely different, third being that didn't exist before comes into being. Creativity, in short, is the core of the Sublime latent in every human being and anything that is worldly. Whenever an actual *creation* takes place, whenever there is *coniunctio*, for example, in each difference between a text and a *created* text, however minute it may be, there is a part of the Sublime that is in action. This Sublime constantly wants to actualise itself – meaning, to become *sublime* – through the ordinary/horizontal. Art is the Sublime blazed through an ordinary form.

As Henry Bergson states, "There will be novelty in our acts thanks only to the repetition we have found in things" (2007, p. 76). Thinking intuition in line with unforeseeable novelty and also immediate consciousness extended within the linear flow of reality, Bergson studies the link between

Expressing the inexpressible   239

the possible and the real and asks if a symphony was possible before it was composed by the musician and became real (Ibid., p. 10). As a novelist, I don't yet know what my next novel is going to be like. But every time I write a novel, looking backwards, I discover that the novel has always lived inside me. My new novel is "new" to me, different than anything I have ever written, yet I see its link to my previous life and works and readily place it within the chain of my other novels once it becomes real.

What we call "unconsciousness" is the vertical side of our consciousness which is horizontal, and art is experienced as an extension of our immediate horizontality towards a vertical direction. I said earlier that everything has both horizontal and vertical dimensions. Words are no exception to this. When we are three and fall, we say "My knee is hurt" and use the word "hurt" accurately in that sentence. No one can claim that the three-year-old who says her knee is hurt doesn't know the meaning of this word. However, word is horizontal, whereas meaning is vertical and therefore limitless.[8] The Turkish novelist Tanpınar once said that we first learn the words, and then their meanings. To put it more precisely, the horizontal meaning of words become more and more vertical as we learn them. With time, we dive deeper and deeper into the meaning of a word, i.e. the word "hurt", and think that we didn't really know the meaning of that word before, even if further verticality of its meaning is still unknown to us. This is how and why our relationship with words determines our relationship with life and vice versa. When we communicate with the essence of a poem or a novel through its horizontal reality which is composed of words and the like, we also become aware that this essence is incommunicable on a horizontal level and sense more of the vertical content that is still unknown to us. The horizontal vessel of the text conceals its essence whilst revealing it at one and the same time. As Oscar Wilde said, "All art is at once surface and symbol." Words, for example, are the surfaces of the Sublime.

Lacanian psychologist Annie G. Rogers also states in her book *The Unsayable*: "Every sentence we speak is continually surrounded by what is not said and may in fact be unsayable. Ironically you can only hear the unsayable through what is *said*" (2006, p. 61), and that "words both reveal and conceal unconscious connections" (Ibid., p. 82). She summarizes Lacan's view of the signifier (the horizontal) and the signified (the vertical) as follows:

> Lacan showed us that a signifier points to something beyond, something that can't be said or represented. What is signified is always "slipping beneath the signifier." Signifiers repeat and connect with one another and can be heard only retrospectively. Even as you construct and hear one signifier, another emerges, and the chain of signifiers always points toward a lack, something that can't be represented. Because they are embedded in ordinary words, signifiers are usually disguised.
>
> *(2011, p. 116)*

Every single word and every single detail is felt as a potential and important with this potentiality within a work of literature. They are, first and foremost, their potentiality. The famous dramatic principle of Anton Chekhov – although it is very much unlike the Chekhovian perspective when taken at its face value – that a pistol should be fired in the following scene if it is ever shown in a preceding scene cannot be taken literally, because, *in a work of fiction, showing a pistol itself already means showing the potentiality of this pistol to fire*. There are no clear distinctions between factual reality and potentiality in fiction. Chekhov himself, actually, is the writer who makes magic out of showing the pistol in the first scene and keeping it unfired during the rest of the scenes. Pistols make strong impact on us by not being fired during Chekhov's short-stories and plays, more than they possibly could if they were ever to be fired. If the camera focuses on a pair of shoes put in front of a stove, we immediately wonder whether the shoes will be burned, and this wonder is kept at its peak during the time our expectation is not met, evolving into our questioning. Horizontal movements invoke questions regarding vertical motives or such during fiction. If a man stands up, walks in the room and looks out from the window in a film, these actions trigger questions at once about why he did these actions and so on and on, although the same actions would remain solely horizontal to us in real life. And stories tell about themselves more by not being told. Learning to tell a story creatively is about learning to tell a story without telling it.

Poet Audre Lorde said: "Poetry is the way we give name to the nameless so that it can be thought". All forms of art are indeed various ways of telling the untellable. *Each* form of art *created* is indeed itself, in a unique way, *created* to tell something that only *it* can tell, if it is a true creation. In *What is Literature*, Sartre stresses that the poet doesn't use the language, and that rather, it is the language that serves the poet (2011, p. 12), and he says: "One might think that [the poet] is composing a sentence, but this is only what it appears to be. He is *creating an object*" (p. 16, italics mine).

> Poets are men who refuse to *utilize* language. Now, since the quest for truth takes place in and by language conceived as a certain kind of instrument, it is unnecessary to imagine that they aim to discern or expound the true. Nor do they dream of naming the world, and, this being the case, they name nothing at all, for naming implies a perpetual sacrifice of the name to the object named, or, as Hegel would say, the name is revealed as the inessential in the face of the thing which is essential. *They do not speak, neither do they keep still; it is something different.*
>
> (Ibid., p. 12, last italics mine)

As Ernst Kris remarked, "The artist does not 'render' nature, nor does he 'imitate' it, but creates it anew. He controls the world through his work" (1953, pp. 51–52). Art is a way to have control over the object/world/reality – in poetry, for example, over words/language –, and therefore, over the world and reality, art naturally overcomes the feeling of being governed by whatever the object of the artwork is – words/language/i.e. – and the reality/world they are associated with. The British aesthetician Louis Arnaud Reid, in *Meaning in the Arts*, suggests that every work of art has a life of its own and "The import of a work of art is its 'life', which, like actual life, is an indivisible phenomenon" (1969, pp. 66–67). As another aesthetician, Susanne K. Langer, states, the sign – the word/language, as in the example by Sartre – is something to act upon, or a means to command action, whereas "the symbol is an instrument of thought" (1941, p. 34).

Putting it in my terms, a symbol is something that has a concrete substance on horizontal reality[9] which functions as a medium towards its verticality through this substance, something that is bigger than its own horizontal reality on the surface. Because we are imposed a certain way to see and understand the world, the intersection points where the horizontal meets the vertical are not always available to our thinking, and we tend to perceive the vertical aspect closer to its horizontal surface. When we can't move much deeper than the horizontal, we perceive the horizontal object as a sign, such as a three-year-old who is aware of the meaning of the word "hurt" even if this verticality is closer to its surface. In that sense, almost all people are aware that there is a meeting point between the horizontal and the vertical, and to some extent, maybe most people are also aware that there is no limit to the verticality (the Sublime) we can take a word or any other horizontal object to. However, creativity is an unforeseeable spark coming out of the clash where the horizontal meets the vertical, and this is why a third *being*, the metaphorical child, is very adept to indicate the nature of creativity. Creativity is a moment, experienced as a vertical movement, either when Cézanne encounters the Tree through the tree as a result of many other moments of creativity through the tree and other trees and many other objects of art, or when Rollo May or any other person with aesthetic sense encounters Cézanne's Tree as a part of many other moments of creativity she/he had encountered before. The poet creates a Language, and through the Language she/he created, the person with aesthetic verticality also goes through a moment or moments of creativity through the Language created, to the extent that his/her aesthetic sensibility in regard to poetry and the general arts allows. The sign – the letter/word/image/object – is still and dead, even if it can be regarded as a celebrated union of the horizontal and the vertical. The sign is transformed into a symbol only when a different, separate, third *being* comes into place, and then, the letter/word/image/object is suddenly *animated*, which is the moment of creativity, either on the side of the creator or the reader/audience. Without this aesthetic sensibility, we read, but we don't read *creatively*, meaning that our reading remains more horizontal, closer to the horizontal surface of the text. The more verticality we have in regard to aesthetic understanding of literature, the more we are open to create ourselves through the text, rather than to become a passive reader of it. The critical difference between a sign and a symbol is this *vitality*. A symbol or a *created* thought/text/object is *alive*, and when I say that art is the magical *revival* of the letter/word/text/language, what I mean can only be valid to the extent that we can be *revived* through the touch of this creation. As Morris Philipson says in *Outline of a Jungian Aesthetics*, "everything that *acts* is actual" (1963, p. 84). The created object is something that *acts*, something that has an independent existence in its own right, and we know it *acts*, only through our own vertical *acting* in response to it. Things become real only when they are *created*. As Kierkegaard notes, truth exists only as the individual himself produces it in action, and creativity is the name we give to this producing in action. Art is not the Sublime animated; the Sublime *is* this animation itself.

When I refer to the metaphorical child, I accentuate that it is a third *being*, because "being should be understood to mean *potentia*, the source of potentiality" (Angel et al., 1958, p. 41), and "when used in a particular sense, such as *a* human being, it always has the dynamic connotation of someone in process, the person being something" (ibid).

Our sense of *being* and vitality, or the Sublime within, is experienced at its peak during the act of creation. Creation is never a one-time event. The *created* object is created by its audience only as long as it continues to be created and revive itself. The object that was once created becomes still and dead the moment it ceases to be created by us. The magical revival of the object is limited to the verticality its horizontality could extend to; once the verticality is experienced, our experience is captured in the horizontal again. Our vertical experience becomes horizontalized.

Like individuation that "does not shut one out from the world, but gathers the world to oneself" (CW 8, par. 432), the particularity of the work of art is the sort of particularity that gives us a better understanding of the generality the particularity is naturally a part of, and through art, we come closer to our own unique self, our own Sublime within, whilst coming closer to the world at the same time. Jung regarded the deepest level of the psyche as simply the "world" (CW 9, par. 291), and this is also the unimaginable deepest depth of the vertical, or, in other words, the Sublime itself.

Notes

1 The quoted paragraph gives the best definition for Rollo May's term "encounter". Rollo May explains encounter as experienced between two poles, that of the artist and that of the objective reality, and says that this is indeed what makes the creative act so hard to study (ibid., p. 78). I hope to bring some clarity to the synergy issued out of these two realms by reviewing it in horizontal and vertical terms.

2 We know that Monet painted the same cathedral at Rouen 33 times.

3 Many people think writers become writers because they are good at expressing themselves, but I think it is the other way round: Writers become writers because they feel and think that they are not able to fully express *a* truth, and engagement in literature or any other form of art becomes a vessel for them to express this inexpressible.

4 Even if arts are the most condensed form of creativity and therefore make it easier to talk about the nature of creativity, creativity can be found in all sorts

Expressing the inexpressible   243

of action. Whatever I say about artistic creativity can be applied to any area other than arts, including psychology, as I will mention soon. Jung also believes that "symbolical art-work serves the same purpose for a society that an individual symbolic experience serves for a patient in therapy" (Philipson, 1963, pp. 127–128).

5 I also suggest that the pre-object, which normally defines the uncompleted work the artist is working on, can also be thought as the yet-to-be self. We are not only our present selves, but we are also the total of all the potential selves we are not yet or we could be even if we don't or didn't become them. There is a very deep link between how we create something and how we create our own selves, and these two situations also blend in together, and everything I say about artistic creation is also true for our self-creation, which is a never-ending process.

6 Donald Kalsched talks about the nature of a true "pregnancy" that occurs between the patient and the therapist as a result of a true union in *The Inner World of Trauma* (1996, p. 164).

7 "Con" means "with", and "to conform" means "to form with". Creativity is not *un*-conformist – as it conforms to itself and brings its own vertical form with it – but *non*-conformist; art is not *un*-realist, but *supra*-realist.

8 In *Trauma and Beyond*, Jungian analyst Ursula Wirtz says that "meaning is always 'on the way'" (2014, p. 59). She also mentions Lao Tzu, who taught that true meaning (*Sinn*) cannot be thought (*ersinnt*), otherwise it would not be true meaning (ibid.). But it is also true that word is meaning and meaning is word. The three-year-old who knows the word knows its meaning simultaneously, only extending it less vertically than she/he will possibly do in the future. In short, horizontal is the vertical and vertical is the horizontal.

9 I use the preposition "on", as I see horizontal reality as something linear. Anything within horizontal reality is perceived, at least by me, as something on a line, including the line of time and space. The horizontal defines the surface of anything.

References

Angel, Ernest, Ellenberger, Henri F. and May, Rollo (Ed.) (1958). *Existence: A New Dimension in Psychiatry and Psychology*. New York: Basic Books.

Barron, Frank (1965). The Psychology of Creation. In *New Directions in Psychology II*. London: Holt, Rinehart & Winston.

Bergson, Henry (2007). *The Creative Mind: An Introduction to Metaphysics*. New York: Dover Publications.

Butor, Michel (1991). *Roman Üstüne Denemeler* [*Essais sur le Roman*]. Istanbul: Düzlem Publications.

Collingwood, R.G. (1958). *The Principles of Art*. London: Oxford University Press.

Giegerich, Wolfgang (2005). *The Neurosis of Psychology: Primary Papers towards a Critical Psychology*, *Volume I* in *Collected English Papers*. New Orleans, LA: Spring Journal Books.

Haedens, Kléber (1961). *Roman Sanatı* [*Paradoxe sur le Roman*]. Istanbul: Varlık Publications.

Harned, David Baily (1966). *Theology and the Arts*. Philadelphia: Westminster Press.

Irigaray, Luce (2014). *Başlangıçta Kadın Vardı* [*Au commencement, elle étatit*]. Istanbul: Pinhan Publishing.

Jung, Carl Gustav (1940). The Archetypes and the Collective Unconscious. CW 9.
Jung, Carl Gustav (1954[1947]). The Structure and Dynamics of the Psyche. CW 8.
Jung, C.G. and Kerenyi, C. (1963). *Essays on a Science of Mythology: The Myth of the Divine Child and the Mysteries of Eleusis*. Princeton, NJ: Princeton University Press.
Jung, C.G. and Kerenyi, C. (1973). *Letters, Vol 2: 1951–1961*. Princeton, NJ: Princeton University Press.
Jung, C.G. and Kerenyi, C. (1980). Psychology and Alchemy. CW 12.
Jung, C.G. and Kerenyi, C. (1995). *Memories, Dreams, Reflections*, Trans. Richard and Clara Winston. London: Fontana Press.
Kalsched, Donald (1996). *The Inner World of Trauma: Archetypal Defenses of the Personal Spirit*. New York: Routledge.
Kris, Ernst (1953). *Psychoanalytic Explorations in Art*. London: Allen & Unwin.
Lacan, Jacques (1957). The Instance of the Letter in the Unconscious or Reason since Freud. In Julie Rivkin and Michael Ryan (Eds.), *Literary Theory: An Anthology* (2nd ed., pp. 447–461). Blackwell Publishing, 1998, 2004.
Langer, Susanne K. (1941). *Philosophy in a New Key: A Study in the Symbolism of Reason, Rite, and Art*. London: Oxford University Press, 1996.
May, Rollo (1975). *Courage to Create*. New York: Bantam Books, 1978.
Philipson, Morris (1963). *Outline of a Jungian Aesthetics*. Northwestern University Press.
Pinkola Estés, Clarissa (1992). *Women Who Run with the Wolves*. New York: Ballantine Books.
Proust, Marcel (1929). *Within A Budding Grove, Vol II*, Trans. C.K. Scott Moncrieff. London: Chatto & Windus.
Read, Herbert (1938). *Collected Essays in Literary Criticism*. London: Faber and Faber.
Read, Herbert (1955). *The Grass Roots of Art: Lectures on the Social Aspects of Art in an Industrial Age*. New York: Faber and Faber.
Read, Herbert (1960). *The Forms of Things Unknown: Essays Towards an Aesthetic Philosophy*. London: Faber and Faber Limited.
Read, Herbert (1965). *The Origins of Forms in Art*. London: Thames and Hudson.
Read, Herbert (1967). *Art and Alienation: The Role of the Artist in Society*. London: Thames and Hudson.
Reid, Louis Arnaud (1969). *Meaning in the Arts*. London: Allen & Unwin.
Ricoeur, Paul (1990). *Time and Narrative Volume I*, Trans. Kathleen Mclaughlin and David Pellauer. London: The University of Chicago Press.
Rogers, Annie G. (2006). *The Unsayable: The Hidden Language of Trauma*. New York: Ballantine Books.
Sartre, Jean-Paul (2011). *What is Literature? [Qu'est-ce que la littérature?]*. Retrieved from www.english.ufl.edu/mrg/readings/Sartre,%20What%20Is%20Literature.PDF.
Scheler, Max (1954). *The Nature of Sympathy*, Trans. P. Heath. London: Routledge.
Wirtz, Ursula (2014). *Trauma and Beyond: The Mystery of Transformation*. New Orleans, LA: Spring Journal Books.

SIXTEEN

The *Nibelungenlied*: a Germanic myth and the sublime

Arthur Niesser

Introduction

I was about ten years old when I was invited to help an elderly lady of a well-educated background to pack up her belongings, as she was moving to a smaller house. I was attracted to her large bookshelves, and the lady allowed me to take one or two books of my choice. My eyes fell on a large volume with the title *Götter und Helden* (*Gods and Heroes*) (Fischer,1934). Significantly, it was published one year after Hitler came to power in Germany. It contains Nordic and Germanic sagas, of which the *Nibelungenlied* was the most prominent one. I was fascinated by it, and it has been on my mind ever since.

The *Nibelungenlied* was most likely written around the year 1200 in a monastery in the area of Passau in lower Bavaria, presumably based on oral tradition. It was popular throughout the Middle Ages but then it fell into oblivion for around 250 years. It was in 1755 that a physician from Lindau on the Lake of Constance studied a library of the abandoned castle of Hohenems, which is located south of the Lake of Constance in what is Austria today. He found a handwritten volume and he was immediately fascinated by this story of the heroes of what we now know as the *Nibelungenlied*. Later on, further copies with slightly different versions were discovered (Müller, 2005).

The initial reception was cool and the Prussian King Frederick II (1740–1786), the Great, as he is known in Germany, judged that the poem was worth not even one shot of gunpowder. However, the situation changed in the time of Romanticism when it was translated into contemporary German, and it came to be regarded as the German *Iliad* and *Odyssey*. It was hailed as being at the foundation of national poetry.

The epic poem is vaguely based on historical events at the time of the Great Migration. In particular, in 436/437 the Burgundian Empire, which had been established along the Rhine river, was destroyed by a coalition of Romans and Huns. The second part of the Nibelungenlied was strongly influenced by these folk memories. The first part, however, drew predominantly on Nordic sagas, such as the Edda, but others as well (Müller, 2005). Winder McDonnel concludes, "It is not until the turn of the thirteenth

245

century that the two major strands of the tradition, the (mythical) death of Siegfried and the (historical) demise of the Burgundians, are brought together in the epic form that has been passed down to us" (McConnell, 1998a, p. 2f). McDonnel draws parallels with *The Iliad* and *The Odyssey* as already mentioned, but also the Indian *Mahabharata*, the English *Beowulf* and the Welsh *Mabinogion*. Richard Wagner, in his composition of the *Ring des Nibelungen*, used similar material, but the epos of the *Nibelungenlied* and Wagner's *Ring* are different poetic expressions and need to be distinguished from one another.

This brief introduction indicates already how the *Nibelungenlied* divides opinions. There are passages which reflect sublime polarities, appealing to the noble attitudes and the finest values, or the opposite, with treachery, murder and slaughter (Burke, 2015). I will demonstrate how these opposites were enacted in German history and thinking, and I will propose a symbolic approach to the myth in line with Jungian concepts.

Summary of the storyline

Here now is a summary of the content: Siegfried, who grew up in Xanten in the Netherlands, comes to the Burgundian court at Worms on the river Rhine to demand Kriemhild, the sister of King Gunther as his wife. He wants to fight against Gunther in single combat. Hagen, a close relative of the king and his first vassal, knows about Siegfried's background and tells the story of his fight with the dragon. Bathing in his blood had made his skin hard and impenetrable. Siegfried had acquired a huge treasure, the Nibelungen Hoard, and came into possession of an invisibility cap.

Siegfried can be appeased, and a friendship develops. However, Hagen remains suspicious. Siegfried helps King Gunther to gain Brunhild as his wife in return for the permission to marry Kriemhild. He does so by deceit. Brunhild, the queen of Iceland, had vowed only to marry a man who could defeat her. Any beaten suitor was killed. Siegfried, using his invisibility cap, overpowers Brunhild under the guise of Gunther. Brunhild followed Gunther to the Burgundian court. However, on the wedding night she ties her husband down and he must spend the night dangling from a hook. Siegfried is asked for help again. The next night he wrestles Brunhild down and takes her ring and her belt from her, which deprives her of her physical strength. Many commentators suggest that he actually rapes her.

Siegfried and Kriemhild, now married, returned to Xanten but visited the Burgundian court again ten years later. During a tournament, Kriemhild basks in the splendour of her husband Siegfried. Brunhild reminds her that Siegfried had declared himself vassal of her husband Gunther. During the ugly quarrel of the queens as to who has the most noble husband, Kriemhild produces the ring and the belt that Siegfried had taken from Brunhild. The latter is deeply humiliated and seeks revenge. She approaches Hagen for help. Hagen and the king together plot the assassination of Siegfried, which they carry out in a cowardly way by Hagen driving a spear into the back of the unsuspecting Siegfried. Kriemhild had been tricked into marking the only area where Siegfried was vulnerable, as he otherwise was protected from injury after his bath in dragon blood.

The second part of the *Nibelungenlied* describes Kriemhild's revenge. She gives in to the courtship of Attila, the king of the Huns, so that she would gain access to a military force. Years later she invites the Burgundians to the court of Attila with the intention to provoke a battle in which Hagen would be killed. It is reported that even after more than ten years she still sheds tears for Siegfried every day. Hagen recognises the trap and warns against the journey. However, when he is called a coward, he consents and leads the party. He knows that nobody will return home alive but he still continues with the enterprise. He provokes and tantalizes Kriemhild and Attila by killing their six-year-old son. A terrible and atrocious battle ensues with unimaginable suffering and many deaths.

The *Nibelungenlied* gives detailed accounts of the fighting action. Kriemhild has set fire to the hall into which the Burgundians retreated. Plagued by the heat and thirst, they resort to drinking the blood of the slain comrades. The Burgundians now call themselves the Nibelungen. Fierce battles between individual heroes on either side are narrated in detail. Even friends are forced to fight one another in single combat as they are bound to their king by duty and oath. In the end Gunther and Hagen are captured alive. Hagen demands the head of Gunther in exchange for revealing the location where he sunk the treasure of the Nibelungen in the Rhine. However, when Gunther is killed, he boasts that now only he himself knows the place and he would never disclose it. In a burst of fury Kriemhild kills Hagen with Siegfried's sword. Hildebrand, a Visigoth at the Hun court, finds it unbearable that such a hero as Hagen should be slain by a woman and he in turn kills Kriemhild (De Boor, 2000).

I had to shorten the story and leave out many details of highly significant symbolic value. Again and again, the author emphasises the splendour, the bravery, the proud spirit and the sense of honour. These are guiding principles for the actions of the individuals, and there seems very little leeway for alternative decisions. The first part, ending in Siegfried's death, is dominated by Siegfried's heroic attitude, which is unfeeling and insensitive and results in his death in an act of realpolitik as Hagen and Gunther feel threatened by Siegfried's power. In the second part, the tragedy unfolds with an eerie necessity, where there seems no way out and the actors are hemmed in by their chivalric ideals, which end in death, destruction and complete obliteration.

Political reception

The eighteenth century saw the emergence of cultural nationalism. The Grimm Brothers as well as Friedrich Schlegel and others were looking for manifestations of "national" poetry and the *Nibelungenlied* seemed to be the perfect expression, especially after the defeat of German forces during the Napoleonic wars. At its core was the idea of a specific German national character (Von See, 1991). A leading representative was the philologist Friedrich Heinrich von der Hagen. He wrote in the preface to his translation from the medieval German into modern language in 1807 during times of Napoleonic occupation:

> Hospitality, conventionality, honesty, loyalty and friendship till death, humanity, clemency and magnanimity during the plight of battle, unshakable steadfastness, superhuman bravery, boldness and willing sacrifice for honour, duty and justice; virtues, which intertwined with the ferocious features and dark forces of revenge, rage, wrath, fury and gruesome zest for death appear all the more lustrous and manifold. They leave us behind, albeit in grief and sorrow, yet also comforted and strengthened, to accept the inevitable, but fill us with courage to word and deed, with pride and trust in the fatherland and its people, with hope in the future return of German glory and grandeur in the world.
>
> *(Ehrismann, 2002, p. 177, own translation)*

The one central virtue as emphasized in the *Nibelungenlied* is the notion of "Treue", which translates as loyalty or faithfulness. In the nineteenth and twentieth century Germanic thinking, loyalty became a doctrine, which mainly meant loyalty to the Sovereign, the State or the Authority. Loyalty was absolute and included joyful acceptance of death. The term Nibelungentreue, the loyalty of the Nibelungen to their king and to one another was regarded as the utmost of German virtues. Paradoxically, loyalty and faithfulness allowed for duplicity, deceit and extreme cruelty as long as it served the loyalty to the sovereign or the authority (Härd, 1996, p. 168); (Hoffmann, 1998). Kriemhild's cruelty was a consequence of her loyalty to Siegfried, and Hagen's murderous actions were justified by his service to the king. "Treue", faithfulness, as a Germanic virtue meant giving up individual liberty and accepting willing sacrifice. In its final consequence, it results in a fight without hope and seeking heroic death.

Thus, in 1909 the Imperial Chancellor, Fürst von Bülow, referred to "Nibelungentreue", i.e. the loyalty of the Nibelungen, to express the firm adherence to the alliance with Austria. As we now know, this alliance resulted in the drama of World War I, the Great War, as it is known in the United Kingdom. During World War II, the drama of Stalingrad was reinterpreted. Hermann Göring, in a speech in 1943, drew parallels between the hopeless battle in Stalingrad and the futile fight of the Nibelungen at the Court of the Huns:

> And from all these gigantic struggles, like an enormous monumental building called Stalingrad, the fight for Stalingrad stands out. The time will come when this will have

been the greatest battle of heroes ever having taken place in our history . . . those fighting there now, against vastly superior forces. . . , again and again, exhausted, drained – we know a tremendous heroic song of an unprecedented struggle. It is called "The Battle of the Nibelungen". They too stood in a hall of blazing fire and quenched their thirst with their own blood – but they fought and fought to the last man. Such a battle is going on there today.

(Heinzle and Waldschmidt, 1991, p. 180, own translation)

There is a faint reminiscence of this determined struggle to the end in the modern myth surrounding football, which has it that German footballing success is down to determination, will and self-sacrifice for the team (Stiftung Haus der Geschichte der Bundesrepublik Deutschland, 2016).

Among all the figures in the *Nibelungenlied*, it is that of Hagen which has always interested me most. In the first part of the *Nibelungenlied*, he is depicted as the dark figure that serves the Court unfailingly and whose attitude can be described as Realpolitik. He has no hesitation to murder Siegfried in an act of cowardly deceit when this seems necessary for the sake of the power and the honour of the Burgundian court. In the second part of the *Nibelungenlied*, the character turns from the villain to the hero, even though Hagen has not changed at all. He is now contrasted not to Siegfried, as in the first part, but to Kriemhild in her destructive search for revenge. He remains cynical, ruthless and arrogant, but it is his unflinching submission to his fate, his proud defiance of death, the loyalty to his cause and the disregard for his scrupulous actions that were admired as heroic. Interestingly, up to the end of the World War I, Siegfried was regarded as the national hero, whereas during the Nazi period, increasingly Hagen took on this role (Härd, 1996, p. 183). He represented qualities which were seen as typically German. He would rather destroy himself and the world than to take a step back. As quoted by Hard, Friedrich W.J. Schelling regarded Hagen's struggle and demise as the sublime in its highest potency: to fight against an absolute power and to succumb in this struggle. While the figure of Hagen in its unyielding determination and strength is impressive, it is "the incarnation of dark and destructive human drives" (Härd, 1996, p. 181). It is a tragedy that over a period of well over 100 years Germany was in the grip of a myth which resulted in death and destruction.

It seems significant that there is no mention of any woman linked to Hagen. Two women stand out in the *Nibelungenlied*: Kriemhild and Brunhild. In the first part, Kriemhild is characterized as most beautiful, charming, noble and lovely beyond measure. However, as her mother reminded her, she can only be a truly beautiful woman through the love of a man. She is enchanted by Siegfried, but she is dependent on her brother giving consent to her marriage. She has no importance on her own, only through her association with the hero Siegfried. This is why the murder of Siegfried not only deprives her of a beloved husband but also of a sense of identity.

She is the wife of the hero; her importance, her *animus*, is projected on to Siegfried. According to Jung, inner images of male (*animus*) and female (*anima*) are unconsciously projected upon the person of the beloved (Jung, 1954[1925]). I understand Kriemhild's drive for ruthless revenge as a distorted search for identity.

As a woman, she has no status in a male-dominated world, and her revenge is the reaction of the wronged feminine. Brunhild is treated even worse. She is deprived of her strength by deceit and rape, hence her bitterness. She should be the equal of Siegfried, but she is deprived of her position by male treachery. As a consequence, she pursues the death of Siegfried. We can say that both main female characters in the *Nibelungenlied* were wronged by male violence. If I translate this into psychological language in line with Jungian terminology, then I would say that *anima* values, which are connected to compassion, feeling and relating (Goss, 2015, p. 108) were suppressed and even violated. This resulted in the *anima* turning negative and murderous.

Anima *neglect*

I would like to expand more on the concept of the *anima* and relate this to the tragedy of the *Nibelungenlied*. Jung described how the *anima* allows access to the world of the unconscious, especially to intuition, feeling and emotions.

I am following Verena Kast's understanding in that "animus and anima are archetypes that can be experienced at any time by both men and women" (Kast, 1986, p. 88). In other words, in contrast to Jung's original concept, men and women both have *anima* and *animus*. Jung describes the *anima* as the "archetype of life itself" (Jung, 1954[1934]). The *anima* enables loving and creative relationships. In contrast, the main male protagonists in the *Nibelungenlied* were cut off from the world of feelings, compassion and genuine relationship. Their lives are dominated by male images of loyalty, chivalric ideals, a code of honour and the will for power. Hagen has opportunities to avert the catastrophe, but it is his pride and ultimately his inability to admit fear that prevent him from doing so.

In contrast to Hagen, Siegfried is depicted as a bright hero throughout. However, he does not know suffering. He can be generous to offer his service, as it does not mean bringing a sacrifice. His heroic deeds are a kind of a sport to him. He is unaware why he should come across as threatening. He lacks these *anima* qualities, which ultimately result in his death. "Any potential for real friendship or comradeship is precluded by the unnerving proclivity of Siegfried to say precisely the wrong thing at the wrong time" (McConnell, 1998b, p. 191). Interestingly, an area between his shoulder blades is the only vulnerable part of his body. It had been covered by a leaf when he bathed himself in the blood of the dragon. It is Kriemhild, his wife, who unsuspectingly points Hagen, his murderer, towards this spot. Seen symbolically, Siegfried's underdeveloped and unconscious *anima* renders him exposed and makes his murder possible.

The *Nibelungenlied* describes friendships between men, but they all end in death. There are Hagen and Volker, who are united in close friendship. Particularly poignant, however, is the friendship between the Burgundians and Rüdiger von Bechelaren. Rüdiger is a close friend of the Burgundians and at the same time vassal to Etzel, the king of the Huns. Kriemhild and Etzel force him to honour his duty as vassal and show loyalty to his king. This, however, stands in opposition to the loyalty he owes to his friends. This is an inescapable conflict and, in the end, Rüdiger is killed by his own sword. Hard writes, "Rüdiger's tragic fate purposefully highlights how political power and political obedience forfeit their moral legitimacy, if they transgress the limits, which are set by humaneness" (Härd, 1996, p. 190).

In my view, *animus* values such as loyalty, duty, bravery and heroism easily lead to tragedy without the mitigating compensation by the *anima*. The most sublime virtues can be distorted by an unfeeling attitude which splits off any sense of compassion.

This is illustrated in an abhorrent manner by Heinrich Himmler, chief of the SS, in a speech in Poland on 4 October 1943:

> Most of you will know what it means when 100 dead bodies are lying together, if there are 500 bodies or if 1000 bodies are lying around. To have gone through this and – apart from some exceptions of human weakness – to have remained decent, that is what has made us hard. This is a never written and never to be written glorious chapter of our history.
>
> *(Himmler, 1943, own translation)*

Himmler, in his ideological fixation, turns mass killing into a virtue and redefines the word "decency" as suppressing human compassion.

I would like to contrast this with the behaviour of another German officer and member of the Nazi Party. Some readers may have seen Roman Polanski's film *The Pianist*. It shows a German officer who helps a Polish Jew to survive. Both the Jewish pianist and the officer are historical figures. The film is based on the pianist Wladislaw Szpilman and the Nazi Officer Wilm Hosenfeld. Hosenfeld was an enthusiastic supporter of Nazi ideals and the hope of a Germanic renewal. But then, as he witnessed the suffering of Jewish people in the Warsaw Ghetto, he wrote, "I see the children and all I want is to cuddle them and to comfort them" (Papsch, 2012, p. 5). He started using his position and influence to rescue Jewish people – overall a small number – but this is not the point. Hosenfeld, in contrast to the dominant ideology, had preserved access to his feelings. In joining the Nazi party and being part of a movement with all the insignia of pomp and circumstance, he was naïve and fell victim to the seductive *anima* aspect which appeals to feelings but sacrifices the thinking aspect. However, he had not lost the ability to feel compassion. He is honoured at the Yad Vashem Shoah Research Centre as one of the few German "Righteous among the Nations" (Papsch, 2012, p. 9).

252 Arthur Niesser

Striving for the highest values and yet getting entangled in injustice, wrongdoing and evil is a theme which was commented on by other writers.

In April 1953, Hannah Arendt (2016) proposed that evil in its most pernicious form appears whenever we strive after a higher good. Thomas Mann said in a speech at the Library of Congress on 6 June 1945: "The Germans could well ask, why their good, in particular, so often turns to evil, becomes evil in their hands" (Mann, 1945, p. 14). He talks about German Romanticism:

> But it cannot be denied that even in its loveliest, most ethereal aspects where the popular mates with the sublime it bears in its heart the germ of morbidity, as the rose bears the worm; its innermost character is seduction, seduction to death.
>
> *(Mann, 1945, p.17)*

Mann talks about German "death pride" and further "there are not two Germanys, a good one and a bad one, but only one, whose best turned into evil" (Mann, 1945, p. 18).

I already mentioned Schelling and the romantic obsession with death and tragedy.

The German historian Herfried Münkler uses the term "Todeserotik", which can be translated as erotic feeling associated with death.

Erich Neumann in his *Depth Psychology and a New Ethic* warns of the danger of a one-sided radical and rigorous ethical attitude when he writes, "Again and again in the course of history we find that the disastrous influence of criminal personalities is matched by that of only one other class of people – the radical idealists, dogmatists and absolutists. Nero and Cesare Borgia are in fact only rivalled by Torquemada and Robespierre" (Neumann, 1990, p. 94).

The German sociologist Werner Sombart wrote a paper in 1915, which he titled "Händler und Helden" ("Merchants and Heroes") (Sombart, 1915). In it he denounced war for the sake of profit, power or a more comfortable life, and he labelled this as the mean English spirit of merchants. In contrast he praised the German heroic soul of the people. The hero does not care about life and he despises anything sensual. The hero seeks transcendence into the spiritual world through heroic fight and death. This is the Faustian idea of uniting with the Gods by renouncing physicality (Sombart, 1915, p. 31).

Goethe's idea of "Stirb und Werde" (Goethe, 1814), "die and be reborn" as the expression of a process of developmental cycles, becomes distorted into a demand for heroic self-sacrifice. The idea of personal growth towards individuation, the sublime in human nature, is distorted into a destructive bloodletting, which causes misery and tears.

The protagonists in the *Nibelungenlied* are guided by high moral values of honour, chivalry, loyalty, firmness, bravery and service to the court. And yet their actions include deceit and murder and result in annihilation.

The *Nibelungenlied*   253

There is much mention of splendour but not of beauty. It seems to me that this refers to the predominance of a moral code which aspires to high ethical values that emanate from a male system of right and wrong. However, these are cut off from *anima* values, from truly relating, from compassion, from human warmth, from fear and from grief. As a result, the *anima* turns against them with vengeance and ultimately a glorification of death. The extermination of Jews then appears as a necessary act of patriotism and the suffering at Stalingrad is glorified as a sublime sacrifice.

I would like to come back to Kriemhild, who is the central female figure in the second part of the epos. She is introduced as adhering to the conventions and ideals of her time. She is completely dependent on her brothers. She plays her role at court and "she is scarcely more than the mere pawn of the kings" (Ehrismann, 1998, p. 21). Her brother, King Gunther, uses her as a bargaining chip to ascertain the help of Siegfried in defeating Brunhild. Following a dream, which her mother interprets as love being inseparable from suffering, she exclaims that she will never marry and she rejects all suitors. By that, she refuses to grow into an adult woman. Her mother reminds her, however, that "you will be valued as a woman only, if God in his goodness grants you a noble knight" (*Nibelungenlied*, 1st Adventure). Contrary to her initial resolve, she falls in love with Siegfried and is happy to marry him. Yet her own standing depends on Siegfried's greatness. Siegfried's death at the hands of Hagen and Gunther deprives her of her own position. Even worse, when Hagen takes away the Nibelungen hoard, he denies her independence, power and potency.

Robbed of her *animus*-husband and her financial means, her *anima* takes on a negative, ruthless quality. All her endeavours now turn towards revenge and she herself uses deceit and power with unspeakable cruelty. She is labelled a "vâlandinne", a she-devil. The archetypal feminine, which has been wronged and violated, turns herself destructive. This can be seen collectively – Medea would be a parallel from the Greek mythology – but also individually as a consequence of abuse and breach of trust.

Conclusion

The *Nibelungenlied* is a Germanic myth and had a great influence on German thinking and self-representation. Wittels calls the *Nibelungenlied* "the representative myth of the Germans" and "an exclusively Teutonic product". He writes, "The representative and dominant myth of a nation, transmitted from generation to generation, seems to be the deepest collective psychological expression of its culture. It contains the philosophy of a nation in the form of a narrative" (Wittels, 1946, p. 91). He refers to Schelling and cites, "A nation comes into existence with its mythology. What is a nation or what makes it a nation? Not only coexistence in space but the unity of its thinking, which means a collective philosophy as presented in its mythology; therefore, its mythology contains the fate of a nation in the same sense as his character is the individual's fate."

After the atrocities of the Nazi era became evident, many inside and outside Germany wondered how a nation with such highly developed cultural values could commit such abhorrent crimes. I suggest that it is the striving for the exalted, the sublime, that creates the opposite as a *shadow*, if it is not counterbalanced by feeling values and relatedness. In the *Nibelungenlied* these *anima* values are suppressed, possibly reflecting a one-sidedness in German cultural development.

It seems to me that following the near total destruction of Germany at the end of World War II, Germany managed to disentangle herself from the Nibelungen myth. Hero images have changed and the *Nibelungenlied* is no longer a compulsory part of the various school curricula. The *Nibelungenlied* is still read and well known in Germany, but rather as a story than as a paradigmatic tale. This is represented in various literary adaptations, which play down the heroic and are of a psychologizing nature (Rolfes, 2005).

I wonder, however, if the denigration of *anima* values is manifest in today's politics. A culture of competition, authority, steadfastness, toughness and other "masculine" values prevails. Decisions have to be rational, hard but fair. Samuels talks about heroic leaders, whose "Führereroticism" turns us on (Samuels, 2015, p. 55).

I ask myself how *anima*-guided political decisions could be different. Maybe our language could change to a more welcoming mindset. We could be curious as to what other cultures could contribute rather than putting up barriers to protect our own way of seeing things. Policies like creating a "hostile environment" for immigrants to deter them from settling in the UK. for example, would no longer be acceptable.

Likewise, the "Monitor" programme on German television reported on 16 August 2018 about a Yazidi young man who had to flee from IS persecution. His whole family was living in Germany and was recognized for asylum, but he faced deportation to Romania under the so-called Dublin agreement, as he was just over 18 years old and had entered the European Union via Romania. Would not *anima*-guided politics recognize the cruelty of separating a young man from his family and leaving him stranded on his own in an unwelcoming environment for the sake of upholding the principle of the Dublin agreement, which requires refugees to seek asylum in the country where they first entered the EU (Reschke and Otto, 2018)? What would an *anima* approach to environmental protection and global warming look like? Would exploitation of nature still be possible? Would there be a more caring attitude towards people living in poverty and those suffering from addictions problems? Jon Mills called for promoting and teaching empathy, based on the personal experience of loving emotional attachment (Mills, 2018).

There was one stanza in the *Nibelungenlied* when I felt that Siegfried came in touch with his *anima* and I find his words moving. In his dying moments he addresses King Gunther, "I am sorry for none so much as my wife, the lady Kriemhild." And, "If you feel at all inclined to do a loyal deed for anyone, noble King, let me commend my beloved wife to your mercy" (Hatto, 1965, p. 132).

Sadly, in the story this change in tone and appeal to the *anima* was not listened to and the tragedy unfolded.

References

Arendt, H. (2016). *Memoirs 1950–1973*, vol. 1, Eds. Ursula Ludz and Ingeborg Nordmann (in Cooperation with the Hannah Arendt Institute Dresden). Munich and Berlin: Piper Verlag Gmbh.

Burke, E. (2015). *A Philosophical Enquiry into the Origin of our Ideas of the Sublime and the Beautiful*. Oxford: Oxford University Press.

De Boor, H. (2000). *Das Nibelungenlied*. Cologne: Parkland Verlag.

Ehrismann, O. (1998). The Reception of Kriemhild. In W. McConnell (Ed.), *A Companion to the Nibelungenlied* (pp. 18–41). Rochester: Camden House.

Ehrismann, O. (2002). *Nibelungenlied: Epoche – Werk – Wirkung* (2nd ed.). Munich: Beck Verlag.

Fischer, H.W. (1934). *Götter und Helden*. Berlin: Deutsche Buchgemeinschaft.

Goethe, J.W.v. (1814). *Selige Sehnsucht in Buch des Sängers, West-Östlicher Divan*. Retrieved from www.lieder.net/lieder/get_text.html?TextId=6619 [Accessed September 13, 2018].

Goss, P. (2015). *Jung: A Complete Introduction*. London: John Murray Learning.

Härd, J.E. (1996). *Das Nibelungenepos*. Tübingen: A. Franke Verlag.

Hatto, A.T. (Trans.) (1965). *The Nibelungenlied*. London: Penguin Classics.

Heinzle, J. and Waldschmidt, A. (1991). *Die Nibelungen. Ein deutscher Wahn, ein deutscher Alptraum*. Frankfurt am Main: Suhrkamp Taschenbuch Verlag.

Himmler, H. (1943). Rede des Reichsführers SS bei der SS-Gruppenführertagung in Posen am 4. Oktober 1943, p. 25. Retrieved from 100(0) Schlüsseldokumente zur deutschen Geschichte im 20. Jahrhundert: https://www.1000dokumente.de/pdf/dok_0008_pos_de.pdf [Accessed September 13, 2018].

Hoffmann, W. (1998). Twentieth-Century Reception of the Nibelungenlied. In W. McConnell (Ed.), *A Companion to the Nibelungenlied* (pp. 127–152). Rochester: Camden House.

Jung, C.G. (1954[1925]). *Marriage as a Psychological Relationship. In: The Development of Personality. CW 17, para 338*. London: Routledge & Kegan Paul.

Jung, C.G. (1954[1934]). Archetypes of the Collective Unconscious. In H. Reid, M. Fordham and G. Adler (Eds.), *CW 9/I* (p. 66). London: Routledge.

Kast, V. (1986). *The Nature of Loving* (1st ed.). Wilmette, IL: Chiron Publications.

Mann, T. (1945). *Germany and the Germans*. Retrieved from https://catalog.hathitrust.org/Record/006168882 [Accessed September 9, 2018].

McConnell, W. (1998a). *A Companion to the Nibelungenlied*. Rochester: Camden House.

McConnell, W. (1998b). The Nibelungenlied: A Psychological Approach. In W. McConnell (Ed.), *A Companion to the Nibelungenlied* (pp. 172–205). Rochester: Camden House.

Mills, J. (2018). *Recognition and Pathos*. Retrieved from www.youtube.com/watch?v=7wTvjSKQfP0 [Accessed August 29, 2018].

Müller, J.-D. (2005). *Das Nibelungenlied* (2nd ed.). Berlin: Erich Schmidt Verlag.

Münkler, H. (2010). *Die Deutschen und ihre Mythen*. Reinbek bei Hamburg: Rowohlt Taschenbuch Verlag.

Neumann, E. (1990). *Depth Psychology and a New Ethics*. Boston and London: Shambhala.

Papsch, G. (2012). *SWR2 Wissen: Ich versuche jeden zu retten*. Retrieved from www.swr.de/swr2/programm/sendungen/wissen/wilm-hosenfeld-wehrmacht offizier/-/id=660374/did=21938062/nid=660374/2uhfbd/index.html [Accessed July 8, 2013].

Reschke, T. and Otto, K. (2018.) *Das Erste deutsche Fernsehen – Monitor*. Retrieved from www.daserste.de/information/politik-weltgeschehen/monitor/videosextern/ angriff-aufs-kirchenasyl-mit-schuetzenhilfe-der-gruenen-zweite-fassung-100.html [Accessed July 31, 2014].

Rolfes, B. (2005). *Helden(bilder) im Wandel (Changing Hero Images)*. Baltmannnsweiler: Schneider Verlag Hohengehren.

Samuels, A. (2015). *A New Therapy for Politics?* London: Karnac Books.

Sombart, W. (1915). *Werner Sombart: Händler und Helden*. Retrieved from www.gleichsatz.de/b-u-t/spdk/19jhd/somb-hanhe1.html [Accessed July 31, 2014].

Stiftung Haus der Geschichte der Bundesrepublik Deutschland (2016). *Deutsche Mythen seit 1945*. Bielefeld and Berlin: Kerber Verlag.

Von See, K. (1991). Das Nibelungenlied – ein Nationalepos? In J. Heinzle and A. Waldschmidt (Eds.), *Die Nibelungen – Ein deutscher Wahn, ein deutscher Alptraum* (pp. 43–109). Frankfurt am Main: Suhrkamp Taschenbuch Verlag.

Wittels, F. (1946). Psychoanalysis and History the Nibelungs and the Bible. *Psychoanalytic Quarterly*, 15: 88–103.

SEVENTEEN

James Joyce's "The Dead" and paleo-postmodernism: a Lacanian/Jungian reading

Catriona Ryan

James Joyce's famous short story, "The Dead" (1992), is a classic modernist text that has been traditionally viewed as one of the most significant examples of great literature in the Irish and global short story canon. "The Dead" is not viewed as a postmodern piece of writing like Joyce's more experimental novels such as *Finnegans Wake* (2012). But the text does have a paleo-postmodern dimension (a term which will be explicated later in the chapter in terms of its of romantic (paleo-modernist) and postmodern influences). The presentation of the main protagonist's gradual disintegration of self can be read in terms of the Lacanian idea that identity is structured through Symbolic language (Lacan, 2007). In the context of "The Dead", the Symbolic is represented as the colonial language of English where Joyce questions the nature of reality and Irish identity. The story has typically been analyzed as an early representation of Joyce's European modernist vision which rejected nationalist cultural narratives in favour of a dissociative existential ontology (Kearney, 1984).

Alternatively, my interpretation of "The Dead" is that it may be viewed as a representation of an archetypal journey which ultimately embraces a Yeatsian revivalist vision of Irish identity. This chapter seeks to argue that Joyce's short story presents a unique linguistic construction and deconstruction of Irish identity incorporating a vision of the sublime, suggesting the possibility of achieving Jungian individuation (Jung, 1981) through a romanticized paleo-modernist Yeatsian trope of the mythical Irish other.

"The Dead" was published in 1914 as part of James Joyce's famous collection of stories, *Dubliners* (1992). The story is concerned with a part-time book reviewer named Gabriel Conroy who attends a Christmas party thrown by his aunts (Kate and Julia Morkin, grand dames in the world of Dublin music) at which he dances with a fellow teacher and delivers a brief speech. As the party is breaking up, Gabriel witnesses his wife, Gretta, listening to a song sung by the renowned tenor Bartell D'Arcy, and the intensity of her focus on the music causes him to feel both sentimental and lustful. Later, Gabriel is devastated to discover that he has misunderstood Gretta's feelings; she has been moved by the memory of a young lover named Michael Furey who preceded Gabriel and who died for the love of Gretta. Gabriel realizes that she has never felt similarly passionate about their marriage. He feels alone and profoundly mortal, but spiritually connected for the first time with others.

The Sublime Vision

The beginning of Gabriel's creative journey of self-discovery occurs when he first meets Miss Ivors, a staunch Irish nationalist. In the following exchange Miss Ivors invites Gabriel on a journey to the west of Ireland which he rejects:

> But you will come, won't you? said Miss Ivors, laying her warm hand eagerly on his arm.
> The fact is, said Gabriel, I have already arranged to go –
> Go where? asked Miss Ivors.
> Well, we usually go to France or Belgium or perhaps Germany," said Gabriel awkwardly.
> "And why do you go to France and Belgium," said Miss Ivors, "instead of visiting your own land?'
> "Well", said Gabriel, "it's partly to keep in touch with the languages and partly for a change.'
> "And haven't you your own language to keep in touch with – Irish?" asked Miss Ivors.
> "Well," said Gabriel, "if it comes to that, you know, Irish is not my language.'
> Their neighbours had turned to listen to the cross-examination. Gabriel glanced right and left nervously and tried to keep his good humour under the ordeal which was making a blush invade his forehead.
> "And haven't you your own land to visit," continued Miss Ivors, "that you know nothing of, your own people, and your country?'
> "O, to tell you the truth," retorted Gabriel suddenly, "I'm sick of my own country, sick of it!"
> *(Joyce, 1992, p. 170)*

Gabriel's rejection of a holiday to the west of Ireland reflects his resentment towards his own culture as he declares his preference for travelling abroad. In the story, Gabriel is a patriarchal figure who thinks he controls the feminine influences around him. He tells his wife what to wear and generally makes decisions for her. In a Jungian context, the path towards individuation involves the subject finding a healthy balance between the *animus* and *anima* aspects of their unconscious selves (Jung, 1981) and consequently overidentification with either disrupts the subject's life-journey towards individuation. At this stage of the story, Gabriel is the embodiment of an

James Joyce's "The Dead" and paleo-postmodernism 259

aspect of the male protagonist (Ryan, 2012) that rejects his *anima* self and has therefore not yet achieved individuation. Gabriel's suppression of his *anima* nature may be viewed as his rejection of an archetypal cultural ideation of Irish identity attributed to Yeats.

From Gabriel's perspective, his wife, Gretta, has a subversive presence, and this is reinforced later in this scene when Miss Ivors refers to the fact that Gretta comes from Connacht, in the west of Ireland; a place linked with a Yeatsian cultural ideology which Gabriel rejects. Through Miss Ivors, the reference to his wife's heritage and the trope of the west of Ireland reveals the beginning of Gabriel's self-doubt in the story. Gabriel's disposition and his agitation belies his attempts to deny a part of his own culture which is part of his identity.

Traditionally, nineteenth-century aesthetic depictions of the west of Ireland are often portrayed in terms of the exotic and the sublime. Its wild topography reflected a stereotype of a primitive culture. Edmund Burke's depiction of the sublime as evincing feelings of "terror and . . . danger . . . and at certain distances . . . may be . . . delightful" has been associated with his experience of the Irish landscape in terms of its association with danger, the unknowable and folk narratives steeped in mythology and magic (Burke, 2008, p. 25; Killeen, 2014, p. 7). As Patrick Duffy notes, "The west was represented as containing the soul of Ireland. In Yeats's construction, it became a fairyland of mist, magic and legend: a repository of Celtic consciousness" (1997, p. 67) (Yeats and Gregory, 1992). Edmund Burke's complex relationship with his own Irish identity in many ways mirrors Gabriel's, whose embrace of Britishness was counterbalanced by a profound sense of alienation and self-doubt. Luke Gibbons makes the point that Burke's development of his aesthetics of the sublime was also informed by the "turbulent colonial landscape of eighteenth-century Ireland" (2009, p. 23). In Joyce's story, the west of Ireland is portrayed on two levels in a feminine context. There is the political dimension associated with the republican activist Miss Ivors who regards Gabriel as a traitor to the Irish Republican movement. She calls him a "West Briton" because he writes for the British-owned *Express* newspaper. This political attack takes a more sublime turn in Gabriel's mystical experience of his wife on the staircase:

> Gabriel had not gone to the door with the others. He was in a dark part of the hall gazing up the staircase. A woman was standing near the top of the first flight, in the shadow also. . . . It was his wife. She was leaning on the banisters, listening to something. . . . But he could hear little.
>
> He asked himself what is a woman standing on the stairs in the shadow, listening to distant music, a symbol of? If he were a painter he would paint her in that attitude.
>
> Distant music he would call the picture. . . . The hall-door was closed; and Aunt Kate, Aunt Julia and Mary Jane came down the hall, still laughing.

260 Catriona Ryan

> – Well, isn't Freddy terrible? said Mary Jane. He's really terrible.
>
> Now . . . the piano could be heard more clearly.
>
> Gabriel held up his hand for them to be silent.
>
> The song seemed to be in the old Irish tonality and the singer seemed uncertain both of his words and of his voice. The voice, made plaintive by distance and by the singer's hoarseness, faintly illuminated the cadence of the air with words expressing grief.
>
> *(Joyce, 1992, pp. 189–190).*

In this scene, Gretta becomes the unconscious aspect of Miss Ivors' nationalist rhetoric. Gretta comes from the west of Ireland and the spectral sublime image of her stance signifies a mystical resonance of her connection to her birthplace. This esoteric potency of the image of Gretta on the stairs is reinforced through a song that has an "old Irish tonality." The Irish writer, Tom MacIntyre, said that the power of the Irish language for the Irish writer has the quality of a "spirit language" that is "roaring from the unconscious" (Ryan, 2012, p. 224). The "old Irish tonality" of the song is the only sound occurring during this scene.

The world of Lacanian Symbolic Language suddenly interrupts the exalted moment when Aunt Kate, Mary Jane and Aunt Julia arrive and Mary Jane says "Well, isn't Freddie terrible?" This question momentarily reverts the attention back to the quotidian banalities of the house party and more specifically concerning Freddie's behaviour. Gabriel's usual highly articulate command of the English language has been subverted as he "said nothing" and "held his hand up for them to be silent." This action refocuses attention on his sublime vision of Gretta on the stairs, the numinosity of which has left him silent. The Lacanian Symbolic language of English has been deconstructed through the sublime haunting presence of the Real as Gabriel "said nothing." The Real (Lacan, 2018) is evoked through the acoustic atmosphere of this scene which is steeped in "old Irish tonality" and evokes a haunting image of a past Irish identitarian space which is rooted in the feminine other.

This scene is reminiscent of Lacan's views of the sublime in his discussion of the Greek heroine, Antigone, the daughter of Oedipus. According to Lacan, she represents "what it is man wants and what he defends himself against" (1992, p. 240). Lacan goes on to say how Antigone "pushes to the limit the realisation of something that might be called the pure and simple desire of death as such. She incarnates that desire" (1992, p. 82). Burke's idea of the sublime becomes most "affecting" in the face of death, of "annihilation" (Smith, 2018, p. 142). Hence Burke emphasises the importance in developing an "aesthetic distance" which can transform that primordial pain into pleasure (Smith, 2018, p. 142). Lacan personifies the pain/pleasure dynamic of the sublime through Antigone, who becomes a representation of the death drive and the rejection of the death drive (1992). In other words, the Real is manifested in the female influence associated with the threat of

James Joyce's "The Dead" and paleo-postmodernism   261

dissolution of the masculine self, which both desires and fears the Real. This is the basis of Gabriel's experience of the sublime in this scene. The Lacanian Symbolic code of English has become deconstructed in the face of this vision which both attracts and scares Gabriel. The representation of the power of the Real as the eternal feminine space of desire is associated with an "old Irish tonality" sounding archetypal context which threatens to subsume Gabriel's identity as he is left silent.

Gretta's feminine power alienates Gabriel, who is desperately trying to comprehend his relationship to such a power by utilizing his limited creativity in terms of controlling the image of Gretta on the stairs aesthetically as the subject of a painting. The other-worldly nature of Gretta's position on the stairs is of the Jungian *anima*. In his autobiography *Memories, Dreams, Reflections*, Jung describes a strange experience with his *anima* self in which he imagined the image had flown away: "If, therefore, one has a fantasy of the anima vanishing, this means that it has withdrawn into the unconscious or into the land of the dead. . . . There it produces a mysterious animation and gives visible form to the collective contents. Like a medium it gives the dead a chance to manifest themselves" (1989, p. 191). Gabriel did not recognize Gretta when he first noticed her at the top of the stairs. He sees her as "a woman standing on the first flight." Gretta has become the supernatural other that is inaccessible to Gabriel. Gretta, as *anima*, embodies the Jungian "land of the dead" (Jung, 1984), the west of Ireland. In the face of this sublime vision, Gabriel's existential sense of self is threatened.

In the short stories of the Yeatsian protagonist, Red Hanrahan, Yeats presents a paleo-modernist vision of the west of Ireland which is seen through Hanrahan, who is described as a "poet of the gael" (Hirsch, 1981, p. 883). According to Edward Hirsch, Hanrahan represents the "archetypal possibilities of the imagination" (1981, p. 883). The main theme in the Hanrahan stories is the border between the mortal and the immortal world. In a story entitled "The Vision of Red Hanrahan", Hanrahan has a vision of the Celtic past. His external vision of legendary Celtic figures such as Deirdre and Grainne represent Hanrahan's acceptance of his *anima* identity. This vision is contrary to Gabriel's view of his wife on the stairs. Gretta represents the Jungian *anima* and consequently becomes an externalization of Gabriel's disconnection from his *anima* nature.

According to the Jungian psychologist Ian Alister, the *anima* has a "critical role in forcing us to pay attention to the *shadow* contents which always draw us into relationship with them . . . often against our conscious will and even when they seem to represent what we most hate and despise" (1998, p. 205). Therefore, Gabriel's disconnection from his *anima* self is reinforced by a separation from his heritage, the ideal of which is represented by Gretta, who symbolizes the Yeatsian paleo-modernist trope of the west of Ireland.

The shadows around Gretta confuse Gabriel who wonders what they were "a symbol of." In a postmodern sense they represent Gabriel's own fragmentation. Since he is alienated from his *anima* he cannot progress in the Jungian process of individuation. Gabriel's misunderstanding of his wife is really a misunderstanding of himself. The image of fragmentation, via the mystical visual aura of Gretta, is a powerful turning point in the story. Rather than completely surrendering in the face of the sublime threat of the Lacanian Real, which in a Jungian context, would have enabled Gabriel to connect with his *anima* to achieve full individuation, Gabriel chose to revert to old habits and control the sublime event from a patriarchal perspective. He imagines himself as a male artist who tries to control the scene aesthetically through a misunderstanding of his own unconscious drives. As a result, Gabriel fails to understand the "old Irish tonal" music as he strains to listen to it. As Gretta is utterly absorbed by the sound which connects her to her past when she lived in the west of Ireland, Gabriel is alienated from the sound which is referred to as "distant music."

Paleo-postmodernism

Paleo-postmodernism (a term I created for my research into the work of Tom MacIntyre) (Ryan, 2012) is partly based on the literary revival's late nineteenth-century paleo-modernist interest in precolonial and pre-Christian ideas of Irish culture which provided a sense of Irish cultural identity for Protestant writers such as Yeats who were alienated in a Catholic-dominated society. The aesthetics of paleo-postmodernism involves a combination of a Yeatsian-styled romantic vision and postmodern deconstruction (Ryan, 2012). It may be argued that Joyce's deconstruction is based on the experience of the Irish writer, who, due to the trauma of colonialism and the subsequent loss of the Irish language, as a first language, is alienated in the colonial language of English. A good example is taken from Joyce's novel *Portrait of the Artist as a Young Man* (1992), when Joyce's autobiographical character, Stephen Dedalus, is having a conversation about language with his Dean of Studies at Trinity College, who is English. In that conversation, Dedalus has an awareness of his own alienation using the language of English, the language of the colonizer:

> The language in which we are speaking is his before it is mine. How different are the words home, Christ, ale, master on his lips and on mine! I cannot speak or write these words without unrest of spirit. His language, so familiar and so foreign, will always be for me an acquired speech. I have not made or accepted its words. My voice holds them at bay. My soul frets in the shadow of his language.
> *(1992, p. 189)*

A sense of alienation is a common experience for the Irish writer as Seamus Deane states, "We've got essentially a colonial heritage that has had some very deep effects on the language. We write in English, but we are haunted by the ghost of a lost language" (1987, pp. 29–30). The sense of alienation experienced by Dedalus and Gabriel point towards a loss of a primal, precolonial Irish identity. The unconscious grief associated with that loss results in alienation and induces an identitarian existential crisis.

Such a crisis in the short story is a central part of Gabriel's defamiliarization of his identity. According to Derrida, "[D]econstruction shows that things . . . do not have definable meanings and determinable positions, ... that they exceed the boundaries they currently occupy" (1997, p. 31). In the context of "The Dead", an indeterminacy of meaning is represented in the gradual dissolution of the main protagonist's identity as mediated through his own silence. In the story, Gabriel is presented as a very self-assured character who overidentifies with his masculinity, which is further symbolised through his intellectual command of the English language. At key moments it is his identification with the language of English that ruptures in the face of two sublime visions which are associated with the Irish cultural stereotype of the west of Ireland and the Irish language. The mystical resonance of these Yeatsian tropes are presented by Joyce as archetypal representations which act as points of subversion that break down the protagonist's use of the English language and replace it with the sublime experience of self-revelation.

Lacan and Jung

Jung and Lacan are central to the paleo-postmodern analysis of Joyce's famous short story. Though Lacan's theories are different to Jung, the former offers a way of studying Joyce's use of Jungian imagery through the Real and the Symbolic which provides a better understanding of how Joyce conjoins Lacanian deconstruction with a sublime, archetypal space (rooted in a Yeatsian desire for a precolonial identity) (Vilar-Argaiz, 2013).

Jacques Lacan's concept of language is relevant to Joyce's work, as it provides a useful framework for understanding the writer's deconstruction of language and how that relates to the psychological motives of his protagonists. Lacan's concept of the Real, the Imaginary and the Symbolic aspects of language is based on Freud's idea of the Oedipus complex (1992). The Real is concerned with an infant's absolute identification with the mother, the feminine other. Once the child leaves the space of the Real, all its drives are directed towards reattaining that original union with the maternal body. As the child matures, the prelinguistic space of the Imaginary is adopted in order to overcome the trauma of separation from the mother, with the child maintaining the fantasy of maternal identification. Through the Symbolic, the child renounces his desire for identification with the maternal space of the Real through the adoption of the patriarchal code of language (2007). Joyce was never influenced by Lacan, but the incorporation of the theorist's ideas is useful in a paleo-postmodern reading of Joyce's prose in order to explore the complexity of the Irish author's English language deconstruction. According to Lacan, it is the construct of Symbolic language that structures a subject's identity and in Joyce's short prose the Lacanian Symbolic may be seen as a metaphor for the alienated Irish subject who uses the colonially imposed language of English. The Lacanian Real in Joyce's story can be read as a representation of the mystical unconscious archetypal feminine domain of the west of Ireland and the Irish language.

The main attribute of the Lacanian Real is its link to the subject's unconscious desire for the maternal body. In Jungian terms the Real shares similar characteristics to the anima. Both are unconscious drives that have a gendered feminine attribute. According to Jung the unconscious space is made up of archetypal male and female qualities known as the animus and the anima (1981). The animus is stereotyped masculinity characterized as the subject's dominant and rational side. The anima is essentialized as a feminine archetypal form (Jung, 1981).

In Jung's view, the goal of individuation is the subject's integration of both the *anima* and *animus*. Joyce's story concerns the main protagonist's overidentification with his *animus* nature. The *anima* in the story is symbolized by his wife Gretta who Gabriel misunderstands until the end of the narrative. As a representation of the Eternal feminine who also symbolizes the west of Ireland and the language of Irish, Gretta becomes an externalization of Gabriel's *anima*.

This analysis of Jung is also Yeatsian as Yeats's paleo-modernist association of the Irish mythological past is based on the archetypal world of the *anima mundi* (Olney, 1975, pp. 40–45) (Yeats, 2002) or in Jungian terms the "collective unconscious" (1981). Therefore, the Yeatsian dimension to the mystical ideology associated with Gretta is rooted in the revivalist fascination with ancient Irish mythology and the Irish language.

The significant link between Jung and Lacan in this analysis of "The Dead" is based on the representations of the archetypal eternal feminine and its association with the sublime. Lacan's concept of the sublime is associated with fear of transcendence: the Real. The Real as a pure force represents the death drive for the subject and as a result threatens the subject's destruction but, at the same time, it is bound up with the subject's desire for the maternal body. In Joyce's "The Dead", this sublime threat is counterbalanced by Gretta's representation of Jung's archetypal *anima*. Jung's *anima* (or *animus*) counters this disintegration of the self with the potential integration of the subject's *anima* or *animus* to achieve individuation. In the story, such an integration is portrayed as a kind of sublime beatific vision. Joyce's main protagonist, Gabriel, experiences both aspects of the sublime (Burke, 2008, p. 25) where the author's gradual destruction of the protagonist's identity mirrors the subject's creative journey, which ultimately causes Gabriel to surrender to an inner existential sublime poetic vision of pure self-knowledge.

Individuation and the paleo-postmodern Self

In "The Dead", the main metaphor that signifies the journey from the fragmentation of Gabriel's overidentification with the *animus* to eventual Jungian self-realized individuation is the snow. According to Carl Jung, snow can be symbolic of the *anima*: "One reported case tells of a young man

James Joyce's "The Dead" and paleo-postmodernism   265

who was being initiated by an older shaman and who was buried by him in a snow hole. He fell into a state of dreaminess and exhaustion. In this coma he suddenly saw a woman who emitted light. . . . Such an experience shows the *anima* as the personification of a man's unconscious" (2002, p. 186). In "The Dead", the snow is also a reflection of the Self. When Gabriel first arrives at the party he is anxious to shake the snow from his person, as he is "scraping his feet vigorously" (Joyce, 1992, p. 152). This is in contrast to Gretta, who Gabriel describes as lacking sense, as she would have no problem walking through the snow.

This oppositional perspective reflects the Jungian *anima* that Gabriel is alienated from. But the situation changes radically at the end of the story:

> Generous tears filled Gabriel's eyes. He had never felt like that himself towards any woman, but he knew that such a feeling must be love. The tears gathered more thickly in his eyes and in the partial darkness he imagined he saw the form of a young man standing under a dripping tree. Other forms were near. His soul had approached that region where dwell the vast hosts of the dead. He was conscious of, but could not apprehend, their wayward and flickering existence. His own identity was fading out into a grey impalpable world: the solid world itself, which these dead had one time reared and lived in. A few light taps upon the pane made him turn to the window. It had begun to snow again. He watched sleepily the flakes, silver and dark, falling obliquely against the lamplight. The time had come for him to set out on his journey westward. Yes, the newspapers were right: snow was general all over Ireland. It was falling on every part of the dark central plain, on the treeless hills, falling softly on the Bog of Allen and, farther westward, softly falling into the dark mutinous Shannon waves. It was falling, too, upon every part of the lonely churchyard on the hill where Michael Furey lay buried. It lay thickly drifted on the crooked crosses and headstones, on the spears of the little gate, on the barren thorns. His soul swooned slowly as he heard the snow falling faintly through the universe and faintly falling, like the descent of their last end, upon the living and the dead.
>
> *(Joyce, 1992, p. 196)*

This beautiful conclusion to the story represents Gabriel's final dissolution of his old self that identified completely with his *animus* archetype. At this stage of the story, Gabriel had finally come to understand the "old Irish tonality" of the "distant music" which he had previously failed to comprehend. It was a song which Gretta's young lover from the past had sung to her before he died in the snow. The "old Irish tonality" of that song (with its Irish linguistic mystical connotations) has transformed into a heightened beatific vision of Gabriel's *anima* nature. Through the metaphor of the snow, Gabriel begins to experience his own *anima* nature, which is connected to the numinous world of the dead. Gabriel decides to take the journey to the west of Ireland as his soul becomes feminised in the action of "swooning". Gabriel becomes the snow itself.

In a Lacanian context, the previous sublime experience of the Real has revealed its apocalyptic nature and has instigated the dissolution of Gabriel's totalized identification with his *animus*. In other words, Gabriel's eloquent spoken English language signification is absent and is replaced by a silent sublime ideological metaphor that is linked to the "old Irish tonality" of the west of Ireland. Though the experience of the Lacanian Real induced an existential deconstruction of Gabriel's identity, it did not destroy him; rather its transformational presence metaphorized as the snow opened Gabriel to his *anima*, to the possibility of achieving individuation. Jung once said that one of his patients' dreams about individuation involved "the most sublime harmony" (1977, p. 204). In other words, the apocalyptic threat of the sublime vision of the Lacanian Real, through seeing Gretta on the stairway, is transformed through Gabriel's acceptance of his own *anima*, and this has resulted in a wholistic sublime experience of self-revelation. In a paleo-postmodern context, the postmodern deconstruction of English language signification has taken place, and instead of nihilism it has found an archetypal space in the paleo-modernist Yeatsian world of Irish cultural mysticism.

Bibliography

Alister, I. (1998). *Contemporary Jungian analysis: Post Jungian Perspectives from the Society of Analytical Psychology*. London: Routledge.

Battersby, C. (2007). *The Sublime, Terror and Human Indifference*. London and New York: Routledge.

Boheemen, C. (2009). *Joyce, Derrida, Lacan and the Trauma of History*. Cambridge: Cambridge University Press.

Burke, E. (2008). *A Philosophical Enquiry into the Origin of Our Ideas of the Sublime and the Beautiful*. New York: Dover Publications, Inc.

Campbell, J. (1971). *The Portable Jung*. New York: Viking Press.

Clark, M. (1971). *Understanding the Self-Ego Relationship in Clinical Practice: Towards Individuation*. London: H. Karnac Books Ltd.

Deane, S. (1987). *Celtic Revivals: Essays in Modern Literature, 1880–1980*. Winston-Salem, NC: Wake Forest University Press.

Derrida, J. (1997). *Deconstruction in a Nutshell: A Conversation with Jacques Derrida*, Ed. John D. Caputo. New York: Fordham University Press.

Duffy, P. (1997). Writing Ireland: Literature and Art in the Representation of Irish Place. In Brian Graham (Ed.), *In Search of Ireland: A Cultural Geography* (pp. 64–84). London: Routledge.

Fink, B. (1995). *The Lacanian Subject: Between Language and Jouissance*. Princeton, NJ: Princeton University Press.

Gibbons, Luke (2003). *Edmund Burke and Ireland: Aesthetics, Politics and the Colonial Sublime*. Cambridge: Cambridge University Press.

Harvey, D. et al. (2008). *Celtic Geographies: Old Culture, New Times*. London: Routledge.

Hassan, I. (1987). *The Postmodern Reader: Essays in Postmodern Theory and Culture*. Columbus, OH: Ohio State University Press.

Hirsch, E. (1981). And I Created Hanrahan: Yeats, Folklore and Fiction. *ELH*, 48(4): 880–893.

Joyce, J. (1992). The Dead. In James Joyce (Ed.), *Dubliners* (pp. 157–203). London: Minerva.

Joyce, J. (1992). *Portrait of the Artist as a Young Man*. London: Wordsworth Classics.

Joyce, J. (2012). *Finnegans Wake*. London: Wordsworth Editions.

Jung, C.G. (1977). *Collected Works of C.G. Jung, Volume 12: Psychology and Alchemy*, Trans. R.F.C. Hull. New York: Princeton University Press.

Jung, C.G. (1981). *Collected Works of C.G. Jung, Volume 9: The Archetypes and the Collected Unconscious*, Trans. R.F.C. Hull. New York: Princeton University Press.

Jung, C.G. (1984). *Dream Analysis 1: Notes of the Seminar Given in 1928–30*. London: Routledge & Kegan Paul.

Jung, C.G. (1989). *Memories, Dreams and Reflections*, Trans. R. Winston and C. Winston. New York: Vintage Books.

Jung, C.G. (2002). *Man and His Symbols*. London: Aldus Books.

Kearney, R. (1984). *Transitions*. Manchester: Manchester University Press.

Killeen, J. (2014). *The Emergence of Irish Gothic Fiction: History, Origins, Theories*. Edinburgh: Edinburgh University Press.

Lacan, J. (1992). *The Ethics of Psychoanalysis: 1959–60: The Seminars of Jacques Lacan*. Trans. D. Porter. New York: Norton.

Lacan, J. (2007). *Ecrits*. Trans. B. Fink. New York: Norton.

Lacan, J. (2018). *The Four Fundamental Concepts of Psychoanalysis*. Trans. A. Sheridan. London: Routledge.

Nolan, E. (1995). *James Joyce and Nationalism*. London: Routledge.

Olney, J. (1975). The Esoteric Flower: Yeats and Jung. In G. Miller Harper (Ed.), *Yeats and the Occult* (pp. 27–54). London: Macmillan.

Ryan, C. (2012). *Border States in the Work of Tom Mac Intyre: A Paleo-Postmodern Perspective*. Newcastle: Cambridge Scholars.

Smith, Craig R. (2018). *Romanticism, Rhetoric and the Search for the Sublime: A Neo-Romantic Theory for our Time*. Newcastle: Cambridge Scholars.

Villar-Argaiz, P. (2013). Organic and Unworked Communities in James Joyce's "The Dead". In P. Martin Salvan (Ed.), *Community in Twentieth Century Fiction* (pp. 48–66). London: Palgrave.

Yeats, W.B. (2002). *Autobiographies*. London: Palgrave.

Yeats, W.B. and Gregory, Lady (1992). *Visions and Beliefs in the West of Ireland*. London: Colin Smythe.

EIGHTEEN

Apostolic actuality: David Jones and sublimation

Luke Thurston

For Jean Laplanche, psychoanalysis remains an "unfinished revolution"—its barrage of concepts constantly outflanked, unsettled, by the relentless "Copernican" otherness flowing from the primal wound of its discovery (Laplanche, 1999[1992]). One of the prominent signs of that unfinishedness is the inadequate Freudian account of aesthetic experience. As Donald Winnicott admitted in 1966: "Freud did not have a place in his topography of the mind for the experience of things cultural" (Winnicott, 2005[1971], p. 128). Thus, "sublimation" in Freud remained little more than an abstract notion, and lacked the epistemological consistency of a genuine concept. As such, sublimation can be seen as a symptom of the aporia, the lack of place or pathway, on which to think about cultural life in psychoanalysis.

Since then, there have of course been many attempts to properly conceptualize sublimation, or at least to locate the "experience of things cultural" in relation to the field of psychoanalysis. I will draw on some of these in my effort to get to grips with what is at stake in the work of David Jones. But vital aspects of Jones's work—those aspects, in my view, that keep it alive and sustain our engagement with it so long after its historical moment has passed—will in turn be seen to challenge and complicate the lexicon of psychoanalytic interpretation.

David Jones (1895–1974) can now, thanks to recent efforts by critics, be seen as a key figure in British modernism, whose work across both visual and textual media inscribes a singular and heroic struggle to sustain itself—perhaps sustain "self" as such—as precisely a location of cultural experience, in a life continually traversed by pathogenic trauma. Let me start with a letter Jones wrote to his friend Jim Ede in October 1927, when his main worry, a decade after serving as a soldier at the Somme, was what to do about the woman he was supposed to be marrying, Eric Gill's daughter Petra. How, Jones fretted, could the circle of his artistic vocation be squared with the "normal" life of a married man? In his anxious, half-informed way (he has obviously been reading some psychoanalysis), Jones accidentally touches on the central problem of Freudian sublimation.[1]

> I agree I think with what you say in your letter to a large extent – It may be I personally am too concerned

with "inhibitions" – the whole question of sublimation –
suppression – "canalization" and the rest is a very vexed
one – and hideously complicated for me – Complicated
largely by there being no general standard of practice, or
accepted ethics in the world at the moment – everyone
means different things by the same words and everyone
interprets ideas and actions so diversely that one is more
scrupulous I suppose than one might normally be if there
were a real civilization builded upon some understood philosophy – were it Catholic, Buddhist, Protestant, pagan or
what you will – but we of the modern world all are a mixture of these "isms" and consequently are shy and alarmed
at each other's notions. *This is probably all nonsense* – at
any rate it is ill put. I *told* you it is no use my writing letters – but I will post it.

(Jones, 1980, p. 44)

The whole question of sublimation, if not "probably all nonsense," is
indeed a very vexed one—but not simply, as Jones thinks, due to the modern
collapse of a "real civilization" that could have furnished some total meta-
language (a fantasy Jones nurtured with his reactionary Catholic friends).
What is "hideously complicated," though, as Jones suggests, is the crucial
question of how sublimation relates to other meta-psychological terms like
those he scare-quotes ("inhibitions", "canalization"). "Because Freud left the
theory of sublimation in such a primitive state," comment Laplanche and
Pontalis, "we have only the vaguest hints as to the dividing-lines between
sublimation and processes akin to it (reaction-formation, aim-inhibition, ide-
alization, repression)" (Laplanche and Pontalis, 1973[1967], p. 433). As it
stands, the unfinishedness of the theory may indeed have been distinctly useful
for Freud, since it mystically squares a circle by seeming to combine satisfaction and inhibition, the unconscious otherness of the drive and a controlling
agency that looks very much like the ego. Although in sublimation the drive
is *zielgehemmt*, "aim-inhibited", it can still achieve a *Befriedigungserlebnis*,
an "experience of satisfaction", as if the constitutive antinomy between the id
and the ego, pitting the otherness of the sexual against the fragile coherence of
the "I", has been conjured away (Freud, 1955[1923a], p. 258).

Now, as I have argued elsewhere, the conceptual incoherence of sublimation derives from a wider problematic in Freudian meta-psychology,
whereby it is secretly governed by an economy of discharge (*Abfuhr*) whose
primary theoretical function is to protect the integrity of psychical structure, its "topographical" coherence, against the disruptive assault of libido
(Thurston, 2003, p. 36). Sublimation can thus be seen to have served to protect the Freudian subject from any "aesthetic" disruption, by mysteriously
discharging libido into the safe vessel of some respectable, sanctioned form
of culture, leaving the ego in peace and translating the drive from its blind
unconscious insistence to some notional zone of legibility and communal
pleasure (thus "secondary", diminished, bound pleasure). Clearly, however,

for Jones, who in 1927 is still very much preoccupied with the daily task of carrying on living after the war, no such utopian space of benevolent cultural mediation existed any longer (though it once *had*, he and his friends were convinced, notably before the "break" which had cut Europeans off from their sustaining Christian meta-narrative – an account reminiscent of T.S. Eliot's "dissociation of sensibility") (Eliot, 1951[1932], p. 288).[2] The fact that there was no longer a meta-language, for Jones, meant that the very possibility of sublimation, which Winnicott will re-conceptualize as its "potential space", had been destroyed, atomized, reduced to a state of hostile cultural fragmentation that threatens the very possibility of artistic communication (Winnicott, 2005[1971], pp. 135–139). The pessimistic, indeed apocalyptic tone of Jones's letter is in tune with the gloomy anti-modernism of his drinking pals. Yet it also unwittingly endorsed the confused economy of Freudian sublimation, where libidinal "discharge" somehow goes directly from the artist's inner unconscious to the external world of art galleries and theatres, with no sense of psychical or intersubjective complexity (why can't everyone do it?), nor indeed any explanation of the mysterious alchemy that supposedly once upon a time had let libido flow into the sacred vessels of a "real civilization", if only that civilization had not been demolished by an iconoclastic, atheistic modernity.

Here we need to turn to some post-Freudian developments about the aesthetic. As we will see, the reprise of those questions in the object-relations milieu of British post-war psychoanalysis, centring on the concepts of play, fantasy and reparation, can shed useful light on some important features of Jones's work as an artist and poet. However, simply to apply this theoretical perspective to Jones would be to risk sharing the tendency of many commentators on his work by producing an interpretation resolutely aligned with what we might call the Jonesian ego, an agency whose project was precisely "regenerative"– both in terms of personal recovery (where, as we shall see, a new definition of sublimation offered by Jean Laplanche is relevant) and of the restoration of an imaginary site of non-alienated, redemptive culture (sometimes known as "Wales"). The trouble with such an account is that it only tells half the story and indeed risks radically falsifying the true status of Jones, turning him into a far less important artist, for the regenerative dimension of Jones's work – much of it beautiful and moving – is far from all it has to offer. Jones's work also insistently inscribes, in full modernist defiance of aesthetic comfort, a troubling encounter with the limits of meaningful representation, a ritual renewal or avowal of a real presence – something that tends initially to "silence" the beholder in wonder or in horror. It is this reopening or renewal of something fundamentally at odds with "reading" that I shall explore. It is what keeps Jones's work alive today in the afterlife of its constitutive context. To approach it, we will need to look in greater depth, and more critically, at psychoanalytic ideas about fantasy and sexuality.

The key to Winnicott's account of human life and of cultural experience is its intersubjective dimension, which is essentially defined by play. Just as, in his view, the analytic relation had to be rethought as no longer a relation of doctor and patient but one of "two people playing together", so the practice of – indeed the very capacity for – artistic expression and understanding "begins with creative living first manifested in play" (Winnicott, 2005[1971], p. 51 and p. 135). Thus play, in all its senses, offered for Winnicott a new pathway for thinking psychoanalytically about cultural life, one no longer focused primarily on art works (as Freud had tended to do), but one that now saw art as a wider process involved in a larger psychical field comprising other processes that were creative but also interpretative and empathic. Creative living, wrote Winnicott, entailed the ability to understand and "enter imaginatively" into another's world (Winnicott, 1987[1970], p. 117). Creative subjectivity was therefore essentially transitional, a space which "in adult life is inherent in art and religion", and which is crucial for negotiating and playfully testing the intersubjective limits of inner and outer realities (Winnicott, 1958[1951], p. 230). This was certainly, Adam Phillips reminds us, a long way from the Freudian view of culture, with its emphasis on libidinal *Zielgehemmung*, "aim-inhibition" (Freud, 1955[1923a], p. 232). For Winnicott, writes Phillips, culture "was only the medium for self-realization" (Phillips, 1988, p. 119).

In terms of thinking about Jones, this seems to free us from the impasse or paradox of non-repressive aim-inhibition, and Winnicott's emphasis on intersubjective play fits well, as we shall see, with how Jones represents one kind of relation between individual and framing context (but it is not the only kind). However, we need to be very careful here not to throw the libidinal baby out with the meta-psychological bathwater, for Winnicott's account of creativity crucially shifts away from Freud's focus on how to link artistic expression and sexuality in an adult subject to the very different domain of pre-Oedipal infancy. Heavily influenced by Melanie Klein's post-war reorientation of psychoanalysis, Winnicott wrote that, when treating children, "[although] I was able to confirm the origin of psycho-neurosis in the Oedipus complex . . . I knew that troubles started earlier" (Winnicott, 1965[1962], p. 172). In engaging with subjectivity and libido before the definitive organization of drives and fantasy during the Oedipal crisis (which usually occurs in an individual between the ages of three and five), Winnicott addresses a very different set of questions than those Freud had asked about sexuality and art. In "The Location of Cultural Experience", he is very clear about this shift:

> It is to be noted that the phenomena that I am describing have no climax. This distinguishes them from phenomena that have instinctual backing, where the orgiastic element plays an essential part, and where satisfactions are closely linked with climax. . . . Psychoanalysts who have rightly emphasized the significance of instinctual experience and of reactions to frustration have failed to state with comparable clearness or conviction the tremendous intensity of these non-climactic experiences that are called playing.
> *(Winnicott, 2005[1971], pp. 132–133)*

Winnicott suffers from the confusion caused by Strachey's mistranslation of *Trieb* as "instinct", which is especially unfortunate here, as the question of *Instinkt*, the biological term Freud sometimes uses, may ultimately be relevant to this topic. Now if we are talking about babies, it is all very well to refer to the intensity of pre-Oedipal existence with all its non-climactic pleasures and pains, but when it comes to considering the adult subject, whose sexuality is defined, from a Freudian perspective, by the unconscious – an unconscious constituted by repression – the question should be quite different. This is why Laplanche, for instance, talks about the "always more or less desexualized notion of 'object-relations'" (Laplanche, 2015[1999], p. 258). It is not that pre-genital, "non-climactic" sexuality does not exist, but to make it the exclusive basis of the account is to evade the Freudian subject, the subject of a post-Oedipal and thus repressed sexuality, a sexuality no longer blissfully and creatively at play in a space between egos, but haunted by the other, impregnated by an enigmatic alien presence.

To desexualize, to sublimate, is to make erotic life ego-friendly, playful, mutually pleasurable and benevolent. This may well be, as Laplanche suggests (Ibid., p. 262), a version of Freud's motto *Wo Es war, soll Ich werden* (Freud, 1960[1933a], p. 80), and it may also be at stake in the obscure transition from the first to the second Freudian topography, whereby in his late work Freud seems at times to privilege the supposedly rational agency of the ego, the very thing that in his earlier work had seemed the principal obstacle to the treatment. But let us take this model of what Winnicott calls the "true self", a subject sustained and ultimately freed from self-division by a benevolent environment created by a caring, and in turn undivided, other subject. Look how Jones, writing in the 1930s about his wartime experience, completely upends our expectations by representing that experience in a way remarkably consistent with such a model. The text is *In Parenthesis*, Jones's great war-poem, which has been described as "one of the foremost works of British literary Modernism" (Dilworth, 2012, p. 13). To set the scene, it is early December 1915, and No. 6 Platoon, B Company, of the 15th Battalion of the Royal Welch Fusiliers is just arriving in Normandy, with Private John Ball (Jones's *persona*) doing his best to keep up. After a hard night trooping "rather as grave workmen than as soldiers", Jones's *persona* reflects:

> [T]here was in this night's parading, for all the fear in it,
> a kind of blessedness, here was borne away with yester-
> day's remoteness, an accumulated tedium, all they'd piled
> on since enlistment day: a whole unlovely order this night
> would transubstantiate, lend some grace to.
> *(Jones, 2010[1937], p. 27)*

The minute particulars of lived reality, its suffering and boredom, are absorbed into a collective order, which as it were blesses the individual by absolving him of his own experience, transubstantiating – or "sublimating' – the real of that experience. Whereas for a Sassoon or an Owen any hint of praising what the military order had done to individual

Apostolic actuality   273

men could be nothing but flagrant hypocrisy, Jones has no qualms about presenting the absorption of the self into a collective, disciplinary cultural space as both an aesthetic and an implicitly religious union:

> Informal directness buttressed the static forms – ritual words made newly real. The immediate, the newness, the pressure of sudden, modifying circumstance . . . brought intelligibility and effectiveness to the used formulae of command; the liturgy of their going-up assumed a primitive creativeness, an apostolic actuality.
>
> *(Jones, 2010[1937], p. 28)*

It is this sense of "apostolic actuality", of the self becoming a vessel for some divine message (*apostolos* is God's postman) that puts Jones's work light years away from that of the canonical war poets, with their outraged rejection of any attempt to ascribe redemptive significance to the mass slaughter of the trenches. The redemptive Jonesian vision of the traumatic real – and bear in mind that he had served as a soldier for more than three years, and must have witnessed an appalling number of deaths and injuries, and indeed caused some himself – is almost surreally at odds with what we expect. What Jones is struggling to do, in fact, despite everything that he had seen and suffered since 1915, is to revive as accurately as possible the lived experience of young Private Ball as he first arrived at the front, a subject still hypnotically bound into the "corporate will" (Ibid., p. 7) or group psychology of the military order (Freud's *Group Psychology and the Analysis of the Ego* (1955[1921c])) was, like Jones's *In Parenthesis*, a response to the war). Perhaps, at first sight, the "primitive creativeness" felt by the soldier as the empty routine of training is filled out by the real of lived experience would seem to have little to do with sexuality at all, as Jones himself would undoubtedly have loudly protested. But I will argue that the relation to the other – be it sacred union or nightmarish entanglement – is fundamentally there as the primal source or primitive creativeness of Jones's art.

Let us go further into Jones's "parenthesis", bracketed off from ordinary life as a ritual or sacramental space. One of the strangest things we find there is a disclosure of the erotic dimension of the wartime catastrophe. Left without a leg to stand on by an enemy bomb, Private Ball realizes that his chances of crawling out of the trench alive will be greatly enhanced if he abandons his heavy rifle. His delirious thoughts spiral back to the voice of his training sergeant when the gun was first issued to him:

> . . .and you men must really cultivate the habit of treating this weapon with the very greatest care and there should be a healthy rivalry among you – it should be a matter of very proper pride and
>
> > Marry it man! Marry it!
> Cherish her, she's your very own.
>
> *(Jones, 2010[1937], p. 183)*

274   Luke Thurston

This libidinal investment, as Freud would say, in the modern equipment of destruction is a striking example of the distortion of human values in war. But that distortion is precisely what structures Private Ball's world as quasi-psychotic, as is shown by the jagged, ruptured text switching between textbook doctrine and sudden fantasmatic commands (the superego, Lacan says, is a sadistic voice commanding "Enjoy!" (Lacan, 1998[1975], p. 10). Getting married to your rifle is a good example of what happens inside a world "moulded by, made proper to, the special environment" (Jones, 2010[1937], p. 91) of the war, inside a "parenthesis" where the repressive rules of ordinary life do not apply.

The creation of a "special environment" in the catastrophic wasteland of the war is thus both a way of conveying the psychical reality of the soldiers and a description of Jones's own literary task in *In Parenthesis*. The world cannot be represented realistically or even rationally there but has to be brought back to life through a "primitive creativeness" that corresponds to the ritual eclipse of ordinary ego-governed existence. Is that creativeness, as Winnicott might see it, a matter of play? An encounter with a "warden of stores" in an unfamiliar trench gives a vivid sense of ritualistic playfulness:

> A man seemingly native to the place, a little thick man, swathed with sacking . . . gorgeted in woollen Bala-clava, groped out from between two tottering corrugated uprights, his great moustaches beaded with condensation under his nose.
>
> *(Ibid., p. 89)*

This strange, anthropoid trench-dweller has a brief exchange with the officer, and then:

> He slipped back quickly, with a certain animal caution, into his hole; to almost immediately poke out his wool-work head, to ask if anyone had the time of day or could spare him some dark shag or a picture-paper. Further, should they meet a white dog in the trench her name was Belle, and he would like to catch any bastard giving this Belle the boot.
>
> *(Ibid., p. 90)*

The trench has become a kind of ontological parenthesis for this man, an environment with its own set of ritual rules and protocols. The requests and instructions he gives out indicate an acknowledgement of a shared playful community with other men expressed by such things as telling the time, sharing social rituals like smoking or reading the paper, and the protection of love objects (Belle the dog is a mock chivalric beloved). But the withdrawal into the "hole" symbolizes an ontological gap between his particularity and the symbolic register of the community outside the war, as if his self-excavated world no longer fully belongs to human reality:

> They watched him vanish, mandrill fashion, into his enclosure. They wondered how long a time it took to become so knit with the texture of this country-side, so germane to the stuff about, so moulded by, made proper to, the special environment dictated by a stationary war.
>
> *(Ibid., p. 91)*

In Parenthesis itself, as the title indicates, is also an enclosure, a special environment withdrawn from the ontologically consistent world of realistic "reality". This textual environment is carved out by Jones "mandrill fashion", in a creative excavation of human subjectivity, exposing the "aboriginal mask" (Ibid., p. 91) of a self that is shaped by an unspeakable world of vital enjoyment. To become such a self "knit with the texture" of the wartime situation is, crucially, to break the rules of the game that define everyday reality, those rules that support the regime of psychical defence constricting and impoverishing the subject's enjoyment of its "aboriginal" libidinal drives. This wartime transgression of the barrier of repression that ordinarily regulates and constitutes the liveable self points inevitably to both a rich creativity and to something powerfully traumatic. But is the transgression in this text, which was written more than a decade after the war itself, no more than a retrospective fantasy, or does it stem from an unforgettable encounter with a traumatic-creative potential foreclosed by "realistic" subjectivity?

For Winnicott, the "true" self is an agency unhindered by the compliant conventionality of the everyday ego and thus able to reassemble "the details of the experience of aliveness" (Winnicott, 1965[1960], p. 148). But the key Winnicottian point is that such a self is not some groundless speculative abstraction but always only part of a situational reality. For the true self to be able to emerge, to discover itself through playful transitional experiment, Winnicott stipulates that a special "holding environment' – maternal care, the analytic setting, perhaps art or religion with their framed spaces – is required (Winnicott, 2005[1971], pp. 149–159). Let us look at a self-portrait produced by Jones in 1927, just before he started work on *In Parenthesis* (see Figure 18.1).

Jones produced this engraving while staying as a guest at the monastery on Caldey Island, off the coast of South Wales. The "holding environment" that offered Jones temporary respite from the sexual problem of Petra and Petra's father, and perhaps allowed him to "sublimate" or regain a sense of psychical centredness, can be seen represented here as a tightly packed series of frames within frames.[3] First, there is the artwork-within-the-artwork, apparently centred on some symbol (a fish, perhaps), then its frame, then the holding figure of the ego-artist-monk, then the enclosing structure of the temple merging with the enclosing ring of animals, then the exterior frame of the image (and then, outside the image, the room in the monastery where

Figure 18.1 *The Artist* (1927)[4]

Jones is working, then Caldey Island itself, ringed by the sea). It is clearly the image of an ego blissfully cushioned from external threats, withdrawn from external reality like the mandrill in his trench and, like him, "knit with the texture" of the environment (the calm proximity of animals is always a sign of happiness in Jones).

One way of understanding the fate of sublimation in the development of Freud's thinking, according to Laplanche, is to see it as a precursor of what the second topography will generalize (and perhaps mystify) as the binding power of Eros, the unifying life drive (Laplanche, 2015[1999]). The main agent of Eros is of course that pre-eminently unifying psychical agency, the ego. In one mode of what Freud may once have thought of as sublimation, Laplanche writes, "the ego imposes unity on what is diverse and anarchic in the drive by way of the ego's unitary and specular form" (Ibid., p. 264). This kind of narcissistic binding by the ego turns the whole field of representation into a series of protective enclosures to ward off the psychical incursion of the drive, to make the other unrepresentable and therefore (according to the imaginary logic of negation) non-existent. In this version of sublimation, the ego has managed to triumph over the libidinal assaults of the other, restructuring the psychical economy as a comfortably legible, concentric "holding environment". In one sense, sublimation in this ego-centred mode proposed by Laplanche can be seen as primarily a defence mechanism, the warding-off or disavowal of decentring sexuality (recall how Winnicott emphasized the "non-climactic" quality of the activities he wished psychoanalysis to refocus on). It is easy to see how such a model of psychical binding and narcissistic self-redemption might correspond to a therapeutic process of recovery from trauma, where artistic techniques are often used highly effectively.

To read Jones according to this theory of sublimation, as self-unifying artistic recovery, however, is to badly simplify and ultimately misconstrue his work, and it may also misrecognize the potential significance of sublimation as a way to think sexuality in relation to artistic and cultural practices. Shortly before Jones began his hugely productive artistic "parenthesis" of 1928–1932, he was commissioned to produce some illustrations for a new edition of Swift's *Gulliver's Travels*. Here are two of these illustrations, showing Gulliver first entering the city of Lilliput (see Figure 18.2) and then being sexually assaulted by a female Yahoo (see Figure 18.3).

These images offer a dialectical inversion of the "holding environment" embedded in the Winnicottian account of self-therapeutic aesthetic play and represented by Jones in his 1927 portrayal of the artist-as-monk on Caldey Island. The redemptive poetic logic of *In Parenthesis*, absorbing, as we saw, the particular suffering of the individual soldier into a collective order of redemptive ritual (an order of "blessedness", of intelligibility and

Figure 18.2   *Gulliver entering Lilliput* (1925)

Figure 18.3 *Female Yahoo embraces Gulliver* (1925)

effectiveness) is reversed, as if in a spirit of bitter parody. Where we might expect to see Gulliver looming triumphantly over the diminutive world of Lilliput, instead we see him trapped halfway into a trench-like enclosure, knit with the texture of the environment not in animal contentment but in claustrophobic terror. The exposed buttocks that echo across both images are not an accident of style: the reversal of narcissistic containment directly links with a traumatic psychical wounding, a being penetrated by the other. What Jones is inscribing in these images is the traumatic return of an invasive sexual real, the other decentring me and reducing me to a passive receptacle.

On one side, then, Jones's work as both writer and artist can be seen, providing we carefully choose which images and passages to consider, as governed by a therapeutic and redemptive teleology consistent with an ego-centred version of Freudian sublimation and perhaps with the Winnicottian motifs of play and culture. If we turn to other parts of Jones's work, though, we see the dominant ego reversed, laid open to a penetrative and enigmatic sexual otherness seemingly at odds with the conscious intentions of the artist to "canalize" that sexuality into redemptive and sacramental artworks.

I want to conclude by looking at a moment where Jones inscribes the opening of the ego in a different sense, one which may have become possible for him due to his religious awakening immediately after the war. Here is a key passage from *In Parenthesis*, where what is at stake is the relation between the soldier-protagonist and his neighbour, the soldier marching alongside him:

> With his first traversing each newly scrutinised his neighbour; this voice of his Jubjub gains each David his Jonathan; his ordeal runs like acid to explore your fine feelings; his near presence at break against, at beat on, their convenient hierarchy.

(Ibid., p. 42)

Here the individual soldier is no longer caught up in the hypnotic magic of the army's corporate psychological structure, nor is he simply isolated, trapped in his own irregular pathology. The presence of the neighbour – the face of the other, Levinas would say (Levinas, 1996[1972], pp. 52–53) – supervenes as ethical demand, traversing and displacing the ego's habitual grammar (look at the inconsistency of pronouns). The narrative voice can only figure this ethical scrutiny through the intertextual web of a paternal culture, in Victorian poetry and the Bible. So "this voice of his Jubjub gains each David his Jonathan": the relation to the other is both uncanny non-sense ("Beware the Jubjub bird") and impossibly direct masculine identification. The allusion is to Chapter 18 of the first book of Samuel in the Old Testament: "And it came to pass, when he had made an end of speaking unto Saul, that the soul of Jonathan was knit with the soul of David, and Jonathan loved him as his own soul" (1 Samuel 18:1). It is this psychical knitting together that language cannot accommodate: it "runs like acid" through the symbolic order, the "convenient hierarchy" of the signifier dully echoed by the military ranks and structures. The "near presence", the psychical intermixing of David and Jonathan, calls for a new inscription of the other: no longer as a presentation before a subject but as an interpenetration, a flowing-across.

What is striking here is the contrast between this ethical inmixing of subjects and the traumatic sexual penetration seen in the Gulliver illustrations. It is very clear that there are no women: it is the all-male hierarchy of the army that allows Jones to envisage (and perhaps even to have somehow experienced a decade before) a psychical proximity to the other, which undoubtedly has a powerful erotic dimension – it burns through discursive protocols "like acid" – but remains shielded from the traumatic real of sexual difference. Perhaps Jones's quixotic dream of "a real civilization builded upon some understood philosophy" indicates that it was only in a patriarchal and homoerotic structure like the army that he could imagine a creative psychical transition that would not entail a traumatic opening to the sexual other.

As we have seen, then, exploring Jones's artwork and writing can help us clarify some of the questions raised by the psychoanalytic engagement with aesthetic experience. The notion of sublimation, with its ill-defined metapsychological status and vague scope, becomes increasingly hard to sustain as a single concept as we work through the various modalities of how artistic practice relates to sexuality in Jones. On the one hand, Jonesian art seems to open a dimension of "blessedness" – be it in celebrating the ritual forms of military order that can somehow "transubstantiate" the horrific reality of war or reinscribing the enclosing layers that protect the artist-monk from psychical contact with the traumatic real of sex, as embodied in Petra Gill's damaged self. We saw how this sense of art as a kind of complex defence mechanism could be linked to Winnicott's interpretation of play and infantile experience, with its "non-climactic" pleasures, and indeed to Laplanche's rereading of sublimation as a process by which the ego effectively insulates itself from having any encounter with unconscious

280 Luke Thurston

sexuality in its properly sexual dimension, that of traumatic otherness. But another aspect of sublimation, the idea that through artistic work the subject precisely can link up with and carnally experience the sexual other as such, without diminishing or taming it, may also be at stake in Jones. It was here that the 1925 engravings for *Gulliver's Travels* seemed exemplary: by showing the subject crushed and constrained by the "holding environment", penetrated and violated by the sexual other, these small icons arguably give voice to the repressed truth of Jones's experiences in the war and in his relationship with Petra. That these images could plausibly be described as examples of *de*-sublimation, or simply of the return of the repressed, reminds us of the central metapsychological problem of sublimation, its impossible dual function as defence against and expression of sexuality. For David Jones, it seems, the only doctrine that pointed to a way out of this antinomy was a religious one, which supposedly allowed an ethical opening undistorted by the travails of sexuality. But his art could not stop blaspheming against that doctrine and raising questions about the very possibility of sublimation.

Notes

1 In the 1920s Jones discussed psychoanalysis quite often with Jim Ede, and since he frequently stayed with the Edes he would have had access to books by or on Freud. In 1947, Jones also stayed for five months at Bowden House Clinic, Harrow, where he underwent psychotherapeutic treatment (see Dilworth, 2017, pp. 108, 240–247).
2 The "break' refers to a split between religious and secular culture, which Jones and his friends discussed in the 1920s and early 1930s and which they located in the nineteenth century. See Wilcockson (1977).
3 Eric Gill had incestuous relations with his daughters, as was first revealed by Fiona McCarthy (1989, pp. 151sqq). On the troubled relationship between Jones and Petra Gill, see Dilworth (2017, pp. 79–80, 100–104).
4 Permission to reproduce the images in this chapter was kindly granted by Bridgeman Images on behalf of the copyright holders of the artistic work of David Jones.

References

Dilworth, T. (2012). *David Jones in the Great War*. London: Enitharmon.
Dilworth, T. (2017). *David Jones: Engraver, Soldier, Painter, Poet*. London: Jonathan Cape.
Eliot, T.S. (1951[1932]). The Metaphysical Poets (1921). In *Selected Essays* (pp. 281–291). London: Faber & Faber.
Freud, S. (1955[1921c]). Group Psychology and the Analysis of the Ego. In J. Strachey (Trans.), *The Standard Edition of the Complete Psychological Works of Sigmund Freud*, vol. 18 (pp. 65–143). London: The Hogarth Press and the Institute of Psycho-Analysis.

Freud, S. (1955[1923a]). Two Encyclopaedia Articles. In J. Strachey (Trans.), *The Standard Edition of the Complete Psychological Works of Sigmund Freud*, vol. 18 (pp. 233–259). London: The Hogarth Press and the Institute of Psycho-Analysis.

Freud, S. (1960[1933a]). New Introductory Lectures on Psycho-Analysis. In J. Strachey (Trans.), *The Standard Edition of the Complete Psychological Works of Sigmund Freud*, vol. 22 (pp. 1–182). London: The Hogarth Press and the Institute of Psycho-Analysis.

Jones, D. (1980). *Dai Greatcoat: A Self-Portrait of David Jones in his Letters*, Ed. R. Hague. London: Faber & Faber.

Jones, D. (2010[1937]). *In Parenthesis*. London: Faber & Faber.

Lacan, J. (1998[1975]). *The Seminar. Book XX: On Feminine Sexuality, The Limits of Love and Knowledge (Encore) (1972-'73)*, Ed. J.-A. Miller, Trans. B. Fink. New York: W. W. Norton & Company.

Laplanche, J. (1999[1992]). The Unfinished Copernican Revolution. In J. Fletcher (Ed.), L. Thurston (Trans.), *Essays on Otherness* (pp. 52–83). London and New York: Routledge.

Laplanche, J. (2015[1999]). Sublimation and/or Inspiration. In J. Mehlman (Trans.), *Between Seduction and Inspiration: Man* (pp. 253–283). New York: The Unconscious in Translation.

Laplanche, J. and Pontalis, J.-B. (1973[1967]). *The Language of Psychoanalysis*, Trans. D. Nicholson-Smith. London: The Hogarth Press.

Levinas, E. (1996[1972]). Meaning and Sense. In A.T. Peperzak, S. Critchley and R. Bernasconi (Eds.), *Basic Philosophical Writings* (pp. 33–64). Bloomington, IN: Indiana University Press.

McCarthy, F. (1989). *Eric Gill*. London: Faber & Faber.

Phillips, A. (1988). *Winnicott*. London: Penguin Classics.

Thurston, L. (2003). Meaning on Trial: Sublimation and *The Reader*. In P. Adams (Ed.), *Art: Sublimation or Symptom*. New York: The Other Press.

Wilcockson, C. (1977). David Jones and "The Break". *Agenda*, 15(2–3): 126–131.

Winnicott, D.W. (1958[1951]). Transitional Objects and Transitional Phenomena. In *Collected Papers: Through Paediatrics to Psycho-Analysis* (pp. 229–242). London: Tavistock.

Winnicott, D.W. (1965[1960]). Ego Distortion in Terms of True and False Self. In *The Maturational Process and the Facilitating Environment: Studies in the Theory of Emotional Development* (pp. 140–152). London: The Hogarth Press.

Winnicott, D.W. (1965[1962]). A Personal View of the Kleinian Contribution. In *The Maturational Process and the Facilitating Environment: Studies in the Theory of Emotional Development* (pp. 171–178). London: The Hogarth Press.

Winnicott, D.W.(1987[1970]). Cure. In *Home is Where We Start From: Essays by a Psychoanalyst* (pp. 112–122). London: Pelican.

Winnicott, D.W. (2005[1971]). *Playing and Reality*. New York: Routledge.

Index

Note: page numbers in *italics* indicate a figure on the corresponding page. Page numbers followed by "n" indicate a note on the corresponding page.

Abrahamic religious traditions 83
abstract art 64; Arp and 71–72; Kandinsky and 69–71; and recovery of spiritual 69–72
"acoustic figurability" 204
Adios, Nonino (Piazzolla) 204
aesthetic education 18–19
affinities: desire 9–11; language 7–8; quaternity 11–12
agalma 7, 119
Akhmatova, A. 179
Alcibiades I (Plato) 20
Alexander the Great 34
Alister, I. 261
American Heritage Dictionary 237
Améry, J. 223
"analogical contiguity" 161
Analytic of the Sublime (Kant) 190
Anaxagoras 47n16
anima 12, 27n10, 50; guided politics 254; and individuation 258, 261; Kast on 250; and *Nibelungenlied* 250–253, 254
anima mundi 111
animus 250–251; "The Dead" 264–266; and individuation 258; inexpressive in music 208
Anna Karenina (Tolstoy) 237
Answer to Job (Jung) 14, 16, 55, 69
Antigone (Sophocles) 15, 175, 176, 180
"antique spirit, the" 46n12
anxiety: milder 31; severe 31; sublime 31–46
apophatic sensitivity 66–67

"apostolic actuality" 273
Archetypes and the Collective Unconscious (Jung) 8
Arendt, H. 251
Aron, R. 231
Arp, J. 64, 67, 71–72
art: described by Raphael 231; as form 235; and horizontal dimension 232; and infinity 231; Kris on 236; and psychic energy 236; and sublime 231–232; and vertical dimension 232; *see also* creativity; music; paintings
Art and Alienation (Read) 234
Art of the Novel, The (Haedens) 235–236
Artist, The (1927) 276, 277
artists, scapegoats 44, *44*
Aufhebung 130–131, 144n16
Augustine, St 9
autochthones, in mythology 167

Babel, I. 179
Bachelard, G. 208
Bacon, F. 103, 146n25
Baldwin, J.M. 40
Balint, M. 236
Bally, C. 43, 47n22
Barreto, M.H. 225
Barron, F. 230
Batum (Bulgakov) 182
Beguines (Mechthild of Magdeburg) 64, 67–68
Bergson, H. 232, 238–239
Berlin Congress of the International Psycho-Analytic Association 47n21
Bernays, M. 201

Bingen, H. von 101–102
blazing sublime, in mystic experiences 100–103
Bloom, H. 53, 129
body of desire *see* hermetic subtle body
Boehme, J. 9, 64, 67, 69–71
Boileau, N. 51, 142n3
Book of Job 55
Borowski, T. 223
Borromean knot 12
boundary breakers, tricksters as 177
Bowie, M. 155
"break" 280n2
Breton, A. 117, 126–127
Brodsky, J. 175, 182–184
Buber, M. 14, 86
Bulgakov, M. 175, 181–182
Bülow, F. von 248
Burgundian Empire 245
Burke, E. 1, 2, 16, 50–51, 53–55, 94, 96, 259
Burston, D. 13
Butor, M. 235

Cage, J. 209
Cahen, R. 1
"Carazan's Dream" 46n7
Carrington, H. 110
Cazenave, M. 14–15
Celan, P. 223
Cézanne, P. 230–231, 241
C.G. Jung: A Biography in Books (Shamdasani) 55
Charlus, Baron de (fictional character) 54
Chasseguet-Smirgel, J. 135
Chekhov, A. 240
"Christ-eroticism" 68
Christianity 50, 83
"Church-within-the-Church" hermeticism 117
Cicero 9
City of God, The (St Augustine) 9
Civilization and Its Discontents (Freud) 2, 124
Clement V, Pope 111
cognitive psychology 98
Cohn, J. 108–109, 142n4, 143n11
coincidentia oppositorum 207
Coleridge, S.T. 24–25, 51, 60
Collaborators, The (Hodge) 181
Collected Works (Jung) 50–51, 57
"common sense philosophy" 96
compensatory otherness 88
compensatory sublime 88
complex pleasure of sublime: "Kant is my philosopher" 55–57; Kant's

concept of sublime 57–61; Longinus and Burke 53–55; notion of sublime and concept of dread 52–53; Otto and Jung 52; overview 50; reflections on sublime 50–51
Concerning the Spiritual in Art (Kandinsky) 70
"Concerning the Sublime" (*Über das Erhabene*) (Schiller) 16–17
"contrived depthlessness" 116
Copernican Revolution 56
Corbin, H. 79
Course in General Linguistics (de Saussure) 47n22
creationism, and tricksters 178
creative destruction, sublimation as 126–134
creative intelligentsia 175, 179
creative subjectivity 271
"Creative Writers and Day-Dreaming" (Freud) 137
creativity: defined 230; and political systems 178; and social climate 184; and Soviet Union 178; and sublime 238; and tricksters 178; as vertical to horizontal movement 236; *see also* art
Crime and Punishment (Dostoevsky) 232–233
Critique of Judgment (Kant) *see* *Critique of the Power of Judgment* (Kant)
Critique of Practical Reason (Kant) 56
Critique of Pure Reason (Kant) 56
Critique of the Power of Judgment (Kant) 37, 51, 56–57, 59, 62
Crockett, C. 109, 117
Culp, A. 81
culture: Freudian view of 271; Winnicott on 271

Dada movement 127
Dalhaus, C. 200
Dangwei Zhou 51
Dauer im Wechsel (Goethe) 20
da Vinci, L. 128
Days of the Turbins, The (Bulgakov) 181
"Dead, The" (Joyce) 257; Lacanian Real in 263–264; overview 257–258; paleo-postmodernism 262–263; sublime vision 258–262; symbolism of snow in 264–265
Deane, S. 262
deathbed visions 100
death drive 220
Deleuze, G. 81
Demosthenes 53

284 Index

Depth Psychology and a New Ethic (Neumann) 252
Derrida, J. 2, 51, 87, 129
Descartes, R. 56, 78
desire 9–11; Jung on 196; Lacan on 196; and *Thunder, Perfect Mind* 196
Destruktion als Ursache des Werdens, Die (Spielrein) 41
Deutsch-Israelitische Gemeindebund 25n2
diamond sublime 77–78, 81, 87, 89–90
Ding 14, 108, 118, 131, 144n18
dissolution: metaphorical 178; metonymical 178; and tricksters 178
Divinity, and Self 186–187
Dog's Heart, A (Bulgakov) 181, 182
Doran, R. 51, 56
Dossier K (Kertész) 220
Dostoevsky, F. 128
Dovlatov, S. 182
Dowd, A. 85, 88
dread 52–53
"Dreams and Occultism" (Freud) 110
"dream thinking" 39
Dubliners (Joyce) 257
Duchamp, M. 103
Duffy, P. 259
Durand, R. 207

Eckhart, M. 64, 67, 68–69
Economist, The 59
Ecstasy of Saint Teresa, The (Bernini) 12–13
ego 13; as an "imaginary function" 13; conscious 80; deconstruction of 13; Freud on 44–45, 65, 272; -ideal 118; ideal- 118; inexpressive in music 208; David Jones on 275–276; Jung on 64, 65; Laplanche on 277; as other 77; and sublimation 277; vulnerable 95–96
Eigen, M. 203–204
Einstein, A. 2
Eliade, M. 110, 129
Ellenberger, H.F. 110
Empedocles 6, 42, 45, 47n20
enantiodromia 88
Energies of the Real 220–221
English philosophy 33
English Romantic movement 51
English Romantic poetry movement 60
English Romantics 62
Enlightenment 109
Eranos Jahrbuch 47n14
Eros 277; described 161, 195; sublime 161–163

"Essay on the Maladies of the Head" (Kant) 37
Estés, C.P. 237
Ethics (Spinoza) 20
evil: Arendt on 252; Jung on problem of 224; Kertész on existence of 222
expressionism 64, 70

Fadeev, A. 179
fascinans 191
Fatelessness (Kertész) 218
Faust (Goethe) 6, 12
feminine sexuality, and *jouissance* 155–157
feminine sublime 163
Fenwick, E. 100
Fenwick, P. 100
Ferenczi, S. 141n2
fertile sublime 192–193
few lines composed above Tintern Abbey, A (Wordsworth) 60–61
Fiasco (Kertész) 223, 226n2
Fichte, J.G. 33
Finnegans Wake (Joyce) 135, 139, 257
form: art as 235; and essence 235; and idea 235
Forms of Things Unknown, The (Read) 234
Four Fundamental Concepts of Psycho-Analysis, The (Lacan) 7, 13
Fraenkel, T. 126
Frankenstein, or The Modern Prometheus (Shelley) 166; and laws of procreation 171; new species, creation of 171–172; sexual theories 173; Victor Frankenstein attraction to electricity 170–171
Franz, M.-L. von 112–113
Frederick II the Great, Prussian King 245
freedom 17, 52–54, 58; artistic 133; creative 133
French Revolution 39, 53
Freud, L. 103
Freud, S. 2, 123, 167, 201; *Civilization and Its Discontents* 2, 124; and *creatio ex nihilo* 139; ego 272; "Creative Writers and Day-Dreaming" 137; "Dreams and Occultism" 110; and Empedocles 47n20; *Instinkt* 272; *Interpretation of Dreams, The* 109–110, 127; mourning as "emptying out" and glimpses of "life in death" as archetypal 87–89; and "oceanic sentiment" 45; *Outline of Psycho-Analysis, An* 125; *Project*

for a Scientific Psychology 144n18;
*Psycho-Analytic Notes on an
Autobiographical Account of a Case
of Paranoia (Dementia Paranoides)*
10; and Rolland 45; sublimation
268–269; telepathy 110, 119; *Three
Contributions to the Sexual Theory*
10; *Three Essays on the Theory of
Sexuality* 128, 130, 134
Freudian sublimation 268–269

Gallop, J. 156–157
Gemelli Marciano, M.L. 26n6
gender 155
German mystical tradition 64
German Romanticism 56, 64
Gestalt *Cycle of Awareness* 85
Gibbons, L. 259
Giegerich, W. 58, 61, 119, 208, 224–225
Gnostic demiurge 108
Gnosticism 12, 192; characteristics of 13;
    Jung and 12–16; Lacan and 12–16
Goethe, J.W. von 6, 68, 128, 252
Göring, H. 248
Gorky, M. 179
Gothic horror 50
Götter und Helden (Gods and Heroes)
    (Fischer) 245
Greek cosmology 41, 47n12, 47n23
Greek philosophy 33
Griffiths, P. 209
Grossman, D. 89
Guattari, F. 81
Gulliver's Travels (Swift) 277,
    277–278, 280
Gumilev, L. 179
Gumilev, N. 179

Hadewijch of Antwerp 68
Haedens, K. 235–236
Hagen, F.H. von der 248–249
Hamann, J.G. 56
"Händler und Helden" (Sombart) 252
Hanslick, E. 200
Harari, R. 219–220
Harned, D. 234
Hegel, G.W.F. 9, 15, 33, 88, 95, 142n3,
    144n16, 191; comparison of poetry
    and music 202
Hegel's Aesthetic: A Critical Exposition
    (Kedney) 95
Heidegger, M. 8, 41
Heraclitus 6, 88
Herbart, J.F. 33, 41, 46n8
hermaphrodite 50
hermeticism 109, 111, 117

hermetic subtle body 108–120
Hesiod 10
Himmler, H. 251
Hinton, L. 224
Hirsch, E. 261
Hirst, D. 103
Hitler, A. 2, 141n2, 223
Hodge, J. 181
"holding environment" 275, 277
holistic pluralism 96
Holocaust 223, 224, 226n3
Homer 18, 35, 53, 233
horizontal reality 241, 243n9; and
    art 232; and novels 232–233; and
    sublime 236
Hosenfeld, W. 251
Hugo, V. 82
Hull, R.F.C. 24–25
human subjectivity 19–20, 275
Humboldt, W. von 25n2
Hume, D. 56
Huxley, A. 129

"Ideal and Life, The" (*Das Ideal und
    das Leben*) (Schiller) 21–22
Idealism 64
Idea of the Holy, The (Otto) 52
Iliad, The (Homer) 233
images: Jung on importance of 186;
    and sublime 78–79
Imbert, C. 36–37, 47n15
impressionism 208
incest 166, 168
individual autonomy 175
individuation 113, 186, 194–195; and
    anima 258, 261; and *animus* 258;
    and paleo-postmodern Self 264–266
"inexpressive" in music 208
In Parenthesis (Jones) 272, 273–275,
    277–278
inscrutability 81, 85–86
instrumental music 200; and
    autonomous status 205–206; and
    sublime 206–209; as symbolic
    function 203–204
intellectual uncertainty 128
Intelligentzia 2
Interpretation of Dreams, The (Freud)
    109–110, 127
"I-Thou" 78, 90

James, W. 96
Jameson, F. 116
Jankelevitch, V. 206–208, 212
Jentsch, E. 128–129
John of Paris 68

Johnston, A. 116–117
Jones, D. 268–270; *ego* 275–276; "holding environment" 275
Jones, E. 124
jouissance 54, 161; defined 153; and feminine sexuality 155–157
Joyce, J. 70, 139, 219, 257
Jung, C.G. 1, 52, 96, 129, 153; *Answer to Job* 14, 16, 55, 69; *Archetypes and the Collective Unconscious* 8; *Collected Works* 50–51, 57; on desire 195; glimpses of "life in death" as archetypal 87–89; Gnosticism and 12–16; on importance of images 186; on importance of music 202; on individuation 113, 186, 194–195; Lacan and 12–16; *Liber Novus* 59; *Memories, Dreams, Reflections* 21, 22, 24, 26n6, 59, 119, 261; mourning as "emptying out" 87–89; *Mysterium Coniunctionis* 113, 202, 205; notion of Self 55, 71, 80–81, 160–162; and problem of evil 224; on psyche and matter 229; representation of psyche 186; *Psychological Types* 6; *Psychology and Alchemy* 234; *Psychology of Dementia Præcox, The* 10; *Psychology of the Unconscious, The* 8–11, 19; *Relations between the Ego and the Unconscious, The* 26n7; *Septem Sermones ad mortuous* 14; on sublime 159; sublime in 108–120; *Symbols and Transformations of the Libido* 8; transcendent function 194–197; *Transcendent Function, The* 60; *Transformations and Symbols of the Libido* 9, 15–16, 25n2; on trickster archetype 176, 180–181; see also *Red Book, The* (Jung); "Ulysses: A Monologue" (Jung)
Jungian *anima* 261, 265; *see also anima*
Jung Institute at Zürich 55

Kaddish for an Unborn Child (Kertész) 221
kairos 35, 46n3, 66, 70
Kandinsky, W. 64, 67, 69–71, 70
Kant, I. 2, 190–191; concept of the sublime 57–61; "phantom" representation 38; sublime with mathematics and 37; "super-sensible destination" 58
"Kant with Sade" (Lacan) 11
Karenina, Anna (fictional character) 237
Kashmir Saivism 103

Kast, V. 250
Kaufmann, P. 14
Kedney, J. 95
Kertész, I.: on existence of evil 222; Real of Auschwitz 221; shame and *sinthome* 222; *sinthome* 219–224; writing 218–219
Kierkegaard, S. 52
Kingsley, P. 6, 14, 26n6
Klein, M. 271
Kleinpaul, R. 40, 47n22
Kojève, A. 9
Kris, E. 240–241
Kristeva, J. 159
Kush, V. 104

Lacan, J. 1, 80, 153; clinical artistry; concept of "*le sinthome*" 219–221; definition of Real 155; definition of sublime 155; on desire 195; *Four Fundamental Concepts of Psycho-Analysis, The* 7, 13; and Gnosticism 12–16; *jouissance* 153, 155–157, 161; Jung and 12–16; "Kant with Sade" 11; on music 202–203; "Response to Jean Hyppolite's Commentary on Freud's 'Verneinung'" 172; *Seminar. Book VII. The Ethics of Psychoanalysis, The* 7, 13–15, 20, 125, 130, 133, 140; sublimation as creative destruction 126–134; sublime and psychoanalytic creativity 134–139; sublime in 108–120; "Subversion of the Subject and the Dialectic of Desire, The" 146n25; Symbolic language 260–261; version of Oedipus complex 167–168
Lacanian Real 172, 262–264, 266
Lacanian Symbolic 260
Langer, S.K. 204, 208, 241
language 7–8
Laplanche, J. 268, 272
laws of procreation 171
Lazarus, M. 25n2
Le Bon, G. 128
Leibniz, G.W. 33, 56
Lemaire, A. 80
Letter to Caesar (Sallust) 9
Lévi-Strauss, C. 166–167, 168, 203
Lévy-Bruhl, L. 89
Lewis, C.S. 129
Liber Novus (Jung) 59
Liber primus 22–23
Liber secundus 24
libido 8–11, 39, 67, 124–125, 196

Life of Language, The (Kleinpaul) 40
"linguistic matrices" 8
Locke, J. 56
loi, La (Vailland) 134
Longinus 16, 32, 35–37, 46n2, 53–55, 94
Lorde, A. 240
"loss of control" metaphor and tricksters 178
Lyotard, J.-F. 51, 53, 95, 104, 209

magnificent sublime 191
Maiello, S. 203
Mandelstam, J. 175
Mandelstam, O. 175, 179, 180–181
Mann, T. 252
Maslow, A. 96
Master and Margarita, The (Bulgakov) 181–182
"mathematical sublime" 37
matter: Jung on 229; and psyche 229
May, R. 230, 235, 237
Mayakovsky, V. 181
Mayer, R. 10
McDougall, J. 135
Meaning in the Arts (Reid) 241
Mechthild of Magdeburg 64, 67–68
medieval scholasticism 117
Mellor, A. 156
melophobia 201
Memories, Dreams, Reflections (Jung) 21, 22, 24, 26n6, 59, 119, 261
Merleau-Ponty, M. 78
Messiaen, O. 104, 199; on music and faith 209; *Quartet for the End of Time* 210–214; techniques for the sublime 209–214; van Maas on music of 210
Meyerhold, V. 179
Michelangelo 128
Milbank, J. 161
Miles, T.H. 108–109, 142n4, 143n11
Miller, J.-A. 144n15
Miller, P.A. 15
Moberly, L.G. 144n13
Molzer, M. 60
Mukhina, V. 179
Mundus Imaginalis (Imaginal World) 79
Münkler, H. 252
music: and deep unconscious processes 204–205; Hegel's comparison of poetry and 202; and idea of sublime 205–209; Jung on importance of 202; Lacan on 202–203; and psychoanalysis 200–203; and psychoanalysts 200–203; Romantic

view of 206; symbolic function of 203–205
Mutter, A.-S. 141
Mysterium Coniunctionis (Jung) 113, 202, 205
Mysterium Magnum (Böhme) 10
mysticism 69–71
mystics 67–69
myths 166–167

NAc (Nucleus accumbens) 99
near-death experience (NDE) 100–101
Near Death Experience Research foundations 100
"negative theology" 219–220
Neoplatonic doctrine of Plotinus 11
Neoplatonism 12, 19, 26n8
neuropeptides 99
neurotransmitters 99
Nibelungenlied: and *anima* 250–253, 254; female characters in 250; Germanic myth 253; notion of "Treue" 248; overview 245; political reception 247–250; storyline summary 246–247
noble sublime 191
nominalism 6

'object-relations' 272
Observations on the Feeling of the Beautiful and Sublime (Kant) 38
Ode to Intimations of Immortality (Wordsworth) 77, 80
Ode to Stalin (Mandelstam) 180
Odyssey (Homer) 35
Oedipus Complex 12, 167–168, 263
Oldenburg, C. 103
"On Grace and Dignity" (Schiller) 26n7
On the Aesthetic Education of Man in a Series of Letters (Schiller) 18
On the Sublime (Longinus) 53
"On the Sublime" (Schiller) 16–17
otherness: compensatory 88; sublime as opportunity for integration of 94–105
Otto, R. 51–52, 81, 129, 187, 191–192
Outline of a Jungian Aesthetics (Philipson) 242
Outline of Psycho-Analysis, An (Freud) 125

paintings 230–231; *see also* art
paleo-postmodernism: aesthetics of 262; "The Dead" 262–263; of Self and individuation 264–266
Paris Review, The 223

288 Index

participation mystique 89
Phaedrus (Plato) 22
phantasia 33–34, *33*, 36–39, 41
phantasia kataleptike 34, *34*, 37
phantasia thinking 39
phantasma 33–34, *34*
phantastikon 33, 39
phantaston 33
Phenomenology of Spirit, The (Hegel) 144n16
Philipson, M. 242
Phillips, A. 53, 271
Phillips, J. 55
Philosophical Enquiry into the Origin of Our Ideas of the Sublime and the Beautiful, A (1757) (Burke) 53
Philosophical Sphere or the Wondrous Eye of Eternity, The (Boehme) 69
Pianist, The (Polanski) 251
Piazzolla, A. 204
Picasso, P. 70, 236
Pigeaud, J. 33
Plato 6, 10, 53
poetic sublime subjectivity 80–81
Poirier, P.H. 187
Polanski, R. 251
Pollock, J. 133
Porete, M. 68
Portrait of the Artist as a Young Man (Joyce) 262
Post-Jungians Today 52
pre-object 236–238, 243n5
prima materia 194
privatio bono 54
Project for a Scientific Psychology (Freud) 144n18
Proust, M. 231
psyche 50, 64, 66–67, 72, 74, 78–79, 83–84, 90–91, 103, 105; Jung on 229, 186; and matter 229
psychic apparatus 31, *32*
psychoanalytic creativity, and sublime 134–139
Psycho-Analytic Notes on an Autobiographical Account of a Case of Paranoia (Dementia Paranoides) (Freud) 10
Psychological Types (Jung) 6
Psychology and Alchemy (Jung) 234
Psychology of Dementia Præcox, The (Jung) 10
Psychology of the Unconscious, The (Jung) 8–11, 19
"pure pleasure-*ego*" 44
Purloined Poe, The (Gallop) 156

Quartet for the End of Time (Messiaen) 210–214; melodic symmetries 212–213; technical innovations 211; "varied periodicity" 212
quaternity 11–12

radical iconoclasm 70
Raphael, M. 231
Read, H. 234–236
Real 2, 12, 15, 39, *43*, 78–79, 84, 111, 116–120; "The Dead" and Lacan's notion of 262–263; and Frankenstein 172; Lacan's notion of 155, 172
realism 6, 175, 179
Red Book, The (Jung) 14, 16, 27n10, 187, 194, 196; desire 9–11; Lacan, Jung and Gnosticism 12–16; language 7–8; quaternity 11–12; Schiller on the sublime 16–19
Reid, L.A. 241
Relations between the Ego and the Unconscious, The (Jung) 26n7
"religious instinct" 209
Renaissance 109, 119
repetition, cycle of, 42, *42*, 45
repression 11
"Requiem for analytical psychology" (Barreto) 225
"Response to Jean Hyppolite's Commentary on Freud's 'Verneinung'" (Lacan) 172
Ricoeur, P. 210
Riklin, F. 60
Rite of Spring (Stravinsky) 211
Robespierre, M. 39
Rogers, A.G. 239
Rolland, R. 45
Roman Catholicism 12
Romanticism, and notion of sublime 86–87
Romantic movement 109
Ronen, R. 25n3
Ross, A. 209
Rostropovich, M. 183
Roudinesco, É. 1
Rousseau, J.-J. 37, 39

Sallust 9
Sandbach, H. 34
Saussure, F. de 47n22
Scheler, M. 234
Schelling, F.W.J. 20, 21, 33, 249
"schema L" 7
Schiller, F. 16–19
Schlegel, F. 247
Schopenhauer, A. 9, 95, 200, 202

Schrödinger, E. 41, 47n14
Schwartz-Salant, N. 113
Secret of Hegel, The (Stirling) 144n17
Seidl, A. 206
Self: and Divinity 186–187; higher
    112; individuation and paleo-
    postmodernism of 264–266; Jungian
    individuation of 103–104; Jung's
    notion of 55, 71, 80–81, 160–162,
    186; masculine 162; as Other 58
*Seminar. Book VII. The Ethics of
    Psychoanalysis, The* (Lacan) 7,
    13–15, 20, 125, 130, 133, 140
"Seminar on the Purloined Letter":
    destruction in 154–155; and
    feminine *jouissance* 156; Gallop on
    156–157
Septem Sermones ad mortuous (Jung) 14
shadow, personality type 194, 196
Shakespeare, W. 128
Shalamov, V. 179
Shamdasani, S. 51, 55, 59
shame: as boundary-making tool 177;
    and Kertész's writing 222; and social
    being 177
Shame and Necessity (Williams) 222
shamelessness, and tricksters 177
Shaw, P. 20, 153
Sholokhov, A. 179
Sigmund Freud Papers 141n1
Silberer, H. 117
sinthome, le 218–224; disruptive energies
    of the Real of 221; and "negative
    theology" 219–220; and shame 222
Siskin, C. 90
socialist realism 175, 179
social parasitism 183
Socrates 6–7, 22, 27n9, 119
Solzhenitsin, A. 179
Sombart, W. 252
Song of Songs, The (Bloch and Bloch) 187
"sonorous envelope" 203
Sophocles 15, 175
Soviet Union: and censorship of
    authors 175; creative people treated
    as tricksters 175; and creative rebels
    179–180; and creativity 178
Spielrein, S. 41, 47n16
Spinoza, B. 9, 20–21, 56
Steinthal, H. 8, 25n2
Stern, D. 78
"Stirb und Werde" (Goethe) 252
Stirling, J.H. 144n17
Studies on Hysteria (Breuer and
    Freud) 140
Sturm und Drang movement 56

subjective sublime 77, 90–91; Freud
    and Jung 87–89; fundamentals of
    "the diamond sublime" at work
    89; glimpses of "life in death"
    as archetypal 87–89; imagining
    sublime as "diamond field" 81–83;
    mourning as "emptying out" 87–89;
    poetic sublime subjectivity 80–81;
    Romanticism and notion of sublime
    86–87; subjective sublime 90–91;
    subjectivity, image and sublime
    78–79; sublime otherness 76–77;
    urban sublime subjectivity 83–86
"subjective thinking" 39
subjectivity, and sublime 78–79
sublation (*Aufhebung*) 123–141
sublimation 11, 268; conceptual
    incoherence of 269; as creative
    destruction 126–134; and *ego* 277;
    Freudian 268–269; stages 193–194;
    unio mentalis 194
sublime 52–53, 65–66; and art
    231–232; compensatory 88;
    and creativity 238; defined 153;
    diamond 77–78, 81, 87, 89–90; as a
    "diamond field" 81–83; dictionary
    meaning of 166; Eros 161–163;
    feminine 163; fertile 192–193;
    image and 78–79; and in-depth
    psychology 96–98; and instrumental
    music 206–209; in Jung 108–120;
    Jung on 159; Kant's concept of
    57–61; in Lacan 108–120; Lacan's
    155; Messiaen techniques for the
    209–214; musically 205–209;
    neuro-physiological understanding
    of 98–99; as opportunity for
    integration of otherness 94–105; and
    psychoanalytic creativity 134–139;
    reflections on 50–51; Romanticism
    and notion of 86–87; Schiller on
    16–19; subjectivity and 78–79; and
    Thunder, Perfect Mind 190–192;
    vision and "The Dead" 258–262
Sublime, The (Shaw) 161
sublime anxiety 31–46; psychic
    apparatus 31, *32*; psychoanalytic
    pathways *32*
'Sublime Object' 15
Sublime Object of Ideology, The
    (Žižek) 15, 116
sublime otherness 76–77
sublime subjectivity 80–81
"Subversion of the Subject and the
    Dialectic of Desire, The" (Lacan)
    146n25

290 Index

"super-sensible destination" 58
Surrealism 127
Swedenborg, E. 102
Symbolic 2, 12, 19, 39–40, 78–79, 84, 117, 219, 257, 260–261, 263
Symbols and Transformations of the Libido (Jung) 8
Symposium (Plato) 6–7, 119
synchronicity 82, 84–86
Synchronicity and Intellectual Intuition in Kant, Swedenborg, and Jung (Bishop) 51
System of Transcendental Idealism (Schelling) 21
syzygy 50
Szpilman, W. 251

Tabula Smaragdina 115
Tarner Lectures 41
terrifying sublime 191
terror tremendum 187, 191
Theology and the Arts (Harned) 234
Theory of the Sublime, The (Doran) 51
"thinking with directed attention" 39
Thomán, I. 123
Thomán, M. 123–124, 135, 139–141, 141n1
"thought-transference" 110
Three Contributions to the Sexual Theory (Freud) 10
Three Essays on the Theory of Sexuality (Freud) 128, 130, 134
Thunder, Perfect Mind: and desire 196; erotic dimension 190; fertile sublime 192–193; overview 187; and sublime 190–192; transcendent function 194–197; as transformative psychic experience 193–194; use of opposites 189; voice of 187–188
Thurston, L. 221
"Time in Subliminal Psychic Life" (Spielrein) 43
"topological dream" 38
tragic transgression 176
transcendental idealism 56, 61–62
Transcendent Function, The (Jung) 60
Transformations and Symbols of the Libido (Jung) 9, 15–16, 25n2
Trauma and Beyond (Wirtz) 243n8
Trial, The (Kafka) 233
tricksters: as boundary breakers 177; creative people labeled, in Soviet Union 175; and creativity

178; dissolution of 178; Jung on 176; Lacan on 176; and " loss of control" metaphor 178; overview 176; physical entrapment in narratives 176–177; and shamelessness 177
Turangalila Symphonie (Messiaen) 199
Tusculan Disputations (Cicero) 9

"*Ulysses*: A Monologue" (Jung) 157–158; figurative detachment 160–161; sublime destructiveness of 159; themes 158–159
"unconscious, the" 7–8, 12, 55, 58
University of Cambridge 1, 47n14, 74
Unsayable, The (Rogers) 239
Unus Mundus 224
urban sublime subjectivity 83–86

Vailland, R. 134
Vases Communicants, Les (Breton) 127
Vermorel, H. 45
Vermorel, M. 45
vertical reality: and art 232; and artistic value of an object 233
Vieira, M. 43
Villa Nova, A. de 111
Völkerpsychologie (Kleinpaul) 47n22
Vorstellung 33, 37, 39, 41–42, 46n1
Vorträge und Aufsätze (Heidegger) 144n18

Wagner, R. 246
War with Catiline, The (Sallust) 9
Western culture 86
White, B. 116
Why War? (Einstein and Freud) 2
Wilde, O. 239
Williams, B. 222
Wilson, S. 200
Winnicott, D.W. 268, 270–271, 275
Wirtz, U. 243n8
Wisdom, J. 47n14
Wordsworth, W. 1, 50–51, 53, 56, 60–62, 76–77, 80–81, 88, 91
Wurth, K.B. 206, 209

Zeitschrift für Völkerpsychologie und Sprachwissenschaft 25n2
Zilcosky, J. 144n13
Zimmer, H. 196
Žižek, S. 2, 15–16, 116, 202–203
Zwingli, U. 6